Praise for *Below the Convergence*

"Alan Gurney's brilliant new study, *Below the Convergence* . . . will delight both the armchair traveler and the intellectual tourist to Antarctica. . . . The author's knowledge is so broad and deep that he graces this history with gems of information. . . . After finishing the final page, the reader will sigh in appreciation for the obvious skill, knowledge, and even joy in Gurney's writing. And then one cannot help indulging an obvious wish. Surely it is not unreasonable, given the title's scope, to hope that *Below the Convergence* will one day (soon?) be followed by another volume, or perhaps even several more, of such delicious reading. The wait will be worth it."
—*Chicago Tribune*

"Mr.Gurney's neatly written, densely detailed prose introduces the concept of deep cold with lyrical precision."
—*The New York Times Book Review*

"Charts, maps, and contemporary illustrations enrich this narrative of men against the sea. Obviously this is the sort of nonfiction to appeal to fans of the Jack Aubrey/Stephen Maturin nautical adventures."
—*The Washington Post Book World*

"For anyone interested in maritime exploration and extreme southern voyaging, *Below the Convergence* is a must. . . . What's more, it's a cracker to read." —*Sailing*

"The treasure-trove quality of this unusual book . . . written for serious sailors, should entertain anyone curious about history's backwater." —*Publishers Weekly*

"Beyond the harrowing adventures one would expect to read about in any narrative of Antarctic discovery, Gurney's articulate story is a welcome portrait of an age driven by great mysteries and simpler technologies than those of today."
—*Kirkus Reviews*

"His fascinating account should appeal to all readers. Highly recommended." —*Library Journal*

PENGUIN BOOKS

BELOW THE CONVERGENCE

Alan Gurney is a yacht designer and photographer living on the Isle of Islay in Scotland. He has lectured on this subject aboard the *Linblad Explorer* on trips to both the Antarctic and the Arctic.

A L A N G U R N E Y

Below the
Convergence

Voyages toward Antarctica
1699–1839

PENGUIN BOOKS

PENGUIN BOOKS
Published by the Penguin Group
Penguin Putnam Inc., 375 Hudson Street,
New York, New York 10014, U.S.A.
Penguin Books Ltd, 27 Wrights Lane,
London W8 5TZ, England
Penguin Books Australia Ltd, Ringwood,
Victoria, Australia
Penguin Books Canada Ltd, 10 Alcorn Avenue,
Toronto, Ontario, Canada M4V 3B2
Penguin Books (N.Z.) Ltd, 182–190 Wairau Road,
Auckland 10, New Zealand

Penguin Books Ltd, Registered Offices:
Harmondsworth, Middlesex, England

First published in the United States of America by
W. W. Norton & Company, Inc. 1997
Published in Penguin Books 1998

1   3   5   7   9   10   8   6   4   2

THE LIBRARY OF CONGRESS HAS CATALOGUED THE HARDCOVER AS FOLLOWS:
Gurney, Alan.
Below the convergence: voyages toward Antarctica, 1699–1839 / Alan Gurney.
p.   cm.
Includes bibliographical references and index.
ISBN 0-393-03949-8 (hc.)
ISBN 0 14 02.7260 7 (pbk.)
1. Antarctica—Discovery and exploration—History.   I. Title.
G870.G78   1997
919.8′9—dc20   96–3911

Printed in the United States of America
Set in Galliard
Designed by Marjorie J. Flock

An old tradition has it that those who have rounded Cape Horn under sail can take their after-dinner drink with one foot upon the table. And those who have sailed across the polar circles can drink with both feet upon the table. This book is dedicated to the latter— past, present, and future.

Contents

List of Maps

Maps follow page 282

The Southern Ocean

Halley's South, 1699–1700

Cook's South, 1772–1775

Bellingshausen's South, 1819–1821

South Sandwich Islands

The Sealer's South, 1820–1823

South Shetland Islands

South Shetland Islands

South Shetland Islands

Weddell's South, 1823

South Georgia

Biscoe's South, 1830–1832

Kemp's South, 1833 and
        Balleny's South, 1839

Balleny Islands

Acknowledgments

IN ADDITION TO the titles listed in the Bibliography, sources for this book have come from the Mitchell Library, Glasgow; the Bodleian Library, Oxford; and the Public Record Office, Kew Gardens. The author is particularly grateful to the Council of the Hakluyt Society for permission to quote from their publications and to reproduce the illustration of the *Paramore*. A debt is also owed to Mr. J. Herman of the Natural History Department, Royal Museum of Scotland, Edinburgh, for his great courtesy in showing me the type specimen for the Weddell seal, and to Mr. A. B. Cruickshank, Director of the Royal Scottish Geographical Society, for permission to reproduce the portrait of James Weddell.

BELOW THE
CONVERGENCE

Prologue

T HE SOURCE of the Nile, the possibility of a Northwest Passage from the Atlantic to the Indies, the existence of a huge southern continent—all, over the centuries, have exercised the speculations, imaginations, and energies of countless geographers, cartographers, and explorers.

In 460 B.C. the mystery of the annual—and apparently ineluctable—flooding of the Nile delta led the historian Herodotus to the first cataract at Aswan. The source, and the answer, was not revealed until the nineteenth century, with the explorations of Burton, Speke, Baker, and Stanley. The search for a Northwest Passage was, perhaps, more parochial: inspired in the fifteenth century by English commercial considerations, continued in the nineteenth by English nationalistic aspirations, and achieved by the Norwegians in the early twentieth century in a spirit of pure adventure.

The unknown southern continent—*Terra australis incognita*—was a different matter. The scope of this book is not to trace in exhaustive detail the reasons for this pertinacious hypothesis, but to sketch some of the voyages by explorers, sealers, and whalers into the Southern Ocean which, over a span of a hundred years, eliminated *Terra australis incognita* from the world's maps and whittled it down to a much smaller continent—Antarctica.

But the hypothesis does have to be explained. And as it starts with the pagan Greeks, it only seems appropriate to adopt a protean form, spin the globe, select certain scenes and actions, and generally play the Olympian eavesdropper.

I

Terra Australis Incognita

The intention of the Voyage has in every respect been fully
Answered, the Southern Hemisphere sufficiently explored
and a final end put to the searching after a Southern Continent, which has at times ingrossed the attention of some of
the Maritime Powers for near two Centuries past and the
Geographers of all ages. That there may be a Continent or
large tract of land near the Pole, I will not deny, on the
contrary I am of opinion there is. . . .

Journals of Captain James Cook, 21 February 1775

I T IS THE FOURTH century B.C. and, in the shaded walkways
of the Lyceum in Athens, Aristotle is strolling with his students
and discussing what is so obvious to the intellectually curious—
the spherical nature of the Earth, as opposed to the flat-disc
Earth of the ancient Homeric Greeks. Aristotle's reasons are based on
observed fact: the constellations change as a person travels north or south,
and during a lunar eclipse the shadow of the Earth that falls on the Moon
is always curved. "The sphericity of the Earth," Aristotle concludes, "is
proved by the evidence of our senses." It follows—due to that sense of
balance, order, and symmetry beloved of the Greeks—that there must also
be a land mass in the south to counterbalance the land mass of the north.
Such theories, perhaps, the young Alexander had heard a few years earlier
when Aristotle had been his tutor at the Macedonian court.

But what of the size of this sphere? A century after Aristotle, in 240
B.C., a brilliant polymath, Eratosthenes, is appointed chief librarian of the
Museum at Alexandria—the most cosmopolitan city and center of learning
in the Mediterranean world. In an experiment elegant in its simplicity,
Eratosthenes sets about calculating the circumference of the Earth. The
instruments for this measurement are ingenious: the Sun, a deep well, and
a vertical obelisk. Near Syene (Aswan), a town south of Alexandria and
some fifty days' camel journey away (about 5,000 stadia), Eratosthenes

knows of a deep well where the Sun, at noon on the day of the summer solstice, shines directly down the well shaft without casting a shadow. Knowing that the Sun on the same day in Alexandria does cast a shadow at noon, Eratosthenes reasons that by measuring the shadow cast by a vertical obelisk near the Museum in Alexandria, then calculating the angle of the Sun's rays to the obelisk, he will be able to calculate the Earth's circumference.

When Eratosthenes bends down to measure the length of the shadow, he is measuring the size of the Earth. The angle is nearly $7\frac{1}{2}$ degrees— about one-fiftieth of a circle. Thus the distance between Alexandria and Syene is one-fiftieth of the earth's circumference ($50 \times 5{,}000 = 250{,}000$ stadia, or 25,000 miles)—very close to the actual polar circumference of 24,860 miles. And so begins, with this imaginative experiment, the science of geodesy—the science of Earth measurement.

A quick spin of the globe and the scene shifts to Spain during the first century A.D. Here a Roman geographer, Pomponius Mela, is borrowing from the works of the Greeks to produce a Latin geography, *De situ orbis*. Herodotus, Eratosthenes, and Parmenides (a Greek philosopher of the sixth century B.C. who had divided the world into climatic zones) are all incorporated. According to Mela, the northern land mass of Europe, Asia, and Africa is separated by an equatorial ocean from a large southern continent. This is the land of the Antichthones—the people of the opposite world. There are five zones of climate in Mela's world. The equatorial zone is so hot as to be uninhabitable and impassable; the two polar zones are so cold as to be uninhabitable; but between these two dreadful regions there is a northern and a southern temperate zone where life is supportable. The groundwork is being laid for centuries of speculation, myth, and misconception.

"In the second century of the Christian era the empire of Rome comprehended the fairest part of the earth and the most civilized portion of mankind." So Edward Gibbon, with classical grace, opens his masterpiece *The Decline and Fall of the Roman Empire*. But if Rome is the political center, the center of learning is still Alexandria. And working among the crowded shelves in the libraries of that bustling city is a scholar by the name of Claudius Ptolemy. He is going to bequeath to posterity a number of volumes and maps which will mark the high tide of classical geographical knowledge. His maps are oriented with the north on the top and the east to the right—as in modern maps; for the location of towns and cities a coordinate system of lines of latitude and longitude is used; the problem of scale is tackled and Ptolemy has short shrift for his contemporaries and predecessors who enlarged land masses to accommodate place names or shrunk them them to avoid blank areas; squarely grasped is the thorny question of how to draw the curved surface of the world on a flat sheet of parchment; he advises that a small-scale map of the world should be supplemented with larger-scale regional maps. In short, Ptolemy is advocating the layout of a modern atlas. Calculating distances is a grave problem and he suggests an astrolabe or gnomon for measuring the Sun's altitude and thereby giving the latitude for north and south distances. But it will be centuries before the problem of longitude—the east to west distance—is solved. An annoyance to Ptolemy are travelers' estimates of distance. These, according to the vexed geographer, are unreliable, as due to "their love of boasting they magnify distances." Ptolemy, in brief, is attempting to place the elements of geography and cartography on a rational scientific footing. But in doing so he is selecting and synthesizing other people's information. Inevitably there are mistakes, and his two massive volumes, one on astronomy and the other on geography, contain a number of errors which will have a profound effect upon later European thought and exploration.

In the third century B.C. Aristarchus of Samos had proposed a theory that the Earth revolved around the Sun. Ptolemy, however, selects the Aristotlean concept of a geocentric universe, with the Sun revolving around the Earth. It is a theory that will accord well with Christian dogma. And the residue left by the other errors will clog the perceptions of European exploration until well into the eighteenth century. Oddly enough, Ptolemy does not choose to use Eratosthenes' estimate of the size of the Earth, but chooses instead the calculations of the Greek astronomer Poseidonius, whose figures make the Earth three-quarters its true size. The Mediterranean on this smaller Earth stretches too far west, and south of the equator Africa stretches east to join with China and so makes the Indian Ocean an inland sea. The mass of land to the south is *terra incognita*. Here then, with supreme irony, are the seeds of the two major misconceptions that formed the premise for two of the world's great voyages. The combined errors of a smaller world and an extended Mediterranean will lead Christopher Columbus to believe that the distance from the Canaries to Japan is only twenty-four hundred miles—it is over ten thousand. And the persistence of the *terra incognita* in the south will send James Cook off on the second of his great voyages around the world.

St. Basil, in the fourth century A.D., sets the tone for the spirit of the new Christian age: "Of what importance is it to know whether the Earth is a sphere, a cylinder, a disc or a concave surface? What is important is to know how I should conduct myself towards myself, towards my fellow man and towards God."

In 391, a few years after St. Basil's death, we watch, with an Olympian shrug of the shoulders, a Christian mob looting and destroying the pagan temples and centers of learning in Alexandria. It is the dawn of a thousand years of Christian dogma that is to cripple any free inquiry into the workings of the natural world. Gibbon will comment sadly that the empty

shelves in the libraries "excited the regret and indignation of every spectator whose mind was not totally darkened by religious prejudice." Ptolemy's works—and others of that intellectually spacious Hellenistic world—
sink quietly into the slough of intolerance. Theology is all, and the explanation of all phenomena can be found in the Scriptures. The world reverts to
the flat-disc theory of the ancient Greeks. For does not the Lord "sitteth
upon the circle of the Earth" and "stretcheth out the heavens as a curtain,
and spreadeth them out as a tent to dwell in" (Isaiah 40:22)? Jerusalem is
the center of this disc, for "I have set it in the midst of the nations and the
countries that are round about her" (Ezekiel 5:5). And any suggestion of a
southern continent is stomped upon with ecclesiastical severity. In 741
Pope Zacharias excommunicates an Irish priest who has the temerity to
preach such a doctrine. "For it would be admitting the existence of souls
who shared neither the sin of Adam nor the redemption of Christ." Further, the Apostles had been commanded to "go ye into all the world, and
preach the gospel to every creature" (Mark 16:15). They had not gone to
the antipodes; therefore the antipodes could not exist. *Terra australis
incognita* was heresy. On such ideaological thinking a future librarian of
the Royal Geographical Society would pass this summary judgment: "It is
an unedifying story."

But religion has not yet finished with the Alexandrian centers of learning. Another monotheistic faith is soon to sweep through Egypt, along the
coast of North Africa and into the Iberian Peninsula: Islam has burst forth
from its narrow desert confines. The Islamic general who captures Alexandria asks the Syrian Caliph Omar what are his wishes for the remaining
libraries. "If these writings of the Greeks agree with the Book of God,"
replies the Caliph, "they are useless and need not be preserved; if they
disagree, they are pernicious and ought to be destroyed." The Caliph's
Catch-22. And destroyed they were—to heat the public baths. But Ptolemy's works, buffeted by the zealots of both religions, survive and are
translated into Arabic. And Islam becomes the custodian and caretaker of
much classical learning.

For the lighthearted, however, all is not unrelieved theological gloom.
During the Middle Ages one of the most popular books is the *Polyhistor* of
a third-century Roman, Gaius Julius Solinus. Borrowing shamelessly from
the Roman naturalist Pliny—Solinus is mockingly known as "Pliny's
ape"—and with fabulous additions of his own as to the animals and strange
humans that inhabit the world, the *Polyhistor* is to have a lasting influence
on the slumbering cartography of the Middle Ages, if only to provide
decorative entertainment. One incensed nineteenth-century geographer,
C. R. Beazley, would fulminate regarding Solinus's influence on medieval
geography that: "no one ever influenced it more profoundly or more
mischievously.'

The thirteenth-century Hereford Map is an ecclesiastical and decorative example of this mischievous influence. The Earth is a circular disc with Jerusalem at its center. The Garden of Eden is located, as well as Noah's Ark. And the lands and islands are peopled with fabulous Solinus creatures. Here are the dog-headed men, the "cenocephali"; here is a horse-footed man, a "hippopod"; here is a man with long ears reaching to his knees; here are cannibals, the "anthropophagi," munching away on limbs; here are men with heads in the middle of their chests; and here are, perhaps most enchanting of all, the "ymantopedes," men with one leg who hop and somersault about and whose feet are so big that they use them as a shade against the sun or shelter against the rain. All is not myth, however, for here also is a drawing of a man holding a long stick and wearing long flat boards on his feet: the first known drawing of skis.

A man very familiar with skis, Fridtjof Nansen, echoing the Royal Geographical Society's librarian, would offer this acid comment on the church's influence on medieval thought: "This was the intellectual food which replaced the science of the Greeks. Truly the course of the human race has its alterations of height and depths."

But the tide is turning. In 1407, to counter the wheel maps of the medieval age, there surface in Europe—via Constantinople—Ptolemy's works on geography and astronomy. Another translation is made, this time from the Arabic into Latin, and within two years these works and maps are available to European scholars. A few years later Prince Henry of Portugal, "Henry the Navigator," founds a school of navigation at Sagres. And from here, overlooking the ceaseless surge of the Atlantic at the westernmost limit of continental Europe, the Portuguese caravels are directed on their extraordinary voyages of exploration.

Souls and spices are an unlikely recipe for exploration. But it is the search for a sailing route to the Spice Islands of the Moluccas, combined with zeal to convert the heathen, that is the driving motive behind these voyages. And also the adamantine will of Prince Henry. For his chosen captains show a certain pusillanimity at being ordered to sail into Solinus-like regions where oceans boil and monsters lurk to devour foolhardy mariners and sink their vessels. But prodded by the visionary Prince, supported by faith, and sustained by a diet of salted meat, salted fish, garlic, olive oil, beans, biscuits, and flour, these tough and resourceful seamen range down the coast of Africa and into the Indian Ocean on their search for cloves, nutmeg, mace, pepper, ginger, cinnamon, and souls.

By 1487 Bartholomew Diaz has rounded the tip of Africa, and a decade later Vasco da Gama has reached India. Ptolemy's landlocked Indian Ocean is a myth. While the Portuguese have been scouting the coast of Africa for a passage east to the Indies, a self-confident and glib-tongued Genoese is persuading the Spanish—having been rebuffed by the Portuguese—to finance an expedition to sail west to the Indies. Based on Ptolemy's maps, and with judicious juggling of figures to salt the mine,

Christopher Columbus estimates that it is only twenty-four hundred miles from the Canaries to Cipangu (Japan). It is ten thousand miles: the rest, as they say, is history.

In 1493 this scramble for gain by the two Iberian powers leads Alexander VI—that most worldly of Popes—to issue, with sublime arrogance and pontifical omniscience, a papal bull dividing the world between Spain and Portugal. The dividing line for this stupendous carve-up is set 100 leagues west of the Cape Verde Islands. After some acerbic haggling between the two beneficiaries, the final dividing line is settled, signed, and sealed by the Treaty of Tordesillas in 1494. The new line is set 370 leagues west of the Cape Verde Islands. All new discoveries to the west are Spanish, all to the east are Portuguese. Not even the nineteenth-century European scramble for Africa, the American move west, or the Russian move east can compare with this colossal real estate effrontery.

Straddling like Apollyon across the way, the New World is to prove a more formidable barrier than Africa to the riches of the Indies. In 1513 a Spanish conquistador, Vasco Núñez de Balboa, marches across the Isthmus at Panama and gazes at the Pacific. In a dramatic gesture—in an age of dramatic gestures—Balboa wades into the ocean and claims for Spain all lands washed by its shores. The sea he names the South Sea. In 1520 the seeingly impenetrable bulwarks of the American continent are breached by Ferdinand Magellan and the discovery of his eponymous Strait. It is to take thirty-seven days for Magellan's three vessels to thread their way through the Strait. The land to the south they name Tierra del Fuego; but they are uncertain if this is part of a large land mass or merely an island. Only one vessel, the leaking, stinking, and barnacle-encrusted *Victoria,* returns to Spain. And eighteen scurvy-ridden seamen, barefooted, dressed in rags, faces hidden by matted hair and beards, stagger in file carrying lighted candles to the Convent of Santa Maria de la Vitoria in Triana. There they give thanks for their safe deliverance, pray for the souls of their dead companions and Ferdinand Magellan, and give penance "for having eaten flesh on Fridays and celebrated the feast of Easter on Mondays, due to their having lost a day in their reckoning." These penitents, the first men to circumnavigate the world, had been caught in the time warp of crossing the dateline. Nevertheless, flat-earth churchmen and the dogmas of faith prove hardy beasts. Centuries later, in 1898, Joshua Slocum in the *Spray,* sailing on the first single-handed circumnavigation, will entertain three Boers in Durban sent by President Kruger of the Transvaal to test the validity Slocum's outrageous claim that he is sailing *around* the world. They will argue to no purpose. Later in the day Slocum will pass one of these gentlemen on the street and make a curving motion with his hands; not to be outdone, the fundamentalist will return with a flat and level movement of his.

In 1578, Sir Francis Drake, that pugnacious, spade-bearded, and arche-

typal fighting Elizabethan seaman—or pirate, depending upon your nationality—thumbs his nose at the Treaty of Tordesillas and slips through
the Strait of Magellan in sixteen days. After entering the Pacific he is blown
south and east by storm-force winds. The winds easing, he sails north and
west to make a landing on—or near—the island that boasts Cape Horn.
Here Drake, in typical cocky fashion, lies down on his stomach, stretches
his arms and torso over the steep face of the cape, and claims, with an
urchin grin, that he is the southernmost man in the world. South of his
outstretched arms lies a glittering sea. Here "the uttermost Cape or hed-
land . . . stands in 56 degree . . . without which there is no maine nor Iland
to be seen to the Southwards, but that the Atlanticke Ocean and the South
Sea, meete in a most large and free scope." Today that body of turbulent
water stretching from Cape Horn to the Antarctic is known as Drake's
Passage. In 1919 the International Oceanographic Conference of London
will fix on the meridian of Cape Horn as the boundary between the Atlantic and the Pacific. Drake, no doubt, would be wondering why it had taken
so long.

What are the cartographers to make of these Spanish, Portuguese and
English voyages? In 1531, a French mathematician, Oronce Finé, publishes an elegant map of the world where Magellan's Tierra del Fuego
forms part of a huge southern continent confidently named *Terra australis
recenter invento sed nondum plene cognita*—"the southern land newly discovered but not yet fully known." In 1570 Abraham Ortelius publishes
his magnificent *Theatrum Orbis Terrarum* (Theater of the World). This
collection of seventy maps eventually runs to forty editions. As in Finé's
map, Tierra del Fuego is shown as part of a vast southern continent, a mass
of land with a coastline sweeping majestically around the earth, complete
with headlands, capes, bays, inlets, and rivers. A year previous to the publication of the *Theatrum Orbis Terrarum*, a friend of Ortelius and fellow
cartographer had published a map of the world with a revolutionary new
projection. Gerhardus Mercator—born Gerhard Kremer—produced this
new type of map for the use of seamen: it was entitled a *New and improved
Description of the World amended and intended for the Use of Navigators*.
But another century will pass before seamen, being cautious conservative
folk, fully appreciate the practicality of a chart where, for the first time,
they can plot a course to a distant landfall with a straight line.

Mercator and Ortelius published their maps in the Low Countries. A
decade after their appearance, the stolid burghers of those watery lands
declare their independence from Spain and the loathed Spanish Inquisi-

OVERLEAF
World map by Abraham Ortelius.
From *Theatrum Orbis Terrarum*, Antwerp, 1570

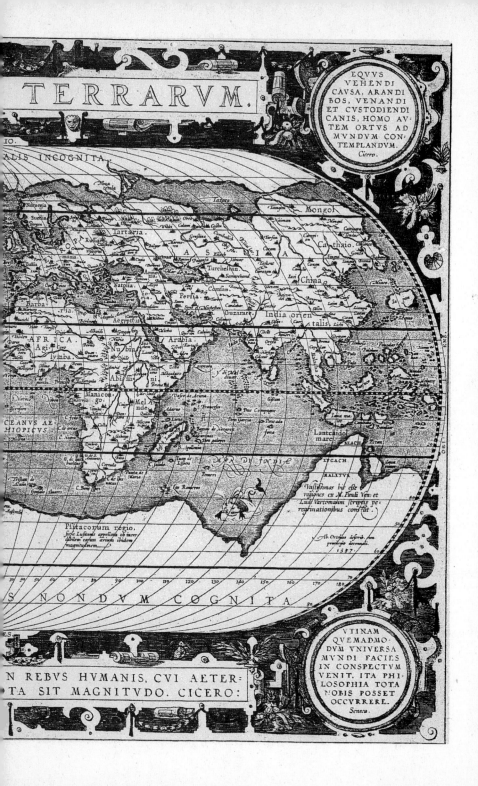

tion. The fifteenth and sixteenth centuries had seen the caravels, carracks, and galleons of the two Iberian kingdoms carving furrows across the world's oceans. The seventeenth century is to belong to the mercantile Dutch, who, in their seaworthy *flyte* and armed *jacht,* oust the Portuguese and the English from the East Indies. The Vereenigde Oostindische Compagnie (Dutch East India Company), founded in 1602, is the formidable company—virtually an arm of the government—that monopolizes the Dutch East India trade. This formidable company, before its dissolution in 1798, is to lay the foundations for the Dutch overseas possessions and etch on the world's maps the islands of the East Indies and the north, south, and west coasts of New Holland (Australia).

The Company, formed for trade and not for exploration, lays down laws for Dutch merchants that only Company ships may sail to the East Indies for trade, going either round the Cape of Good Hope or through the Strait of Magellan. The legislators, perhaps, have been influenced by those maps showing Tierra del Fuego as part of *Terra australis incognita.* One man believes otherwise. Isaac le Maire, a founder member of the V.O.C., has grown rich—and disenchanted—with the Company. Monopolist companies breed within them men who become stifled by the giant they have created. Such a man was le Maire.

The Strait of Magellan was banned to all but Company ships. Therefore, reasons le Maire, create a new company—Australische Compagnie—and look for a passage to the Indies south of the Strait. Drake's headland where "the Atlanticke Ocean and the South Sea . . . meete in a most large and free scope" might be no more than seamen's tavern gossip. But there could be truth in it.

In June 1615 two vessels lie at anchor off Texel in the Netherlands: the 220-ton *Eendracht,* commanded by Wilhelm Cornelius Schouten, and a 110-ton *jacht,* the *Hoorn,* commanded by Jan Cornelius Schouten. In overall command of the Australische Compagnie expedition is Jacob le Maire, old Isaac's son. The *Hoorn* is to be lost by fire on the Patagonian coast; but on 29 January 1616 the *Eendracht* rounds and names the southernmost cape of Tierra del Fuego and sails from the Atlantic into the Pacific. Schouten writes in his log: "Cape Hoorn in 57° 48′S. Rounded 8 p.m." With this laconic entry the fearsome cape makes its debut into nautical tale, legend, and saga.

The Dutch voyage jolts the Spanish into a galvanic reaction to this end run around their precious Strait of Magellan. With commendable speed the Spanish India Office orders two tough, battle-hardened, and sagacious brothers, Bartoleme and Gonzalo Garcia de Nodal, to the command of two 80-ton caravels. Their crew are impressed Portuguese and the two brothers sail from Lisbon during September of 1618 carrying orders to either prove or disprove the Dutch voyage around the end of South America. They can, of course, only confirm the truth of it. But, driven by gales away from Cape Horn, they discover, on 12 February 1619, a desolate group of islands that lie fifty-six miles south-southwest of the cape. Islas Diego Ramirez are named after the expedition's cosmographer. These bleak, wind- and wave-battered islands are to be the most southerly recorded land for a 156 years. The cartographers dutifully adjust their world maps to show the new passage into the South Sea; and the shores of *Terra australis incognita* inch south.

Twenty-six years after the rounding of Cape Horn, two more Dutch ships sail from Batavia (Djakarta). This is no maverick expedition, but one that sails under the flag of the Dutch East India Company. It is part of a comprehensive plan to discover "the Southern portion of the world all round the globe, and to find out what it consists of, whether land, sea, or icebergs, and all that God has ordained there." The architects of this expedition are Anthony Van Diemen, the great governor-general of Batavia, and Frans Jocobszoon Visscher, the most brilliant of the Dutch East India pilots. The two vessels are the jacht *Heemskerch* and the flyte *Zeehaen*. In command is Abel Janszoon Tasman, with Visscher as "pilot major."

On 13 August 1642 Tasman is issued his instructions and the two ships sail next day, bound for the Dutch possession of Mauritius. The instructions are enlightened ones. The natives of any land discovered are to be treated with courtesy and the Dutch are counseled to "be patient and long-suffering, no ways quick to fly out." This admirable advice, however, is not to affect a certain amount of dissembling on the part of the Dutch. This is, after all, a commercial venture. There is canny advice to Tasman that if the natives "offer you gold or silver in exchange for your articles, you will pretend to hold the same in slight regard, showing them copper, pewter, or lead and giving them an impression as if the minerals last mentioned were by us set greater value on."

The two ships spend a month at Mauritius outfitting for their voyage south. The plan is to sail south to between 52 and 54 degrees south latitude and search for land; if no land is discovered, to run east to the longitude of the eastern extremity of New Guinea, then north to elucidate questions raised by Dutch and Spanish voyages. There is also a contingency plan to continue sailing east to the coast of Chile. Here the gold- and silver-bearing provinces of Chile and Peru exert a double allure to the Dutch: they can satisfy their hunger for precious metals and have the satisfaction of tweaking the beards of the hated Spanish.

Loaded with their cargo of trade goods, by early November they reach latitude 49°4'S. Snow, hail, gales, and the cold felt by the crew force a return to more temperate latitudes, and they run their easting down in 44°S. Toward the end of November land is sighted and by 1 December thay come to anchor in a protected bay. The land is named Van Diemen's Land (Tasmania). No inhabitants are seen, but traces of them exist, for cut into the tree trunks are notches spaced five feet apart. These natives could be giants. In truth they are not giants; but the descendants of these shy natives quietly watching the Dutch are to have a melancholy history. Their story is terrible and shameful. Tasmania would be settled by the British in 1803 as a penal colony, and the natives, displaced from their ancestral lands, would fight back with their primitive weapons. One settler wrote: "The natives have been very troublesome and treacherous . . . the only alternative now is, if they do not become friendly, to annihilate them at once." In 1830 Tasmania would be put under martial law and the pogrom started. This included a massive sweep of the island, with a line of armed settlers attempting to drive the natives, like a herd of game, into the cul-de-sac of the Tasman Peninsula. Needless to say, most of the natives, with their superior fieldcraft, managed to avoid the blundering British. But the settlers won in the end—removing the natives to Flinders Island in the Bass Strait. The last pure-blooded native died in 1876.

Tasman's stay is short. By 4 December the two ships sail from this land that is "not cultivated but growing wild by the will of God" and continue their easterly course.

On 13 December more land is sighted. It proves to be a cloud-capped, mountainous one, with surf beating in a white fringe along its shores. Sailing along this inhospitable-looking coast they eventually reach a low-lying shore that offers hope of a protected anchorage. At sunset on 18 December the two vessels are anchored. An hour later, twinkling in the evening shadows, lights are seen on shore, and then two canoes slip from the shore to the ships. They stop a short distance off, call out to the Dutch in an unknown language, and blow what sounds to the Dutch like a Moorish trumpet. The Dutch shout back and, not to be outdone, play European instruments. This impromptu concert reaches its finale with the fall of darkness. So ends the first contact between Europeans and the Maoris of New Zealand.

The natives of Van Diemen's Land had proved shy, elusive, and mysterious. The following day the natives of this new land are to prove of a different kidney. The next morning the Dutch find themselves encircled by canoes. Suddenly, without warning, one of the larger canoes, the natives furiously paddling, rams into a launch carrying a message between the two ships. In a frenzy of violence, four of the launch's crew are clubbed to death. The *piacevole* overtures of the previous evening have been replaced by the *feroce* chords of an all too familiar tragedy. The two ships weigh anchor and sail from this ill-fated refuge, which the Dutch name Murderers' Bay, and for three weeks coast north along the shores of the land they have named Staten Land. Contrary winds prevent them following the land when it trends east and Tasman sails north deeper into the Pacific. The expedition finally returns to Batavia ten months after leaving. The Directors of the company receive the news of his discoveries with marked unenthusiasm. The voyage has brought no trade or profit and, sniff the

Directors, Tasman "had been to some extent remiss in investigating the situation, conformation and nature of the lands and peoples discovered, and left the main part of this task to be executed by some more inquisitive successor."

Nevertheless, Tasman's voyage has sliced off a great segment from the coastline of *Terra australis incognita*. And the world is to wait eighty-five years before the birth of the inquisitive successor.

The year of Tasman's discoveries, 1642, sees the death of Galileo Galilei, astronomer, mathematician, physicist, and founder of experimental science. A few years earlier Galileo had been forced by the Inquisition to abjure, on his knees, his heretical views that the Earth moves around the Sun. Legend has it that after making his recantation and while rising to his feet, he murmured sotto voce "E pur si mouve" (nevertheless it does move). 1642 is also the year of the birth of Isaac Newton. The blinkered vision of the Jesuit priests and the narrow byways of Christian dogma are to be illuminated by a new age of scientific inquiry.

In 1660, at a meeting in London, a group of inquiring and learned gentlemen found a society for "Physico-Mathematical Experimentall Learning." The nascent Royal Society is symptomatic of an age when the advances in mathematics, optics, and astronomy lead to improvements in navigation that will be pivotal for exploration in the next century. But practical advances go hand in hand with speculation. Tasman's account of his voyage is printed in English in 1694, and three years later William Dampier's *New Voyage Round the World*—dedicated to the President of the Royal Society—is published and, such is its success, runs to three editions within a few months.

Dampier's portrait hangs in the London National Portrait Gallery. It shows a rather morose face with heavy underlip and brooding eyes. Underneath is the legend *Captain William Dampier: Pirate and Hydrographer*—an intriguing title which is to give generations of children a hint of romance and adventure among the more earnest and stuffier figures of British history. Buccaneer he was—but also a man with a scientific bent and an inquiring eighteenth-century mind under the seventeenth-century Carolean fall of hair. In 1699 Dampier publishes his *Discourse of Winds, Breezes, Storms, Tides and Currents in the Torrid Zones,* a work which is to receive the praise of yet unborn seamen such as Cook and Nelson. Dampier's publisher, having a keen nose for his public and with the sweet smell of the successful *Voyage* lingering in his nostrils, brings out further volumes of voyages by buccaneers.

The spate of journals fuels the speculations of academics as to the size, shape, location, inhabitants, and possible trade with *Terra australis incognita*. An age's literature reflects its fads, fashions, and concerns; it is no wonder, then, that Swift's Lilliput is located to the northwest of Van Diemen's Land. Swift—no mean pricker of sententious balloons—turns his keen eye and sharp pen on the authors of these weighty leather-bound volumes of geographic speculation. Swift takes deadly aim with his *Project for the Universal Benefit of Mankind*. "The author," he writes, "having laboured so long, and done so much, to serve and instruct the public, without any advantage to himself, has at last thought of a project, which will tend to the great benefit of all mankind, and produce a handsome revenue to the author. He intends to print by subscription, in 96 large volumes in *folio*, an exact description of *Terra australis incognita* collected with great care and pain from 999 learned and pious authors, of undoubted veracity. . . . This work will be a great use for all men, and necessary for all families, because it contains exact accounts of all the provinces, colonies, and mansions of that spacious country, where, by a general doom, all transgressors of the law are to be transported. . . .'

From our Olympian viewpoint, the full, ripe maturity of *Terra australis incognita* is approaching: from Ptolemy's egg, through larva, through pupa to a most beautifully realized, if flawed, imago. But, as in the life cycle of the loveliest of butterflies, the final elegant imago stage is also the most fleeting. One of the creators of this closely reasoned chimera is Alexander Dalrymple. A portrait of Dalrymple in middle age shows him to be of corpulent figure with petulant lips, beefy face, and choleric eyes that glare accusingly at the viewer. This is a Scot with a grievance, and one who will nurse it to keep it warm. Dalrymple admitted to being "priggishly precise," an attribute admirable in the Admiralty's first Hydrographer—for this he became in 1795—but not one to smooth and lubricate the vagaries of personal relationships.

Born into a distinguished legal and political Scottish family, Dalrymple enters into the East India Company's service in 1752 and at the age of fifteen is sent out to Madras. The East entrances him. Here, for the next thirteen years, with indefatigable zeal he rummages the libraries for charts and details of the spice trade and Pacific voyages. Geography, discovery, and astronomy are all grist to his powerful intellect. And with the industry, energy, and collecting ability worthy of the Australian bowerbird, Dalrymple builds an entrancing hypothetical structure for a huge, fertile, and populous unknown southern continent. Founded, walled, and buttressed with material from Spanish, Portuguese, and Dutch voyages, and roofed by apparently unassailable logic borrowed from French academics, it is an imposing structure.

In 1765 Dalrymple, now a Fellow of the Royal Society, returns to England. In 1767 he prints *An Account of the Discoveries made in the South Pacific Ocean Previous to 1764*, followed in 1770 and 1771 by the two volumes of *A Historical Collection of Voyages . . . in the South Pacific Ocean*. Here is contained all his research and his case for a huge unknown continent in the South Pacific. Its northern coastline lies somewhere close to 28°S latitude, and at 40°S latitude the land stretches through 100° of longitude, or 4,596 geographic miles, "a greater extent than the whole civilized part of Asia, from Turkey eastward to the extremity of China."

The advocate in Dalrymple argues that trade with a continent of this size can replace trade with those two million ungrateful wretches in the American colonies. For without a doubt there must live in this great southern continent at least fifty million inhabitants, and "the scraps from this table would be sufficient to maintain the power, dominion, and sovereignty of Britain by employing all its manufacturers and ships." The reason that no one has discovered this continent and all its glories is due to the pusillanimous behavior of some of the explorers. A new Columbus, a new Magellan, is needed and Dalrymple considers himself well fitted to the task. His chance is to come.

Dalrymple's return to England coincides with a time when the scientific gentlemen of Europe are greatly excited by the approaching transit of Venus across the disc of the sun. Sir Isaac Newton's theory that the Earth is not a perfect sphere but bulges at the equator has been confirmed by two French expeditions to measure the arc of a meridian in Peru and Lapland. The circumference of the Earth, it is calculated, is some forty-two miles shorter along a polar circumference than along the equatorial circumference.

The transit of Venus, however, transcends the measurement of earthly things, for it concerns the first step in the measuring of the solar system and the universe—the distance between the Earth and the Sun. Edmond Halley, a half century earlier, had predicted, proposed, and urged that the two transits of Venus on 6 June 1761 and 3 June 1769 should be measured from widely separated observation stations set around the Earth. The next opportunities would not come until 1874 and 1882, followed by 2004 and 2012. Halley knew that he would never live to see the eighteenth-century transits, but wished the astrononers all imaginable success. A hundred twenty observers from nine nations gaze into the heavens on 6 June 1761. But the hazards of travel, war, weather, and inadequate instruments prove formidable stumbling blocks, and when the results of the observations are compiled the answer proves unsatisfactory. There is still 1769; and it is to this transit that the Royal Society bends its considerable prestige influence and patronage.

The Society, with a certain degree of urgency, appoints a Transit Committee who in turn recommend that observers be sent to Hudson Bay, the North Cape, and into the Pacific. The Astronomer Royal, the Reverend Nevil Maskelyne, suggests a trapezium-shaped area in the Pacific for the best observation site. Lying between latitudes 5°S and 35°S and longitudes 172°E to 124°W in the north, and 139°W to 172°W in the south, it is in the area of Dalrymple's interests; indeed, part of the trapezium overlaps Dalrymple's unknown southern continent. And the Royal Society think that Mr. Dalrymple is a proper person to send to the South Seas, being "an

able Navigator and well skilled in Observation." Maskelyne, meanwhile, is
interviewing other candidates who are eager to observe the transit. Mr.
Charles Green is willing to go south at £300 per annum and expenses; Mr.
William Wales to a warm climate on the same terms. Green does indeed go
south, but poor Wales is sent to shiver in Hudson Bay. But Mr. Green's
and Mr. Wales's conditions pale beside those of Mr. Dalrymple. They are
nothing less than the absolute command of a King's ship and the selection
of all the officers; and "if in the common course of accident" he should
lose this ship before the arrival in the South Seas, the government had to
undertake to provide another. Simple terms, according to Dalrymple, but
the only ones that would satisfy him. In this matter he has the backing
of the Royal Society and of a certain Mr. Adam Smith, a fellow Scot, a
philosopher, and an emerging figure in the field of economics. It is also
patently obvious that for Dalrymple the transit of Venus is of secondary
importance to the primary one of finding his great southern continent.
In a letter to the Society's Secretary, breathtaking in its condescension,
Dalrymple notes that "Wherever I am in June 1769 I shall most certainly
not let slip an opportunity of making an Observation so important to
science as that of the Transit of Venus." The new Magellan, the new
Columbus, is laying down his terms.

But these terms are fit to choke their Lordships in the Admiralty who
are providing the ship and crew for the South Seas voyage. The First
Lord, Sir Edward Hawke, swears that he would suffer his right hand to
be chopped off rather than sign such a commission. Their Lordships'
sentiments are made known to the Royal Society; Dalrymple sticks fast to
his demands—an untenable position—and refuses to serve under any but
his conditions. The new Magellan, the new Columbus, loses his chance
and Sir Edward Hawke saves his right hand.

The Royal Society resigns itself to providing advice, instruments, and
Mr. Green as an observer, and the young and wealthy Mr. Joseph Banks—
complete with an entourage of eight persons and two greyhounds—to
study the natural history of the Pacific Islands and lands. Their Lordships
quietly congratulate themselves and appoint an obscure master in the
Royal Navy—now raised to the rank of lieutenant—to command their
exploration vessel bound into the South Seas. The *Endeavour* and James
Cook are about to enter history.

In hindsight Cook appears to be the obvious and logical choice. But in
that April of 1768, a scant few days after the small east-coast collier *Earl of
Pembroke* had been purchased by the Admiralty for £2,800 and renamed
the *Endeavour,* there were few men who would have lighted on the name
of James Cook as her commander. It was, perhaps, the English equivalent
of Kirke Simpson's "smoke filled room" and an instance of the singular
English way of arriving at decisions commented upon by another Ameri-

can, Henry Thoreau: "The government of the world I live in was not formed, like that of Britain, in after-dinner conversation over the wine." Cook was indeed known to the Royal Society—he was appointed by them as the second observer with Green—for his observations of the 1776 eclipse of the Sun while surveying the coasts of Newfoundland; and had earned the Society's acknowledgement that he was "a good mathematician and very expert in his business." And in the Admiralty he was much esteemed by a handful of knowledgeable administrators for his impeccable surveys of the Labrador, Newfoundland, Nova Scotia, and St. Lawrence coastlines. One administrator, Philip Stevens, Secretary to the Admiralty, can be credited with suggesting Cook's name from the dozens of qualified candidates. He was backed in his choice by Newfoundland's Governor—another Royal Navy man—Sir Hugh Palliser.

On 20 May 1768 Captain Samuel Wallis and the *Dolphin* anchor in the Downs after a circumnavigation that has taken 637 days. He brings news of the discovery of a new island within Maskelyne's Pacific trapezium. The geographical position of King George III's Island (Tahiti) was accurately fixed at latitude 17° 30'S and longitude 150°W. The longitude was arrived at by "taking the Distance of the Sun from the Moon and Working it according to Dr Masculine's Method which we did not understand." Wallis's description of the island, the inhabitants, and the position persuades the Royal Society and the Admiralty that here is the ideal site for the observation of the transit of Venus.

The *Endeavour* sails from Plymouth on 26 August 1768. Packed on board are ninety-four souls, provisions for over eighteen months, spare blocks, canvas, spars, cordage, and the finest instruments available for taking astronomical observations of the transit. The *Endeavour*, like a space shuttle, is launched on her mission. The instructions for this mission, signed by their Lordships on 30 July, enjoin Cook to sail for Tahiti, set up his observatory, and measure the transit. "When this Service is perform'd," continue their Lordships, "you are to put to Sea without Loss of Time, and carry into execution the Additional Instructions contained in the inclosed Sealed Packet."

The sealed packet addresses the question of Dalrymple's great southern continent. Some of the crew of the *Dolphin* thought they had seen, south of Tahiti and at sunset, the tops of mountains. Could those evanescent peaks be part of the Southern Continent? Their Lordships, pragmatic men, are circumspect in approaching this subject: "Whereas there is reason to imagine that a Continent or Land of great extent, may be found to the Southward of the Tract lately made by Captn. Wallis in His Majesty's Ship the Dolphin (of which you will herewith receive a Copy) or of the Tract of any former Navigators in Pursuits of the like kind"; having got this off their chests, their Lordships continue in the time-hallowed phraseology of

the Admiralty and Cook is "hereby requir'd and directed to put to Sea
with the Bark you command so soon as the Observation of the Transit of
the Planet Venus shall be finished and observe the following Instructions."

The instructions are a model of their kind—concise, precise, but not
too restrictive. They had been drafted with care.

You are to proceed to the southward in order to make discovery of the Continent
above-mentioned until you arrive in the Latitude of 40°, unless you sooner fall in
with it. But not having discover'd it or any Evident signs of it in that Run, you are
to proceed in search of it to the Westward between the Latitude before mentioned
and the Latitude of 35° until you discover it, or fall in with the Eastern side of the
Land discover'd by Tasman and now called New Zealand.

If Cook does fall in with the continent, he is to survey the coastline;
note the products of seas, rivers, and land, the wildlife, the minerals; and
bring back specimens of the seeds of trees, fruits, and plants. Any natives
are to be treated with friendship tempered with caution. No continent
being discovered, he is to explore and survey the coastline of New Zealand,
reprovision at some known port, and return to England round either the
Cape of Good Hope or Cape Horn.

Three years later, mission accomplished, the weather-beaten *Endeavour* anchors in the Downs and Cook repairs to London to lay before the
Admiralty the reports of the voyage. It is an astonishing account. Here
are contained adventures and perils, romantic islands, and near-disastrous
shipwreck. The transit of Venus has been observed; great slices have been
taken off any theoretical southern continent; five thousand miles of new
coastline have been surveyed, with New Zealand and the east coast of
Australia firmly marked on the world's maps. Their Lordships are extremely gratified, as is the Royal Society. Never has any expedition brought
back so many samples of natural history: over a thousand new plants,
hundreds of new fish species, skins of birds, skins of mammals, and "Insects
innumerable." If the sailors in the Admiralty and the learned gentlemen
of the Royal Society are well pleased with this bounty, the flighty levels of
London society are enraptured with the tales of the native Tahitians and
their compliant womenfolk. Oh, how appropriate it is that this is the island
where Venus was observed! And there is much salacious whispering behind
fluttering fans on the amatory adventures of the young Mr. Banks.

As well as providing titillating gossip, Banks brings to London skins of
the kangaroo. And George Stubbs—the celebrated painter of horses—
exhibits a painting of this strange creature at the Royal Academy. It is,
perhaps, this painting, or talking with Banks, that encourages Dr. Samuel
Johnson, during his tour with Boswell of the Highlands and Hebrides,
after a good dinner, to demonstrate to the assembled company the appearance and habits of this curious animal. Standing erect, gathering his coat
to imitate the pouch, and then putting his hands out like feelers, the grave

Doctor takes vigorous bounds across the room. One would have liked to be there. Johnson's views on the "insects innumberable" brought back by Banks are less complimentary: the Doctor thinks that there are insects enough in England for study.

But amidst all the acclaim for this historic voyage, one dissenting voice can be heard. Alexander Dalrymple considers that Cook lacked perseverence in his attempts to find the southern continent. The strength of Dalrymple's spleen can be measured in an example from his writings. Indignant italics spatter the page like ink spots from a hard-pressed quill pen. "The point," fulminates the incandescent Dalrymple, "is not yet determined *whether there is or is not a* SOUTHERN CONTINENT? Although four voyages have been made *under their auspices* [the Admiralty's], at the same time I dare appeal, even to them, that I would *not have come back in Ignorance.*" Dalrymple had constructed his southern continent—his bowerbird structure—with gleanings from many sources. But in the bowerbird world a rival can appear who can trample down the elegant structure.

There were indeed vast unexplored areas of the ocean that could still contain a southern continent. And Cook, unknown to Dalrymple, was quietly formulating a plan to either find it or dispose of it. Thomas Huxley, a century after the *Endeavour* voyage, would write that one of the great tragedies of science is the slaying of a beautiful hypothesis by an ugly fact. The beautiful hypothesis of *Terra australis incognita*, centuries old, was about to meet its fate.

II

The Haven-Finding Art

Though the latitude's rather uncertain,
And the longitude also is vague.

W. J. Prowse, *The City of Prague*, 1856

I only report the longitude (of Hispaniola) to warn the reader
that nothing is more uncertain and that no method used up
to the present to find longitude has produced anything fixed
and certain.

Père Labat, *Memoirs*, 1693–1705

THE DISCOVERIES of the fifteenth and sixteenth centuries, entailing long voyages across the oceans, brought new and vexing problems to the mariner. Diet was one of them, and accurate navigation the other. The three *l*s of coastal navigation—log, lead, and lookout—were insufficient for the precise plotting of new landfalls and discoveries. The European seamen, then, as soon as they had left their familiar capes, headlands, and narrow seas, were presented with the thorny question of finding their position. And the oceans of the world are trackless wastes where the only signposts are moving ones—the Sun, Moon, stars, and planets.

Log, lead, and lookout still remain the Holy Trinity of the sailor's creed, and it is a foolish mariner who fails to hold fast to the triple tenets of his faith. Only the means have changed over the centuries. The playthings of today's weekend yachtsmen are arrayed with satellite navigation systems, knotmeters, depth sounders, and radars—the digital read-out microprocessor electronic versions of a sandglass, block of wood, knotted line, and weighted line.

The log of this trinity contains within itself another three elements: the triune of speed, time, and direction. The simplest method to estimate a vessel's speed is known as a "Dutchman's log." Knowing the distance between the bow and stern, a small chip of wood is thrown into the sea at the bow and the seconds are counted off until it reaches the stern. A simple calculation gives the vessel's speed.* It is probably the way that the *Victoria*'s speed was estimated during the world's first circumnavigation. A more sophisticated method, and one that has given the word "knots" to indicate a ship's speed, works on the same principle. This simple device first appeared in the mid-sixteenth century and was still used in the twentieth. A lightly weighted quadrant of wood is fastened to a line that has knots tied into it spaced at a known distance apart. The log is heaved into the sea and when the first knot enters the water a half-minute sandglass is turned. When the sand has run out, the line is checked and the number of knots that have entered the water are counted, giving the speed in knots— nautical miles per hour. The log on a well-run vessel was heaved every hour, and the speed and compass course were entered on a slate or traverse board, and finally into the logbook at the change of watch every four hours.

The patent log is a development of the common log or knotted line log. Foxon's "perpetual log" was tried in 1773 on the Arctic voyage of Captain Constantine Phipps, and James Cook used one—for the first time—aboard the *Resolution* on the passage from St. Helena to England. The patent log works on the Archimedes screw principle. At the outboard end of the log line is a finned torpedo-shaped rotor; this spins in the flow of water, turning a geared mechanism mounted aboard the ship, and the distance run is shown on a dial. Replaced with electronic gadgetry at the vessel end, it is still being used aboard small yachts.

But even the roughest of estimates for the daily run means little unless the direction is known. The northern hemisphere is blessed with the lodestar, or Polaris, which for purposes of crude navigation appears to be stationary in the heavens. For night sailing it is the fixed beacon signaling north. For sailing during the daylight hours the Sun makes another but far more erratic beacon. For ocean navigation in unfamiliar waters something extra is required. The marine magnetic compass was invented by the Chinese, moved west with Arab traders, filtered through the Islamic countries, and is first mentioned in the works of Alexander Neckam, an English monk at the University of Paris, about 1180–90. The compass more than any other invention—equaled by the cannon, another Chinese invention— enabled the Europeans to dominate the world's oceans for over four centuries.

The lead is a humbler device, measuring both the depth of water and the type of bottom. Elegant in its simplicity, this tapered length of lead is fastened to a line marked in fathoms.† The bottom of the lead is hollowed to hold a lump of tallow which picks up the type of bottom—coarse sand, fine sand, sand and shell, mud, etc.—an indicator of vast importance to the

---

* For speed in knots the formula is $.6d \div s$, where d is the distance and s the time in seconds.

† A fathom is six feet—the length, fingertip to fingertip, of an average man's outstretched arms.

sailing coastal skipper intimate with the creeks, bays, inlets, and coastline of his watery domain. To this type of seafarer, the lead was the most important of the navigating trinity.

The sea is no respecter of nationalities and most sea anecdotes, no matter in which language they are told, have common themes. Such a one is a sly tale about a small coastal trading vessel owned by a skipper so knowledgeable of his coast that he could tell exactly where he was by looking at, then smelling, and finally tasting the bottom sample brought up by the lead. On one trip, carrying some chickens from Mr. Brown's farm, and slipping along in a thick fog, the skipper called for the lead. The mate, as a joke, armed the lead with tallow and also with some chicken manure from the coops. The lead was heaved, the depth called out, and then the skipper looked at the tallow, smelled it, and finally tasted it—and then looked up, shouting, "My God lads, quick, luff up! luff up! something terrible has happened, we're over old Brown's farmyard!"

But the subtleties of the essence of tallow only suffice for coastal navigation. Pathfinding across unfathomable and uncharted oceans requires the two *l*s of latitude and longitude; and this grid, or coordinate, system of the Earth's surface calls for observations of the heavens rather than of the sea floor.

This grid system, with the parallels of latitude running east-west and the meridians of longitude north-south, was formulated in the second century B.C. by Hipparchus, the Greek astronomer, mathematician, father of trigonometry, and the bane of generations of inky schoolboys. An observer's position along a line of latitude was a solvable problem: by measuring the altitude of Polaris or the Sun above the horizon the latitude of the observer can be calculated. The instruments for measuring the altitude were simple ones: the disc-shaped astrolabe, the quadrant, and the cross-staff or Jacob's staff (improved in 1595 by John Davis into the English quadrant or backstaff, where the observer was saved from squinting into the sun). Declination tables for the calculations were available by the fifteenth century. Thus armed, the mariner could, given good weather and reasonably calm conditions, calculate his latitude within a few miles. The heaving deck of a small vessel is not the ideal platform for astronomical observations, and calculated latitudes, even by the best of navigators, could be wildly innacurate.

But finding the latitude only placed the mariner somewhere along the length of a line running around the globe. To find the exact location along this line another position line is required—preferably perpendicular to the latitude line—and where they cross is the position of the observer. *X* marks the spot. But that position line—longitude—was a far more serious and apparently insoluble conundrum.

One sixteenth-century writer dismissed it as a problem of little account. "Now there be some that are very inquisitive to have a way to get the longitude," he wrote, "but that is too tedious for seamen, since it requireth the deep knowledge of astronomy, wherefore I would not have any man think that the longitude is to be found at sea by any instrument; so let no seamen trouble themselves with any such rule, but (according to their accustomed manner) let them keep a perfect account and reckoning of the way of their ship."

The method for keeping "the perfect account and reckoning" was to note the vessel's speed and compass course steered and then make allowances for drift, leeway, and current. All these were usually estimations. The method is known, rather ominously, as "dead reckoning" ("dead," however, being used in the sense of exact or unbroken). And a mariner who failed to keep his exact reckoning was liable to end among the breakers. On long voyages the dead reckoning of longitudinal positions could be hundreds, even thousands, of miles in error. Magellan's pilot, for instance, after the horrifying passage across the Pacific, made an almost 53-degree error in the longitude of the Philippine Islands—three thousand miles. In short, dead reckoning is guesswork: informed guesswork, but guesswork nonetheless.

The loss of life, ships, cargo, and trade was recognized by the governments of the seafaring nations. Prizes for the solution of the longitude problem were offered by the governments of France, Holland, Venice, and Spain. In 1598 Philip III of Spain pledged 6,000 ducats and a life pension of 2,000 ducats to anyone who could find a practical solution. No one did.

The solution appeared to be tantalizingly simple. The Earth spins on its axis through 360 degrees every twenty-four hours. Every hour, therefore, the Sun moves across 15 degrees of longitude. If the mariner knows the time at, say, London, Paris, or Madrid (call this the prime meridian—"meridian" meaning midday), and by observation of the Sun knows the time of noon at his meridian, he can then calculate his distance east or west of the prime meridian. He has found his longitude. But he needs two very accurate measuring instruments—one to measure the altitude of the Sun and the other a paragon of a clock keeping impeccable time. Timekeepers aboard vessels in the fifteenth and sixteenth centuries were sand clocks turned every half hour. Egg timers.

In 1675 the Reverend John Flamsteed, appointed as the first Astronomer Royal to the newly built Royal Observatory at Greenwich, took up residence in his Wren-designed house. His task was to rectify "the tables of the motions of the heavens and the places of the fixed stars, so as to find out the so much desired longitude of places for perfecting the art of navigation and astronomy." The seeds had been sown for zero-degree longitude—the prime meridian—passing through Greenwich Observatory and Greenwich mean time forming the basis of the world's time zones.

In 1707 the fleet of Vice Admiral Sir Cloudesley Shovell, on a passage from Gibralter to England, was wrecked on the Isles of Scilly. The admiral and two thousand seamen were drowned. Ironically, this catastrophe had little to do with longitude and more to do with latitude. Nonetheless, it enouraged efforts to solve the longitude problem; but national governments, being bureaucratic institutions, are lumbering tardigrade creatures, and it was not until 1714 that a bill passed through Parliament "for providing a publick reward for such person or persons as shall discover the longitude at sea." In an age when a skilled craftsman was lucky if he earned £26 a year, an able seaman in the Royal Navy £14 a year, and his captain £100 a year, the prize for longitude was a munificent one:

£10,000 if the method was accurate to within 1 degree, or sixty nautical miles;

£15,000 if the method was accurate to within ⅔ degree, or forty nautical miles;

£20,000 if the method was accurate to within ½ degree, or thirty nautical miles.

A Board of Longitude was constituted, consisting of twenty-two commissioners; and when a majority of those commissioners thought the method "useful and practicable," half the reward would be paid. "Useful and practicable" is an ambiguous phrase and promised to lead to acerbic wranglings among the claimants and the Board. Less ambiguous was the payment for the residue of the reward. A ship, using the proposed method, should sail from a port in the British Isles to a port in the West Indies and, depending upon the degree of accuracy as laid down in the act, the remainder of the prize would be awarded.

Sir Isaac Newton, asked to serve as one of the commissioners on the Board "for finding the longitude at sea," in an obviously irreverent mood replied that he had not realized that it had been lost. But serve he did, and the board over the next few decades scrutinized over three hundred methods for the finding of longitude.

The reward offered was, inevitably, an invitation for numerous cranks and eccentrics to present their offerings to the Board. A Mr. Owen Straton was interviewed by the Board, as he claimed to have "an Instrument of his invention" for the finding of longitude. It was a sundial. Longitude became the early-eighteenth-century equivalent of the crossword. Hogarth satirized it in *The Rake's Progress* where, in the madhouse scene, an inmate is shown serenely working away on the longitude problem, surrounded by his lunatic bedlamite companions.

Hogarth's lunatic had two ways of solving the longitude problem: the mechanical and the astronomical / mathematical. For the mechanical approach to succeed, a watch or timepiece had to be manufactured of such precision and quality that on extended voyages it would tick away at a uniform rate in extremes of temperature and the violent movement aboard ship. At the first meeting of the Board of Longitude, no such exemplar of the clockmaker's craft existed. A hundred of the proposals studied by the Board dealt with an astronomical / mathematical solution—the Hogarthian lunatic's way. It called for measuring the distance between the relatively fast moving Moon and the fixed stars. The "lunar-distance" method had its drawbacks: the calculations were complex, the measurements had to be precise, and the whole hinged on the accuracy of a book of astronomical tables.

Precision in astronomical measuring at sea took a major step forward in 1731, when John Hadley invented the reflecting quadrant, an instrument far easier in use and far more accurate than the backstaff, astrolabe, or cross-staff. By 1757 the Hadley quadrant had been improved still further by Captain John Campbell and evolved into the sextant. By 1777 the brilliant engineer and instrument maker Jesse Ramsden had built a "Dividing Engine" for graduating arcs and linear scales to a precision then unknown. By 1792 Ramsden was making sextants that in accuracy, and with their telescopes, vernier scales, shades, and mirrors, are indistinguishable from today's instruments.

Hadley's invention had seemingly stacked the scales to the advantage of the lunar-distance method: in an age of gambling, if you were a gambling gentleman the lunarian approach would appear to be the odds-on favorite to win the prize.

The principles of lunar distances had been put forward in 1474 by the German astronomer Regiomontanus. But it was to be nearly three hundred years before another German, Tobias Mayer, calculating on Newtonian principles, produced a set of accurate lunar tables for finding the longitude. Mayer, ironically, was concerned not with finding longitude at sea but with accuracy in cartography. He wrote in 1747 that "it is only too well known in geography that very many, indeed most, of the numerous known and note-worthy places need to have their latitude and longitude more accurately determined. To achieve this is one of the most important objects of astronomy. . . ." It was therefore a German cartographer / astronomer / mathematician who had never been to sea—in fact had never seen the sea—who, in a 1755 memorial to the President of the Board of Longitude, claimed the reward.

Mayer's tables were used by Dr. Nevil Maskelyne—a future Astronomer Royal—on a voyage to St. Helena to study the 1761 transit of Venus. The results were encouraging and seemed capable of finding the longitude at sea to within one degree, or sixty nautical miles. Mayer died in 1762 and a year later his tables were incorporated by Dr. Maskelyne into *The British Mariners Guide (Containing Complete and Easy Instructions For The Discovery of the LONGITUDE at Sea and Land, within a Degree, by Observations of the Difference of the Moon from the Sun and Stars, taken with HADLEY'S Quadrant ... by NEVIL MASKELYNE, A.M. Fellow of*

TRINITY COLLEGE, CAMBRIDGE, and of the ROYAL SOCIETY).
No mention is made by the Reverend Doctor of Tobias Mayer.

In 1765 Parliament passed an act that gave Mayer's heirs £3,000—even though the lunar-distance method and the accompanying tables devised by Mayer warranted half the £10,000 reward. The same act also awarded the balance of half the maximum award to a certain John Harrison—but for Harrison to receive his money, Parliament made changes to the 1714 act that, in effect, altered the position of the finishing post. Harrison had to make at least two more of his "Time-Keepers" and also, perhaps even more galling, make public his long- and hard-earned skills and expertise to three skilled mechanics and three rival watchmakers.* The race for finding the longitude at sea was running neck-and-neck between the lunar-distance method and the watchmakers, or as Maskelyne—a partisan of the lunar method—condescendingly called them, the "Mechanics."

In 1661 Christian Huygens, the Dutch physicist and astronomer, had completed the first pendulum clock specifically designed for finding the longitude at sea. In this Huygens had been assisted by Alexander Bruce, the second Earl of Kincardine, then living as an exile in Holland. Bruce, upon the Restoration of Charles II to the British throne, took two of these clocks back to England, where they were tested aboard the royal yacht by Robert Hooke, the English physicist and curator of experiments at the Royal Society. It was obvious, however, that a pendulum clock was incapable of keeping accurate time on a rolling and pitching vessel.

By the time of the 1714 act, even with refinements to the mechanism of clocks that included the pendulum's being replaced by a balance spring, and an auxiliary spring that kept the machine running at a constant rate while the mainspring was being rewound, nothing had been constructed of sufficient accuracy—and robustness—for use at sea.

The same year as the founding of the Board of Longitude, an English inventor, Jeremy Thacker, coined the word "chronometer" to denote a marine timekeeper or watch.† When Thacker's newly minted word appeared in his 1714 pamphlet *The Longitude Examined,* John Harrison, a Yorkshire-born carpenter, was twenty-one years old. Before his death in 1776, he and his brother James were to devote the greater part of their lives to constructing and perfecting a practical chronometer.

Although set in the eighteenth century, the story has all the ingredients of the moralizing self-improving children's fable so beloved by the Victorians. It starts with the humble birth of John Harrison into a poor carpenter's family in the Dickensian-named hamlet of Foulby in Yorkshire. To entertain the infant after an attack of smallpox, Harrison's parents rest a

---

* Harrison had been told of these extra requirements at a meeting of the Board of Longitude in 1765. And had stormed out swearing that "I will never consent to it so long as I have a drop of English blood in my body."

† It was not until 1782 that the word "chronometer" crept into the minutes of the Board of Longitude.

ticking clock on the convalescent's pillow. Young John's course is set. Following in his father's footsteps, he learns the carpenter's trade and also earns extra money by surveying and—the self-improving touch—in the evenings, by guttering candlelight, studies mechanics and physics. At twenty-one, he is repairing and making clocks. His native genius asserts itself and he invents the gridiron pendulum—an ingenious solution to the expansion and contraction to the length of the normal pendulum—and the "grasshopper" escapement. In 1728 he makes a decision to enter the arena for the longitude reward with a marine clock. Packing up models and drawings of his inventions, he travels to London looking for financial backing. A leading clockmaker, George Graham, plays the role of benefactor and finances Harrison from his own pocket.

With the financial backing of George Graham, John Harrison, helped by his brother James, took seven years to construct his first "sea-clock," completing it in 1735. It now sits in the Maritime Museum at Greenwich. It weighs over seventy-two pounds and will just fit into a three-foot cubic box. Its four dials indicate the day of the month, hours, minutes, and seconds. The wheels are made of wood. With all its brass counterlevers, weights, wires, springs, cams, and cogs, it looks faintly comic. It is known as H1. For use at sea, the whole contraption was mounted in gimbals in a wooden case suspended by spiral springs at its corners.

Five members of the Royal Society inspected H1 and recommended that it be given a trial at sea. The Board of Longitude accepted their advice, and Harrison sailed with his creation aboard HMS *Centurion* on a voyage to Lisbon. The results were sufficiently encouraging that the Board advanced the Harrisons money to construct an improved version. The Harrisons' new creation, known as H2, never went to sea. Taller and heavier than its predecessor, it combined a number of refinements—but not enough to satisfy the Harrisons. Another offspring, H3, took seventeen years to design, construct, and perfect, with John Harrison working alone on its creation. At the same time, he was working on his masterpiece, the incomparable H4. The ancestors of H4 had been large, heavy, and cumbersome machines. This was a masterly leap in design, mechanism, and appearance—from a seventy-two-pound behemoth to a five-inch-diameter watch that could be comfortably held in the hand or slipped into a coat pocket. (It looks like a large fob-watch.) It was the design equivalent of, say, taking a clanking, weighty 1874 Remington typewriter to a modern, slim, and portable Olivetti.

In 1761 Harrison requested sea trials for his two latest creations. In the event, only H4 was tested at sea on a voyage to Port Royal in Jamaica and back. Harrison's son William accompanied H4 on the sea trial and convinced a skeptical captain, with the accuracy of the landfalls at Madeira and Jamaica, of the practicality of the "sea-clock." Convincing the Board was another matter.

The results, according to the Board, were negative. The longitude of

Port Royal calculated by the watch (1.25 minutes' difference from the accepted one) was questioned on the rather niggling grounds that this accepted longitude (calculated eighteen years previously, from the observation of a transit of Mercury) was itself suspect. After a stormy passage back to Portsmouth, the longitude of that navy town as calculated by H4 was only eighteen miles from the accepted one. An indignant Harrison pointed out to the Board that after a five-month voyage, H4 had an error of less than 2 minutes. And—more to the point—that the *rate* at which a watch gained or lost time should also play an important part in assessing its qualities.

A second sea trial was ordered for H4, with William Harrison again acting as chaperone to the precious mechanism. John Harrison had written a declaration that he expected H4 to keep perfect time at 72 degrees Fahrenheit and gain or lose one second a day for every ten degrees fluctuation. He also estimated that H4 would gain—for the duration of the voyage—one second per day. In March 1764 HMS *Tartar* sailed for Madeira and Barbados. Harrison's estimations were triumphantly confirmed and, with H4 quietly and competently ticking away the seconds, longitudes were calculated to ten nautical miles. The £20,000 prize called for accuracy to thirty nautical miles. It would appear, on the surface, that Harrison was fully justified in claiming the £20,000.

At Barbados H4's performance had been checked by Nevil Maskelyne with observations of Jupiter's satellites. Maskelyne, who had sailed some months earlier, used the lunar-distance method and Mayer's tables to find the longitude on his voyage across the Atlantic. The Board now had two systems to assess—Harrison's and Mayer's—and on which to pronounce judgment. But the commissioners were now impaled on the horns of the proverbial dilemma. And the twin horns were those words "useful and practicable."

Harrison's watch and the lunar-distance method were both useful—but were they practicable? Could, in fact, someone other than Harrison make a sufficiently accurate watch? And, more to the point, what would be the cost? As to the lunar-distance method and its proponents, Nevil Maskelyne—the Astronomer Royal—admitted to taking up to four hours to work through the complex calculations. Few masters in the Royal Navy, and even fewer merchant sea captains, were likely to greet that item of information with any show of enthusiasm. And so, in the manner of all committees, the Board made a ruling that satisfied no one. Mayer's heirs and supporters thought the £3,000 award piffling, and it took months of persuasion to bring Harrison around to agree with the new rulings of the new 1765 act.

A further irritant to Harrison was the Board's request that H4 undergo more testing at the Greenwich Royal Observatory, where Nevil Maskelyne, the newly appointed Astronomer Royal, would act as judge and jury.

Harrison, with some justification, did not believe that Maskelyne—pro-lunar-distance man—could, or would, act as an impartial judge. And such was the case. "Mr Harrison's watch," pronounced the oracular Astrono-mer Royal, "cannot be depended upon to keep the longitude within a degree in a West India voyage of six weeks; nor to keep the longitude within half a degree for more than a fortnight, and then it must be kept in a place where the thermometer is some degrees above freezing."

As this pronouncement flew in the face of H4's actual performance on two West Indian voyages, it was not long before Harrison pointed out that the obtuse Astronomer Royal had failed to take into account the *rate* of the watch. "It is not necessary that a Watch should perform it's Revolutions precisely in that Space of time which the Earth takes to perform her's," snapped Harrison, "it is only required that it should invariably perform it in *some known Time,* and then the constant Difference between the Length of the one Revolution and the other, will appear as so much daily gained or lost by the Watch, which constant gain or loss, is called *the Rate of its going,* and which being added to or deducted from the Time shown by the Watch, will give the true Time, and consequently the Difference of Longitude."

While this exchange of broadsides was taking place, Maskelyne pub-lished the first edition of the 1766 *Nautical Almanack* (based on Mayer's tables and reducing the computation time of lunar distances); Harrison had started on a fifth watch; five hundred copies of Harrison's pamphlet describing the construction of his "Time-Keepers" (thirty-one pages long and with fifteen drawings) had been printed and published "By Order Of The Commissioners Of Longitude"; and Mr. Larcum Kendall was requested by these same commissioners to make a replica of H4.

By 1770 Harrison had completed H5 and Larcum Kendall his copy of H4. Kendall had taken three years to make his copy; been paid £500 by the Board of Longitude; and been complimented by William Harrison on the craftsmanship of this elegant, beautiful, and what was to become historic watch. It is known—inevitably—as K1.

In 1771 Lieutenant James Cook and the *Endeavour* returned to En-gland after the adventurous three years' voyage around the world. Joseph Banks, the wealthy young naturalist on the voyage, became the darling of English society and was feted at balls, levees, soirees, and receptions in the tonier parts of west London. Cook was raised—an infinitesimal step—to the rank of commander and returned to his home, wife, and two sons at Mile End in the east of London. And moves were quietly made for a second exploratory voyage. On the *Endeavour* Cook had used the lunar-distance method for finding his longitude at sea. The proposed new voyage—an-other circumnavigation—offered the ideal opportunity to give the newfan-gled watches their ultimate test.

Harrison made an appeal to the Board requesting that H4 and K1 be taken with Cook on his new voyage. On the accuracy of these two watches he would base his claim for the residue of the £20,000 award. The appeal fell on deaf ears. But it was a selective deafness. Nevil Maskelyne by October of 1771 was subtly maneuvering to have two observers from the Royal Observatory aboard for the next voyage and "the Watch made by Mr Kendall by order of this Board and now in the possession of the Astronomer Royal. . . ." Other watches of a new design made by John Arnold were to keep K1 company.

Enter His Majesty King George III. That much-maligned monarch, keenly interested in the longitude problem, had already given an audience to John Harrison and his son. Harrison now appealed to his sovereign and stated his case in the long-drawn-out battle with the Board. Legend has it that King George, having listened to the watchmaker, growled, "By God, Harrison, I'll see you righted." And H5, Harrison's latest creation, was given a ten-week trial at the King's private observatory in Richmond. After ten weeks the watch was only four and one-half seconds in error. The King's interest was keen, and, more to the point, his influence helpful. On 6 May 1773, with the monarch's personal backing, Harrison presented a petition to Parliament requesting the outstanding £10,000. Less than two months later the eighty-year-old inventor was voted not £10,000, but £8,750. The Board and Parliament were still showing their miserly penny-pinching ways; and Harrison could well write that "I hope I am the first, and for my country's sake, shall be the last that suffers from pinning my faith on an English Act of Parliament."

Three years later, John Harrison was dead. But not before the return of Cook and the *Resolution* from the 1772–75 voyage that circumnavigated the world and Antarctica. For that voyage Cook had carried Larcum Kendall's copy of Harrison's masterpiece. And Cook was affectionate in his praise of "our trusty friend the Watch," and "our never-failing guide the Watch." But perhaps the truest vindication of John Harrison's genius came on the last leg of the voyage. After three years sailing Cook had such trust in the watch that on leaving Cape Town and bound for St. Helena in the company of the East Indiaman *Dutton,* he wrote: "Depending on the goodness of Mr Kendall's Watch, I resolved to try to make the island by a direct course, it did not deceive us and we made it accordingly on the 15th of May at Day-break. . . ." Indeed, such was Cook's confidence in the watch that a young midshipman on the *Resolution* wrote: "The day before we saw St Helena, the *Dutton* spoke us, and said they were afraid that we would miss the Island, but Capt Cook laugh'd at them, and told them that he would run their jib-boom on the Island if they choose. . . ."

The day after the *Resolution* had dropped anchor at Spithead, Cook's "trusty friend the Watch," in the care of the ship's astronomer William Wales, was being carried by post-chaise to Greenwich and the care of Nevil Maskelyne. The Astronomer Royal, faced with the outstanding performance of K1 on a three-year voyage, was now haunted by his dismissive comments on H4. But powerful and influential men, schooled in the ways of committees and privy to the ear of other powerful men, can bend policy to their liking. Such a one was the arch-lunarian Maskelyne. The success of K1 led to the repeal of all the acts relating to longitude. In 1774 a new Longitude Act—formulated mainly by Maskelyne—was passed by Parliament. The conditions for any watchmaker were daunting, and financially the rewards were halved. Plus—a brilliant stroke of legislative gamesmanship—a *two-thirds* majority of the commissioners had to approve the method. Maskelyne could well satisfactorily remark that he "had given the Mechanics a bone that would crack their teeth."

K1 was to circumnavigate the world again on Cook's third, last, and fatal voyage. Another Kendall chronomter—K2—was destined to be carried by Captain Bligh on his voyage in the *Bounty*. When Bligh and his companions were set adrift in the launch, the mutineers prudently kept K2 and used it to find Pitcairn Island. There it remained from 1789 until 1808, when an American sealer, the *Topaz,* Captain Mayhew Folger commanding, came upon the island. To Folger's amazement the island was inhabited. The mutineers' hideaway had at last been found. In an exchange of gifts between the Americans and the descendants of the mutineers—only John Adams, calling himself Alexander Smith, was left alive from the *Bounty*—Folger received the *Bounty*'s azimuth compass and the Kendall chronometer. The *Topaz* sailed from Pitcairn and shaped a course for the sealing islands of Juan Fernandez. This might perhaps be thought of as enough adventures for K2—but at Juan Fernandez the *Topaz* was plundered by an avaricious Spanish governor and K2 vanished from sight. It next turned up at Concepción in Chile, where it was bought for three doubloons by a Spaniard named Castillo. On his death in 1840 the watch was sold to Captain Herbert of HMS *Calliope,* who brought it back to England. Over half a century had passed since K2 had been put aboard the *Bounty*.

In that half century Maskelyne's attempts to bolster the lunar-distance method against the inroads of the despised "Mechanics" had been slowly eroded away. But the process had been a long one. The innate conservatism of seamen is proverbial, and costs alone were in favor of the lunarians. For government and private shipowner alike, a 10-shilling investment in a yearly *Nautical Almanack* has more attractions than £100 spent on a newfangled watch. And it was not until 1825 that chronometers were standard issue to ships of the Royal Navy.

The Board of Longitude was dissolved in 1828. In the 114 years of its existence it had laid the foundations of scientific navigation with the chronometer and the lunar tables working together. The chronometer was eventually to reign supreme, but it was not until 1908 that the lunar tables were dropped from the yearly *Nautical Almanack*.

Foreign navies were not slow in grasping the advantages of the chronometer. In 1819 Captain Thaddeus Bellingshausen, commanding the two Russian expeditionary ships the *Vostok* and the *Mirny,* sailed to England—then the world's leading country in the manufacture of surveying and navigational equipment—to collect chronometers, sextants, transit instruments, artificial horizons, planimeters, achromatic telescopes, and charts. The expedition was at the start of a historic voyage that would circumnavigate Antarctica and be the first to sight land below the Antarctic Circle.

The Russians' care in selecting their instruments stands in marked contrast to a contemporary English admiral who queried one of his officers bringing aboard a suspicious-looking box. On being told that it was a chronometer, the admiral ordered it back ashore, saying that there would be "no necromancy" aboard *his* flagship.

But perhaps the last word should go to an American, who, nearly two centuries after John Harrison's death, rose to his feet after a dinner at 10 Downing Street and proposed a toast to the long-dead watchmaker. His invention, said the proposer, had led to the charting and mapping of the Earth with precision. It was the precursor of navigation systems that would take men to the Moon. The speaker was Neil Armstrong.

III

The Plague of the Sea

The destiny of nations depends on how they nourish themselves.

Jean Anthelme Brillat-Savarin, *The Physiology of Taste*, 1825

The disease which we in England call the Scuruie and Scurby, and upon the seas the Skyrby.

Gerard's Herbal, 1597

CORBUTUM, . . . Scorbute . . . Scuruie . . . Scurby . . . Skyrby . . . scurvy. Call it what you will, this was the disease that over four centuries killed more seamen than cannonball, musket fire, drowning, and shipwreck combined. It was the Black Death of the sea. And the symptoms were as loathsome as the symptoms of the Black Death. Let Richard Hakluyt, chronicler of the 1589 best-seller *The Principal Navigations, Voyages and Discoveries of the English Nation*, describe it: "By reasons of Navigation, the sailors fall with sundry diseases; their gummes waxe great and swell, so they are faine to cut them away, their legges swell, and all the body becometh sore, and so benumed that they cannot stirre hand nor feet."

To the sixteenth-century mariner scurvy was yet another affliction to add to the Pandora's box of maladies that included smallpox, the pox (venereal disease), ague (malaria), bloody flux (dysentery), ship fever (typhus), black vomit (yellow fever), and bubonic plague. It was an age when disease was accepted as one of the normal hazards of life, as immutable as the rising and setting of the Sun, as birth and death, and in extreme cases such as the Black Death, as the manifestation of a particularly dyspeptic divine retribution on mankind for its sins. St. Cyprian's words had a terrible ring of truth: "Are you molested with death and famine? Is your health crushed with raging diseases? Is mankind generally tormented with epidemical maladies? 'Tis all for your sins."

Divine punishment aside, there were various theories as to the cause of scurvy. It was perhaps some miasma, some effluvium in the air over oceans, some insalubrious change in climate once across the equator. . . . Whatever the cause it was part and parcel of long voyages at sea. Sir Richard Hawkins (who had sailed around the tip of South America into the Pacific in 1593) wished that "some learned man would write of it, for it is the plague of the sea and the spoil of mariners."

Vasco da Gama's 1497–99 voyage from Portugal to India and back was an ominous portent to the mariner of a new peril in a perilous calling. Two-thirds of da Gama's men were to die from the plague of the sea, and da Gama was forced to abandon two of his four ships due to these deaths and the weakness of the remaining crew. Some passages on the voyage were over ninety days long. By contrast, Columbus's longest passage across the Atlantic was fifty days and the shortest twenty-two.

Of the five ships and 265 men who sailed with Magellan in 1519, only one ship and 18 men returned to Spain. On the dreadful passage across the Pacific, where they were three months and 20 days without refreshment from any kind of fresh food, 19 men died from scurvy. The remainder, barely alive, were reduced to drinking putrid yellow water, eating biscuit powder crawling with weevils and stinking of rat's urine, sucking sawdust, gnawing at the ox hide (used as an antichafing material) ripped from the yards, soaked in salt water for five days, and then grilled over the embers of a fire—as were the rats auctioned off to those who could afford them. On the homeward voyage from the Spice Islands the *Victoria*, loaded with spices, was to make one passage of 148 days without revictualing. The result was the death from scurvy of half the crew, some of them natives from the East Indies. And so, with the smell of death mixed with the scent from cloves, cinnamon, nutmeg, and mace in their nostrils, the living launched the dead into the sea, where, as noted by Pigafetta, the indefatigable Italian diarist of the voyage, the Christians appropriately floated face upward toward Heaven and the heathens face downward toward Hell.

Scurvy was not limited to the sea. But its swift approach, its greater malignity, and its dreadful toll made it appear to those early mariners making their long passages across the oceans as some new type of disease. In 1675 Gideon Harvey, physician to Charles II, was splitting scurvy into mouth scurvy, leg scurvy, acid scurvy, joint scurvy, stomachic scurvy, land scurvy, and sea scurvy. He termed it the "disease of London," thought it infectious, and thought that babies became scorbutic from being kissed by doting and scurvy-infected parents. Sir Richard Hawkins, with twenty years' sailing experience behind him, estimated that ten thousand men had died from the disease. Hawkins believed, like many others, that the cause was prolonged exposure to sea air. To counteract this the decks should be washed with vinegar and the ships fumigated by the burning of tar. The best cure was "the air of the land; for the sea is natural for fishes, and the land for men." But there was another cure—sour oranges and lemons. And, wrote Hawkins, "This is a wonderful secret of the power and wisdom of God, that hath hidden so great and unknown a virtue in this fruit, to be a certain remedy for this infirmity."

But it was not only oranges and lemons that cured scurvy. Jacques Cartier, with three ships and 110 men from St. Malo, spent the winter of 1535–36 in Canada at Stadacona (Quebec City). During that winter the local Huron Indians were suffering and dying from a disease—a disease that soon appeared among the Frenchmen. Cartier's description of this disease—and the cure—identifies it as scurvy.

The said unknown sickness began to spread itself amongst us after the strangest sort that ever was either heard or seen, insomuch as some did lose all their strength, and could not stand on their feet, then did their legs swell, their sinews shrink as any coal. Others also had all their skins spotted with spots of blood of a purple colour: then did it ascend up to their ankles, knees, thighs, shoulders, arms and neck: their mouths became stinking, their gums so rotten that all the flesh did fall off, even to the roots of the teeth, which did also all fall out.

If the disease, to the Frenchmen, appeared to have come from the Indians, so did the cure. That spring, with at least fifty Indians and twenty-five Frenchmen dead, the miraculous remedy appeared. The Indians showed the French how to make a brew from the bark and leaves of a tree that they called *Ameda* or *Hanneda*. This potion effected an almost instant cure, a cure that "wrought so well, that if all the physicians of Montpellier and Louvain [leading medical schools of Europe] had been there with all the drugs of Alexandria, they could not have done so much in one year, as that tree did in six days."

It is probable that the *Ameda* was a northern white cedar, also known as the tree of life, arbor vitae, Lebensbaum, Thuia du Canada, and, scientifically, *Thuja occidentalis*. Cartier, delighted with this magic tree, had some young saplings dug up and transported them back to France, where they were transplanted into the royal gardens at Fontainebleau.

Cartier had been searching for a Northwest Passage to China. Sixty years after his wintering in Canada, a Dutch expedition led by Willem Barents and searching for a Northeast Passage to China spent an even more harrowing winter in the Arctic Ocean on the bleak island of Novaya Zemlya at 76°N. It was the farthest north that any Europeans had ever wintered. Their ship trapped and crushed by the ice, sixteen men and a young cabin boy built a small hut from the ship's timbers and driftwood. The carpenter and the cabin boy died from scurvy. In the June of 1597, showing all the signs of scurvy after their winter, the survivors took to open boats and sailed six hundred miles toward the Russian coast. It is one of the remarkable and lesser-known small boat voyages and deserves to rank with those of Bligh and Shackleton. Willem Barents, their "chief

guide and only pilot on whom we reposed ourselves next under God,"
died on the passage. On landing at Vaygach Island they found a cure for
their disease.

. . . [I]n this island we found great store of Leple leaves,* which served us exceeding well, and it seemed that God had purposely sent us thither: for as that we
had many sick men, and most of us were so troubled with scouring in our bodies,
and were thereby become so weak, that we could hardly row, but by means of those
leaves we were healed, whereat we could not choose but wonder, and therefore we
gave God great thanks for that, and for many other his mercies showed us, by his
great and unexpected aid lent us, in that our dangerous voyage: and so as I said
before, we eat them by whole handfuls together, because in Holland we had heard
much spoken of their great force, and as then found it to be much more than
expected.

The Leple leaves were those of the scurvy grass—*Cochlearia officinalis.*

A fruit, a tree, a flowering plant. Three certain cures for the plague of
the sea. Other recommended cures and preventions were based on the
belief that the secret was in the sourness of the oranges and lemons. It
followed, therefore, that the more bitter the taste, the better the cure.
These astringent and dubious remedies included vinegar, seawater, and oil
of vitriol (sulfuric acid)—and for the fortunate sailors of Bistol, a mouthful
or two of hot water that gushed from a well at the River Avon's shoreline.
The cures for landsmen were less drastic, more effective, and more palatable: purslane *(Portulaca oleracea),* watercress *(Nasturtium officinale),*
brooklime *(Veronica beccabunga),* parsley *(Petroselinum crispum),* chervil
(Anthriscus cerefolium), strawberry *(Fragaria vesca),* dame's rocket
(Hesperis matronalis). But the most widely used was scurvy grass.

In 1676 there was published in London a slim volume entitled *Cochlearia Curiosa: or the Curiosities of Scurvygrass* by Dr. Andreas Valentinus
Molimbrochius (Moellenbrock). It had originally been written in Latin—
the universal language of scholars and gentlemen—and had been "En-
glished" by Thomas Sherley, M.D. Moellenbrock gave sage advice on his
subject:

. . . [T]ake of Scurvy Grass very small cut or minced, and add of juice of Lemons
or sour Oranges, and so you will have a sauce pleasant to the taste, and effectual
against the Scurvy, for these kind of sauces are mighty advantageous in the Scurvy,
insomuch that the people of Norway are preserved from this disease by the use of
them. . . .

Lord William Howard bought "Skirvie grasse for my Lady"; the Earl
of Bedford paid 4 d [pence] for "scurvy grass to put in the children's
ale"; and, showing that scurvy grass was not an aristocratic perquisite, the

---

*Lepelbladen, or spoon leaves. A Dutch physician, Forestus, in the middle of the sixteenth
century prepared a cure for scurvy with a concoction made from Lepelbladen (scurvy grass) and
Beekpunge (brooklime).

patients of St. Bartholomew's Hospital in London were given scurvy grass ale—provided it was ordered by the doctor. And ale was the most popular way of getting the benefits of the plant. Here is a recipe for a seventeenth-century brew:

Of the juice of scurvy-grass one pint; of the juice of water-cress as much; of the juice of succory [chicory], half a pint; of the juice of fumitory, half a pint; proportion to one gallon of ale; they must be all tunned up together.

The wealthy pill-taker was also catered for by Dr. John Pechy, who advertised his patent cure for scurvy in 1696:

Excellent purging Pills prepared by John Pechy M.D. . . . . They cure the Scurvy, the most reigning Disease in this Kingdom. . . . The price for each Box is One Shilling Sixpence with Directions for use.

Pechey's pills—whatever their ingredients—were not cheap. The price of a box would support a laborer and his family for a week.

Learned European physicians, Wierus (1567), Forestus (1595), Euga-lenus (1604), and Sennertus (1624), all published works on scurvy, and ascribed its cause with as many reasons as their advocated cures: "over-flowing of black bile," "obstruction of the spleen," "corruption of the humours," "gross melancholy," "serious ichorous humour," "unwhole-some air," "vitiated texture of the blood," and, for the sailor, "a necessary consequence of an idle life, and a feeding on salt beef and pork." This in 1696 from Dr. William Cockburn, physician to the Fleet.

Today we know that scurvy is a deficiency disease, caused when some element is lacking in the diet. In 1912 a British biochemist, Professor Frederick Hopkins, published a paper suggesting that besides the carbohy-drates, proteins, fats, minerals, and water in food, there were other sub-stances necessary for good health. He named them "accessory food factors." The same year, the Polish-born Casimir Funk, with a brilliant choice of names worthy of Madison Avenue, coined the word *vitamine* for these accessory food factors and presented his theory of vitamin deficiency diseases. But it was not until 1932 that the final piece was pressed into the complicated scurvy jigsaw puzzle. The Hungarian scientist A. Szent-Gyorgi, working on an entirely different problem, isolated a crystalline substance in adrenal glands and, appropriately enough, in paprika. The same substance was also isolated in lemon juice. Vitamin C—ascorbic acid—had been found. After tests on guinea pigs, it proved to be an anti-scorbutic. Over four hundred years had passed since Sir Richard Hawkins had made his observations on oranges and lemons.

The term "antiscorbutic" had been coined two hundred years prior to the elucidation of the mystery. In 1734 there was published in Leyden—home of the famous Dutch university and a center of medical learning—a slim eighty-five-page volume entitled *Observtiones circa Scorbutum* by

Johannes Bachstrom, M.D. Every page breathes a cleansing and refreshing air. Banished were the medieval "black biles" and "ichorous humours"; banished too were all the various types of scurvy. It was all one disease, and Bachstrom was positive and precise as to its cause and its cure: scurvy was a result of a deficiency of fresh vegetables in the diet. The only cure—the "anti-scorbutic," in his words—was fresh vegetables, fresh herbs, fruits and berries. Sailors were advised to store more vegetables; besieged soldiers to grow antiscorbutic plants on the ramparts; landsmen to eat as much vegetable food as possible.

If the drowning of two thousand seamen of Sir Cloudsley Shovell's fleet triggered the founding of the Board of Longitude and the invention of a practical chronometer, another disastrous voyage of the Royal Navy led to medical reforms, an epithet for a nation, and changed the course of history.

On the last day of 1600 Queen Elizabeth signed a charter licensing a new company to trade with the East Indies. The East India Company had been born. It was a "joint-stock" company with nearly two hundred investors. Headed by the Earl of Cumberland, it included Nicholas Barnsley, grocer, £150; James Deane, draper, £300; Sir Richard Saltonstall and his children, £200; Sir Stephen Seame, Lord Mayor of London, £200. The East India Company fleet that sailed from London in January 1601 was commanded by James Lancaster, an experienced Elizabethan seaman who had already voyaged to the East Indies. His flagship carried some bottles of lemon juice—and it was the only ship of the five-strong fleet that did carry it. Scurvy appeared, followed by the inevitable deaths. The flagship *Red Dragon* was the least affected, with Lancaster administering a teaspoonful of lemon juice a day: "The juice worketh much better if the party keep in short diet and wholly refrain salt meat, which salt meat, and being at sea, is the only cause of the breeding of this disease."

All East India Company ships after this initial voyage carried lemon juice. Captain John Smith—the founder of Virginia—echoed Lancaster's sentiments in his 1627 *Seaman's Grammar,* where he recommended that ships carry spices, Dutch cheese, bacon, wine, mutton, marmalade, and "the juice of lemons for the scurvy. Some it may be will say I would have men feast than fight, but I say the want of these necessaries occasions the loss of more men than in any English fleet hath been slain since eighty-eighty."*

Pragmatic English seamen were not alone in realizing the benefits bestowed by lemon juice. The Dutch Wilhelm Schouten and Jacob le Maire bought twenty-five thousand lemons "all for a few beads and some poor Nuremberg knives" from the natives of Sierra Leone before embarking on the historic 1616 rounding of Cape Horn. The Spanish by the

* 1588, the year of the Spanish Armada.

early seventeenth century were stocking their ships sailing between the Philippines and Mexico with "agrio de limon" (lemon juice) and "jarabe de limon" (lemon syrup).

The Admiralty in London appeared impervious to previous experience, the advice of English seamen, and the practices of the East India Company ships. They were, after all, only merchant seamen and therefore relegated to the shadows, untouched by the light of a King's Commission. In 1740 the Admiralty sent out a squadron of five men-of-war, one sloop-of-war, and two victualing ships with a complement of 2,000 men. The commander was Captain George Anson and the aim was to break the Spanish hegemony in the Pacific. And bring back booty. Power politics and plunder. With baffling imbecility, the Admiralty foisted on the able and long-suffering Anson 260 infirm Chelsea Pensioners (most of them sixty to seventy years old) and over 200 raw marine recruits to act as land forces. Anson had originally been promised 500 Pensioners, but "all those who had limbs and strength to walk out of Portsmouth deserted." The remnants—veteran soldiers all—embarked with "the concern that appeared in their countenances, which was mixed with no small degree of indignation to be thus hurried from their repose into a fatiguing employ." It was also a death sentence.

The outfitting and provisioning of the squadron can only be described as criminal. Four years later, one ship and fewer than 200 men returned to the shores of England—but the captured treasure was valued at half a million pounds. The cost was a thousand men lost to scurvy, over 300 to typhus and dysentery, 4 in action, and the remainder to shipwreck, accident, starvation, and desertion. Anson was raised to the peerage and Richard Walter, M.A., chaplain of His Majesty's Ship the *Centurion,* wrote a best-seller, *A Voyage Round The World*.

The appalling losses of this expedition prompted a twenty-eight-year-old Royal Navy surgeon, Dr. James Lind, to investigate. His first task was to study the world literature on the subject of disease and then the accounts of expeditions. There were also some puzzling questions to be resolved regarding the Anson voyage. Why, for instance, did the sick men landed from the *Centurion* at Juan Fernandez continue to die, while the even sicker men—too sick to move—remaining aboard the *Gloucester* recover? The answer appeared to be that the men on the *Gloucester* had been fed fresh greens, as it was thought that the land air alone would cure the *Centurion*'s men.

All Lind's researches pointed to citrus fruit as the best combatant against scurvy. In 1747, aboard the *Salisbury,* Lind had the chance to test his hypothesis. In medical circles it is considered the classic controlled experiment. Twelve scurvy-ridden seamen were selected for this clinical investigation. All the patients were kept in the same quarters and all were fed on the same provisions—but with varying additions. Two were given a quart of cider each day; two took twenty-five drops of *elixir vitriol* three times a day; two took two spoonfuls of vinegar three times a day; two drank half a pint of seawater a day; two took a paste mixture "the bigness of a nutmeg" made of garlic, mustard seed, horseradish, balsam of *Peru,* and gum myrrh; two took two oranges and one lemon a day which "they eat with greediness, at different times, upon an empty stomach." One of the orange-and-lemon patients was back on duty within six days, the other a few days later, followed by the cider men.

In 1753 Lind published the results of his findings in the epochal *A Treatise of the Scurvy* and recommended that there be an issue of lemon juice aboard all Royal Navy ships. The advice was received by the Admiralty with glacial indifference. Instead, their Lordships elected to place their faith—a compound of hope over experience—in two substances of questionable antiscorbutic value. One of them, sauerkraut, was recommended to the Admiralty by a surgeon who wrote that it was "a German dish . . . which is nothing but cabbage cut small, pressed down, and preserved in a manner to keep it a long time. This dish is much esteemed by His Majesty, and it would surely be no handicap upon the sailors to be obliged to eat with their meat whatever their Sovereign esteems a delicacy." Sauerkraut has negligible antiscorbutic value. The Admiralty's other choice had nil. This was an extract of malt conceived by Dr. David MacBride, and it became the standard antiscorbutic of the Royal Navy. In 1767 the Sick and Hurt Board (the Admiralty arm concerned with the navy's health) stated that it considered oranges and lemons an ineffective antiscorbutic. At the same time Spanish and Portuguese medical men were in complete agreement with the findings of Lind that "the juices of lemons and bitter oranges are a most sovereign remedy and a sure means for the prevention" of scurvy. And "it would be superfluous to praise to intelligent Portuguese the virtues of lemons and bitter oranges, for they all know that they are the most sovereign remedy against the diseases of seafarers."

The Admiralty might have thought oranges and lemons ineffective, but the efficacy of their chosen antiscorbutics can be measured by the 2,400 cases of scurvy that were landed from the Channel Fleet during the spring of 1780. This after a six-week blockading cruise off the French coast. But the Admiralty was not completely peopled by blue-coated obscurantists. In 1795, after being bombarded by the advice of Sir Gilbert Blane (a Commissioner of the Sick and Hurt Board and a disciple of Lind) and Dr. Thomas Trotter, physician to the Channel Fleet, the Admiralty finally hauled down its colors and ordered that an issue of lemon juice and sugar be served aboard His Majesty's ships.

The ounce of juice and ounce and a half of sugar usually went into the rum allowance. In 1760 there had been 1,754 cases of scurvy in the Naval Hospital at Haslar. In 1806 there was 1. It was fifty years after Lind's recommendation and two hundred years after the East India Company had adopted an issue of lemon juice. Other merchant ship owners proved as obdurate and tightfisted as the Admiralty: it took two acts of Parliament (1854 and 1894) to coerce the shipowners into issuing a daily dose of lemon or lime juice to their seamen. The British "lime-juice sailor" was created and then the American, slightly derogatory, term "limey" for all of today's Brits.

During the long-drawn-out Napoleonic Wars, with the Royal Navy stretched to breaking point, Admiral Nelson purchased fifty thousand gallons of lemon juice (at 1 shilling a gallon) from Sicily for the seamen of the British blockading fleets. Sir Gilbert Blane, who estimated that "fifty lemons might be considered as a hand to the fleet," pointed out, after the defeat of Napoleon, that had the Royal Navy suffered the same rate of deaths from disease as during the American War of Independence, the fight against Napoleon at sea would have been lost. (And if lemon juice had been issued in 1753—as was Lind's advice—the war in America might have had a different result). The lemon had proved as powerful as the carronade broadside.

This story of scurvy grass, oranges, and lemons has been given—deliberately—a smooth, if slow in human terms, evolutionary development. But social evolution is full of as many crochets and quirks as biological evolution. And one of the ironical quirks is that the seaman whose paramount concern was the health of his men was also the man who—unwittingly—helped delay the introduction of the 1795 lemon-juice issue.

Not one man died from scurvy on a ship commanded by James Cook. It was a record without precedent. On the *Endeavour* he had indeed lost men from dysentery and malaria; but that was at Batavia, *fenua mate,* the land that kills. For the impeccable health record on the *Resolution* he was made a Fellow of the Royal Society and awarded the Copley Medal. Sir John Pringle, in his presidential discourse for the award, and in full rhetorical sail, said, "if Rome decreed the *Civic Crown* to him who saved the life of a single citizen, what wreaths are due to that Man, who, having himself saved many, perpetuates . . . the means by which Britain may now, on the most distant voyages, preserve numbers of her intrepid sons, her Mariners. . . ." One of those mariners was Thomas Perry of the *Resolution,* who, in part of a nine-stanza lower-deck ballad, paid his simpler tribute to Cook:

> We were all hearty seamen no cold did we fear
> And we have from all sickness entirely kept clear
> Thanks be to the Captain he has proved so good
> Amongst all the Islands to give us fresh food.

Thomas Perry had got it right. Cook had been supplied by a liberal Admiralty with many items thought to be antiscorbutic: sauerkraut, essence of malt, marmalade of carrot (recommended by Baron Storsch of

Berlin as a "Very great anti-scorbutic"), portable broth, rob of lemons and oranges, essence of spruce. The last two require some explanation. "Rob" comes from the Arabic *robb,* meaning a fruit syrup: it was a method recommended by Lind as one way of preserving orange and lemon juice; and it was made by condensing the juice by heating—a process guaranteed to nullify its antiscorbutic value. The essence of spruce echoes Cartier's magic Canadian tree. Lind had drawn attention to the Russian and Swedish treatment of scurvy with a beer made from young pine needles and shoots. MacBride also recommended it: "dry spruce, if boiled in water about one hour and a half, will make a good *Chowder-beer* . . . the spruce may be kept in any dry place for two or three years after cut." The resulting brew must have been both unpalatable and useless.

Cook, on the other hand, had most certainly been exposed to freshly made spruce beer during his years on the Canadian coast. And he never failed to start a brew when the opportunity arose to gather fresh shoots from the shores of any newly discovered coastline. Spruce beer was still made in the USA at the end of the nineteenth century; and the laconic style of the following recipe bears witness to its "down-east" origin.

One pint good spruce extract, 12 lb molasses, 3 gallons of water. Boil all and let stand 1 hour. Add 3 or 4 gallons of water, 1 pint of yeast (the water should be hand warm). Pour into a 10 gallon cask. Fill her up. Let her work. Bung her up. Bottle her off.

Cook's provisions, in truth, were insignificant as antiscorbutics. It was Cook's tireless and unremitting efforts in keeping his vessels clean, dry, fumigated, warm, ditching stale water from the casks and refilling with fresh at every opportunity, and gathering anything that swam, flew, walked, and grew, for the table, that preserved his men's health. As Cook noted, "We came to few places where either the art of man or nature had not provided some sort of refreshments or other, either in the animal or vegetable way, and it was first care to procure them by every means in my power and obliged the people to make use of them, both by example and authority." Few officers in the Royal Navy were capable of this singlemindedness. And his seamen cursed him for these gastronomic adventures. And wished, as one of them wrote, "that he might be obliged to eat such damned stuff mixed with his broth as long as he lived. Yet for all that there were none so ignorant as not to know how right a thing it was." And by his example those tough, rough, and unlettered lower-deck hands would trail back aboard like schoolchildren from an outing "with a handkerchief full of greens," just to please their captain.

Cook's brilliant achievement—and his advice—reinforced the Admiralty's belief that their choice of sauerkraut and essence of malt were the correct ones. Other nations were also influenced by Cook's example. And in 1789 we can look on rather wryly as the brilliant and clever Alessandro

Malaspina diligently supervises the making of sauerkraut and essence of malt in Cadiz—a port overflowing with oranges and lemons—prior to the Italian-born seaman's leading a five-year Spanish expedition into the Pacific and Alaska. It was a voyage that made no new discoveries, but was distinguished for its survey, hydrographic, and scientific accomplishments—and for an impressive health record, with no man dying from scurvy. But then Malaspina did carry the citrus fruits of the south, as well as the sauerkraut and malt of the north.

There is a final O. Henry twist to the story of lemon juice. The rob method of preserving lemon juice had been abandoned and replaced (no doubt with the seamen's wholehearted approval) by a 25 percent addition of rum to the fresh juice—the alcohol being the preservative agent. This obligatory issue in the Royal Navy virtually eliminated the plague of the sea. Indeed, scurvy had become such a rare disease that one eminent surgeon, in 1830, diagnosed a scurvy case as one having cancer of the gums: he was unfamiliar with scurvy symptoms.

After the Napoleonic Wars the Royal Navy, flush with victory, pride, men, and ships, turned its attention to the Arctic. The Northwest Passage beckoned once again, this time for reasons more resonant with romance than crass commercialism. There was also simple power politics. The Russian bear had stretched its paws across the Bering Strait and grasped parts of the North American continent, with trading posts and settlements stretching nearly as far south as San Francisco.* From 1818 to 1852 the Royal Navy sent its ships into the Arctic with kegs of lemon juice spiked with rum—to lower its freezing point—and the seamen, for the most part, remained free from scurvy.

In the 1860s the Admiralty ceased buying its lemons from Sicily, Malta, Portugal, and Madeira and started purchasing West Indian limes—within the Empire, and cheaper. In 1875–76 a Royal Navy Arctic expedition under Captain George Nares, with two ships and a 121 men, was decimated by scurvy. The plague of the sea had returned. And lime juice lost favor as an antiscorbutic.

Today we know that lime juice has half the vitamin C of lemon juice. For a seaman living on preserved provisions with little or none of the essential ascorbic acid, the daily ounce of lemon juice will just keep scurvy at bay. The ounce of lime juice will not. Indeed, in 1911, William Bruce the Scottish polar explorer and scientist, dismissed lime juice as "doing no harm" and "that it may or may not be useful in other directions." Bruce ascribed scurvy to the then medically fashionable theory of ptomaine poisoning, and canned food was to be used only to add variety to the diet.

---

*There was a Russian settlement at the mouth of the Russian River some sixty miles north of San Francisco. The border between Russian and British Arctic territories was settled in 1825 at 141°W.

The prevention and cure in the Antarctic regions was to live off the land and "feed on the excellent flesh of the seals and fish . . . and on the eggs and flesh of the innumerable penguins and other birds." It is the voice of James Cook.

Scurvy is inextricably linked with diet. And from the time in the fifteenth century that the Portuguese call the "Discoveries" to the early nineteenth century, the provisions aboard sailing ships changed little. Shakespeare's Master, Swabber, Boatswain, Gunner, and his Mate, could have exchanged places with C. S. Forester's counterparts and noticed small difference—except that Hornblower's men would have gulped rum rather than brandy.

The reason for this apparent inertia was the age-old problem of preserving food. And, until the first decades of the nineteenth century, the preserving of food had hardly changed for close to three thousand years. Preserving by drying with sun or smoke was known to our early ancestors; Homer wrote of salting; pickling with vinegar, mustard, salt, and honey was known by the first century A.D.; and the Romans used ice. Cheese is a way of preserving milk, and, carrying it further, beer of barley, wine of grapes.

In the middle of the sixteenth century, before Spain, England, Holland, and France had made any settlements on the North American continent; before the English had formed The Mystery and Company of Merchant Adventurers for the Discovery of Regions, Dominions, Islands and Places Unknown and sailed to Archangel and then journeyed overland to Moscow (the first small step in that extraordinary enterprise that was to lead to dominion over a quarter of the Earth's land, nearly a quarter of the Earth's peoples, and to bequeath them an international language)—before all this, the scale of provisions laid down for a seaman of Henry VIII's England was one pound of biscuit, one gallon of beer, one pound of meat for four days of the week, with cheese and dried fish for the remainder.

During the second decade of the nineteenth century, when Moscow was in flames and looting French soldiers prowled the outskirts; when Washington was put to the torch and sacked—the pickings were poor—by the British, the scale of provisions as laid down for a seaman of George III's Royal Navy was one pound of biscuit and one gallon of beer daily; two pounds of salt pork, four pounds of salt beef, twelve ounces of cheese, eight ounces of butter, two pints of dried peas, and three pints of oatmeal a week. There were three meatless days a week—"banyan days," named after the vegetarian Banian caste in India.

For longer voyages south, the butter (it turned rancid and ended up greasing the blocks) was replaced by olive oil, the oatmeal by rice, and the beer (it soon went stale) by wine and brandy. The issue of cheese was the notorious Suffolk and Essex cheese, a cheese so hard—it kept better—that it was carved into coat buttons by the sailors. It was known as "Suffolk Thump" or "Suffolk Bang" and is immortalized by Samuel Pepys, who wrote that his wife was angry "at her people for grumbling to eat Suffolk cheese." Half the price of better cheeses, its reputation earned it the following lines of doggerel:

> They that made me were uncivil
> For they made me harder than the devil,
> Knives won't cut me, fire won't sweat me
> Dogs bark at me but won't eat me.

James Cook, having served his time on the lower deck and endured this villainous cheese, insisted that his ships be supplied with the more palatable Cheshire cheese.

In an age when the poor of England subsisted on bread, cheese, and dried peas, the seaman's rations appear—if nutritionally disastrous—at least better than his fellow landsman's. But ration allowances on paper differed markedly from those in the cask. After 1776, with a magic conjuring trick, the ship's purser was allowed to reduce the rations by an eighth to compensate him for wastage and seepage. The pursers—perhaps the best-hated warrant officers in the Royal Navy—were primarily businessmen out to make a profit; indeed, the more venal of them regularly sold the ship's stores and lined their pockets with the proceeds. The successful petition to the Admiralty by the pursers to issue rations at fourteen ounces to the pound was an effort to recover the loss "of Bread by its breaking, and turning to Dust: of butter, by that part next to the Firkin being not fit to be issued: of Cheese, by its Decaying with Mold and Rottenness, and being eaten with Mites, and other insects: of Peas, Oatmeal and Flower, by their being eaten by Cockroches, Weavels and other Vermin." The petition is a telltale indication of the quality of the provisioning. The Admiralty victualing yard at Deptford was known sardonically as "Old Weevil."

Rancid pork, putrescent beef, stale beer and water, weevil-ridden biscuits, this was the common fare of the sailors—navy, whalers, sealers alike—who ventured into the Southern Ocean. Fresh meat was sometimes carried. On the hoof and claw sailed sheep, bullocks, hogs, goats, and chickens—most of them destined for the afterguard's table. One of these animals, a goat, achieved fame by twice circumnavigating the world. Shipped aboard for its milk—officers only—she had sailed with Captain Samuel Wallis and the *Dolphin* on the 1766–68 voyage, when Tahitians first laid eyes on Europeans and a goat. It was a memorable experience for the Tahitians; the goat butted one of the natives in the backside and he jumped overboard in terror "and all the rest, upon seeing what had happened, followed his example with the utmost precipitation." The goat returned to Tahiti with Cook on the *Endeavour* and then to contented browsing in Cook's garden at Mile End, around her neck a silver collar

inscribed with a couplet composed in her honor by Dr. Samuel Johnson—
in Latin and with classical references. What else would one expect from the
Doctor?

> Perpetui, ambita bis terra, praemia lactis
> Haec habet, altrici Capra secunda Jovis.*

She died on 28 March 1772. Before her death it is claimed—and one
hopes that it is true—that the Admiralty signed a warrant admitting her as
a pensioner to the seamen's hospital at Greenwich.

There was one source of fresh meat available on all ships, one not
sanctioned by any administrative body, and unknown to the purser's scales.
These were rats. They were eaten by Magellan's men on the first circumnavigation; they were eaten by Bougainville's men (deck hands and officers
alike—the Prince de Nassau paying six sous a piece and finding them
excellent) on the first French circumnavigation of 1766–69; in 1792 a
seaman on the *Active* wrote that the crew skinned and grilled them and
that they tasted much like rabbit; they were relished by officers, for Baron
Raigersfeld, writing at the same time, bought biscuit- and cheese-fed
rats—peppered and grilled, they made a change from the gobbets of fatty
salt pork. The American explorer Dr. Elisha Kent Kane ate them in the
Arctic when his ship was frozen in for two winters. Having first tried to
exterminate them with a makeshift and nearly disastrous gassing experiment, he eventually resorted to eating them: "The repugnance of my
associates to share with me the table luxury of 'such small deer,' gave me
the frequent advantage of a fresh-meat soup, which contributed no doubt
to my comparative immunity from scurvy." The empirical Kane had hit
upon a truth: for the rat harbors a remarkable enzyme that synthesizes
vitamin C—eating the abhorrent animal is an effective antiscorbutic measure. Indeed, eating most meat, freshly killed and either eaten raw or *juste
à point,* will cure scurvy. Only guinea pigs, monkeys, and humans lack the
enzyme that synthesizes ascorbic acid.

Lobscouse (stew), skilligolee (oatmeal gruel), burgoo or Scotch coffee
(oatmeal gruel with salt meat), pease pudding (dried peas boiled in a
bag), duff (boiled dough and raisins), cracker hash (soaked biscuit and salt
meat), hard tack (biscuit and salt meat), soft tack (soft white bread and
butter—officers only)—this was the limited litany of the sailors' fare. The
salt beef—"old horse" to American sailors—had to be soaked in a "har-
ness-cask": yet another wry comment as to its contents. The more inedible
pieces served in the fo'c'sle were stabbed with a sheath knife and held aloft
to the following rhyme:

---

* Translated by Boswell into a quatrain:
> In fame scarce second to the nurse of Jove
> This Goat who twice the world has traversed round
> Deserving both her master's care and love,
> Ease and perpetual pasture now has found.

> Old horse! old horse! what brought you here?
> From Sacarap' to Portland pier
> I carted stone for many a year.
> I laboured long and well, alack,
> 'Till I fell down and broke my back.
> They picked me up with sore abuse
> And salted me down for sailor's use.
> The sailors they do me despise,
> They pick me up and damn my eyes,
> They eat my flesh and gnaw my bones
> And throw the rest to Davy Jones.

A sailor's palate, hardened by this coarse fare, was as callused as his hands. Good cooks were rare. "God sends meat and the devil sends cooks" summed up the sailor's attitude; and in this the Royal Navy was worse served than merchant ships. In 1704 the Admiralty gave orders, in respect to the appointing of cooks, "to give the preference to such cripples and maimed persons as are pensioners of the chest on Chatham [a seaman's hospital]." The cook's duties were succinctly laid down as follows:

OF THE COOK

1. He is to take upon him the Care of the Meat in the Steeping-tub.
2. In stormy Weather he is to preserve it from being lost.
3. He is to boil the Provisions and deliver them out to the Men.

James Cook wrote a letter of protest to the Navy Board on the appointment of his ship's cook: "The man you have been pleased to appoint cook on His Majesty's Bark the *Endeavour,* is a lame infirm man, and incapable of doing his duty without the assistance of others; and as he doth not seem to like his appointment, beg you will be pleased to appoint another." The Navy Board, in its wisdom, did appoint another, one John Thompson, who had lost his right hand. Cook protested once again, but the Board was adamant, and so the *Endeavour* sailed with a one-handed cook.

There was, however, one provisioning item that was consumed with relish and universal approval: rum. It was an age of hard drinking—an age of Hogarth's *Gin Lane* for the city poor; bottles of claret, port, champagne, and brandy for the city gentlemen; and four bottles of wine at a sitting for the country Squire Westerns and Parson Supples. In an age like this the sailor's rum was served in prodigious quantities and any attempt to tamper with the issue led to "murmurings within the Fleet." In 1740, Admiral Vernon (whose habit it was to wear a boat cloak of coarse grogram cloth that earned him the nickname *Old Grog*) in an effort to drive "that Dragon Drunkenness out of the Fleet," had the courage—or temerity— to order the dilution of the neat rum issue. The daily half pint of rum, served at noon and at six o'clock, was to be diluted with a quarter pint of water. The hands, perhaps in admiration of Old Grog's nerve in meddling with their rum, promptly called it "grog." By Nelson's day the grog issue, served at noon to the lively tune of *Nancy Dawson* or *Drops of Brandy*, had been reduced to one gill (quarter pint) of rum with three gills of water, and in subsequent years it was reduced even further. Finally, in 1970, this old and hallowed tradition of the Royal Navy ended—and with it went "sippers" and "gulpers," the liquid currency of the lower deck.

In 1806 the French Navy was sampling preserved meat, fruit, and vegetables that had been packed in glass jars. It was a process invented by a confectioner, Nicolas Appert, and in 1809 a grateful Napoleon awarded Appert 12,000 francs and the title "Benefactor of Humanity." The Appert process was to heat the foodstuffs to high temperatures in glass jars and then seal the jars with layers of cork. The idea crossed the Channel and by 1812 the Donkin & Hall factory was at work in the Blue Anchor Road, Bermondsey, making preserved meat in tinned iron containers—not glass jars—resembling tea canisters. The canisters were labeled with the French word *bouilli* (boiled meat). The canned food industry had started and "bully beef" was born. By 1813 canned food was being supplied to the Royal Navy, and four years later a Donkin & Hall brochure was quoting testimonials from such luminaries as Sir Joseph Banks, Admiral Cochrane, and Lord Wellesley.

British Arctic expeditions from 1814 were supplied with canned beef, mutton, veal, and vegetables. The Russian Arctic expedition of 1815–18 under Otto von Kotzebue carried Donkin & Hall products and found them excellent. A Russian Antarctic expedition under Thaddeus Bellingshausen stopped off in England to supply themselves with charts, navigation instruments, and "Mr Donkins . . . specially preserved fresh soups with vegetables and beef tea." The French corvette *Astrolabe* on the 1826–29 voyage into the Pacific carried Appert's preserved food—in cans, not glass jars; it was not a success, as the greater part of the canned braised chicken turned out to be putrid. The commander of that expedition, Dumont d'Urville, returned to the Pacific and the Antarctic in 1837–40 provisioned with canned goods by Noel & Taboureau, using a new process. The meat, in thirty-kilogram containers, proved even less of a success than Appert's braised chicken, for the drums started to explode seven weeks after sailing from Toulon.

The British were more successful with their canned provisions. In 1839 the *Erebus* and *Terror* were being loaded with twenty-six tons of canned provisions before sailing to the Antarctic. They included beef, mutton, veal, ox-cheek, vegetable soup, carrots, parsnips, beetroots, onions, and turnips. After the completion of this voyage Sir James Clark Ross recommended that canned provisions be issued to all ships of the Royal Navy. The Admiralty reacted with far more speed to the advice from Ross than it had done to that of Lind. The same year, 1847, canned goods became part of the standard provisioning (they had been part of the ship's "medical comforts" since 1831). But the new type of provisioning, like lime juice, was soon to fall from favor. The scale of the provisions ordered by the Admiralty led the manufacturers to increase the size of their canisters. Two- to six-pound packs became ten- to fourteen-pound packs. And the contents of the larger-size containers were the ones found putrid. Such was the scale of the wastage (in one year, in one victualing yard, from one manufacturer, over fifty tons of canned meat had to be condemned) that a Select Committee was appointed to investigate. One of its conclusions was to limit the size of the container to six pounds and for the Admiralty to set up its own canning factory at the Deptford Victualling Yard.

The limit on the size of the canister was an empirical but wise choice. Louis Pasteur had yet to publish his findings on the part microorganisms play in fermentation and putrefaction, and it was thought sufficient to exclude air from the can in order to preserve the contents. We now know that the center of the large packs of meat were insufficiently heated— bacteria remained alive in the center ready to contaminate the rest.

A nation's eating habits, its regional differences—and its attitude toward food—defined the provisions aboard vessels in the days of sail. For French sailors their scale of provisions remained unchanged for over one hundred years. Laid down in 1689 by Jean Baptiste Colbert, it consisted of biscuits, salt beef, salt cod, bacon, cheese, dried peas, dried beans, oil, vinegar, wine, and brandy, with pickled vegetables reserved for the officers and the sick. By some strange gastronomic quirk the French sailors preferred English salt beef to their own. And when an English ship was taken as a prize, the beef was one of the first items that found a new home.

In 1647 Estienne Cleirac called Frenchmen *gastrolâtres*—men devoted to their stomachs. It is a description reinforced by a reading of *The Memoirs of Père Labat*. This amiable and convivial priest sailed to the West Indies in 1693, and the Lucullan feasting aboard the *Loire* could have only happened aboard a French ship. Breakfast consisted of fresh-baked bread, butter, cheese, ham or pâté, a ragout or fricassee, and "very excellent wine." Dinner at noon was chicken broth, Irish beef *du petit salé,* mutton or veal, fricassee of chicken, two ragouts, two salads, cheese, jams, stewed fruits, and nuts. Supper was much the same as dinner, only with more wine. On board there were two large earth-filled boxes planted with chicory (and guarded night and day by a sentry to thwart thieving rats and common sailors). When the chicory was finished, the box was sown with lettuce and radish seeds.

The same civilized attitude can be seen a few years later. Sailing between the West Indian islands aboard a French barque armed with two cannons but only one cannonball, the good father noted that the one round could not be fired, as it was used to crush the mustard seeds to dress their *cochon boucanné*. A perfect example of La Rochefoucauld's aphorism: "To eat is a necessity, but to eat intelligently is an art."

Compare Labat's *Memoirs* with an incident from the *Memoirs of William Hickey* aboard the East India Company ship *Plassey* bound from England to India. No freshly baked bread, but only hard biscuit "uncommonly bad and flinty." So hard that a 5-guinea wager was made that one of Hickey's companions would be unable to eat a biscuit—teeth only and no water—within four minutes. It was gobbled, with a near choking in the process, with six seconds to spare. Eating is turned into a game.

Labat and Hickey exemplify their respective countries' attitudes toward food. If Brillat-Savarin's aphorism "Tell me what you eat, and I shall tell you what you are" is taken to its logical conclusion, a nation's eating habits can be measured by the consumption of its consumers. Fifty years before Labat, De Rochefort in his *Histoire Naturelle des Antilles de l'Amerique* described the Carib Indians' gastronomic rating of the Europeans. The Spanish were virtually uneatable, being tough and full of gristle; the Dutch were dull and tasteless; the English little better; but the French were considered tasty and delicious.

Aboard American ships—navy, whalers, and sealers—the provisions could have found a place in the Conestoga wagons and prairie schooners of the pioneers: casks of salt pork, flour, molasses, beans, coffee, rum, and whiskey. At Rio de Janeiro, on the first leg of the 1838–42 United States Exploring Expedition, 125 gallons of whiskey was found to have leaked from the *Vincennes* casks. Knowing the ingenuity of sailors at tapping casks, it is unlikely that the leak was natural.

The gargantuan consumption of wine, beer, and spirits by eighteenth- and nineteenth-century seamen is one of the most staggering aspects of their nutritionally disastrous diet. Measuring the energy intake—the fuel—in calories, the glaring fact emerges that over half their energy came from alcohol. P. G. Wodehouse's immortal pig, the Empress of Blandings, in order to preserve her prize-winning shape, consumed 57,800 calories a day. The human body requires less—about 3,500 calories for an active male. Without the wine, beer, and rum, the sailor's diet lacked sufficient calories to power the quill of a sedentary clerk sitting at an Admiralty desk.

Today's health evangelists, the fervent apostles of diet and exercise, whose creed is more concerned with the temporal body than with the soul, whose icons are jogging shoes and exercise machines, and who, if wine, beer or spirits ever pass their lips, puritanically quantify it in "units," would, using this measurement, classify these seamen as chronic alcoholics. It is a sobering thought, that His Brittanic Majesty's ships were manned by irredeemable drunks. But it seems appropriate that this navy of lushes, after winning the battle of Trafalgar, preserved their Admiral's body in a cask of spirits for his last passage to England.

IV

The Southern Ocean

I firmly believe that there is a tract of land near the pole,
which is the source of most of the ice which is spread over
this vast Southern Ocean.

Journals of Captain James Cook, 6 February 1775

LMOST three-quarters of the Earth's surface area is covered by
salt water. Guides to this vast area—the Baedekers of the
oceans—are published by the Hydrographic Departments of the
United States and Britain. The American *Sailing Directions* are
printed in loose-leaf ring binders held in paper covers. The British *Pilots*
are well-bound volumes worthy of any bookshelf. The contents of both
are similar.

The *Pilots* number seventy-three volumes all told, and cover the coasts
and seas of the world, from the *Africa Pilot* (no. 1) to the *Ch'ang Ch'iang
Pilot* (no. 73). Bound in sober navy blue cloth with gilt lettering and
numbered off like parading sailors on the chart room bookshelves, they
make an impressive display of nautical information, hard-won learning,
and experience. If such an item as a nautical *vade mecum* exists, these
publications admirably perform this function. Full of sage advice as to
tides, currents, reefs, shoals, and anchorages, they are not noted for their
lyrical prose. Hilaire Belloc, however, found a sentence in one that he
committed to memory. The qualities are Homeric: "But the mariner will
do well to avoid this passage at the approach of the turn of the tide, or the
wind be rising, or darkness falling upon the sea."

Volume no. 9 in this series is the *Antarctic Pilot*. And the full title on
the front cover gives a whiff of high adventure and voyages fit for an
Odyssey. It reads thus:

THE

ANTARCTIC PILOT

COMPRISING

THE COAST OF ANTARCTICA

AND

ALL ISLANDS SOUTHWARD OF THE USUAL
ROUTE OF VESSELS

The *Antarctic Pilot,* in short, is the seaman's guide to the Southern Ocean. Captain James Cook, the first man to lead an expedition into the high southern latitudes, so named the ocean after realizing the uniformity of this vast circumpolar body of water: its climate, wind patterns, currents, and wildlife. But what are the limits to this ocean? Particularly, what is its northern boundary?

The second edition of the *Antarctic Pilot,* published in 1948, has no problem with the question. In a forthright manner it states: "The name 'Southern Ocean' has been adopted for all the portion of the globe bounded southward by a line joining the southern parts of South America, Africa, Australia and New Zealand, and southward by the coast of Antarctica." By the fourth edition, in 1974, a havering and vacillating note is struck: "Southern Ocean is the term generally adopted by British scientists, but as yet not universally agreed, for the circumpolar body of water lying N of the Antarctic Continent, the N limits of which are not precisely defined but approximately Latitude 55°S."

Russian oceanographers side with their British brethren and lean toward the second-edition definition. The United States Hydrographic Center in its *Sailing Directions for Antarctica* cunningly sidesteps the issue and makes no mention of a Southern Ocean—or even of an Antarctic Ocean, for that matter. U.S. scientists are advised to spell Southern Ocean in lower case—southern ocean. The International Oceanographic Commission of UNESCO writes "Southern Oceans"—plural—which makes no sense at all. Chile and Argentina, due to political reasons (they regard the southern Pacific and Atlantic as their own private bailiwicks) will have no truck with the name.

The vastness of this ocean is easier to deal with than the semantics. A lone and resolute sailor setting his vessel's bow toward the rising sun and leaving astern the shouldering bulk of Cape Horn can sail around the globe along the 56°S latitude and arrive back at Cape Horn, tanned by wind and sun, having sailed across more than 12,000 miles of ocean without sighting land, his only companions being seabirds, whales, dolphins, and perhaps the lone iceberg.

A like-minded sailor sailing east from the rocky shores of Labrador in 56°N latitude will have a short sail of 1,850 miles before being stopped by the island of Jura lying off the west coast of Scotland. From here his journey round the globe will be more land than water. If of an inquiring mind, he can, on this eastbound 56°N odyssey and with small diversions, take in the isolated farmhouse on Jura where George Orwell wrote *1984;* listen to the piper on the battlements of Edinburgh Castle and absorb culture at the Festival; pace, like Hamlet, through the passages of Elsinore

Castle; ponder on Lenin's Tomb in Red Square; cross the path of the ninth- and tenth-century Viking trade routes on the Volga River and visit Kazan University, where Lenin and Leo Tolstoy were students; traverse the huge and sinister-sounding Vasyugan Swamp of Siberia; ease his journey with a ride on the Trans-Siberian Railway; cross the mountainous Stanovoy Range of eastern Siberia; take to the sea again with a short passage across the Sea of Okhotsk, followed by an even shorter land journey across the Kamchatka Peninsula, and another sea passage, across the Bering Sea, before being blocked by the formidable bulk of the Coast Mountains of the Alaska panhandle; travel through Dawson Creek and the terminus of the Trans-Alaska Highway; and finally cross that great stretch of Canada that appears more water than land, before arriving back on the coast of Labrador. He would have a skin dappled with the finest collection of insect bites in the northern hemisphere, a mind stuffed with impressions of history, culture, politics, and literature, and a bag bulging with tourist kitsch items—impulsively bought and regretted at leisure.

The southern voyager would have crossed an apparently sterile stretch of ocean, devoid of history and interest. Only the soaring albatross might have brought back dim schoolroom memories of Coleridge's ancient Mariner and the fate of that benighted sailor. Or, if he was of a larger literary turn of mind, perhaps the vastness and open immensity of the Southern Ocean would have called to mind Dante's world, where the northern hemisphere was land and the southern hemisphere water, with only the slopes of Mount Purgatory rising from the ocean's depths. He would, however, be spared the universal blank and stoney-eyed stare of the uniformed officials at all the frontier crossings—a look that is slipped on with the uniform, and which, with the rubber stamp, forms part of the bureaucratic armament in officialdom's battle to harass and cow the anarchic public.

Nevertheless, frontiers would have been crossed. Not those marked by warning signs, flags, fences, and uniformed guards, but ones of a more enduring kind, related to rivers, deserts and mountain ranges. Snaking around Antarctica some eight hundred miles off the coastline and weaving between 50°S and 60°S latitude, two bodies of water of differing temperature and salinity converge. Here, at this meeting place, the near-freezing surface waters surrounding the continent slip below the warmer waters of the sub-Antarctic. Oceanographers know it as the Antarctic Convergence.

For the crew of a ship sailing south, the frontier is well defined. Within a few hours the water and air temperature take a precipitous drop and hover near the freezing point, and the fog and mist close in. If the shivering deckhand knows that a boundary has been crossed, so will a marine biologist and oceanographer studying hauls from the plankton net and bottom dredge; the Convergence is a definite biogeographical frontier with differing forms of planktonic life and bottom sediment on either side of the frontier.

The most dramatic example of the Convergence's influence can be seen in the climatic differences between two islands in the Southern Ocean. Staten Island, trailing off the scorpion tip of South America, is one thousand miles distant from South Georgia, but lies in the same latitude. Staten Island is well wooded, wet, windy, and cool. South Georgia is treeless, windy, over half covered with permanent ice and snow, and has glacier snouts nosing into the sea. In the meridian of South Georgia the Convergence, due to sea-bottom configuration and currents, takes a sweep north, engulfing South Georgia while leaving Staten Island in more temperate waters.

Sometimes an animal, by reason of its perfect fitness in a harsh and hostile environment, becomes identified in the popular mind as representing that environment—becomes in effect its heraldic beast. As the polar bear is for the Arctic, the penguin for the Antarctic, and the camel for the desert, so for the Southern Ocean the most fitting emblem is the wandering albatross. This magnificent bird, with its eleven-foot wingspan, soaring effortlessly over the white-capped waves, is the pure essence of these southern waters. A young wanderer, tentatively launching itself into the air from its birthplace in South Georgia at the start of its three- to five-year hegira before returning to its ancestral home, will endlessly circle the globe and the waters of the Southern Ocean, its curiosity perhaps only piqued by the occasional sighting of a lone ship or isolated island.

No other continent is so surrounded by such a vast body of water. The swells, waves, and set of this ocean, under the urging of the prevailing westerly winds, endlessly circle the continent, the only constriction being the 620-mile-wide bottleneck between the tips of South America and the Antarctic Peninsula.

Experiments with drift bottles and drift cards indicate an east-flowing current of between five and eighteen miles a day. But nature can perform its own drift experiments: on 5 March 1962 a submarine eruption thirty-five miles northwest of Zavodovski Island, the northernmost of the South Sandwich Islands, spewed out millions of tons of pumice. Nine days later, HMS *Protector* reported two thousand square miles of ocean covered with pumice particles thick enough to block the ship's water intakes. The pumice reached the shores of New Zealand by early 1964, the larger pieces, like buoyant bathtub playthings, sailing before the wind at sixteen miles a day. A more sophisticated and expensive approach was used in 1978–79 in a study of temperature and atmospheric pressure when a large number of drift buoys were released in the Southern Ocean. The buoys transmitted their position and climate information several times a day to a passing satellite: the average drift was thirteen miles a day. The same conclusion was reached nearly 150 years earlier by Captain James Clark Ross in the *Erebus* and the *Terror.* After sailing from Kerguelen Island bound east for Tasmania, it was noted that the ships were twelve to sixteen miles by observation in advance of their daily reckoning. In one two-day period with no observations they found themselves fifty-eight miles to the east of their reckoning. In these days of satellite navigation systems, reading extracts like this illuminates the perils of sailing-ship navigation based on sun or lunar sights and dead reckoning: it conjures up visions of sudden and catastrophic shipwreck on any of the bleak islands set like traps in the Southern Ocean. On one such group, the Auckland Islands lying to the south of New Zealand and on the course of ships bound from Australia to Cape Horn, nine ships and over a hundred lives were lost over the short space of 40 years.

The unrestricted fetch of the Southern Ocean urged on by the prevailing westerlies—the "roaring forties" of the square-rigger days—builds up a heavy swell and big seas. Through James Cook's daily record of his months in the Southern Ocean runs a litany of "very high swell," "great swell," "vast swell," "prodigious swell," "prodigious sea," "sea ran prodigious high." Cook was not a man given to exaggeration, and his laconic entries are borne out by U.S. satellite information showing "significant wave heights" of thirty-six feet every few days in some part of the Southern Ocean. Now the significant wave height is the average height of every third wave taken over a twenty-minute period: the maximum wave height during that period is often twice the "significant wave height." The Russians in their wave maps of the Southern Ocean suggest maximum wave heights of between eighty and one hundred feet near Kerguelen Island. Monster hundred-foot breaking waves are the stuff of which seamen's nightmares are made.

The continent that is wrapped around by this formidable ocean has even more implacable defenses than mere winds and waves. During the winter months over half of the ocean below the Convergence gradually freezes over and locks the continent in an iron grip.

The Inuit of the Arctic have a large vocabulary to describe types of snow. Seamen in their turn have also evolved an extensive glossary to catagorize the many types and conditions of sea ice: anchor, bergy bits, brash, floe, floeberg, nilas, fast, frazil, grease, growler, hummocked, pressure ridge, flooded, breccia, ice cake, pancake, rotten, shuga, slush, and pack. Even submariners have evolved their own recondite terms, seeing the ice, as it were, from underneath: friendly, skylight, bummocks, hostile, and canopy.

Due to its salt content, sea ice forms and acts differently from freshwater ice. In the felicitous imagery of the *Sailing Directions for Northern Canada,* "Two inches of fresh-water ice will support a heavy man walking; two inches of sea ice will not support a child crawling." And the stages of newly forming sea ice make a chanted refrain that would appeal to the ears of a child: frazil, grease, slush, shuga, pancake. The last-named is the most decorative and instantly recognizable. A gentle swell, breaking the newly forming and fragile frozen surface, rubs and jostles the pieces into roughly circular shapes with upturned edges—the surface of the sea magically covered with frozen lily pads. The next phase is for the pancakes to weld together, and with freezing temperatures and calm weather the ice quickly thickens into floes and pack ice. The frozen sea at its peak—consolidated pack ice—covers some seven million square miles of the Southern Ocean—a mass of ice the size of South America. After September, with the return of the spring and summer sun, the cordon around Antarctica slowly loosens and the weakened and rotting ice floes drift away on the ocean's currents; but over a million square miles of sea ice defies the summer sun and remains as an iron-like rim blocking off large stretches of Antarctica's coastline from any approach by sailing ship.

Such a sailing vessel, having crossed the Convergence on a southbound course, will come across large areas of the drifting pack ice and then spend a frustrating and dangerous time threading its way through the ever-changing maze of floes. But the ice a seaman sees first, often before even crossing the Convergence, is the "ice islands" of the early voyagers: the tabular icebergs spawned by Antarctica's ice shelves. These distinctive icebergs, so different from those of the Arctic, are flat topped and often miles in length; with waves crashing at the base of their high cliff faces they can well be mistaken for islands.

The early voyagers, particularly those coming from civilian life and not part of the ship's company proper—the "experimental gentlemen" of the sailors when talking of the artists, naturalists, and astronomers—tended to describe these icebergs through the lens of the new Romantic movement in literature and the arts—particularly the effect of scenery upon the "sensibilities" of the viewer. "Feelings of awe and admiration," "majesty of size," "inconceivable grandeur," "delicately beautiful," "strangely terrific aspect" are the tenor of these descriptive passages. And the quintessential "sublime" of the Romantic period is scattered through this prose like currants in a plum duff pudding.

To the jaundiced and pragmatic eyes of seamen, not given to the high-blown fancies of literary gentlemen of the Romantic period, with their Rousseau-esque notions on the "noble savage," simple peasant life, and inspiring scenery, the icebergs merely represented another dangerous and unpredictable hazard: their only advantage, if large enough, as a place for shelter in the lee, and, if small enough, as providing chunks of ice to be melted for fresh water.

The seasonal pattern and the timetable for the breakup of the winter pack ice determined the position of the early discoveries along Antarctica's coastline. Indeed, until the period after World War II and Antarctic photographic mapping flights, most of Antarctica's coastline lay hidden in mystery and conjecture—tentatively indicated on maps by the broken line of cartographic uncertainty.

These lengths of the coastline, rimmed by permanent pack ice, are the last strongholds of Antarctica's defense system. But they are counterbalanced by weak points where, during the months from December to March, a ship can reach the coast with relative ease. The South Shetland Islands, parts of the Antarctic Peninsula, the east coast of the Weddell Sea, and, most famous of all, the Ross Ice Shelf and Ross Island are typical of these.

The summer months in the South Shetlands have average temperatures above freezing—a fact that has earned them the condescending soubriqet of "banana belt" from personnel who man stations in more frigid climates. This relative warmth, combined with the frequent depressions that sweep across the Peninsula bringing strong winds, leads to a quick breakup of the winter ice. The case is different in the eastern sector of the Weddell Sea. There, easterly winds and a comparatively warm subsurface current running from the Indian Ocean help in the breakup of the sea ice. But, as if to balance this, a plume of pack ice streams eastward from the tip of the Peninsula, making a barricade for any entry into the Weddell Sea until late summer. It is this stream of ice that confronted Cook's *Resolution* and *Adventure* in 1773, and whalers of this century. As to the Ross Sea pack ice, wind and current open up a corridor roughly following the 180-degree meridian into the heart of the Antarctic: a route followed by the ships of Ross, Scott, Shackleton, Amundsen, and Byrd that led them to Ross Island and the Ross Ice Shelf—as far south as a ship can sail.

This remote and hostile ocean, with its monstrous waves and swells; its constant pattern of depressions endlessly circling the continent and following fast one upon another; its icebergs and pack ice; its surface waters near freezing; its scattering of bleak and inhospitable islands—all this, set thousands of miles from the great concentrations of population in the northern hemisphere, seems an unlikely magnet for the fleets of ships and thousands of men who over the last two hundred years have made the long voyage south in a cycle of recurring invasions. Some came on voyages of exploration, but for the most part the lengthy voyage was made for the hunting of seals and whales.

The Southern Ocean below the Convergence, although having a surface appearance of sterility, is in fact a fecund and rich broth supporting different species of animals noted more for their sheer quantity than for their diversity. An observer peering over the rail of a ship shouldering its way through the pack ice and upending the floes on its passage can see the foundation of this richness in the yellow-brown stains on the underside of the floes. One such algae, *Phaeocystis poucheti,* blooms in such abundance that it can clog a plankton net with a jellylike mass: in the days when marine biologists swore, drank strong liquor, chewed and smoked tobacco, it went by the name of "Dutchman's 'baccy juice."

Here is the pasture of the ocean—the phytoplankton—that is browsed upon by the small creatures of the ocean—the zoöplankton. And one of the zoöplankton, the two-inch-long, shrimplike crustacean *Euphausia superba,* in its turn provides food for the seabirds, penguins, seals, and whales. The old whalers knew the blue whale, *Balaenoptera musculus,* as the "sulphur-bottom" whale due to the film of yellow-green phytoplankton that shaded its natural color. A sighting of a blue whale feeding in the Southern Ocean dramatically illustrates an extraordinary short food chain in one glance—from phytoplankton to zoöplankton to the largest mammal ever to live on this planet.

> Big floes have little floes all around about 'em,
> And all the yellow diatoms couldn't do without 'em.
> Forty million shrimplets feed upon the latter,
> And *they* make the penguin and the seals and whales
> Much fatter.

So wrote Thomas Griffith Taylor, a geologist on Captain Robert Falcon Scott's second (1910–11) Antarctic expedition. Eleven species of Griffith Taylor's shrimplets—or "krill," the Norwegian word for whale food—are found in the Antarctic: but it is *Euphausia superba* that dominates them all. Distributed around the continent below the Convergence with the largest congregations near the South Shetland Islands, South Georgia, and west of the South Sandwich Islands, they mass together in such huge swarms that the sea is tinted pink by their sheer numbers. In these extraordinary concentrations the billions of krill swim with military precision, all in parallel alignment and all with heads in the same direction. In 1981, off Elephant Island, a monstrous swarm of krill was seen and estimated to be more than 2.5 million tons (70 million tons of fish is roughly the world's annual total fish catch). This swarming habit of krill makes them easy prey for the blue whales—or any other predator, for that matter, including man—during the four months of feeding time: but then an adult blue requires about 4 tons of krill a day.

Today the chances of sighting a blue whale in Antarctic waters are remote. The massive slaughter of over thirty-one thousand blues during the 1930–31 season dealt the stocks a mortal blow, and they are now reduced to a pitiful number—perhaps 2 percent of their original population.

The whales most likely to be seen, particularly in the krill swarming areas, are the fin, Sei, Bryde, minke, humpback, sperm, and killer whales. All these, except for the last two, are filter feeders of krill. The humpback, among these filter feeders, is perhaps the most distinctive, with its enormously long flippers—one-third the body length—and its characteristic diving sequence: a slow, wheeling, humpbacked rotation, and then the languid raising of the tail flukes high into the air before the final slide into the depths. A sight never to be forgotten is to watch a humpback, apparently at play, lie on the surface with one giant scalloped flipper raised like a sail, then roll over with the flippers extended, for all the world like a child spinning with outstretched arms; and then to watch the slow sinuous dive followed, if you are lucky, by the whale's exploding from the water in a giant backward somersault leap—forty tons of airborne exuberant whale.

A whale that does evoke a passing and, from man's point of view, unjustified apprehension, is the killer whale. Linnaeus gave it the name *Delphinus orca*—the demon dolphin—and it has managed to collect for itself a rather fearsome reputation. Seeing a pack of killers with their tall fins scything the water as they patrol the edge of the pack ice does invoke a frisson of fear. It is the menace associated in countless World War II movies, with the camera shot across the sea focusing on the telltale wake of a U-boat periscope . . . underneath the sinister periscope—or fin—something terrible lurks.

The killer whale is a relatively small animal, only about twenty-five to thirty feet long, and its most distinctive feature is the high dorsal fin, which can be six feet tall in an adult male. The body is beautifully and distinctively marked in a black-and-white pattern, with the Antarctic whales having their white patches tinted yellow by a film of algae. Favorite hunting areas are the leads in pack ice and among ice floes, for their eating habits are predatory and omnivorous—seals, penguins, squid, fish, and even other whales.

Like most pack hunting animals, they are possessed with high intelligence and work together in groups. A lone seal lying on an ice floe will have its resting place tilted from underneath and slide helpless to its death. The writer has seen six killers in line ahead, led by an adult male, swim fast toward a floe on which rested a somnolent seal; the whales turned quickly at the floe's edge, setting up a series of waves that washed across the floe and swept the seal into the water.

This hunting acumen was demonstrated to Scott and the expedition photographer, Herbert Ponting, in 1911. At the time, the *Terra Nova* was moored to the fast ice and busy unloading stores for the winter quarters on Ross Island a mile and a half away. Ponting, eager for photographs of some icebergs held in the fast ice, was packing a sledge with his camera equipment; nearby, two sledge dogs were tethered to the wire stern hawser of the ship. Also nearby, but prowling the water at the ice edge, were half a dozen killer whales. Scott shouted to Ponting and pointed out the whales. The whales to Ponting were the perfect photograph; to the whales Ponting and the dogs were strange but possibly tasty morsels. The whales dived under the ice and rose with loud "booming noises." The ice split asunder and Ponting, clutching his camera, leaping from floe to floe, racing for safety, recollected thinking that no doubt the first bite would be very unpleasant but it would not matter much about the second. It would have been of small consolation to Ponting to have the assurances of knowledgable marine biologists that no human has been eaten by a killer whale. Lieutenant Victor Campbell—known as the "Wicked Mate" to his *Terra Nova* companions—wrote in his diary on the incident: "What an irony to be eaten for a seal and spat out because one was a man. . . ." A little more caustically, in a letter to his sister, "a man" was changed to "only a photographer."

Some seven miles to the north of Ponting's terrifying experience, at Cape Royds on Ross Island, lay the empty winter quarters hut of Shackleton's—by now Sir Ernest Shackleton's—expedition of 1907–9. The hut lies in a hollow among the volcanic rocks of the island, cheek by jowl with the southernmost Adélie penguin colony in Antarctica. Fifty miles distant from Cape Royds, on the opposite side of Ross Island at Cape Crozier, lay what was then the only known emperor penguin colony. Both breeds, perhaps, are the best known and most famous of penguins: the emperor due to its size—it's the largest living penguin—and the Adélie, with its black-and-white livery reminiscent of a tubby gentleman in a dinner jacket, a boon to cartoonists and thus immortalized into Antarctica's archetypal penguin.

The scientific names for animals and plants can be guaranteed to produce a glaze-eyed look in the lay reader, followed by a quick turning of the page. But rummaging through the ragbag of vernacular and scientific names for Antarctica's animals is a rewarding, salutary, bewildering, and sometimes amusing experience. *Homo sapiens,* being a quantifying, cataloguing, and bureaucratic species, seeks to bring order to an apparently anarchic world. It makes it less threatening. The Swedish naturalist and physician Carolus Linnaeus, born in 1707 as Carl von Linné, strove manfully to bring order to the flora and fauna by fathering the modern system of scientific nomenclature. His Latinized name was a bow to an age where Latin was the lingua franca (a merchant's language used in the Levant and a mixture of Italian, French, Greek, Spanish, and Turkish) of the scientist (a term not coined until the middle of the nineteenth century). Linnaeus arrived at a binomial system, with two words describing the genus and species of flora and fauna; the language used is a barbarous compound of pseudo-Latin mixed up with Greek roots.

The derivation of the vernacular name "penguin" is lost in the mists of time, in this case northern mists. Funk Island off the coast of Newfoundland was known to English sixteenth-century sailors as Penguin Island—so named, it is thought, after the now-extinct flightless great auk, which nested on the island in vast numbers. Such helpless prey was easily killed and the meat, either fresh or salted, used in provisioning ship. Thus the name for the northern flightless bird was transferred by English sailors to the flightless bird of the south.

But "penguin" is an odd word. Some authorities claim it comes from the Welsh *pen gwyn,* meaning white-headed—but the great auk had a black head; others claim it comes from the Latin *pinguis,* meaning fat; others from the English "pin-wing," in reference to the small wings. On one sixteenth-century map, Funk Island appears as Puanto—"stinking"—Island, in reference to the guano deposits from huge numbers of other breeding seabirds. Perhaps some long-forgotten Welsh sailor, chattering away in his own language, named the island "white-headed" after this covering of guano—and the name was then transferred to the great auk.

We now enter an *Alice in Wonderland* and *Through the Looking Glass* world. The scientific name for the extinct great auk is *Pinguinus impennis,* meaning featherless penguin. The great auk was not featherless, nor is it a member of the *Sphenisciformes*—the order of all penguins (penguins are distinguished for having an order and a family—*Spheniscidae*—to themselves). Now the word *spheniscus* is a Latinized form of a Greek word meaning wedge; but little about the penguin is wedge-shaped except for a wedge-shaped tail and, stretching the imagination, the short stumpy wings.

No matter; the first time the word "penguin" is used to describe the southern bird occurred during the 1586–88 third circumnavigation of the world by Thomas Cavendish in the *Desire.* Cavendish stopped at the same island in the Straits of Magellan that Sir Francis Drake had anchored off nine years previously. Here Drake had "found great store of fowl which could not fly, of the bigness of geese, whereof we killed in less than one day 3,000 and victualled ourselves thoroughly therewith." Cavendish and his men followed Drake's example and "killed and salted great store of Penguins for victuals." Over the next two centuries the name penguin became common currency in other languages. It so annoyed the French eighteenth-century naturalist Comte de Buffon—ignorant English seamen mistaking a quite different southern bird for the northern great auk—that he proposed naming the southern bird *manchot,* meaning "one-armed" in French. As the penguin has two distinct wings—or arms—it was not a happy choice by the eminent naturalist. The name penguin has determindly held its own: *pinguino* in Spanish, *pinguin* in German, *pingvin* in Danish and Swedish, and the French, finally admitting defeat, bowing to *pingouin,* with *manchot* coming in as an also-ran.

But what of the vernacular and scientific names for each species of penguin seen by those early sailors in the Southern Ocean? Let us first take the emperor penguin, *Aptenodytes forsteri.* The genus *Aptenodytes,* in barbarous Latin with Greek roots, means "featherless diver"; but although the emperor does dive—like all penguins—it is by no means featherless.

The first emperor penguin skins and carcasses—preserved entire in casks of strong pickle—came to Europe for the first time aboard the *Erebus* and the *Terror* in 1843. In London they were declared a new species by John Gray, Keeper of Zoology at the British Museum, and Gray gave them the specific name *forsteri* to honor Johann Forster, who had sailed aboard the *Resolution* as naturalist—though it is doubtful if Forster had ever seen an emperor penguin during the voyage with Cook.

Ross and the naturalists aboard the *Erebus* and the *Terror* found these doughty birds so hard to kill that they resorted to rather unusual methods:

During the last few days we saw many of the great penguins, and several of them were caught and brought on board alive; indeed it was a very difficult matter to kill them, and a most cruel operation, until we resorted to hydrocyanic acid, of which a tablespoonful effectually accomplished the purpose in less than a minute. These enormous birds varied in weight from sixty to seventy-five pounds. The largest was killed by the *Terror*'s people, and weighed seventy-eight pounds.

Next in line in this regal avian hierarchy is the king penguin, *Aptenodytes patagonicus,* slightly smaller than the emperor. Johann Forster had killed some of this species on South Georgia, and the specific name stemmed from the erroneous belief that the birds bred in Patagonia.

What of the smaller breeds of penguin found by those early sailors of the Southern Ocean? Oliver Goldsmith, just before his death in 1774, compiled a book on natural history and noted that "our sailors . . . give these birds [penguins] the very homely, but expressive name of arse-feet." Not only sailors. The generic name of the three species of *Pygoscelis* penguin is a Latinized version of the Greek *pygo,* "rump," and *scelos,* "leg": the "rump-legged" penguin.

The specific name of *Pygoscelis antarctica,* the chinstrap penguin, gives a nod of recognition to the fact that this bird, after the emperor and Adélie, is the southernmost breeding penguin in the Antarctic. The vernacular name comes from the distinctive black line under the chin, rather like the chinstrap of a helmet. Breeding even further south than the chinstrap is *Pygoscelis adeliae,* the Adélie penguin, named after the wife of the French Antarctic explorer Dumont d'Urville. *Pygoscelis papua,* the Gentoo penguin, was given its specific name by Johann Forster; and here we have him floundering badly in the mistaken belief that the birds also bred in Papua or New Guinea. The vernacular name Gentoo first surfaces in the Falkland Islands during the nineteenth century, and it appears a bizarre word to describe a penguin. The word itself is an anglicized version of the Portuguese *gentio,* meaning "gentile," and used in India by Muslims to describe Hindus: in one English travel book of the eighteenth century a reference appears to the "Jentoo dancing girls of Madras." Perhaps the colorful head of the Gentoo penguin, with its red bill and white flashes over the eyes, brought back to some sailor in the Falklands the memories of a warmer climate and the gestures of the painted nautch-girl dancers of India.

Also breeding on the Falklands are the rockhopper penguins, *Eudyptes crestatus*, and the macaroni penguins, *Eudyptes chrysolophus*. The generic name *Eudyptes* means "good diver." Both these species have yellowish crests above the eyes; *crestatus* stands for "crested" and *chrysolophus* for "golden crested." Once one has seen a rockhopper penguin emerge from the sea and hop its way up a rocky cliff face to its breeding colony, the common name becomes obvious. "Macaroni" is a little more recondite. In the days of the eighteenth-century grand tour, young English exquisites would return from their continental travels affecting the extravagant dress, hairstyles, and manners of the continent and also make much ado about foreign, particularly Italian, food. In 1764 Horace Walpole wrote in one of his many letters about "the Maccaroni Club which is composed of all the travelled young men who wear long curls and spying-glasses." The parading affectations of these young fops amused the common folk, and again some forgotten sailor must have given the name "macaroni" to the penguin with the fancy crest. For Americans the word is immortalized in one of the verses from *Yankee Doodle:*

> Yankee Doodle came to town
> Riding on a pony;
> Stuck a feather in his cap
> And called it macaroni.

The Magellanic penguin is the last in our list. Breeding in the Falklands and southern South America, it bears the family name *Spheniscus* and the specific name *magellanicus,* referring to one of its breeding areas, the Strait of Magellan. Due to its asslike bray, it is also known in the Falklands as the jackass penguin; to the ornithologically pure, however, the jackass is a similar but slightly different species breeding in South Africa. Nevertheless, the Magellanic or jackass penguin, from either South America or South Africa, was certainly the first penguin ever seen by Europeans.

It is only on land, at their breeding sites, that penguins appear the dominant bird. On some of the Falkland Islands, South Georgia, Macquarie Island, Kerguelen Island, Heard Island, and the South Shetlands, they provided meat, eggs, and oil for the sealers. Except for the unsuitable feathers, they performed the same function in their day as the all-important domesticated geese of northern Europe. Their only appearance at sea would be the startling sight of a group of penguins bursting from the water like short dumpy projectiles in low trajectory flight, or, if close to the pack ice, as a group standing in solemn convention. The *Terra Nova,* on her way to Ross Island in 1910 and held up by the pack ice of the Ross Sea, often came across such groups of Adélie penguins. The men would gather together on deck and sing one of the popular music-hall songs of the day, with one of its lines running "for she's got rings on her fingers, bells on her toes, elephants to ride upon wherever she goes." Cecil Meares, whose voice was full but flat, would then end the serenade with "God Save the King," and the penguins, having been entranced with the musical-hall song, would scuttle off. This small icescape episode distills the essence of the fascination held by man for these very humanlike creatures with their upright gait and bustling active colonies, for all the world like a busy city. I can think of no other animal inspiring the efforts of a male chorus.

For the seaman aboard his vessel, sailing across the lonely reaches of the Southern Ocean, the albatross and petrels were the constant companions. Sailing-ship sailors were masters at improvisation. Albatross shot or caught at sea bear mute witness to this characteristic. Nimble and patient fingers would turn the hollow bones into pipe stems and the large webbed feet into tobacco pouches. The smaller birds were spared this transformation and served as friendly companions, bringing an air of freedom, to men confined by the narrow spaces of shipboard life. Here, from the center of their world bounded by the circle of the horizon, the men would watch the small, dainty, and fluttering storm petrels that appeared to walk upon the water; the ghostly gray-backed prions flitting in fast and erratic flight just above the surface of the ocean waves and troughs; the stocky diving petrels with whirring wings bursting into and out of waves like bullets through a target; flocks of the beautifully black-and-white-patterned Cape pigeons sporting with the breaking wave tops and great followers of ships; and, if near icebergs and pack ice, the ethereal pure-white snow petrels gliding like phantoms in the icescape.

Here amidst the pack ice, swimming between the leads or hauled out on the ice floes, are four of Antarctica's six species of seal. The one most likely to be seen from ships threading their way through the pack ice is the crabeater seal. Contrary to the name, these seals are not eaters of crabs but consumers of vast quantities of krill. As a result of this diet, hauled out on the ice floes, they stain the ice and snow a deep reddish pink with their excrement. In order to cope with the krill the seal has developed a set of instantly recognizable teeth: complex cusps interlock to form a strainer so that when a mouthful of krill and water is taken the jaws can be closed and the water expelled, leaving the krill in the mouth. It is an elegant variation of the baleen plates of the filter-feeding whales. Crabeaters also have the distinction of being the most numerous seal in the world: over half the world's total seal population is made up of these creatures of the ice floes. As the crabeaters lie out on the ice floes, an observer will notice a large proportion of them marked with deep, twin, parallel scars on their pelts. These are the lucky seals: as young seals they managed to escape from the jaws of another seal—the leopard seal.

Resting on the pack ice the leopard seal is unmistakable with its distinctive domed head, humped outline, and long slit of a mouth. "Reptilian" and "dangerous" are adjectives that spring to mind. Like the killer whale, it is an opportunistic predator with a varied diet. On patrol in the waters off a penguin colony, it will snatch an unwary adult or uneducated younger penguin. But warm-blooded animals are not the exclusive prey. Nearly 40 percent of its diet is made up from the ubiquitous krill. To cope with this varied diet, the leopard seal has developed teeth similar to the crabeater's, but, like the wolf's in the fairy tale, larger and sharper. These are teeth that serve as a strainer, to grab fish and to rip apart flesh.

Compared to this lean, hungry, Cassius-type seal, the Weddell seal would be the type sought out by Julius Caesar. The Weddell is a sleepy, portly fellow, and, like an affable and well-fed London clubman, one that tends to stick to his habitat—in this case, the fast ice. The Weddell is the archetypal seal: round head, big round eyes, tubby figure; it is a seal with all the babylike qualities required by conservation organizations to extract money from a neotenous animal–loving public (Walt Disney, in transforming a rodent into the round, babylike Mickey Mouse, knew what he was doing).

Never far from a hole in the ice or near the ice edge, the Weddell is a gregarious creature, and when hauled out is usually found in groups of a dozen or more. To keep its tubby form filled out, the Weddell feeds on fish, squid, and bottom invertebrates, which it locates in the darkness of the depths and the gloom of the long winter. Sedentary on the land or ice but active in the water, this remarkable seal can dive to two thousand feet and stay under water for over an hour. To maintain their openings in the ice—and they have to do this constantly during the winter—they use their teeth in a swinging sawlike motion, which eventually wears the teeth down to the gums. For the Weddell seal it is the quietus.

The most elusive seal of the pack ice is the Ross seal. In January 1841, during the *Erebus* and *Terror* expedition, a strange seal was sighted on the pack ice. As in so many cases when an unusual animal is first seen, the end result was bloody. A sergeant of the Royal Marines was first onto the ice floe and brained the seal with a handspike, followed by a shot through the head. Three skulls of this strange-looking seal were taken back to England, declared a new species, and named after James Clark Ross, the expedition commander. For a hundred years, only fifty other sightings were reported: not that it is particularly rare seal, but one just rarely seen, for its favorite habitat is the unvisited heavy pack ice. When it is seen, with its short muzzle and large eyes set on a wide head, the closely studied drawings and photographs of the creature spring to life: the head is raised, the jaws open wide, and the neck and torso inflate like a pouter pigeon. Clap a blond wig on the head, stick a spear under a flipper, and you have a large-bosomed, polar Valkyrie about to burst into a Wagnerian aria.

All these seals, being creatures of the pack ice, were spared the slaughter visited upon two other species—the elephant seal and the Antarctic fur seal. These two, the first for its oil and the second for its pelt, and both due to their breeding pattern on land, were the magnet that first drew men to the Antarctic. Their natural history and destiny is so intimately bound up with man and the early explorations in the Southern Ocean that it cannot be dismissed in a paragraph. This book, in short, is about them as well as about their hunters.

Behold, then, this ocean below the Convergence as it was during the last half of the eighteenth century: huge, hostile, fecund, and teeming with life, surrounding an empty, cold, and sterile continent. Here indeed was the ultimate barrier at the uttermost part of the world where both sea and land lay uncrossed by man since *Homo sapiens* began its extraordinary exodus from Africa and the sixty thousand years of global wandering. Since that exodus, this colonizing and gregarious biped had spread north to the rims of the lands circling the Arctic Ocean; south to Australia and Tasmania; made extraordinary voyages to populate the scattered islands of the Pacific and New Zealand; east through Asia to the Americas and then down to the southernmost cul-de-sac of Tierra del Fuego, lying at the very frontier of the Southern Ocean. The species was now spread across the globe from the Etah Inuit at 78°N in Greenland to the Fuegian Yamana at 56°S near Cape Horn. And, as if to buttress themselves and reinsure their uniqueness in a hostile world, living on the edge of extinction, both Inuit and Yamana called themselves "the people."

The impact of another member of this wandering species, this *wandervogel,* on the waters, life, and lands south of the Yamana happened with alarming and ferocious speed. In the middle of the seventeenth century, James Ussher, Archbishop of Armagh and preacher at Lincoln's Inn, after exhaustive study of Holy Writ and the writings of Martin Luther and Johann Kepler, proclaimed in *Annales Veteris et Novi Testamenti* that Earth and man were created on 23 October 4004 B.C. And with Calvinistic certitude he even went so far as to give the precise hour—noon. He is buried in Westminster Abbey. But it is as well not to snigger at this generous and good prelate. In our own century other eminent authorities ridiculed the idea of continental drift—and lived to be proved wrong.

Following in the prelate's footsteps, a date and time can be given for the end of Antarctica's immemorial isolation. Over a century after the Archbishop's revelation, between eleven o'clock and noon on 17 January 1773, two ships and over two hundred men crossed the Antarctic Circle for the first time in recorded history. Later that day, unknown to themselves, they lay some eighty miles off the Antarctic continent, halted by pack ice. Captain James Cook, with the men of the *Resolution* and the *Adventure,* was opening a new chapter in polar exploration.

V

Edmond Halley and the Pink "Paramore"

He gott leave and a viaticum of his father to goe to the Island of Sancta Hellena, purely upon account of advancement of Astronomy, to make the globe of the Southerne Hemisphere right, which before was very erroneous, as being donne only after the observations of ignorant seamen. There he stayed some months. At his returne, he presented his Planisphere, with a short description, to his Majesty who was very well pleased with it; but received nothing but Prayse.

John Aubrey, *Brief Lives*, published 1813

RCHIMEDES and the bath, Newton and the apple, Halley and the comet, Darwin and the ape, Einstein and $E = mc^2$. All a mother lode for the cartoonist's pen, and all immortalized for the man in the street and posterity. But Edmond Halley, friend of Sir Isaac Newton, only swims into the public consciousness and arrives on the cartoonist's drawing boards every seventy-six years, when his eponymous comet makes its approach to the Earth. It is a supreme irony that Halley's prediction of the periodicity of the comet is the only achievement remembered from a brilliant career that spanned eighty-five tumultuous years, from the Commonwealth of Oliver Cromwell through the reigns of six British sovereigns.

Edmond Halley was more than an astronomer. In an age of polymaths he was the polymath supreme: astronomer, mathematician, geophysicist, meteorologist, surveyor, cartographer, hydrographer, inventor, navigator, and sailor. Born in 1656 into a prosperous trading family—his father was a soap boiler and salt merchant and collected a thousand pounds a year on his rental properties—Halley showed his scientific precocity at sixteen by measuring the variation of the magnetic compass from true north. At seventeen, "well versed in Latin, Greek and Hebrew," the young Halley entered Queen's College, Oxford. But it was the cold logical beauty of the mathematical language and astronomy that attracted Halley. Years later Halley wrote: "From my tender years I showed a marked bent towards mathematics; and, when, about six years ago (1672) I first devoted myself wholly to astronomy, I derived so much pleasure and delight from its study as anyone, inexperienced therin could scarcely believe."

While still an undergraduate at Oxford Halley published his first scientific paper on the elliptical orbit of planets in the Royal Society's *Philosophical Transactions*. It was the first of eighty contributions. As an undergraduate he approached the Secretary of the Royal Society with a proposal to catalogue and position the stars of the southern hemisphere. His would be a companion to the star catalogues of the northern hemisphere compiled by Hevelius in Danzig, Cassini in Paris, and Flamsteed in England. The philosophical gentlemen of the Royal Society approved the proposal, King Charles II endorsed it, Halley's father funded £300, and the East India Company provided transportation. It was all a most satisfactory arrangement.

Halley, overjoyed at his good fortune, set about the assembling of suitable measuring instruments. "And so, being now certain of going, I had a sextant made with a radius of 5½ London feet; the framework was of iron and the limb and enclosing radii and the scales were of brass. It is equipped with telescopes in place of open sights, and, so that all necessary motions can be conveniently imparted, it is mounted upon two toothed semi-circles placed at right angles to each other turned by endless (or Archimedean) screws, serve with little trouble to adjust the plane of the sextant to that of any two selected stars. Moreover, I have a quadrant about 2 feet in radius. . . ."

The twenty-one-year-old Halley and an assistant sailed for St. Helena (that small island of volcanic origin set in the South Atlantic and the future island of exile and death for Napoleon Bonaparte) in November 1676, burdened with that very serious-sounding sextant, quadrant, micrometers, several telescopes—one of them twenty-four feet long—and a pendulum clock. A year was spent on the island, and Halley's harvesting of the heavens produced 341 stars. On his return to England Halley set about cataloguing his harvest and produced the first printed volume of telescopically measured star positions, the *Catalogus stellarum Australium*. Halley astutely named a southern constellation after King Charles and presented a copy to that rakish and devious monarch. King Charles answered in kind— if not in specie—and pressed Oxford University to award Halley "the degree of M.A. without any condition of performing any previous or subsequent exercises for the same." That same year, 1678, Halley was elected a Fellow of the Royal Society. His career was launched on its long and brilliant trajectory.

The next two decades saw Halley visiting the astronomer Hevelius in

Danzig; an obligatory grand tour of Europe that included time spent with Jean Cassini, Director of the Paris Observatory, an institution where he left a memory of being "a charming man of rare intelligence"; then, on a more personal note, marriage in 1682 to Mary Tooke. Two years after his marriage Halley traveled to Trinity College, Cambridge, to consult with Isaac Newton. The meeting fostered a friendship and mutual esteem that had momentous repercussions. Halley's visit with Newton was prompted by the desire for mathematical proof on planetary motion. Kepler's laws

Portrait of Edmond Halley by Thomas Murray.
Courtesy of the President and Council of the Royal Society

were all very well, but *why* was the question. Newton—fourteen years older than Halley—had the answer and the proof for the eager young man. It was somewhere among his papers but had unaccountably been lost. No matter; Newton would work it all out again and send the proof to Halley.

A few months later Newton's calculations arrived in London, and Halley—
no mean mathematician himself—was astounded and delighted by its ele-
gance. He returned to Cambridge and, in further talks with Newton,
found himself in the position of an archeologist working at a dig and
happening upon discoveries of outstanding originality and beauty. The
discoveries had to be made public.

Newton, a shy and retiring man, had been buffeted by the harsh winds
of controversy that had roared around his theory that white light was a
mixture of light of all colors, and was consequently loath to publish more
of his works. But Halley was determined that these treasures should see
the light of day; and with charm and diplomatic skill the younger man set
about persuading Newton to weave together the diverse strands of his
work into a great disquisition for the greater glory of science.

Three years after that first meeting between Halley and Newton, the
Philosophiae Naturalis Principia Mathematica (The mathematical principles of natural philosophy), or the *Principia,* as it came to be known, was
published. It had been nursed, edited, and paid for by Halley. Embodied
in this great scientific treatise of seventeenth-century Newtonian physics,
the work of a great intellect and quill pen, were the principles that would
be used for the space program by twentieth-century scientists and comput-
ers. Of Halley's efforts a nineteenth-century commentator reflected that
but for him the *Principia* "would not have been thought of, nor when
thought of written, nor when written printed."

Having steered the *Principia* through to its destination, Halley turned
next to the undersea world, with the invention of a practical diving bell.
Halley reported that his bell, lowered over the side of a navy frigate, "kept
3 men 1¾ hours under the water in ten fathoms deep without any the least
inconvenience and in as perfect freedom to act as if they had been above."
The inventor went diving himself and found it cold working under the sea
and "fortified" himself with a primitive dry suit made from "a double or
triple flannel or knit woolen westcoat and excluded the water by a very well
liquored [oiled] leather suit made fitt and close to the body." His inventions for working under water proved so successful that he formed a public
company to salvage wrecks—a company whose shares were quoted in
newspapers.

Salvaging wrecks was all very well, but the nagging problem of finding
the longitude at sea was a matter of even greater importance. Neither
Halley nor Newton thought that a clock mechanism could be made of
sufficient accuracy for navigation at sea. The answer lay in the stars and
planets—or perhaps the variation of the magnetic compass needle from
true north.

In March of 1693 a close-written sheet of paper lay before the gentlemen of the Royal Society. On its cover, in elegant copperplate script, was
written "Proposal of Mr Middleton and Mr Haley to compass the Globe

for Improvement of Navigation." The proposal was brief and to the point. It asked the assistance of the Royal Society to use their good offices in obtaining a small vessel—no larger than sixty tons—for a voyage east to west "through the great South Sea," the purpose of the voyage being to study the magnetic variation in the world's oceans and any other practicable methods of determining longitude at sea. The costs of the expedition would be borne by Mr. Middleton and the observations would be taken by Mr. Halley. And so, in a proposal of about three hundred words, the first voyage of purely scientific exploration was under way.

The good offices of the Royal Society proved effective, and events moved with remarkable speed. Within three months the Admiralty were ordering their Deptford Yard to begin construction of an eighty-ton vessel, and eight months later Deptford informed their Lordships that the "New Pinke building here well be ready to Launch any day. . . ." The little pink was duly launched on the spring tides and, christened the *Paramore,* entered into the Royal Navy. The designation "pink" is of Dutch origin and described a vessel as unpretentious as a Dutch clog; pinks in the Royal Navy usually served as victualing vessels and spar transports. For an exploration vessel this tweeny of the Fleet was small: sixty-four feet in length, eighteen feet in beam; three-masted, with a narrow stern, bluff apple-cheeked bows, much tumblehome (sides bulging out above the waterline and then back in toward the deck); flat-bottomed and with shallow draft. It was not a shape to inspire much confidence in clawing off a lee shore.

After the initial burst of activity there followed a two-year hiatus before the expedition gained momentum. On 4 June 1696 Halley received his commission as master and commander of the *Paramore*. On the same day warrants were granted for the appointment of boatswain, gunner, and carpenter. The frugal Admiralty regarded this vessel as "going on a private Affaire" and, as such, would supply the crew and vessel, but Captain Halley—or the Royal Society—had to stand surety for the crew's wages over a twelve-month period. And then, surprisingly, the finances having been settled, the Admiralty ordered the *Paramore* to be laid up in wet dock. Halley had been appointed to the Mint at Chester to oversee the taking in of old, debased, and clipped coins and the minting of the new milled-edge coins, a position rife with opportunities for the dishonest and therefore requiring a man of probity and integrity.

For two years the *Paramore* languished in her dock at Deptford while Halley organized the Chester Mint. And then, early in 1698, the improbable, larger-than-life figure of the twenty-six-year old Tsar of Muscovy appeared on the scene. Traveling under the thinly veiled incognito of Peter Mikhaylov, the Tsar, accompanied by a large coterie of Russian drinking companions, arrived at Sayes Court near the Deptford shipyards to study shipbuilding as practiced by the English. For Peter I—to go down in history as Peter the Great—the incognito was a pleasing fiction that caused

acute embarrassment in the protocol-conscious countries visited by the
Russian "Great Embassy." So did the boisterous manners of these strange
Russian visitors. Sophia, Electress of Hanover, wished drily that the Tsar's
manners were "a little less rustic." It was a sentiment perhaps shared by
the English government, who footed the large repair bill for Sayes Court

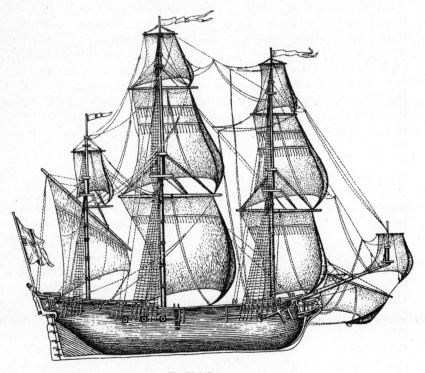

The Pink *Paramore*.
Courtesy of the Hakluyt Society

after the destructive and exuberant Russian visit. But, notwithstanding
the incognito, suitable deference had to be shown to royal wishes. The
advantages to the Tsar of the incognito were obvious. As Peter Mikhaylov,
he could enjoy the low-life pleasures of drinking and smoking at a tavern
on Great Tower Street; and as Peter I, he could make requests of the
English government that would most certainly have been refused for plain
citizen Peter Mikhaylov.

One of these was a request for a meeting with Halley to talk over
matters concerning science and ships—two great interests of the Tsar. And
Peter found the astronomer such good company and so entertaining a
conversationalist that they often dined together at Sayes Court. It was

perhaps after one of those dinners that Peter sent another request to the English government, asking that the *Paramore* be readied and rigged for sailing; and so, with the Tsar at the helm, the *Paramore* had her first sailing trials. Sailing the *Paramore* might have been the event leading to Peter's comment that he would "rather be an admiral in England than Tsar in Russia."

Halley was now finished at the Mint; and after the long wait in the royal dockyards and brief sailing interlude with the Tsar, the *Paramore* became a hive of activity resounding to the clunk of shipwright's mallets, the hoarse cries of seamen, and the trundling of barrels as the hogsheads of salt beef, salt pork, flour, cheese, and dried peas were stowed in the hold. For orders had come from the Admiralty that as "His Majesty has been pleased to lend his Pink the Paramour to Mr. Hawley for a Voyage to the East Indies or South seas, Wee do hereby desire and direct you, to cause her to be forthwith Sheathed and Fitted for such a Voyage, and that she be furnished with Twelve Monthes Stores proper for her. . . ." A few days later, on 19 August 1698, Halley received his second commission to be master and commander of the *Paramore*.

The decision of the Admiralty to place a landsman in charge of a royal ship appears to be a surprising one. But then, even with her six three-pounders and two one-pound swivel guns, the *Paramore* was not a man-of-war but a vessel on "Private Service." And Halley, whatever he lacked in seagoing experience, certainly made up for it in navigating expertise. It was also a navy in a transitory stage of its history: there still hung about it the more egalitarian and raffish airs of the privateering Tudor navy and Drake's injunction that "I must have the gentleman to haul and draw with the mariner, and the mariner with the gentleman." Nor had it petrified into the rigid, hierarchic, and class-conscious service of the nineteenth century, the navy satirized so affectionately by Gilbert in *H.M.S. Pinafore*.

Nearly two months after Halley had received his commission, another officer was appointed to the *Paramore:* Lieutenant Edward Harrison, an officer with eight years' service, commissioned as mate and lieutenant. It was to prove an unhappy choice of their Lordships.

In 1694 Harrison had submitted a paper to the Royal Society on a solution to the problem of finding longitude at sea. It had met with a cool reception, and Halley—then acting as Clerk to the Royal Society—had thought the idea impractical. Harrison had expanded the paper into a book published in 1696 entitled *Idea Longitudinis*. And in this book the choleric Harrison, still smarting from the Royal Society's rebuff, made some acid comments to the effect that "there are some Persons in *England,* whose Duty it is (being paid for it) to improve *Navigation* and *Astronomy,* and from whom much is expected, and little or nothing appears." The book met the same reception as the paper.

This then was the officer, still nursing his grudges, appointed to take

orders from a landsman; the landsman, moreover, rubbing salt in the
tender wounds, who had, in Harrison's eyes, been instrumental in damning his magnum opus. The unsuspecting Halley knew nothing of the offended naval ego.

A few days after Harrison took up his posting Halley received his orders
and instructions from the Admiralty. They came as no surprise, for they
were based on his recommendations. In part they read as follows:

Wheras his Matjy. has been pleased to lend his Pink the Paramour for your proced-
ding with her on an Expedition, to inprove the knowledge of the Longitude and
variations of the Compasse, which Shipp is now compleatly Man'd, Stored and
Victualled at his Mats. Charge for the said Expedition; you are therefore hereby
required and directed, forthwith to proceed with her according to the following
Instructions.

You are to make the best of your way to the Southward of the Equator, and
there to observe on the East Coast of South America, and the West Coast of Africa,
the variations of the Compasse, with all the accuracy you can, as also the true
Scituation both in Longitude and Latitude of the Ports where you arrive.

You are likewise to make the like observations at as many of the Islands in the
Seas between the aforesaid Coasts as you can (without too much deviation) bring
your course: and if the Season of the Yeare permit, you are to stand soe farr into
the South, till you discover the Coast of the Terra Incognita, supposed to lye
between Magelan's Streights and the Cape of Good Hope, which Coast you are
carefully to lay downe in its true position.

Halley was also to visit the English West Indian Plantations "to lay
them downe truely in their Geographical Scituation" and "omit no opportunity of Noteing the variation of the Compasse, of which you are to keep
a Register in your Journall."

There is no mention of girdling the globe, and Benjamin Middleton,
like the Cheshire cat, has faded from the scene.

The *Paramore*, with her complement of twenty men, slipped down the
Thames on 20 October 1698. The next few weeks were to prove frustrating
ones for Halley and his new command. Although launched in 1694, and
except for the outings with the young Russian Tsar, this was the pink's
maiden passage, and, as in many maiden passages with new vessels, problems appeared with alarming frequency. The *Paramore* proved a poor per-
former to windward but, even worse, she leaked badly and the sand ballast
choked the hand pumps. Halley made for Portsmouth and the naval dockyards, where the leaking seams were recaulked and the ballast was changed
to shingle. On 22 November, the repairs completed, the *Paramore* joined
the fleet of Rear Admiral John Benbow anchored off the Isle of Wight and
waiting for a fair wind to carry them down Channel and on to Madeira
and the West Indies. The fleet would give the lightly armed *Paramore*
protection from the predatory Barbary pirates; for as Halley noted in a
letter to the Admiralty, "Our people were somewhat doubtfull of going

alone for meeting with a Sallyman." Halley's people were not being over-fearful. For in any meeting with the "Sallymen"—the predatory Moorish pirates sailing from the Moroccan port of Sale—the lightly armed *Paramore* could have easily been taken and the crew put up for sale in the slave markets of the North African coast.

At Madeira, Benbow's fleet sailed for the West Indies, leaving the *Paramore* to take on board the obligatory Madeira wine. The barrels on board, Halley set a course for the Cape Verde Islands, where, ironically enough, the *Paramore* came under some poorly aimed cannon fire from two nervous English merchant ships who mistook them for the dreaded Sallymen. The islands provided wood and water at "a very extravagent price," according to Halley, and then the *Paramore* headed out into the Atlantic. The next seven weeks were to be frustrating ones. Bedeviled by calms, head winds, and a northward-setting current, the *Paramore* made but poor progress to the south. Water was rationed to three pints a day, and Halley decided to head for Fernando de Noronha Island, some three hundred miles south of the equator and two hundred miles off the Brazilian coast.

It was during this frustrating passage that the resentful Harrison, nursing his wrath to keep it warm, found a receptive ear and an ally in the boatswain. The first hint of crew problems came in the middle of February, when Halley, coming on deck in the early hours of the morning, found the boatswain's watch steering a course, contrary to orders, north of Fernando de Noronha. Halley surmised that this was done "with a designe to miss the Island, and frustrate my Voyage, though they pretended the Candle was out in the Bittacle, and they could not light it." A day later they made their landfall at the island to find no water, only "small Turtle Doves and Land Crabbs in abundance." Anchored off the island, Halley set about improving the sailing qualities of his unweatherly craft by altering the rake of the masts, setting up the shrouds, and scrubbing the weed- and barnacle-encrusted bottom. A few days later they sailed for the coast of Brazil and fresh water. Here, on the river Paraiba, they watered and were told by the Portuguese that they were the first English ship in thirty years. As the season was late for venturing into the Southern Ocean in search of the elusive *Terra incognita*, Halley toyed with the idea of wintering on the Brazilian coast. But "his officers shewing themselves uneasy and refractory," Halley decided to sail for the West Indies in the pious hope of replacing the more mulish and uncooperative of his officers with men from the West Indian fleet.

In the West Indies came a repeat of the Fernando de Noronha incident. This time the subversive Harrison showed his own true colors and, out of sheer perversity, changed Halley's orders to sail south of Barbados to reach the anchorage on the southern shore, and brought the unweatherly *Paramore* on the wind to attempt a passage north of the island. Halley, noticing the change in motion of the *Paramore,* came on deck, confronted an abusive Harrson, and ordered the *Paramore* back on course. It was now obvious that Harrison's malign influence on some of the warrant officers threatened the conduct of the whole voyage, and Halley, finding replacements for the malcontents impossible in the West Indies, set sail for England, "finding it absolutely necessary to change some of my officers." During the voyage home Harrison again proved insubordinate, forcing Halley to relieve him of his watch and duties and to take over the complete running of the *Paramore.* On 22 June 1699 they were anchored in the Downs. By 3 July Harrison and some of the warrant officers were being tried by court-martial aboard the seventy-gun *Swiftsure.* Presided over by the unfortunate Sir Cloudesley Shovell,* the court, finding no case of flagrant disobedience but only some "grumbling among them as there is generally in Small Vessels under such Circumstances," acquitted the accused with a severe reprimand.

It was this day that the unsuspecting Halley found out the true reasons for Harrison's animosity. Halley, according to the resentful officer, had been the reason for the lukewarm reception of his paper and book on longitude: four years in the festering, the resentment had found its outlet on the voyage. Harrison, realizing that he had lost any chance of promotion, left the Royal Navy and joined the merchant service.

For Halley the voyage had been a grave disappointment; but determined to continue his investigations, he applied to the Admiralty for a second voyage. Their Lordships agreed.

The *Paramore,* altered to improve her sailing qualities, sailed from the Downs on 27 September 1699 accompanied by the *Falconbird* of the Royal African Company, bound for the Guinea coast. The *Falconbird,* well armed with thirty guns and a large crew, would provide protection against the Sallymen. On board the *Paramore* were twenty-four men, nine of them from the previous voyage. The extra crew were aboard at the request of Halley, for the Admiralty, with a touch of grim humor, had appointed to the *Paramore* a one-armed boatswain. Halley's orders and instructions from the Admiralty were virtually a carbon copy of those for the first voyage. But the search for *Terra australis incognita,* at the request of Halley, was given extra emphasis. He was directed to search for the "unknowne southlands between ye Magellan Streights and ye Cape of good hope between ye latitudes of 50 & 55 South. . . ."

As the two vessels sailed down Channel it soon became obvious to Halley that the changes to the *Paramore* had improved her sailing abilities.

---

* The reader may recall from chapter 2 that it was the loss of life in the wrecking of Admiral Cloudesley Shovell's fleet on the Scilly Islands in 1707 that had forced the English government into setting up the Board of Longitude. The admiral's death in the disaster was not by drowning. A very fat man, he floated ashore to a sandy beach and, lying there semiconscious, was murdered by a local woman for the large emerald ring on his finger.

And there were more encouraging signs: the officers and men worked well and were "as forward this time to serve me, as they were backward the last, so that I now proceed with great satisfaction. . . ."

There was of course, as well as the usual hazards of seafarers, the worry and ever-present threat of the Sallymen. A week out from the Downs, the two vessels sailed past a fleet of eighteen homeward-bound Danish vessels who reported a Sallyman over the horizon. It turned out to be a lone English sloop from Dartmouth. The following day a rakish-looking craft appeared over the horizon, "exceeding Sharp and promised to Saile like the Wind," according to Halley. It was another false alarm. She turned out to be a Dutch vessel flying French colors and carrying a cargo of figs from Faro in Portugal.

On 12 October the *Paramore* parted company from the *Falconbird*, the Royal African Company vessel heading for the Guinea coast with her cargo of rum, firearms, gunpowder, knives, tallow, copper pans, and cloth to be exchanged for redwood, hides, ivory, gold, and slaves. The *Paramore*, now alone in an empty ocean, headed for Madeira to load with barrels of wine. But she failed to reach the island. Although in the same latitude as Madeira, they were downwind and far to the east—which meant a tedious time beating to windward in the Sallymen's bailiwick. And so, prudence overcoming thirst, Halley bore away for the Cape Verde Islands to take on board the less palatable but more essential water.

Tragedy struck on the passage to the islands when Manley White, the ship's cabin boy, fell overboard and drowned. Young Manley had been a great favorite of Halley and the loss of life—the only one of all Halley's voyages—deeply affected the astronomer, who could never mention the accident without tears coming to his eyes. The watering in the islands was a somber affair. But the water butts filled, the *Paramore* stood south through the Atlantic, crossed the equator, and slanted toward the Brazilian coast and Rio de Janeiro. Here, in the shadow of the Sugar Loaf Mountain, they took on board wood for the galley stove, replenished the water butts, and, in lieu of the Madeira wine, hogsheads of rum. On 29 December the *Paramore* weighed anchor and sailed out between the sheltering headlands into the Atlantic, bound south for the Southern Ocean.

Halley was following the usual peremptory tones of Admiralty instructions: "you are without loss of time to sett sail . . . and proceed to make a Discovery of ye unknowne southlands. . . ." But the voyage still remained one to plot magnetic variations and to use these as a possible solution to finding the longitude. Now this presents a similar problem as the hoary chicken-and-egg riddle. The calculations for magnetic variation are relatively simple; but now the variation has to be accurately plotted on a chart using the coordinates of latitude and longitude. How to find the longitude with sufficient accuracy?

In 1610 Galileo, peering through his homemade telescope—he had

heard of this newly invented Dutch instrument and built one himself—
discovered the faint pinpricks of light that are the planet Jupiter's satellites.
Twenty-four years later, and after countless nights of observation, he wrote
of their positions and eclipses as a possible method of finding longitude. It
was a method never used. Another Italian, Giovanni Domenico Cassini,
took the idea further and improved and expanded Galileo's tables. Invited
to France in 1669 on the strength of this work, the forty-three-year-old
astronomer and surveyor was persuaded to work at the newly founded
Royal Academy of Science. The invitation was not entirely altruistic: Louis
XIV and his scientifically minded minister of finance, Jean Baptiste Colbert, had long harbored impressive ideas for the first accurate mapping of
France. Galileo's idea, perfected by Cassini, would be the method for
finding longitude. By 1676 Cassini and other astronomers had refined the
tables for the Jovian satellites to the point of practical use. Newton had
invented the reflecting telescope—a vast improvement over Galileo's
model. Trained astronomers and surveyors were sent into the field, and
the great work began. It was, however, a complicated and time-consuming
operation to find the longitude from the satellites, one rife with possibili-
ties for error, and totally impractical at sea.

The *Paramore* sailed south—buffeted by gales, languishing in calms,
and scudding before squalls, with the magnetic variation being recorded
at every opportunity. By the end of January Halley was noting the increasing cold, "scarce tollerable to us used to the warm Climates. . . ." They
were at 50°S, just north of a line between the Falkland Islands and South
Georgia. The next few days were spent creeping along under reduced sail
and taking soundings every two hours, for they were now in thick fog and
had sighted swimming penguins, a sign—perhaps—of land. From Halley's
description the penguins were probably Gentoo and king penguins, two
of the species that breed on the Falklands and South Georgia.

A few days later at 51°30′S (London is at 51°30′N) Halley was finding
the climate abominable, with "misty rainy uncomfortable weather, though
the hight of Sumer here." Temperatures were now well below freezing,
and the crew were put on a full allowance of provisions and rum.

On 1 February, at 52°24′S, they sighted what appeared to be three
islands: "Flatt on the top and covered with Snow . . . milk white, with
perpendicular Cliffs all around them . . . the great hight of them made us

conclude them land, but there was no appearance of any tree or green thing on them. . . ." To the crew these islands reminded them of the south-east coast of England and the white chalk cliffs of Beachy Head and North-Foreland. And so they were named.

Halley's rudimentary charts showed no islands near their position. Either he was drastically wrong in his navigation or these islands, extraordinary as it might seem, were made of ice. Nightfall was soon upon them and Halley, loath to approach too closely to these islands, with darkness falling and the wind rising, stood off and on and waited for the dawn of the following day. It came with thick fog; not until noon did the visibility clear and the islands reveal themselves to be ice, not land. And what an immense mass of ice. The largest island was estimated to be five miles in length, and Halley, his fingers chilled by the cold, sketched the islands into the *Paramore*'s logbook—the first drawing of an Antarctic tabular iceberg.

The next few days were to prove hazardous ones. They were now sailing in thick fog and hemmed about by fast-moving icebergs, growlers, and floes. It was as if they were threading their way, part blindfolded, across a gray sea of bewitched islands and reefs that possessed a disconcerting habit of magically changing position. The Paramores were only too well aware of their dangerous situation. "This danger," wrote Halley, "made my men reflect on the hazards wee run, in being alone without a Consort, and of the inevitable loss of us all, in case we Staved our Shipp which might soe easily happen amongst these mountains of ice in the Fogg, which are so thick and frequent here." The cold was bad enough but worse still was the all-pervasive damp: "So penetrating a moysture that our linnen, our Cloathes, our papers etc feel wett with it, even in our Cabbins."

When they had first sighted the tabular icebergs, the *Paramore* had been a scant two days' sail from the island of South Georgia, an island not plotted on any of Halley's charts and one which would wait three-quarters of a century before Captain James Cook landed on its shores. But now the *Paramore* was standing north, away from this depressing area where they had only been warmed by a brief flicker of pale sun and where Halley, for ten consecutive days, had been unable to plot any magnetic variations. The last of the ice was seen at 50°S, and for the first time in weeks the Paramores, much to Halley's relief, had "a very sereen Night."

On 14 February Halley estimated that the islands of Tristan da Cunha, those isolated pinnacles of volcanic rock set about halfway between South America and Africa, lay some 360 miles to the northeast—and Halley had a mind to see them. A few days later, right on the *Paramore*'s bow, they appeared over the horizon. It was a pretty piece of navigation by Halley; for this was not a case of sailing to the islands' latitude and then sailing along the latitude—running the latitude down—until the islands were reached, but rather a question of sailing at a diagonal to the latitudes direct to the islands.

The Tristan da Cunha group of islands are the sole breeding grounds—except for a very small colony in the Falklands—of the great shearwater, a seabird that flies north on a migration route almost as long as the 22,000 miles clocked up by the Arctic tern. High seas made a landing on the islands impossible, and Halley bore away for the Cape of Good Hope some 1,500 miles away and almost due east. A week after the peaks of the shearwater's breeding grounds had slipped below the horizon, the *Paramore* was struck by storm-force winds from the south. Under a scrap of canvas and in less control of their course than a great shearwater, the *Paramore* was swept helplessly before the storm; even the tiny sail proved too much in these survival conditions, and the *Paramore* broached in the mountainous seas. But in Halley's heartfelt words, "it pleased God she wrighted again." They now ran before the storm under bare poles. On 27 February Halley found his latitude well to the north of the Cape of Good Hope.

They had now been nine weeks at sea and were running short of water. The storm conditions that had flooded Halley's cabin knee-deep in water had also found their way below into the bread room and a considerable amount of biscuit, flour, and cheese was found unfit to eat. The wind was foul for the Cape but fair for St. Helena, and with the storm moderating Halley altered his plans and set his course for that familiar island, where he could water and provision.

The storm had effectively destroyed any reasonable estimate of longitude, and so Halley was forced back to the traditional latitude navigation: sail north to the island's latitude and then, wind permitting, west for St. Helena. By 12 March they were at anchor off the island's small capital of Jamestown in twenty-three fathoms of water.

A quarter of a century had made little change to St. Helena since Halley's year there as a young man. It was still owned, settled, and administered by the East India Company, garrisoned by Company soldiers, and provisioned by Company ships. This state of affairs was to last until 1834, when the island passed into the hands of the Crown and became a British colony. One peevish and critical visitor dismissed it as a most barren and wretched island affording few comforts, scarce fruit, and no fresh butter. But for the East India Company vessels it afforded a most welcome stop on the long passage from India or China.

The *Paramore,* provisioned with what supplies the island could offer and her butts filled with brackish water, sailed from St. Helena on 30 March. Halley had left with the Governor a letter addressed to Josiah Burchett, the Secretary to the Admiralty in London; it would be put aboard the next homeward-bound vessel calling at the island. The letter was a precautionary measure, a prophylactic against the hazards of the sea: if the *Paramore* disappeared with all hands their Lordships would have at least some small account of the voyage's progress up to the arrival at St. Helena.

The letter informed the Admiralty that the *Paramore* had reached 52½°S and 35°W and found great islands of ice which Halley—erroneously—thought to be aground. At these latitudes "it froze both night and day, whence it may be understood how these bodies of Ice are generated being always increased and never thawing." Halley may be forgiven his theory, for the vast ice shelves that had spawned these prodigious islands of ice were years away from discovery. Halley ended his letter by reporting his progress on the magnetic variations and that he had in hand "a generall Theory which I am in great hopes to settle effectually."

The shearwater is named after its dazzling aerobatics over the surface waters of the oceans. It is a bird that dances with waves. And in this lovely partnership the bird's wings occasionally slice into the wave's surface, shearing the water.

The *Paramore* was now homeward bound. And with her sails spread to the favorable breeze, the small pink performed her own more matronly rolling dance with the waves of the Atlantic. Some two thousand miles further south the first flocks of great shearwaters were leaving the islands of Tristan da Cunha on the first stage of their annual migration to the rich feeding grounds of the North Atlantic. Their course first takes them to the eastern littoral of the Brazilian coast, then north across the equator, then past the West Indies and Bermuda to the waters of the Grand Banks off the Newfoundland coast. From here they fly across the Atlantic to the coastal waters off southwest Ireland and the approaches to the English Channel, where they arrive during the months of August and September.

The *Paramore*'s course was a virtual surface bound copy of the shearwater's. From St. Helena Halley set course for the mysterious island of Trinidade off the coast of Brazil, "to see if there be any such isles as the Maps lay down." Halley found it, landed on it, exchanged his brackish St. Helena water for the sweeter Trinidade water, claimed the island for His Majesty King William III, left the Union flag flying, and to accompany it, and for the use of any future shipwrecked mariners, fresh meat on the hoof and wing in the form of breeding pairs of goats, hogs, and guinea hens. The descendants of the goats and hogs were still roaming the island two hundred years later.

Four months after sailing from Trinidade, the *Paramore* anchored in Plymouth Sound. On the passage Halley called at Brazil, the West Indies, Bermuda, and Newfoundland. The last entry in Halley's *Paramore* journal is for 9 September 1700. It reads: "Deliver'd the Pink this evening into the hands of Captn. William Wright Master of Attendance at Deptford."

The passage had not been without incident. But the problems sent to

try Halley came not from the crew or weather but from the shore. At
Pernambuco (Recife) Halley had been arrested as a suspected privateer in
the home of a Mr. Hardwick, an alleged English consul. To add further
insult to the dignity of a captain in the Royal Navy, his command was
rummaged for contraband. The Portuguese hinted to Halley that the putative consul was no consul at all but an agent for the Royal African Company
and was merely seeking to feather his nest with prize money. Halley's
Admiralty commission eventually convinced the covetous Hardwick of
his gross error. At Barbados the Governor warned Halley of the disease
sweeping the island. They sailed as promptly as possible, but Halley and
some of the crew were struck down by the illness—either yellow fever or
typhoid fever. All recovered. Bermuda proved a pleasant relief after Brazil
and Barbados. Here the *Paramore* was careened and scrubbed, the decks
recaulked, and the weathered wood repainted. Newfoundland was smothered in its endemic fog and at Toad's Cove the *Paramore* was fired upon
by a nervous cod-fishing vessel hailing from Bideford in Devon. The *Paramore* had once again been mistaken for a pirate. But Toad's Cove provided
sweet fresh water and birch wood for the galley stove, and from here it was
but eighteen days to soundings off the coast of England.

It was now two years since Halley had first sailed from England on his
voyages of scientific investigation. Now it was time to work through his
findings and present them to the public. But first there was the tedious
matter of the accounts to be settled with the Admiralty clerks, and the not
so tedious meetings with old friends at the King's Arms on Ludgate Hill—
Halley was ever a convivial man. By the end of October Halley was presenting to the Fellows of the Royal Society a précis of the results from the
two voyages and showing them the first draft of a chart "curiously laid
down with Marks." It was the first mention of Halley's considerable contribution to cartography: for these marks, or in Halley's words, "Curve-
Lines," were lines joining the points of equal magnetic variation. These
lines used to graphically represent equal values became known to Halley's
contemporaries as Halleyan lines. Today they are known as isolines. Today's newspaper readers, if they glance at the weather map, sees Halleyan
lines as isobars marking the curves of equal air pressure or isotherms marking the curves of equal temperature.

In 1703 Halley expanded his Atlantic chart to encompass the whole
world. This new chart, with the sonorous title of *A New and Correct* Sea
Chart *of the* Whole World *Showing the Variations of the* Compass *as they
were found in the year M.D.C.C.,* went through several editions and revi-
sions and was in use for a century. The only area showing no variation was
the Pacific, for as Halley noted, "I durst not to presume to describe the like
Curves in the South Seas wanting accounts thereof." It was a lack put to
rights by James Cook.

Halley's command of the *Paramore* was not completely severed. During the summer of 1701, at his request, the pink was put back into service for Halley to investigate the tides of the English Channel. The resulting chart, like his world chart, was to be in use for a century.

From 1702 until his death in 1742, Halley continued to interest himself in navigation and cartography, although his major contributions were in astronomy and mathematics. His service at sea, however, had obviously made its mark, for the Astronomer Royal, the Reverend John Flamsteed, wrote that "Halley . . . now talks, swears, and drinks brandy like a sea captain. . . ." Notwithstanding the Astronomer Royal's censorious comments, Halley became the second Astronomer Royal on Flamsteed's death.

Halley himself died at the age of eighty-five, much loved and respected. One of his small legacies had been to introduce John Harrison to George Gresham, the London watchmaker who then funded Harrison to continue his work on a practical marine chronometer. The introduction could be considered but a small gesture, but it was one typical of this generous and amiable man.

Halley is buried, appropriately enough, near the Royal Observatory and the Greenwich meridian. The grave is now rank and overgrown. But in the nineteenth century the original tombstone was let into the wall of the old Observatory, and part of it reads: *As when living he was so highly esteemed by his Countrymen, gratitude requires that his memory should be respected by posterity.*

A far more significant memorial is the British Antarctic Survey station named after Halley, set on the Brunt Ice Shelf bordering the Weddell Sea. It is not beyond the bounds of possibility that the icebergs that so impressed Halley and which he sketched into the *Paramore*'s journal were spawned from this ice shelf. More importantly, it was Halley Station, specializing in atmospherics, that spotted the depletion in the now famous ozone layer. Halley would have approved.

VI

Mr. James Cook

I gave him an account of a conversation which had passed between me and Captain Cook, the day before, at dinner at Sir John Pringle's; and he was much pleased with the conscientious accuracy of that celebrated circumnavigator, who set me right as to many of the exaggerated accounts given by Dr. Hawkesworth of his Voyages. I told him that while I was with the Captain, I catched the enthusiasm of curiosity and adventure, and felt a strong inclination to go with him on his next voyage. JOHNSON: "Why, Sir, a man *does* feel so, till he considers how very little he can learn from such voyages."

James Boswell, *The Life of Samuel Johnson*, 1776

N THE LAST SUNDAY of the July of 1775, a small, weather-beaten three-masted ship, the white ensign of His Brittanic Majesty King George III fluttering at the stern and the long white-and-red commissioning pendant drooping from the mainmast head, dropped anchor amid the morning bustle of small boats scurrying like water beetles across the ruffled waters of Spithead. To an observer with a spyglass scanning the time-hallowed Royal Navy anchorage off Portsmouth, the bluff-bowed new arrival would have appeared out of place when compared with the gun-ported warships of His Majesty—a humble carthorse among a field of thoroughbreds.

The tide swings the stern of this homely-looking vessel to the curious inspection of the spyglassed observer. He notes a modest amount of gilt-painted carvings surrounding seven gracefully proportioned stern windows and two quarter-windows set along the hull port and starboard. Two small ports, one on each side, bracket the red-painted rudder post as it vanishes into the hull just below the stern windows. A slight focus of the spyglass above the two ports and below the windows . . . and the ship's name springs clear in the glass: RESOLUTION.

The watcher, having rested his eyes and taken a pinch of snuff, raises the spyglass again and muses on the inordinate amount of activity on deck and behind those elegant stern windows. And also comes a stirring in the observer's memory. And then excitement. Here is Captain James Cook! Returned at last—no doubt about this—from yet another of his brilliant, exciting, and adventurous voyages. The spyglass is shut with a snap and pocketed, and the observer makes a mental note to scan with even keener attention the future contents of the London newspapers and magazines. And perhaps refresh his memory with a quick glance through his own copy of Hawkesworth's account of Cook's voyage in the *Endeavour.* Somewhat prosy, thinks the observer—but that can be laid at the doorstep of Dr. John Hawkesworth, who thinks himself another Dr. Johnson. Sniff.

This critical observer would have been right on all counts.

Later that day the tall, big-boned commander of the *Resolution* was rattling toward London crammed into a post chaise with the expedition's two naturalists, the artist, the astronomer, and a young midshipman. How a midshipman had come to share the post chaise with his commander and the "experimental gentlemen" is surprising. But young Richard Grindal, a "steady clever young man" according to one of his messmates, had only been married one hour before joining the *Resolution* and setting off on the three-year voyage. His captain, perhaps, was speeding him toward the long-delayed honeymoon. Cook, however, was bound for their Lordships at the Admiralty with the reports, logbooks, journals, and manuscript charts of this, his second, circumnavigation. Only then would he make his way to Mrs. Cook at their home in Mile End, some five miles east of the Admiralty.

So ended a most remarkable three-year voyage: a voyage that demolished any high-blown theory of a huge, populated, fertile southern continent; proved the accuracy and reliability of Mr. Harrison's new watches; rediscovered and placed in their correct position numerous Pacific islands; discovered new land; and, most pleasing to Cook, all this with no deaths from scurvy. In a way the *Resolution*'s voyage was Cook's own personal expedition. He had suggested it, planned it, organized it, virtually written the official orders for it, and led it. To be sure, from the conception to the day of sailing in 1772, the busy months had produced some bizarre episodes, a certain amount of acrimony, some waste of public funds, the use of vast quantities of ink, and much sharpening of goose-quill pens. But all this was nothing compared to the final results of the voyage.

In order to understand this voyage one must now step back and look at this rather formidable and severe-looking man surrounded by his expedition companions—one of them a constant irritant for three years—as they sway and bounce their way to London.

Three months short of his forty-seventh birthday, James Cook is a commander in the Royal Navy and will shortly be raised to post-captain— a rank, if Cook lives to ripe old age, that almost guarantees an admiral's post and all the social éclat that trails in its wake. Indeed, young Grindal, trying to make himself as inconspicuous as possible in the post chaise, will eventually reach the rank of post-captain, command the *Prince* at Trafalgar under Nelson, and retire as Vice Admiral Sir Richard Grindal. But a glance at the weathered face of Cook, with those intelligent brown eyes, suggests little stock would be put by this man on a high rank achieved only by age and not by ability. Excessive vanity is absent.

In a few months' time Joseph Banks is to commission the artist Nathaniel Dance to paint a portrait of Cook. It hangs today in the Maritime Museum at Greenwich. Significantly, Cook is not portrayed surrounded with stylized classical Greek and Roman allusions—the usual convention of this Augustan age. The perceptive Dance realized that such a setting ill fitted his sitter's character. Cook is seated, bent forward, wearing his uniform with buttons undone and looking rather rumpled, as if he had dressed hastily—more important things are on his mind. The right hand rests on an opened chart, the left grasps its edge, and Cook gazes out of the picture over the right shoulder of the viewer. And the viewer sees a resolute face, strong-featured, a trifle stern: the face of a man who has made many decisions, is used to command—and expects to have the commands promptly obeyed. In short, it is the face of a very capable and competent man, a judicial man, a reliable man, a man to have on your side in a crisis. People are to say that Dance has caught the very likeness of Cook.

The portrait shows Cook at the peak of his career. He has one more great voyage before him—again in the *Resolution*—into the northern hemisphere and the Arctic Ocean. Then the final closing scene, a Shakespearian tragedy, of death in the bloodstained waters of Kealakehua Bay on the west coast of Hawaii. A tragedy indeed for a man who wrote of the Pacific islanders: "We debauch their morals . . . introduce among them wants and perhaps diseases which they never before knew and which serves only to disturb that happy tranquility they and their forefathers had enjoyed. If any one denies the truth of this assertion let him tell me what the natives of the whole extent of America have gained by the commerce they have had with Europeans."

It would be the last decade of his life that was to gain Cook his almost mythic stature as the greatest sailor-explorer of his age—or any other age, for that matter. To have achieved this legendary quality after being born in a clay-walled, thatch-roofed, two-room cottage in the north of Yorkshire is astounding. Baptized in the village church on 3 November 1728 as "James, ye son of a day labourer," the infant was the second of eight children born to James and Grace Cook. This was an age where death walked close and only the strong survived: by the time the seventeen-year-old James Cook was working in a grocers and haberdashers' shop in the Yorkshire fishing village of Staithes, his mother had watched over the death of four of her children.

The measuring out of ribbons, the careful weighing of pins, sugar, salt, and spice was an unlikely start for Cook's future mastery in seamanship, navigation, and survey. The young Cook must have thought so. Outside the shop window lay the horizon of the North Sea: its fishing cobles, herring busses, and the constant parade of colliers taking the coals of the north to London and the continent.

Cook stuck to the shop assistant's life for eighteen months and then

Portrait of Captain James Cook by Nathaniel Dance, 1776.
Courtesy of the National Maritime Museum

made the first of his decisions that set him on the path to fame and the beach in Hawaii. The long apprenticeship that culminated in the great triptych of voyages was about to begin.

In 1746 the grocery boy was indentured as a "three-year servant" to a

Mr. John Walker. John and his brother Henry were highly respected—and highly respectable—Quaker shipmasters, shipowners, and coal shippers from Whitby. Now the North Sea collier trade was no ordinary trade, and the ships no ordinary ships. And the North Sea and the colliers in which he learned his seamanship were to have a significant influence upon the young apprentice. The trade and ships require explaining.

It has become a cliché to describe this seaborne carrying of coal from the north to London and beyond as the "nursery of seamen." But what a hard and ruthless nursery. The North Sea is a shallow, treacherous sea set with sandbanks and fast-running tides. The English coast fronting this sea is equally inhospitable, the harbors, for the most part, drying out, or set on rivers with shifting harbor bars. Navigation along this coast was by lead, lookout, log, and local knowledge. Storms and gales extracted their usual grim toll. On one dreadful night in 1692 two hundred vessels and over a thousand lives were lost. And every decade produced its tragedy, with hundreds of sailors' bodies washed up on the sand and shingle shores.

The "sea-cole" trade started in the sixteenth century, and by the time Cook first sailed aboard the Walkers' *Freelove* in 1746 the trade employed thousands of seamen sailing in over a thousand ships. Whitby men alone owned over two hundred ships. A century later, three-quarters of the coasting fleet was made up of collier brigs bringing two and a half million tons of coal annually for London's fireplaces and gasworks. In 1838 one observer noted "nearly 2,000 vessels lying windbound in Yarmouth Roads. They got underway on November 1, and were followed by another 1,000 from the southward; in all 3,000 sail went through the Roads in five hours, so that the sea could hardly be seen for ships."

To carry the black diamonds of the north the trade developed its own distinctive type of vessel. Its hold was capacious to carry the cargo; it was strongly built to take the ground when alongside a quay with a full load and the natural support of the sea vanished with the ebbing tide; was easily handled in narrow channels; and, when empty of her cargo, drew stability from the underwater shape so that the minimum of ballast need be loaded for the passage home. The result was the "cat," a name describing the shape of the vessel and not its rig. Where the name comes from is unknown. In Cook's day the cats were square-rigged, with three masts set in a bluff-bowed, flat-bottomed vessel. No figurehead adorned the stem, the only nod to any sense of the aesthetic being in the proportions of the stern windows. As to the size, Cook's first vessel, the 341-ton *Freelove* can be considered typical: 106 feet in length and 27 feet in beam, manned by a master, mate, carpenter, cook, five seamen, and ten apprentices.

When not learning the practicalities of sailoring at sea, Cook lived with the Quaker family in Whitby and studied, at the behest of John Walker, the theoretical side of navigation. Cook probably needed no prodding, and Mary Prowd, the Walkers' housekeeper, provided him with a special table and a supply of candles. A quarter of a century later, when Cook, now a famous figure, returned to Yorkshire to visit his old father and the Walkers, Mary Prowd, in the Walker home, would throw her old arms around the man that the gentlemen of Whitby had ridden out to meet, crying, "Oh honey James! How glad I is to see thee!"

By 1750 Cook's apprenticeship was over and he signed on for the first time as a seaman. Voyages to Norway, the Baltic, down Channel, and the Irish Sea followed; by 1752 he was sailing as mate. Three years later John Walker offered him the position of master of the *Friendship*. Nine years from the start of his apprenticeship to pacing the deck of his own command and perhaps, in the future, the pacing of the deck of his own ship. The farm laborer's son had come far indeed.

But on 17 June 1755, Cook made an apparently irrational decision: he volunteered into the Royal Navy as a seaman. One must now look at a larger world than the one bounded by the horizon as seen from a collier's deck. Which is perhaps what Cook did—and the view offered more exciting prospects than the coastal trade of the North Sea.

Great Britain was poised on the edge of another of her interminable wars with her greatest trade rival, France; the other European states were performing their usual intricate and bewildering contortions before selecting their allies; further east, in India, the rival French and British East India Companies were performing their own dance steps with the local rulers, and the alliances brought open warfare on the subcontinent; across the Atlantic the French-Indian wars were smoldering, with the French making threatening moves down the Ohio Valley from Canada. Indeed, a young colonel in the Virginia militia, one George Washington, on 4 July 1754, had surrendered to the French at Fort Necessity. Benjamin Franklin, in order to counter the French threat, orchestrated the only solution, as he saw it. "There is no repose for our thirteen colonies," he wrote, "so long as the French are masters of Canada." His exhortation was soon to be gratified.

Europe, India, North America, the West Indies: here was a worldwide conflict in the making. In 1755 the Royal Navy was on a war footing with the hated navy press-gangs out on the streets. Not that Cook had much cause to worry: colliers were allowed four men per hundred tons free from the press—usually the master, mate, carpenter, and one or more seamen. But legalistic niceties as to which men were free from the press tended to be pitched overboard with a "hot press" sweeping the streets and anchorages. The Briton's much vaunted "freedom" vanished once aboard a warship.*

In such an atmosphere, then, with the clouds of war gathering across

---

* Impressment was a method used—and abused—by the state authority of many countries to recruit men for their armies and navies. It gained its greatest notoriety in Britain during the Napoleonic Wars with the navy press-gangs forcibly "pressing" men off the streets and sailors out of merchant ships. Certain trades carried "protection" from impressment, but when a "hot-press" was ordered the protection became a worthless scrap of paper.

the horizon, did James Cook volunteer into the Royal Navy. The officer in charge of the press at Wapping must have been thunderstruck at his great good fortune in getting such a prime hand as this tall, healthy, capable seaman. John Walker's loss became King George's gain.

Within a month, able seaman James Cook of the sixty-gun *Eagle* was promoted master's mate. Two years after joining the navy, most of the time having been spent at sea in the approaches to the English Channel and blockading the French coast, Cook took, and passed, an examination to be appointed master. He was now the most important warrant officer aboard a warship. This position in the Royal Navy hierarchy requires some explanation.

The rank of master is one that no longer exists, and even in Cook's day it represented something of an anachronism. Centuries before, when no such thing as a permanent fighting navy existed, the monarch of the day chartered a merchant ship complete with master and crew, then put aboard the gentlemen and soldiers for the fighting. The master's job was to bring his vessel alongside the enemy or put them ashore and then let the armored and chain-mailed hooligans slug it out. By the eighteenth century the method was slightly more sophisticated. The monarch—in name—now owned the vessels, but the master's responsibilities still bore traces of the older days—and also the subtle social ranking of caste. Navy officers with commissions from the Admiralty were the "high caste" gentlemen who led their men into battle; the master who piloted the ship into battle still remained the "low caste" seaman with only a warrant from the Navy Board. No matter; the "low caste" master aboard a First-Rate* earned more than the "high caste" lieutenants.

The duties of a master in the eighteenth-century Navy were comprehensive, time-consuming, and embraced the working fabric of the entire ship. He was the man who navigated the ship; kept the logbook; noted shoals, rocks, and reefs; took responsibility for masts, yards, sails, and rigging; oversaw the vessel's trim and ballasting; and, finally, signed all accounts and vouchers. In short, he earned his pay.

James Cook was a master for eleven years, and in those years, nearly all spent in the waters off North America, he built the solid foundations of his brilliance as a surveyor and a seaman, and, not least of all, honed his qualities as a leader of men with a vigilant concern for their health and well-being. Cook, having served on the lower deck, was only too aware of the improvident and feckless character of seamen. He had also seen too many deaths from scurvy. Cook regarded the men in the same light as he regarded the precious navigational and surveying instruments: both were

---

* Admiral Lord Anson, during his first term as First Lord of the Admiralty (1751–56), introduced the system of rating warships by their number of guns. First-Rates carried 100 guns upward; Second-Rates, 85 to 100; Third-Rates, 70 to 85; Fourth-Rates, 50 to 70; Fifth-Rates, 32 to 50; Sixth-Rates, any number of guns up to 32 if commanded by a post-captain, but rated as sloops if commanded by a lower-ranking commander.

precious and both needed maintenance—a seaman dead from disease was just as dead as one by cannon fire.

By the May of 1756 the undeclared war between the French and British in North America, finally, inevitably, became a declared war. Benjamin Franklin was about to have his wish—one to cost thousands of lives—come true. Two years later Cook was at Halifax in Nova Scotia serving as master aboard the sixty-four-gun *Pembroke,* commanded by Captain John Simcoe. It had been a long two-month passage from England, during which twenty-six seamen had died and large numbers had been put into hospital at Halifax after their arrival. Cook had seen the ravages of scurvy during the months of blockading off France, and now he saw the *Pembroke* a useless instrument, with most of her crew in hospital.

A few months later, the men recovered, the *Pembroke* was at the siege and taking of Louisburg on Cape Breton Island. In the aftermath, on going ashore, Cook noted a military officer working with an unusual-looking instrument, measuring angles and scribbling the results into a notebook. The two men struck up a conversation and Cook found he was talking with Major Samuel Holland, a military engineer and surveyor who was making a plan of the fortifications. The instrument was a plane table. Cook, according to Holland, "expressed an ardent desire to be instructed in the use of the Plane Table . . . I appointed the next day in order to make him acquainted with the whole process." This fortuitous meeting in Louisburg—Cook and Holland obviously found each other genial and like-minded companions—was to have a profound effect on Cook's future career.

Next day, aboard the *Pembroke,* Cook was instructed in the theoretical use of the plane table. The following day, Holland having spent the night aboard the warship—one would have liked to be there to listen to the conversation—Holland, Cook, and two young midshipmen were ashore using the plane table in a practical demonstration. Simcoe—a most unusual naval officer—encouraged Cook in the military methods of surveying and draftsmanship. On returning to Halifax, the *Pembroke*'s great stern cabin was converted into a drafting office. Let Holland pick up the tale: "During our stay at Halifax, whenever I could get a moment of time from my duty, I was on board the *Pembroke,* where the great cabin, dedicated to scientific purposes and mostly taken up with a drawing table, furnished no room for idlers. Under Capt. Simcoe's eye, Mr Cook and myself compiled materials for a chart of the Gulf and River of St Lawrence. . . . These charts were of much use as some copies came out prior to our sailing from Halifax for Quebec in 1759."

But before the plucking of French feathers at Quebec, and during the long, cold winter, Cook, encouraged by Simcoe, set about learning spherical trigonometry and absorbing the contents of Charles Leadbetter's *A Compleat System of Astronomy* and *The Young Mathematician's Companion.* Despite the primary-school tone of the title, the latter was a comprehensive volume dealing with arithmetic, geometry, plain and spherical trigonometry, astronomy, and surveying. Now all this was most unusual reading for a master in the Royal Navy. Most masters' navigational skills started with the lead line and ended with dead reckoning and latitude sights. As Cook honed his navigational and surveying skills during that winter of 1758–59, the British planned their attack upon Quebec.

During the summer of 1759, in a masterly combined operation with 35 warships and 119 transports, the navy took the British army up the St. Lawrence to the French fortress city. The French had removed the navigation aids along the dangerous and tortuous parts of the river and believed it impossible for the British to even bring their warships close to the citadel. Cook's job, along with all the other masters, was to sound and mark the channel—to act as pathfinders. In a way it was a reversion to their ancient role of bringing soldiers to battle.

A marvelous vignette of a small part of this operation appears in *An Historical Journal of the Campaigns in North America,* by the army captain John Knox. The captain sailed aboard the transport *Goodwill* commanded by a merchant master "old Killick." At one of the more hazardous stretches, the mate was put at the helm and "old Killick" ambled forward with a speaking trumpet:

I went forward with this experienced mariner, who pointed out the channel to me as we passed, shewing me, by the ripples and colour of the water, where there were ledges of rocks (to me invisible) from banks of sand, mud, or gravel. He gave his orders with great unconcern, joked with the sounding-boats who lay off on each side, with different-coloured flags for our guidance; and, when any of them called to him, and pointed to the deepest water, he answered, "aye, aye, my dear, chalk it down, a d-d dangerous navigation—eh, if you don't make a sputter about it, you'll get no credit for it in England, &c." After we had cleared this remarkable place, where the channel forms a complete zig-zag, the Master called to his Mate to give the helm to somebody else, saying, "D—— me, if there are not a thousand places in the Thames fifty times more hazardous than this; I am ashamed that Englishmen should make such a rout about it."

After the fall of Quebec, Cook was made master aboard the seventy-gun *Northumberland*. Three years were now spent with the North American squadron and his surveying work continued. And it was soon obvious to his superiors that Mr. James Cook was rising high above the common level of masters. In 1761 he was awarded an extra £50 for "making himself Master of the Pilotage of the River Saint Lawrence." His name was singled out for praise in letters going to the Admiralty. In October 1762, the long war over, the *Northumberland* returned to England and one of the last acts of her captain—now Rear Admiral Lord Colville—was to write a letter to the Admiralty:

Mr Cook late Master of the Northumberland acquaints me that he has laid before their Lordships all his Draughts and Observations, relating to the River St Lawrence, part of the coast of Nova Scotia, and of Newfoundland.

On this Occasion, I beg leave to inform their Lordships, that from my Experience of Mr Cook's Genius and Capacity, I think him well qualified for the Work he has performed, and for greater Undertakings of the same kind. These Draughts being made under my own Eye I can venture to say, they may be the means of directing many in the right way, but cannot mislead any.

The letter is dated 30 December 1762.

This December was an important watershed in Cook's life. A few days before Colville wrote his letter, we have an image of Cook—and what a pleasing domestic image it is, when compared to the male-oriented years at sea—of his walking arm in arm with a handsome slip of a girl across green meadows to the parish church of Barking. Here, after the wedding ceremony in St. Margaret's, the twenty-one-year-old woman signed her new name into the church register: "Elizabeth Cook late Batts."

In her old age Elizabeth Cook loved to tell of that walk across the meadows. As I write this I'm gazing at a portrait of Mrs. Cook painted in her old age—she lived to be ninety-three—and the beauty and spirit of the girl that won James Cook's heart gazes back at me through the integuments of age. A rather formidable lady, one thinks, and a lady with a developed sense of the proprieties. She wore a ring with a lock of her husband's hair in it, and if any person's conduct met with her disapproval, the comment "Mr Cook would never have done so" became the inevitable yardstick for censure.

Elizabeth Cook had only four months with her husband before he sailed for North America. During those four months, momentous events took place. The Treaty of Paris, marking the official end of the Seven Years' War, was signed and vast new territories in North America were dropped into the laps of the harried and overburdened officials in London. Of utmost importance was the accurate surveying of these new acquisitions. Newfoundland, although a British possession prior to the war, was but poorly charted, and Cook was chosen by the Admiralty to carry out the survey along the coast of this strategic and important island—important for its fishing and timber, strategic for its position flanking the Gulf of St Lawrence.

Newfoundland has six thousand miles of tortuous, complex, and intricate coastline; the season for surveying was short and the coast bedeviled with fogs. To accomplish his task Cook spent weeks—and £68 11s 8d—on surveying instruments that included a theodolite, "a brass telescopic quadrant made by Mr John Bird," azimuth compasses, flags and poles, deep-sea leads and lines, tallow, axes, pickaxes, and two "common deal tables to draw upon." As an assistant Cook asked for a draftsman from the Tower—the headquarters of the Ordnance Office and military map-making.

It is plain that Cook did not intend to use the navy method of a "running survey" for Newfoundland's coast. This one, weather and time permitting, would be carried out using the military methods of triangulation based on land—a theodolite is useless at sea—and boats for taking soundings at sea. The traditional naval running survey was carried out from sea, with the vessel sailing along the coast on a set course, the distance sailed carefully logged, and prominent coastal features noted. It was a method open to gross error. Later in life, Cook defined his terms for a proper survey: "Surveying a place, according to my idea, is taking a geometrical plan of it, in which every place is to have its true situation. . . ."

Five years were spent in Newfoundland. Spring, summer, and fall were spent working along the coastline, and the winters were spent in London. His vessel was a sixty-eight-ton schooner the *Grenville,* ex-*Sally,* built in 1754 at a Massachusetts yard. During the winter of 1765–66 the *Grenville* was converted to a square-rig brig as Cook, in a letter to the Navy Board, explained that "schooners are the worst of vessels to go upon any discovery, for in meeting with any unexpected danger their staying cannot be depended upon, and for want of sail to lay-a-back thay run themselves ashore before they wear."

But Cook was gathering more skills than those of seamanship and surveying along a dangerous coastline. Antiscorbutic remedies were learned with the making of "spruce beer" and "essence of spruce"; berries were collected and the diet varied with fresh game, fish, and birds; during the summer of 1776 an observation was made of an eclipse of the sun. When worked out and compared with an observation of the same eclipse taken at Oxford, it would give an exact longitude for the Newfoundland observation. Indeed, the results were communicated to the Royal Society by Dr. John Bevis and appeared in the Society's *Philosophical Transactions.* Mr. Cook was becoming known to the scientific gentlemen of London.

The winter months were spent working on manuscript charts and sailing directions at Cook's home in Mile End. Permission was granted by the Admiralty for their publication by Cook—but he had to pay for their engraving and printing and then arrange for their sale by London's map sellers. It was a curious fact that the most powerful navy in the world still had no hydrographic department for the publishing of charts. The French were far ahead of the British, with cartographers and geographers at work in their Depôt des Cartes et Plans de la Marine, instituted in 1720. Not until 1795 did the British create a Hydrographic Department—with Alexander Dalrymple as Hydrographer—and the first Admiralty chart was not published until 1801. Even then the department was little more than a glorified storeroom. However, in 1808, Captain Thomas Hurd took over as Hydrographer and persuaded the Admiralty that charts should be sold to the public, and organized a naval surveying service. As a young man he had worked under Holland and Des Barres—another military engineer—

in the surveys of North America. The navy, obviously, was learning something from the army.

Cook, during six winters in London, perfected his techniques in dealing with obscurantist and dilatory civil servants at the Admiralty; searched in London map shops on behalf of Newfoundland's Governor, Captain Hugh Palliser—his old captain in the *Eagle*—for evidence of French fishing rights on the island; organized improvements to the *Grenville;* met with—an unheard of occurrence for a lowly master—the First Lord of the Admiralty and the Secretary of the Treasury. Cook, in short, was coming to the notice of men of power and influence who, in their turn, recognized the ability of this impressive, quiet-spoken man.

The winter of 1767–68 was spent working on "A Chart of the West Coast of Newfoundland . . . by James Cook, Surveyor," and the sailing directions to go with the chart. The engraver was Mr. J. Larken, who had engraved Cook's previous works, and it was published in 1768, along with the sailing directions, all being sold by "J. Mount and T. Page, on Tower Hill, Thos. Jefferys, the corner of St Martin's Lane, in the Strand, and Andw. Drury, in Duke's Court, near St Martin's Church." The *Grenville* had to be prepared for the coming season's work and Cook requested that a surgeon's mate be added to the crew. In the spring he asked for reimbursement to the repair of instruments and the cost of stationery. But their Lordships had other work for Mr. Cook. And Mr. Michael Lane—Cook's assistant—was appointed in his place aboard the *Grenville* to continue the Newfoundland survey.

On 25 May 1768, their Lordships resolved "that Mr James Cook be appointed first Lieutenant of the Endeavour Bark." The Admiralty had made a brilliant choice, and James Cook sailed into history. Those hard years in North America had finally brought forth their reward.

The practical result, the fruit as it were, of those years rests in the charts. And masterly, magnificent works they are. The manuscript charts, those worked on at home in Mile End, are large—one is ten feet long, another eight feet by five feet, another six feet by three feet—colored, and contain topographic details not included in the engraved versions: these are also a delight and pleasure to the eye. But more importantly, they are accurate. Let Captain Bayfield who, in the nineteenth century, followed in Cook's footsteps in the updating of the North American surveys, have the final word. In a letter of 1848 to Captain Beaufort—the Hydrographer at the Admiralty—Bayfield wrote: "I have not in the least exaggerated the defects of the old charts of the Gulf, Cape Breton and Nova Scotia. There are none that can with any degree of safety be trusted by the seaman, excepting those of Cook and Lane."

The three-year voyage of the *Endeavour* ended in July 1771. And overnight Mr. Banks and Dr. Solander, the naturalists during the voyage, be-

came the lions of London society. Mr. Banks was presented to the King at
St. James's Palace . . . Mr. Banks and Dr. Solander met with the King at
Richmond . . . Mr. Banks was seen at court . . . Mr. Banks presented His
Majesty with a feather-rimmed gold coronet from Chile . . . Mr. Banks and
Dr. Solander were made honorary doctors of civil law at Oxford University
. . . Mr. Banks was to have two ships from the government to pursue his
discoveries in the South Seas . . . the celebrated Mr. Banks would shortly
make another voyage to St. George's Island, in the South Seas, and it was
said the government would allow him three ships . . . the Swedish naturalist Linnaeus suggested that New South Wales be named Banksia. . . . The
twenty-seven-year old Banks was getting a vastly overinflated opinion of
himself.

Cook's activities went unremarked by London's gossips. At Mile End
he found a grieving but stoical wife. Two sons, James and Nathaniel, were
hale and hearty, but his four-year-old daughter, Elizabeth, had died three
months prior to his return. And a son, Joseph, never seen by Cook, had
been born, baptized, and buried within a month of the *Endeavour*'s sailing. The activity inseparable from the ending of the long voyage acted as
an anodyne to the personal loss.

Two months after his return Cook was promoted to commander and
received his commission from the hands of His Majesty. Not forgotten by
Cook was his old friend and mentor John Walker; the Whitby Quaker
received letters describing the *Endeavour*'s voyage. In one, almost casually,
Cook mentioned the possibility of another voyage, this time with two
ships, and his belief that "the command will be confer'd upon me."

The question of a large southern continent still nagged at Cook's mind.
He and Banks, in the stern cabin of the *Endeavour,* had had many conversa-
tions on the subject: Banks mentions the question in his journals and
Cook, in a postscript to the *Endeavour* voyage, outlined a plan to settle the
problem using New Zealand as a base for the search.

The Admiralty, pleasantly surprised at the public's reception of Cook's
voyage and basking in the reflected glory, saw merit in Cook's proposal. It
would also spike the guns of Alexander Dalrymple—still fuming over his
rejection as commander of the expedition, and still firing his cannonades
of invective.

The decision being made, Cook was ordered to look over vessels in the
Pool of London suitable for service "in remote parts." Two were required.
Cook would have been happy with the *Endeavour* as one of the vessels,
but she had been sent to the Falklands as a store ship. The collier had
proved an ideal exploration vessel, and Cook soon selected three vessels of
the same type. By early November the Admiralty had bought two: the 462-
ton *Marquis of Granby* and the 340-ton *Marquis of Rockingham*. Both
were under two years old and their breeding was impeccable—they had

been built by the Fishburn yard at Whitby, the builders of the *Endeavour*.

By the end of the month the Admiralty had changed their names to *Drake* and *Raleigh* and registered them as sloops-of-war, with *Drake* to carry twelve guns and 120 men, and *Raleigh* ten guns and 90 men. Affairs now moved at a rapid rate. The voyage to "remote parts" was due to sail in March and the two vessels had to be converted to their task. Stowage was needed for stores, provisions, gunpowder, and shot; ordnance had to be installed and gunports fitted; accommodation needed to be made for officers and crew; an underdeck galley built to replace the primitive deck galley used in the coasting trade; masts, yards, sails and rigging overhauled; an extra sheathing of planking laid to act as a sacrificial barrier for the teredo worm.

Cook was now plunged into all the multifarious details of the coming voyage. And the skills learned in dealing with lethargic civil servants during the *Grenville* years were once more brought into play. On only one item did Cook meet with defeat: a request for brass fittings on the furniture in the great cabin was denied by a faceless clerk in the Navy Board as having no precedent. Cook paid for the fittings himself. Considering the changes that were being made on the two vessels, the clerk's diktat touches on the farcical.

As the vessels were converted, their names also went through a transformation blown on the tactful winds of diplomacy. Was it not probable that two such evocative names as *Drake* and *Raleigh* could do nothing but give offense to the rather prickly Spanish? So ran the feelings in the corridors of power—particularly as these ships were bound into an ocean the Spanish, laughably enough, still considered their own private preserve. The names were changed. When Cook heard of it he wrote to the ships' original owners that "the Admiralty have altered the names of the ships from Drake to Resolution and Raleigh to Adventure which, in my opinion are much properer than the former." *Endeavour, Resolution, Adventure*: somewhere in the Admiralty was a man gifted with a sense of the appropriate.

On his previous voyage Cook had navigated across hazardous seas strewn with uncharted reefs, shoals, and islands. He had suffered and survived near-total shipwreck on the Great Barrier Reef. Disease and death had been the *Endeavour*'s lot in fever-ridden Batavia. But as he made his preparations for the new voyage, ahead of him loomed dangers that threatened to wreck the expedition before it even began.

The hazard came in the shape of Joseph Banks. He and Solander had accepted the invitation to voyage again with Cook: but such had been the adulation in London that the young man conceived himself to be the guiding star. First and foremost, Cook's choice of the two colliers met with his adamant disapproval—Banks's thoughts ran more on the lines of a forty-four-gun warship or an East Indiaman. He was, however, stuck with the smaller and cramped *Resolution*. No matter; energy, charm, and good connections are potent forces and he brought to bear his friendship with the First Lord of the Admiralty, the rake, gambler, and politician John Montagu, Fourth Earl of Sandwich. Orders were soon issued for additional alterations on the *Resolution* to accommodate Banks's burgeoning personal party, which grew apace with his mushrooming ego. The Banks entourage now numbered seventeen—including two horn players. Banks was falling into the trap of believing that this was *his* voyage, that Cook was merely a pilot with Banks in command.

To house Banks's bloated party, the *Resolution*'s upper works were raised a foot, an extra deck was added over the waist, and, as the Banks party were to take over what would have been Cook's great stern cabin, a roundhouse was added over the after part of the quarterdeck for the commander's accommodation. Cook, being a highly competent seaman, knew full well what the reckoning would be: the extra weight and windage would make for a seagoing disaster. Powerless in the face of this hurricane of influence and folly, like a good seaman, he waited out the storm.

In late April—the March sailing date had slipped by with all these changes—the two vessels were ordered down to Long Reach to take on powder and shot. Here the "young gentlemen" of both ships, full of the high spirits and exuberance of youth before the beginning of a great adventure, "kept the nearest villages in constant alarm by getting leave to go ashore to buy things and drink tea and so on, and sometimes staying on shore all night for the sole pleasure of removing the signs, shop boards, and so on, and placing them on other houses in the night." For these and other excesses the boisterous youth—some were only fourteen years old—suffered a severe reprimand from Cook. But Cook was soon to have more important matters on his mind than coping with the pranks of his young midshipmen.

The day of reckoning arrived during May, with the *Resolution* being ordered to the Downs. In the passage down the Thames she proved so crank, so tender, so in danger of capsizing that the pilot refused to take her any further than the Nore. She was changed from Cook's description as "the fitest for Service she was going upon of any I had ever seen" to what his first lieutenant succinctly called "an exceeding dangerous and unsafe ship"; another lieutenant wrote with insouciant bravado: "By God I'll go to sea in a Grog Tub, if desired, or in the Resolution as soon as you please; but I must say I think her by far the most unsafe ship I ever saw or heard of."

The Admiralty, only too aware of the disastrous results of their Banks-inspired folly, ordered the *Resolution* to the nearest shipyard, at Sheerness. Here a horde of shipwrights and carpenters descended upon her and the catastrophic changes were ripped out. Visiting the ship and seeing the work in progress, an incandescent Banks exploded in such a fit of petulance that a young midshipman later wrote of the scene: "When he saw the Ship, and the alterations that were made, He swore and stamped upon the Warfe, like a Mad Man, and instantly ordered his Servants and all his things out of the Ship." Banks had often threatened to leave the enterprise at the remotest hint of his desires' being thwarted. This time the Admiralty, heaving a collective sigh of relief, took him at face value and looked for replacements in the scientific staff.

The changes to the *Resolution* now became a public cause célèbre. The fashionable world had flocked to see the *Resolution* undergoing her changes to accommodate the celebrated Mr. Banks. And the shipwrights had cursed as the ladies stepped delicately through the shavings. And now Mr. Banks was no longer going! The rumor mills began their endless fabrications.

Cook continued the seemingly interminable preparations for the delayed voyage as a verbal war rumbled between Banks and his supporters on one side and the Admiralty on the other. Quivering with self-righteous indignation, Banks dashed off a letter to Sandwich giving his reasons for declining to go on the voyage. In it Banks was foolish enough to complain that he had not been consulted on the type of vessel chosen and that the *Resolution* would be, "if not absolutely incapable at least exceedingly unfit for the intended voyage." This was not all. The ship would be overcrowded without the extra deck and therefore unhealthy. The forty-four-gun *Launceston* would be a better ship and he knew many commanders "who would willingly undertake to procede in her in the intended Expedition, ambitious of shewing the World, that the Success of such an undertaking depends more upon the Prudence and Perserverance of the Commander than upon any particular built of the Ship that may be employed." The slap at Cook was mean-spirited and unwarranted. All in all, the letter was the silliest that Banks ever wrote—the inevitable result of a publicity-fattened ego.

Sandwich sent the letter to the Navy Board, who failed to look kindly on gratuitous advice from a landsman. The first paragraph of their opening broadside rumbled: "Mr Banks's first Objection to the Ship respected only the Conveniences for himself and was no more than this, 'that the forepart of the Cabin was an Inch or two too low.' As to the proper kind of Ship, and her fitness and sufficiency for the Voyage, his Opinion was never asked, nor could have been asked with any propriety, he being in no degree qualified to form a right Judgement in such a matter; and for the same reason his Opinion now thereon is not to be attended to." One by one more broadsides demolished Banks's specious arguments and reduced them to wallowing hulks.

Sandwich now joined battle with his friend and composed a twenty-page letter refuting all of Banks's charges. It ended with a deadly ironical riposte, skewering Banks to the wall:

Upon the whole I hope that for the advantage of the curious part of Mankind, your zeal for distant voyages will not cease, I heartily wish you success in all your undertakings, but I would advise you in order to insure that success to fit out a ship yourself; that and only that can give you the absolute command of the whole Expedition; and as I have a sincere regard for your wellfare and consequently for your preservation, I earnestly entreat that the ship may not be an old man of war or an old Indiaman but a New Collier.

Banks did not indeed go on another voyage. In July, having chartered the 190-ton brig *Sir Lawrence,* he and his party sailed for Iceland.

Amidst the noise of hammer, saw, mallet, and caulking irons, the *Resolution* reverted back to the ship "fitest for service she was going upon." And for Cook the endless details of the coming voyage continued. The memorandums, orders, counterorders, questions, and suggestions flew back and forth between Cook, the Navy Board, the Victualling Board, the Sick and Hurt Board, and the Admiralty Secretary. The Victualling Board proved to be in a gratifyingly helpful and experimental mood, and hastened to comply with Cook's requests. Salted cabbage, sauerkraut, beef, pork, suet, butter, peas, wheat, salt, oil, mustard seed, tongue, sugar, portable soups, rob of lemon and orange, extra oatmeal, stockfish, cheese, bread, strong pickle, four barrels of experimentally cured beef, kegs of Baron Storsch's marmalade of carrot, Mr. Irving's apparatus for distilling fresh water from seawater, Dr. Priestly's device for sweetening water by passing "fixed air" through it, Lieutenant Osbridge's machine for rendering "stinking water sweet," Mr. Pelham's wort of boiled-down malt for making beer, Mr. Hales's recipe for making fresh yeast, Dr. James's fever powder—that eighteenth-century specific for all manner of ills. The Victualling Board regretted that French brandy was unavailable in Guernsey; would Spanish brandy—recommended by their agent—suffice? Barrels of spirits, port wine, puncheons of double-proof spirit for the preservation of natural history specimens, new canvas for awnings and sails, better seine nets for fishing, canvas bags for the seamen instead of their usual sea chests—storage space aboard the vessels was shrinking alarmingly—ice anchors, warping machines, croaks and pins for the blocks, extra tools, caulking irons, coopers tools, new butts, puncheons, hogsheads, barrels, half-hogsheads, casks, and kegs. The list appeared endless. For the seamen the Admiralty provided two jackets and trousers each made of fearnought (a sturdy woolen cloth also used as the covering for the gunpowder room doors) for wearing in the cold they were bound to. The natives of the islands were not forgotten. Kegs of nails, tools, looking glasses, combs, beads, kettles, hammers, "fine old sheets," whetstones, and grindstones were added to the overburdened vessels. Also included were two thousand medals struck by Messrs. Boulton and Fothergill of Birmingham (showing the two ships and the optimistic *Sailed from England March MDCCLXXII*)—"to be distributed to the natives of such new discovered countries as the sloops may touch at."

Cook, the Victualling Board, and the Sick and Hurt Board were keenly interested in testing possible antiscorbutic remedies. Cook had carried sauerkraut aboard the *Endeavour* and found the men—conservative creatures wedded to their salt pork, salt beef, and plum duffs—reluctant to eat it. In the early stages of the voyage Cook had ordered the flogging of two men for refusing to eat *fresh* meat. Such refusal was looked on as mutiny. Later in the voyage he used subtler methods of persuasion in his efforts to preserve the health of his men:

The Sour Krout the Men at first would not eate untill I put in practice a Method I never once knew to fail with seamen, and this was to have some of it dress'd every Day for the Cabbin Table, and permitted all the Officers without exception to make use of it and left it to the option of the Men either to take as much as they pleased or none atall; but this practice was not continued above a week before I found it necessary to put every one on board to an Allowance, for such are the Tempers and disposissions of Seamen in general that whatever you give them out of the Common way, altho it be ever so much for their good yet it will not go down with them and you will hear nothing but murmurings gainest the man that first invented it; but the Moment they see their Superiors set a Value upon it, it becomes the finest stuff in the World and the inventer a damn'd honest fellow.

For these seamen of the eighteenth century, life in the Royal Navy was hard, stern, and often brutal. But then, the period, viewed from today's perspective, with its tender and selective sensibilities, appears a brutal one. Nearly two hundred offenses committed by His Majesty's subjects were punishable by hanging—and the executions provided public entertainment: the gallows, whipping post, and pillory were the governing class's instruments in controlling its turbulent people. Flogging with the cat-o'-nine-tails, the naval instrument, is the punishment that lingers on in modern memory. The naval cat, ominously kept in a blood-red baize bag, had a two-foot-long handle of either wood or rope to which was attached the nine "tails" of two-foot-long, quarter-inch-diameter line. The complete assembly weighed about one pound and in the hands of an expert boatswain's mate it could knock a man down. In the metaphorical hands of an insecure and brutal captain it became a sadistic instrument of unparalleled savagery. Such captains boasted of having left-handed boatswain's mates who could cross the cuts made by the right-handed man. To seamen serving in ships with humane and decent officers the cat was just another hazard of service life that numbered storms, shipwrecks, maiming, disease, bad food, late pay, and death.

Some of the men who had eaten the sauerkraut and slung their hammocks on the *Endeavour* were aboard the *Resolution*. Indeed, some who were serving aboard other ships wrote to Cook and asked to sail with him. Where possible, an obliging Admiralty saw to the transfer. For the most part the men were typical of the lower deck: young, illiterate, tough, sentimental, good seamen, inured to hardship—and drunk when possible. Marines were requested who could play the bagpipe, fife, violin, and drum. A year later the Tahitians and Maoris were to be entranced by the marines' musical offerings.

Cook, never a man to strew compliments like a farmhand broadcasting grain, later wrote of his seamen that "they shewed themselves capable of surmounting every difficulty and danger which came their way." And this opinion is reinforced by John Elliot, who sailed as a midshipman and wrote his memoirs "at the request of his Wife, for the use and amusement of his Children *only*." The memoirs throw a light on incidents and personalities that reveals aspects hidden by the more circumspect prose of the official journals. Elliot on the men, then: "I will here do them the justice to say that *No Men* could behave better, under every circumstance than they did, the same must be said of the officers; and I will add that I believe there never was a Ship, where for so long a period, under such circumstances, more happiness, order, and obedience was enjoy'd."

The memoirs carry a delightfully quirky quick reference guide for his children, with short "Remarks" on the "Officers and Gentlemen on the Quarter Deck." Cook is a "Sober, brave, humane and expert seaman and officer." The first lieutenant, Robert Palliser Cooper, receives a "Sober, steady, good officer" in the Remarks column. The second lieutenant, Charles Clerke, is "A brave and good officer & a genal favorite." Clerke's own journal and his letters to Joseph Banks reveal a distinct personality. Lively, intelligent, amusing, Clerke would make an ideal dinner companion. It was he who would happily sail to sea in a "Grog Tub"; he had sailed aboard the *Endeavour* and was to sail with Cook again on the third and last circumnavigation, take command after Cook's death, die of consumption aboard the *Resolution,* and be buried in the remote Kamchatka Peninsula of Imperial Russia.

The third officer was Richard Pickersgill. This would be his third circumnavigation, his having sailed aboard the *Dolphin* and *Endeavour*. Very competent, he was to be much used by Cook for small boat work when approaching unknown anchorages. His was a rather romantic and brooding temperament, and in an age of hard drinking, Elliot's comment is illuminating: "A good officer and astronomer but liking ye Grog." It never, however, affected his judgment during the coming voyage. Only later in life did drink cause his dismissal from the navy and, according to one source, his death by drowning in the Thames.

As to the midshipmen, it was considered "a great feather in a young

Man's Cap, to go with Capt. Cook." And among them were two who achieved fame later in life: the fourteen-year-old George Vancouver—an explorer in embryo—Elliot's "Quiet inoffensive young man"; and the twenty-one-year-old James Burney, son of Dr. Charles Burney, brother to Fanny Burney, and friend of Joseph Banks, Dr. Johnson, and Charles Lamb. He was "Clever & Excentric," according to Elliot—although no indication is given of the eccentricities. Elliot himself would benefit from having the "great feather" in his cap. The voyage over, he was examined by the Directors of the East India Company for a position aboard one of the company ships, and the interview consisted of "Their saying that they suppos'd I had been with Cook, that having been a Pupil of his, I must be a good sailor; asking me how my Uncle did, and telling me to withdraw." Elliot got the post.

Joseph Gilbert, the master of the *Resolution*, aged forty, was one of the older men aboard. Like Cook he had spent time surveying the Newfoundland and Labrador coasts, and Cook came to have a high opinion of his abilities. He was, according to Elliot, "A steady good officer."

The smaller *Adventure* was commanded by Tobias Furneaux, a Devon man. He had been the second lieutenant aboard the *Dolphin* under Samuel Wallis when the sailors had been the first Europeans to see the peaks of Tahiti rising above the horizon. Although a capable seaman, Furneaux lacked the exploring instinct, the taste for navigation and geography, the questing spirit, the inquiring nature, so apparent in Cook.

During the *Endeavour* voyage Cook had obtained his longitude by the lunar-distance method. It was to be used again on this second voyage, but the Admiralty saw an opportunity to test four of the newfangled "Watch-Machines." Three had been made by John Arnold and one, a duplicate of John Harrison's award-winning H4 watch, by Larcum Kendall under Harrison's supervision. This was K1, close to three years in the making, and about to enter nautical history.

Two watches—one of them K1—went to the *Resolution* and two to the *Adventure*. The watches nestled in mahogany boxes fitted with three locks. Each lock had its own key. During the voyage the winding and use of these watches were attended with almost religious overtones as the three officiating priests—the captain, first lieutenant, and astronomer—each with his own key, gathered together for the ritual opening and winding. It was an eerie presage of the rituals for the firing of nuclear missiles.

Two astronomers were appointed by the Board of Longitude. Aboard the *Resolution* went William Wales, a thirty-eight-year-old Yorkshireman, plain-spoken, of ready wit and humor, complete with Yorkshire accent. "An Able steady man," according to Elliot. Wales had observed the 1769 transit of Venus at Hudson's Bay for the Royal Society. After the *Resolution* voyage he became master at the Mathematical School of Christ's Hospital.

And here we come across the literary offshoots of the voyage: Charles Lamb, Leigh Hunt, and Samuel Coleridge were all numbered among his pupils.

Lamb remembered Wales as "that hardy sailor, as well as excellent mathematician, and co-navigator with Captain Cook . . . with a perpetual fund of humour, a constant glee about him which, heightened by an inveterate provincialism of north-country dialect, absolutely took away the sting from his severities." Leigh Hunt described him as "a good man of simple plain manners, with a heavy large person and benign countenance. When he was at Otaheite, the natives played him a trick while bathing and stole his small-clothes; which we used to think a liberty scarcely credible."

But his lasting mark was on Samuel Coleridge. Schoolboys have an instinct for tapping the hobbyhorses of masters, then quietly settling back to let the flow of words wash over them and so avoid the drudgery of lessons. Wales's voyage provided a mother lode of stories. So much so that Dr. Bernard Smith, in a 1956 issue of the *Journal of the Warburg and Courtauld Institutes,* notes many affinities between Wales's journal and the words and images of the "Rime of the Ancient Mariner." Overshadowed by the impressive Wales was the *Adventure*'s astronomer, William Bayly. He also had observed the transit of Venus—but from the North Cape.

The fuming and indignant Banks, having stamped off in a huff dragging his party behind him, left a vacuum in two essential areas: natural history and art. John Zoffany, the artist picked by Banks, was replaced by the landscape painter William Hodges, who was entered, with a pleasing fiction, on the ship's strength as an able seaman. The twenty-eight-year-old Hodges' talents lay in landscapes, ice, and seascapes. But in 1986, a portrait of Cook by Hodges came to light at an Irish country-house sale. It is a more powerful and somber painting than Dance's classical Augustan Age portrait. Here is the same jutting nose and chin, the same firm curved mouth—but Cook's stern resolve and indomitable will, leap out to the viewer with greater force. Those three years aboard the *Resolution* obviously gave Hodges ample opportunity to study his captain.

Finally we come to the last of the supernumeraries, the men chosen by the Admiralty to replace Banks and Solander. And here we find one of the most contentious figures—except perhaps for the American Charles Wilkes—in the history of Antarctic exploration: Johann Reinhold Forster, who was accompanied by his son George Forster. Forster had arrived in England with his eleven-year-old son in 1766, his English at the time as limited as his purse—3½ guineas. Johann was a year younger than Cook, Prussian born; and through his veins ran a potent mixture of English, Scottish, Polish, and Prussian blood. A Lutheran pastor with wide interests in geology, geography, ethnology, antiquities, ancient history, Egyptian languages, natural history, and the collecting of books, he had arrived in

England to seek his fortune and recoup the loss of his inheritance—mostly spent on books. In England, through his connections with German émigrés, Forster was introduced to the island's world of science and scholarship. Years were spent teaching in provincial schools; papers, pamphlets, letters on natural history, geology, geography, and antiquities flowed from his copious pen. His son George worked on translations. Forster's correspondence was vast and his Prussian erudition excited the admiration of influential figures in the scholarly world. And then his chance arrived. Banks vanished and the Admiralty, prodded by Forster's connections, picked him for the expedition. He would be the naturalist, with his son as assistant. Along with the commission went a munificent grant of £4,000. (Wales was being paid £400 and Cook £110 per annum.)

The curriculum vitae indicates a wandering pedagogue of wide, if grasshopper-like, interests. But what of the man himself? The late Professor J. C. Beaglehole* calls him an incubus. At the other extreme is a comment by Georg Lichtenberg—a contemporary of Forster's—who wrote: "If Forster and not Cook had commanded the *Resolution* the learned world would have known three times as much." The idea, needless to say, is so preposterous, so absurd, so extravagant, that one can only laugh in disbelief at the ingenuous German's suggestion.

Elliot's opinion lies in between: "A clever but litigious quarelsome fellow." He also gleefully related that Mr. Burr (the master's mate) knocked down "Old Forster" for calling him a liar and that Cook had been known to show Forster from his cabin. The amiable Clerke, goaded beyond endurance, threatened to shoot him; Forster, inflated by self-importance, thought he should have Mr. Gilbert's cabin and so embroiled himself in a perpetual state of war with the master; between Wales and Forster lay an unbridgeable gulf of antipathy; the crew mimicked him in word and gesture. Forster may have been clever, but he was also pedantic, humorless, much given to Latin quotations, pathologically suspicious. In short, Forster, his own worst enemy, made for a most unfortunate shipmate on a long and often tedious voyage. Young George—"A clever good young man," according to Elliot—spent much of his time acting as a buffer between the Resolutions and his prickly father. One wishes, purely to ease the burden on Cook, that Banks had managed to control his overblown ego, and sailed aboard the *Resolution*. But Forster's abrasive persona lay all in the future for the unsuspecting crew.

On 15 June Cook wrote to the Navy Board requesting permission for the rebuilding of "two fore-mast Cabbins under the Quarter Deck" for the Forsters. On the twenty-first he bade farewell to his wife and children and joined the *Resolution* at Sheerness, sailing on the next day's tide down

---

*All Cook followers owe an eternal thanks of gratitude to the Hakluyt Society and the worthy professor for his masterly work on Cook's journals and for the definitive biography.

the Thames bound for Plymouth. Here the *Adventure* had been waiting since May. The *Resolution,* much to the relief of all, performed admirably on the passage down Channel.

In February, before the *Resolution* imbroglio, Cook had sent Sandwich a memorandum expanding his original plan for the elucidation of the hypothetical southern continent. He had realized that not only the Pacific and Indian Ocean sectors had to be quartered, like a spaniel searching a covert, but also the Atlantic sector. His expanded and revised suggestion was to sail from the Cape of Good Hope and run with the westerlies in a high southern latitude. The ships and men would recuperate in New Zealand and then spend the winter months in the Pacific islands. The following summer would again be spent in the high southern latitudes of the Pacific sector, a call would be made at Cape Horn, then on into the Atlantic sector before returning to the Cape of Good Hope. Cook attached a map of his proposed course along with the memorandum. This method, Cook was convinced, would finally put an end, one way or the other, to the centuries-old hypothesis.

At Plymouth Cook received his final instructions—a virtual carbon copy of his own plan—and found nothing to surprise him: "Indeed I was consulted at the time they were drawn up and nothing was inserted that I did not fully comprehend and approve of."

After fresh provisions were loaded, one final symbolic act was performed. All the chronometers with the portable observatories were taken ashore, checked, and started. Early next morning, on 13 July 1772, the *Resolution,* with a total complement of 118, and the *Adventure,* with 83, both loaded with livestock, stores, and provisions for two years, sailed with a light northwest breeze and set a course of southwest to clear Ushant, bound for Madeira. The great voyage had started.

VII

The Voyage of the "Resolution" and "Adventure"

I have two ladies to read to, sometimes more, but never less. At present we are circumnavigating the globe, and I find the old story with which I amused myself some years since, through the great felicity of a memory not very retentive, almost new. I am however, sadly at a loss for Cook's voyage, can you send it? I shall be glad of Foster's too. These together will make the winter pass merrily, and you will much oblige me.

William Cowper, letter to Joseph Hill, 20 October 1783

As for the *Resolution*, that honest product of Mr Fishburn's yard at Whitby, she proved one of the great, one of the superb, ships of history; of all the ships of the past, could she by magic be recreated and made immortal, one would gaze on her with something like reverence.

J. C. Beaglehole, Introduction to *Journals of Captain James Cook*, 1969

 LL LONG VOYAGES, from the Egyptian fifteenth-century-B.C. passage to the fabled land of Punt to a twentieth-century yacht sailing across the Atlantic, have the same rhythms. The months of preparation segue into the last frantic loading of provisions and stores, the last farewells, and then the severing of ties to shore as mooring lines are cast off or anchor weighed. The widening gap of water between vessel and shore marks the Rubicon: no person experiences it untouched.

Now the voyager's world has shrunk to an insignificant man-made artifact let loose upon a most insubstantial and changeable element. With the cutting of the umbilical ties to shore comes the perception that the irritants of land life, its annoyances, hustle and bustle, crowds, have been left behind. But the new, smaller world at sea is to be replaced by a different and often more rigorous discipline than can be found on land. A seaman's life is a cenobitic one and marked with monastic regularity: the Angelus bell being replaced by the ship's bell marking the hours and changes of watch. And if small heed is paid to the condition of the seaman's soul, great attention is paid to the fabric of the ship: its masts, spars, sails, rigging, hull, and deck—and, as was the case with Cook in particular, the health and cleanliness of the acolytes under the captain's command.

As the Devon and Cornish coast dropped below the horizon, Lieutenant Pickersgill wrote a valedictory "Farewell Old England" in his journal, and Cook no doubt heaved a sigh of relief at leaving the shore's problems astern and turned his mind to the problems ahead. The long passage to the Cape would provide an opportunity to initiate the *Resolution*'s crew to his style.

The sixteen-day passage to Madeira proved relatively uneventful. Pickersgill noted that the *Resolution* appeared to be a faster and handier vessel than the *Adventure*. The Forsters complained about their accommodation and dosed themselves with mulled port wine as a specific against seasickness. But even this concoction failed to ease the younger Forster's disquiet "that mankind were not meant to be amphibious animals and that . . . our present situation was an unnatural one."

At Madeira the two vessels took on fresh water, fruit, fresh beef, a thousand bunches of onions, and four hundred gallons of Madeira wine. Cook also learned, much to his amusement, that a young person going by the name of Mr. Burnett had just left the island after a stay of three months. The supposed Mr. Burnett had been waiting for Mr. Joseph Banks and the *Resolution,* but had departed the island after receiving a letter from Mr. Banks. But the nub of the tale rested on the fact that the putative Mr. Burnett had been discovered—by a maidservant—to be a woman. Obviously Banks had been hoping to add to his creature comforts aboard the *Resolution*. In this he was only following in the footsteps of another naturalist, Philibert de Commerson, who sailed with Bougainville on the first French circumnavigation of 1766–68. Commerson had been discreetly accompanied by a valet named Baré. It was not until arriving at Tahiti, where the natives immediately spotted Baré for a woman, that the subterfuge was discovered: more *femme de chambre* than valet. Elliot adopted a censorious note on Banks's stratagem: "For unless this Lady had been *very prudent indeed* she might have been the cause of much mishief." With the news of Banks's plan happily circulating around the ships, the two vessels sailed from Funchal.

Cook's style began to show. The men were put on a three-watch system rather than the usual two watches of four hours on deck and four off. With the new regimen the crew had four hours on duty followed by eight hours off. The ship was smoked and aired below decks;* at every opportunity the hammocks, bedding, and linen were inspected and aired on deck; after the daily pumping of the ship a foot of salt water was poured down the pump well—it helped, as Cooper noted, to lessen "the stench of the Bilge water which was exceedingly offensive"; Mr. Pelham's experimental "Inspissate Juce of beer" was hauled on deck—and a few days after the cold water had been added the fermentation proceeded with such vigor as to blow out bungs and even the head of one cask. The only creatures to benefit by this abortive brewing were the goats, who licked up the beer from the deck— and became "quite inebriated & lay panting and breathing on deck, as if they were dying; but soon after they recovered and grew fat."

To the sound of bursting casks, the *Resolution* and *Adventure* sailed south for Porto Praya in the Cape Verde Islands. Here they took on more water—brackish, it must be admitted, and obtained with much labor, as the surf on shore was so violent that the full casks had to be hauled through the breaking waves to a launch anchored offshore. In the words of Clerke, it was "a damn'd bad watering place . . . what water we got was none of ye best, however, 'twas tolerable." Through the surf went one unfortunate bullock, fruit, pigs, goats, and fowls. Monkeys also came aboard—bought as pets by the midshipmen and seamen. Mischievous, dirty, and verminous, they soon offended Cook's highly developed sense of hygiene with their insanitary ways, and he had them destroyed.

One animal, hidden by John Elliot, escaped Cook's eye. It did not survive long. At the Cape of Good Hope it committed its last mischievous act by throwing ink over a letter being written by the master's mate, John Whitehouse. The infuriated Whitehouse, goaded beyond endurance, reached for his pistol and "blew him out of the window." Elliot grieved over his lost pet—which perhaps accounts for his characterization of Whitehouse as a "Jesuitical, sensible but insinuating litigous mishief mak- ing fellow."

An incident just north of the equator shows Cook's style when dealing with his seamen. According to James Burney, writing—rather delicately— to his sister Fanny Burney, two men "by way of fun made an house of office of a pair of breeches belonging to our armourer." The armorer complained, and Cook decided the two men should pay equal shares for the trousers and then toss a coin to find a "winner." The winner, now the loser, would wear his new purchase. Which he did, "after many wry faces," accompanied by many scatological jokes from the amused and watching sailors.

---

* Smoking ship was a primitive type of fumigation much used by Cook. Charcoal, pitch, or brimstone fires were lit belowdecks and then, with all hands on deck, the hatches and scuttles were closed.

They arrived at the Cape of Good Hope—then a Dutch colony—on 30 October. During the passage from England the *Resolution* had lost one man overboard and the *Adventure* two midshipmen from sickness. The men of both ships were unscathed when compared to the crew of two outward-bound Dutch East Indiamen that arrived a few days later. The Dutch had lost almost two hundred men to scurvy, with sixty more being sent into hospital ashore.

The British spent nearly a month at the Cape. The crew were given fresh-baked bread every day, with fresh beef or mutton and "as much greens as they could eat." They were rotated ashore in groups "to refresh themselves." Cook was building up his men to face the rigors ahead. The ships were caulked and painted; fresh provisions, wine, and brandy ordered. The astronomers took ashore the portable observatories and watches to make their abstruse calculations. Of the four watches the Harrison-Kendall was proving the most accurate and reliable, with the Arnolds rather erratic and untrustworthy. The Forsters botanized and met a twenty-four-year-old Swedish botanist, Anders Sparrman, who had studied under Linnaeus; they persuaded the young Swede to sail aboard the *Resolution* as their assistant, with Forster paying his keep plus a small stipend. Cook found himself "strongly importuned" by Forster to accept yet another naturalist—and yielded with good grace. Sparrman, in fact, turned out to be a self-effacing young man: a little rigid, prim, prudish, censorious, and easily shocked by the oaths, blasphemy, and boisterous behavior of the British seamen. "A clever steady man," according to the invaluable Elliot.

November at the Cape was a busy letter-writing month for Cook. The Admiralty was brought up to date on the state of the expedition, and a graceful letter was written to Banks, with the opening paragraph running: "Some Cross circumstances which happened at the latter part of the equipment of the Resolution created, I have reason to think, a coolness betwixt you and I, but I can by no means think it was sifficient to me to break of all corrispondance with a Man I am under many obligations too." Details of the passage to the Cape are given and Cook signs off as "Your most Obliged Humble Servant."

John Walker from Whitby days is remembered. The letter is worth giving in full as we find Cook, about to set off into the unknown, in a philosophical mood.

Dear Sir   Cape of Good Hope 20th Nov 1772
   Having nothing new to communicate I should hardly have troubled you with a letter was it not customary for Men to take leave of their friends before they go out of the World, for I can hardly think my self in it so long as I am deprived from having any Connections with the civilized part of it, and this will soon be my case for two years at least. When I think of the Inhospitable parts I am going to, I

think the Voyage dangerous, I however enter upon it with great cheerfullness, providence has been very kind to me on many occasions, and I trust in the continuation of the divine protection; I have two good Ships well provided and well Man'd. You must have heard of the Clamour raised against the Resolution before I left England, I can assure you I never set foot in a finer Ship. Please to make my best respects to all Friends at Whitby and beleive me to be with great regard and esteem

Your Most affectionate Friend

JAM^S COOK

It could be one Quaker writing to another.

On the afternoon of 22 November the two vessels weighed anchor and headed south into the unknown. Or "new and awful scenes," according to George Forster.

Cook's orders after leaving the Cape of Good Hope were to look for "Cape Circumcision, which is said by Monsr. Bouvet to lye nearly in the Latitude 54°00′ South, and in about 11°20′ of longitude East from Greenwich." The oddly named cape—present-day Bouvet Island—had been sighted on the feast day of the Circumcision, 1 January 1739, by Jean Bouvet de Lozier, commanding two ships of the French East India Company, the *Aigle* and *Marie*. They were searching for the sixteenth-century land of Sieur de Gonneville: a land that much attracted the French, as de Gonneville claimed to have lived there for six months and brought back a "prince" to prove it. Where the land lay was open to conjecture; somewhere south of the equator, most certainly. And with this frail evidence French cartographers moved it around the globe with facile ease according to whim. It was most probably Brazil. No matter; from the French point of view any land found south of the Cape of Good Hope would serve as a staging post to the East Indies. They found a steep, fog-shrouded cliff face, ice-capped and inhospitable. Bouvet, unable to land, stayed ten days in the vicinity—his pilot thought it a small island—without discovering anything further.*

This was not the only French discovery that Cook intended to investigate. During the month at the Cape of Good Hope, Cook had collected news of another, more recent French voyage. As far as he could gather, some eight months previous to his arrival at the Cape, two French vessels had sailed south from the island of Mauritius and somewhere close to 48°S latitude had come upon land. Scanty information, but Cook felt obliged to investigate. The ships' names were known but not their commanders.

The unknown commander was the Breton Yves de Kerguelen-Tremarec. Louis XV had dispatched him with two ships, the *Fortune* and the

---

* Bouvet Island, some four miles across, is rather unique. And Bouvet's coming across it was a feat very similar to finding the proverbial needle in a haystack. It is the most isolated island in the world—the nearest land being a thousand miles away. Bouvet's longitude for his Cape Circumcision bears no relationship to its true position—54°25′S and 3°24′E.

Gros-Ventre, to continue Bouvet's search for de Gonneville's tantalizing land; rich, fertile, and perhaps, with judicious colonizing, one to replace the lost Canada. But where exactly did this southern land lie? Bouvet had found an icy cliff face, but this could not, by any stretch of the imagination, be transformed into the fabled land, the new Garden of Eden.

On 12 February 1772, after sailing south from Mauritius, Kerguelen found what he thought to be the mythic land. No landing could be made due to bad weather, and in the same vile conditions, losing sight of his consort, Kerguelen sailed back to Mauritius and then to France. The commander of the *Gros-Ventre* did manage to get foot ashore at an inlet he named Sea Lion Cove—today's Gros-Ventre Cove on Kerguelen Island.

Kerguelen's report to Louis XV bore little relation to facts. The Breton named the land South France and claimed it would be vital for the route to India, the Moluccas, China, and the South Seas. Its climate was suitable for settlement and, no doubt, the land would yield timber, mines, diamonds, rubies, semiprecious stones, and marble. As to any natives: "We shall at least find natural human beings, living in a primitive state, free from defiance and remorse and ignorant of the artifices of civilized man. In fact South France will furnish a wonderful exhibition of moral and physical specimens." All this owed more to the doctrines of Rousseau, the cult of the "noble savage," and an overheated Celtic imagination than to common sense—particularly when this new Garden of Eden had only been glimpsed in foul and foggy weather.

Nevertheless, it was all believed and Kerguelen sailed from France in command of a small fleet of three ships, the *Rolland,* the *Oiseau,* and the *Dauphine,* bound for the new land of South France, set in the equivalent latitude of Paris. Poor Kerguelen; one feels a pang of pity for the wishful-thinking Breton and his approaching nemesis. Kerguelen made his landfall on 14 December 1773 and spent the rest of the year exploring the northwest coast. By the first week of January, his ships in a parlous state, the men ravaged by scurvy, the saddened Breton quit the dreadful coast—no longer the optimistic South France, but now the Land of Desolation. Worse was to come. Back in France he suffered the usual fate of bearers of bad news. Awkward questions were also being asked. Why had he abandoned the *Gros-Ventre* on the first voyage? Was it necessary to smuggle aboard a pretty girl at Brest for his own pleasures on the second voyage? And what were the wife and daughter of the governor of the island of Bourbon doing aboard his flagship? The outcome was dismissal from the service and prison—not, indeed, in the Bastille, but at a small château near Saumur.

All this, mercifully, was in the future for Kerguelen as he headed south to disillusionment. Cook, meanwhile, one day out from the Cape and some twenty-five hundred miles west of Kerguelen and his little fleet, was imprinting his style on the *Resolution.* The water allowance was rationed and he set an example by washing and shaving in salt water. The officers were allowed a quart of water a day for tea. Sparrman and the Forsters suffered the pangs of seasickness—with Forster Senior dosing himself with the invaluable "mulled red Wine with sugar & Pimento."

And the weather was vile as the two ships plunged south, the men constantly changing sail, the decks swept by seas, and the deck seams leaking abominably after all those structural changes in England. Cook issued the fearnought jackets and trousers, which went some way to alleviate the men's discomfort. Forster complained bitterly about the sodden conditions in his cabin and scribbled invectives against Mr. Gilbert into his damp journal—but in truth Forster was no worse off than anyone else aboard the *Resolution*.

On the last day of November the Resolutions suddenly found knee-deep water swirling across the lower deck. A quick sounding of the pump well showed twenty inches of water in the bilge, and a search revealed the inside scuttle of the boatswain's storeroom stove in on the leeward side and pouring water. One of the quartermasters volunteered to go over the side on a lifeline to force in the outside scuttle, "which he effected after being three times washed up into ye fore chains." One hopes that Cook gave him an extra tot of the Spanish brandy.

The "pinching cold" weather, as Cook laconically called it, and the gales now took their toll of the livestock—sheep, goats, hogs, and poultry. "Not a night passes without some dying, however, they are not wholly lost for we eat them notwithstanding." Later in the voyage one of the surviving sows farrowed only to have her young lost in severe weather. Sparrman, something of a gourmet, mentioned to Cook that he had drunk pig's milk in tea and coffee while in China. Cook, gastronomically adventurous, ordered the milking of the sow. It was one of the few orders given by him ever disobeyed—the sow had such an evil disposition that no one dared even try.

The gales drove the ships far to the east of the supposed longitude of Cape Circumcision. On 10 December, close to 51°S latitude—nearly the equivalent latitude of London—they came upon their first iceberg. They were only twelve days from the southern midsummer and sailing in foggy conditions with frequent snow and sleet showers, and the nighttime temperatures falling below freezing. If the Antarctic is defined as the sea and land lying south of the Antarctic Convergence, the *Resolution* and *Adventure* had entered it five days previously—on the day Cook commented that "the air begins to be pinching cold."

The next day, neophytes as yet in Antarctic waters, the Adventures made the signal for land in sight—but they were soon disillusioned: it was their second large iceberg. And Forster, amazed at the size of it, scribbled calculations into his journal in an attempt to estimate the cubic feet of ice.

The next few days were spent creeping through the fog, snow, and sleet, the navigation made hazardous by numerous icebergs. The water froze in the scuttlebutt on deck, the sails and rigging grew icicles, the running rigging froze in the blocks. No gloves could be worn in reefing sails, trimming yards, and striking topgallant masts. The men worked bare-handed, with cut and blistered fingers and palms. Cook issued an extra tot of brandy in the mornings. On 14 December, with four inches of snow on deck, they came across their first great expanse of pack ice. Stretching across the horizon to the west and south, it prevented any progress to the west in their search for Cape Circumcision. But ice was brought on deck and found, when melted, to give fresh water. Cook had found his method of watering.

A few days before Christmas, having been forced east by the pack, they rounded the end of the ice and headed south. On Christmas Day, at 57°50′S and 29°32′E, Cook, knowing his men had been saving their issue of spirits, brought the *Resolution* under short sail, "least I should be surprised with a gale of wind with a drunken crew." Officers, petty officers, and supernumeraries crowded into the stern cabin, with the overflow going to the gunroom mess.

Sparrman, a victim of Nordic nostalgia, missed the traditional Swedish Christmas Eve celebrations, noting that the "supper consisted of the usual piece of cheese and the same kind of biscuits." Christmas Day met with his approval—the stern cabin filled with a "warmer, livelier atmosphere produced with punch, porter, port and Madeira, Bordeaux, Cape, and other wines."

The men celebrated forward in their own style—with "savage noise and drunkenness," according to George Forster, followed by boxing matches. Sparrman went forward to watch this alien sport of the "British savages." The seamen, as the ship was rolling a little, sat stripped to the waist on sea chests and traded punches to the head. Sparrman had seen British sailors in China standing up and boxing. One of the rules, a point of honor, was not to hit below the belt—"an unfair blow" or an "Irish blow"—"Because," as Sparrman noted, "that brutal nation, according to its standards of etiquette, does not avoid but rather aims at this tender place." Later that day the *Adventure* ranged alongside and gave three cheers. They too had been celebrating.

The last days of 1772 were spent sailing west through the icebergs, with the pack ice to the north of them, back toward the longitude of Cape Circumcision. On 3 January, positioned south and west of the supposed cape, Cook came to a decision. Visibility was excellent—about seventy miles from the masthead—but no indication of land lay to the north. Enough time had been spent looking for Bouvet's cliff face: Cook was of the opinion that the Frenchman had been deceived—as they had been—by icebergs surrounded by pack ice. A new course was set, the orders were given, and in closing visibility with snow and sleet, the two vessels bore away on an easterly course. The search for land in the high southern latitudes between their present position and New Zealand had started in earnest.

On 9 January 1773, in 61°S, the two vessels took on twenty-four tons of that precious commodity, fresh water, in the form of ice—an instance, as one man noted, "of drawing fresh water out of ye ocean in hand baskets." Hodges, as the seamen's arms became encased in ice lifting the chunks of precious water into the baskets, busied himself recording the scene in watercolor—the sea calm, the vessels' maincourses brailed up, the ice being lifted aboard, a caverned iceberg floating serenely nearby.

Cook now altered course and started sailing south. On 15 January, with "five tolerable Good days succeeding one another," plenty of fresh water aboard, the men's clothing and linen washed and dried—"a thing that was not a little wanting"—they lay close to 40°E longitude and 150 miles north of the Antarctic Circle. On 17 January, shortly before noon, they crossed it, the first men in recorded history to do so. They were escorted across the line by flights of Antarctic petrels and snow petrels. A few hours later, after sailing in comparatively clear water, they came upon a great mass of solid pack ice stretching across their path to the south. At 67°15′S Cook reluctantly gave the order to steer northeast, away from the impenetrable pack. Eighty miles to the south, guarded by the pack and hidden by hazy weather, lay the coast of Antarctica.

The northeasterly course was designed to take them to the reported position of the land discovered by the *Gros-Ventre* and the *Fortune*. The search, during the last days of January and the beginning of February, revealed nothing. "We've been these 6 or 7 days past cruzing for the Land the Frenchman gave intelligence of at the Cape of Good Hope," wrote an exasperated Clerke; "if my friend Monsieur found any Land, he's been confoundedly out in the Latitude & Longitude of it, for we've search'd the spot he represented it in and its Environs too pretty narrowly and the devil an Inch of Land is there." Kerguelen, in truth, had been confoundedly out in the longitude. It lay some 480 miles to the east of the *Resolution* and the *Adventure*.

The ships, now on the borders of the Antarctic Convergence, were being much bedeviled by fogs. On 8 February, the fog quickly thickening, the vessels lost contact, swallowed by the murk. They tacked back and forth, fired guns, lighted flares, but all to no avail. After two days of playing this peculiar form of blindman's buff, both commanders realized that contact had been irretrievably lost. No matter; Queen Charlotte Sound in New Zealand had been designated as the rendezvous for just such an eventuality.

But before New Zealand, the search for land in the high southern latitudes had to continue.

Before their separation, the ships had spent two months sailing south of the Convergence. Forster and Cook both recorded the types of birds seen, shot, and sometimes eaten. Penguins, virtually armor-plated against shot by their close-packed feathers, had proved a tougher proposition to dispatch. One chinstrap, his head blown away by ball, weighed eleven pounds. During January Forster had winged an albatross swimming in the water and it was brought on board alive. The seamen called this species a

The *Resolution* and the *Adventure* watering by taking in ice at 61° S.
Water-color drawing by William Hodges, January 1773.
Courtesy of the State Library of New South Wales

Quakerbird, after its sober plumage. Forster, excited, thought it a species never before described and named it *Diomedea palpebrata*—the light-mantled sooty albatross—and one of the loveliest albatross on nest or in flight.

Four days after the separation, the *Resolution,* now sailing on a south-easterly course, passed huge numbers of penguins porpoising across their course. The prodigious numbers raised hopes of sighting land. Cook was not as sanguine on that score as his brother officers. After listening to their opinions as to its possible situation, some saying to the north and others to the east, Cook noted, no doubt with a grim smile, that "it was remarkable that no one gave it as his opinion that any was to be found to the South which served to convince me that they had no inclination to proceed any farther that way. I however was resolved to get as far South as I conveniently could without looseing too much easting altho I must confess I had little hopes of meeting with land, for the high swell or Sea which we have had for some time from the West came now gradualy round to SSE. . . ."

Cook was mistaken in thinking that no land lay nearby. About 45 miles to the northeast lay the small and grim Heard Island and the even smaller McDonald Islands. The penguins were Gentoos heading toward their colonies. Cook, however, was right in thinking that no large land mass lay to the north or east. And, having passed south of Kerguelen's discovery, he had also divorced that land from being part of any southern continent.

As the *Resolution* sailed southeast, Furneaux and the *Adventure* were sailing east and passing between Heard Island and Kerguelen Island. Furneaux was headed toward Tasmania—as Cook suspected.

By 24 February the *Resolution* had reached 61°52′S. Winds were from the east-southeast, with a high sea running from the same direction. Around the ship and glimpsed through the snow and sleet lay sixty to seventy icebergs. It had been Cook's intention to cross the Antarctic Circle once more before heading to the rendezvous in New Zealand. The lateness of the season, the danger from icebergs, the sea littered with growlers—almost impossible to pick out from the breaking waves and as dangerous as striking rocks—persuaded him to abandon his intention. But the change of plan was no craven attempt to head for more temperate latitudes: for the next three weeks the *Resolution* held a course close to 60°S latitude. To the south, almost paralleling their course, lay the coast of Antarctica, some 250 to 300 miles away.

During those three weeks, in the middle of a gale, the sow farrowed her nine piglets—all of which died from the cold. This was the sow the crew had baulked at milking. The weather set Forster scribbling apposite Latin tags into his journal. From Virgil's *Aeneid* came "Nimborum in patriam, loca faeta furentibus Austris."* The death of the piglets drew forth more lines from Virgil's *Georgics:*

> Ergo omni studio glaciem ventosque nivales,
> Quominus est illis curae mortalis egestas,
> Avertes.†

---

* In the land of the storm clouds, regions filled with frenzied winds.

† Therefore the less they [goats] need a man to look after them, the more carefully you should protect them from frost and snowy winds.

They were lines gleefully seized upon by the Resolutions and ones which Forster came to regret. During March, in order to protect them from Virgil's frost and snowy winds, two ewes, a ram, and five goats were re-housed on either side of Forster's cabin—with only a thin deal- and chink-ridden partition between Forster and the animals. "Who on a stage raised up as high as my bed, shit & pissed on one side, whilst 5 Goats did the same afore on the other side." One almost feels sorry for Forster.

During this period of sailing close to the 60°S line of latitude, Cook kept a close eye on the state of his crew. Noticing their clothes in a ragged condition, he issued needles, thread, and buttons. Like scruffy schoolboys, their hands were inspected and if found dirty a punishment far worse than a pedagogic caning or a navy flogging was inflicted on the culprit: his issue of grog was stopped. Cook knew his men. Symptoms of scurvy, described by Forster as "bad Gams, livid spots, Eruptions, difficult breathing, con-tracted limbs & a greenish greasy Scum on the Urine," were treated with "sweet wort" and the "marmalade of carrots." Forster, no stranger to sauerkraut, also thought the German cabbage dish helped. Forster's next-door companions, the sheep, also showed signs of scurvy—and were treated with boiled wheat and rice. A midshipman and a quartermaster unknowingly treated themselves with an antiscorbutic. The quartermas-ter's cat, well trained, captured ship's rats and brought them to her master. The cat was rewarded with the foreparts and the back parts were cleaned, roasted, and peppered and then shared between the midshipman and quar-termaster. It made a welcome change from salt beef.

On 17 March Cook resolved to haul north for Australia and New Zealand, his objective being to see if Van Diemen's Land (Tasmania) formed part of New Holland (Australia). Two days later the prevailing northwesterly winds made it impossible to reach Tasmania and the *Resolu-tion* eased away for New Zealand. Sometime between 20 and 21 March they passed north of the Convergence and out of the Antarctic. And Cook noted the difference in temperature. The Resolutions had been sailing in the Antarctic for fifteen weeks and the physical and mental hardships were showing. As Wales remarked, Forster, on one pretense or another, had quarreled with practically every man aboard.

The decision to head north prompted Cook to write an apologetic paragraph in his journal. It is a revealing paragraph, as it shows an unchar-acteristic Cook—one slightly worried that a potential reader might con-sider him lacking in determination:

If the reader of this Journal desires to know my reasons for taking the resolution just mentioned I desire he will only consider that after crusing four months in these high Latitudes it must be natural for me to wish to injoy some short repose in a harbour where I can procure some refreshments for my people of which they begin to stand in need of, to this point too great attention could not be paid as the Voyage is but in its infancy.

A more likely reaction, as Professor Beaglehole, Cook's biographer, succinctly puts it, is that the reader is more likely to be baffled by the conscience that thinks explanation necessary.

With the *Resolution* sailing toward New Zealand, Cook had a mind to find his harbor of refreshment at Dusky Sound, lying in the southwest corner of South Island. He had noticed it during the *Endeavour* voyage— but not investigated. At ten o'clock on the morning of 25 March the lookout at the masthead hailed the deck that the peaks of New Zealand were in sight. By afternoon, close to shore, the weather turned hazy and the *Resolution* lay off for the night under shortened sail and with a heavy swell rolling in from the southwest.

Next day they ran with a fair wind, the great swell surging them forward to the entrance of Dusky Sound. And there must have been some anxious moments as they drove toward the fjord's opening, the seas foaming around the tree-covered rocky cliffs, islands, and islets, the leadsman calling out the soundings. The water shoaled to forty fathoms and then deepened to sixty fathoms, Cook drily noting that "we were however too far advanced to return and therefore pushed on not doubting but we should find anchorage, for in this Bay we were all strangers. . . ."

By three o'clock in the afternoon they had found an anchorage and the *Resolution* at last came to rest after 122 days at sea and over eleven thousand miles, gently tugging at her anchor cable, in fifty fathoms of water. Within minutes, boats and men were over the side to gather fish, fowl, seals, and wood for the galley. Cook went searching for a better anchorage and sent Pickersgill off on the same mission in the opposite direction.

Enough fish was caught to feed all hands and Pickersgill reported that an excellent anchorage, completely sheltered and close to fresh water, lay but two miles away. Pickersgill had found his harbor. The *Resolution* sailed across the sound next day and Cook found the anchorage exactly as described by Pickersgill. Within hours the *Resolution* lay moored bow and stern to the trees, the yards interlocking with the branches of the forest, a fallen tree acting as a gangplank to shore. A hundred yards from the stern ran a gin-clear stream of fresh water; they were surrounded by wood for the galley fire; the water and land would provide fish, lobster, seal meat, and birds for the pot. After the dangers, cold, and monotonous diet of their first dip into the Antarctic, here indeed the Resolutions could, as Cook gently noted, "enjoy with ease what in our situation might be called the luxuries of life."

Pickersgill Harbour, except for a small wooden boardwalk installed by the New Zealand Parks Department, remains virtually unchanged from the days of the *Resolution*'s visit. The rain still falls on the close-packed trees and drips through the canopy onto the ground cover of shrubs, ferns, and moss. The stream that provided fresh water still babbles and swirls into the small bay. Of all the world's anchorages graced by the *Resolution*, this is the one where her presence and the shades of Cook, his officers, the crew, and the experimental gentlemen can be felt. And, appropriately enough, seen. On the hillside above the mooring place lies a clearing in the forest. Here, during the last days of March 1773, the trees were felled to clear space for the portable observatories. Today, the fallen trunks lie on the rain-sodden ground and the moss-covered boles bear the axe marks of the seamen-turned-lumberjacks. And not only seamen. Wales cheerfully recorded "that before Dinner I had cut down and destroyed more Trees and curious shrubs & Plants, than would in London have sold for one hundred Pounds."

Standing in that clearing, it takes little imagination to hear the astronomer's rich Yorkshire accent; the laughter and chatter of the seamen as they set up a forge to repair ironwork and boilers for the brewing of Spruce Beer (Sparrman, the gourmet, added rum and brown sugar to the beer and found it tasted much like champagne); the splash of oars as the boats bring back the daily catch of fish and lobster; the puff of smoke and flat thump of muskets and fowling pieces as seals, ducks, and shorebirds fall for science and the pot.

The *Resolution* spent six weeks in Dusky Sound before sailing to the rendezvous point in Queen Charlotte Sound at the northeast corner of South Island. By the evening of 13 May she lay anchored in Ship Cove close to the *Adventure*. Furneaux was aboard the *Resolution* before she came to rest, and in the stern cabin he gave his report of the happenings since the separation on 8 February. As Cook suspected, Furneaux had sailed toward Tasmania, but had kept a course south of Tasman's route of 1642. They had landed and considered—mistakenly—that the land formed part of Australia. They had been moored in Ship Cove since 7 April. Such were the bare bones of the story. And here they lay, topmasts and yards struck down, all prepared for a snug winter in the sheltered cove, waiting for the arrival of the *Resolution*. Poor Furneaux. As with Kerguelen, one feels a pang of pity for him. That meeting at Ship Cove has all the ingredients of countless comedy scenes in novels, plays, and films. The rather ineffectual schoolmaster slumps in the common-room armchair after an arduous day with the young hooligans, when in bursts the keen headmaster, brimming with energy, ordering him out for an evening's work to referee the louts on the football field. Worse, the headmaster finds that some of the pupils are in poor health. And, indeed, the *Adventure* had cases of scurvy.

Cook gave orders to Furneaux to prepare his ship for sea. They were not going to "Idle away the whole Winter in Port" but were going to explore the unknown parts of the Pacific to the east and north. At dawn next morning Cook was ashore with a boatload of seamen gathering "sellery and Scurvy grass," and gave orders for it to be served twice a day. And made a rather testy entry into his journal that "I took care that this order was punctualy complied with at least in my sloop." Furneaux had been found wanting in the care of his men.

Cook made a mistake in relying upon Furneaux's opinion that Tasmania formed part of Australia. Nevertheless, the results of the first stage of the search for *Terra australis incognita* were conclusive. Between them the two vessels, like brooms sweeping across the ocean, had laid to rest any possibility of a continent's lying in a temperate latitude between the Cape of Good Hope and New Zealand. Any land would certainly have a most disagreeable climate and be of small extent—nothing more than small islands. They had both crossed the Antarctic Circle close to midsummer: one could only shudder at the thought of midwinter in any land lying below the Circle.

To dismiss Cook's first tropical sweep through the Pacific with a paragraph comes close to *lèse-majesté*. Only the first part of the seventy-two-hundred-mile voyage through the South Pacific forms part of the search for *Terra australis incognita*. Sailing from New Zealand on 7 June, the two vessels steered an easterly course for six weeks and crossed twenty-five hundred miles of empty ocean. It was a track calculated to either prove or disprove Dalrymple's conjectures on a southern continent. The empty sea provided the answer. Having blown away the fog of conjecture, Cook altered course for the north.

A few days later, the idle and dirty cook of the *Adventure* died of scurvy and Furneaux reported twenty more cases of the disease aboard his ship. The news struck at the very foundations of Cook's own methods for combating the disease and brought forth a rather testy entry in Cook's journal on the difference in health of the two vessels. The lack of initiative—and leadership—in the gathering of fresh greens while the *Adventure* lay idle in Queen Charlotte Sound was the obvious cause.

The sweep through the South Pacific took them through the dangerous reefs and islets of the Tuamotu Archipelago; near shipwreck on a Tahitian reef; meetings with old friends from the *Endeavour* days at Matavai Bay; through the Cook Islands; on to Tongatapu (named the Friendly Islands by Cook); and then, loaded with hogs, fruit, yams, and poultry (the seamen set the birds to cockfighting as a diversion during the dogwatches—but with no great success); south again to New Zealand and Queen Charlotte Sound to prepare for the second exploratory voyage into the polar regions.

A violent reception met them off the east coast of New Zealand. Storm-force winds exploded sails; the *Resolution* lost her fore-topgallant mast; both vessels lay a-hull, with breaking seas sweeping the decks and pouring below to reduce the living quarters to squalid and sodden chaos. The sailors cursed and swore in their habitual manner—a most effective catharsis when dealing with flogging sails, wildly thrashing blocks, heavily loaded sheets, braces, guys, and tackles. The three naturalists, superfluous in times like this, lay clutching the sides of their waterlogged bunks. And later penned prim comments on the sailors' "horrible vollies of curses and oaths," clucking that, "without any provication to serve as an excuse . . . [they] execrated every limb in varied terms. . . ." Forster, needless to say, found an apposite quotation in Virgil's *Aeneid: Insequitur clamorque virum, stridorque rudentum.**

After a week of nearly unending gales, near Cape Palliser off the entrance to Cook Strait and only forty miles from the haven of Queen Charlotte Sound, the *Resolution* lost sight of the *Adventure*. The next three days were spent tacking back and forth across the strait—beating their heads against the wall of the prevailing northwesterlies. A short time was spent anchored at the entrance to present-day Wellington's harbor, but, the wind turning fair, Cook promptly got under way and within a few hours the *Resolution* entered Queen Charlotte Sound and on 3 November lay quiet in Ship Cove. The anchorage was empty. The *Adventure* was missing.

Unworried at first, Cook set about preparing the *Resolution* for the second dip into the Antarctic. All the sails were unbent for repair; rigging, masts, and yards were overhauled; decks and topsides recaulked; tents set up on shore for the sailmakers, coopers, and blacksmiths; water casks cleaned and filled; the portable observatory erected; firewood cut and forges and ovens fired; provisions inspected. The last found over four thousand pounds of bread to be so moldy as to be uneatable—the barely eatable being rebaked in the shoreside ovens.

The Maoris appeared in their canoes, exchanged fish for cloth, stole everything unguarded—one old rogue of a chief even picking Cook's pocket of a handkerchief. But Cook, who had noticed the figging law practiced by the old man, quietly retrieved it from the thief's cloak. It led to rueful mutual laughter and an invitation to dinner in the *Resolution*'s stern cabin.

The vegetable garden, planted before they had left for the South Pacific islands, had to be inspected: the radishes and turnips were found gone to seed, the peas and beans eaten by rats, the potatoes dug up by the Maoris, the cabbage, carrots, onions, and parsley well grown and prolific. For an untended garden, the results were surprisingly satisfactory.

The passing days, as the naturalists botanized, shot birds, scribbled in journals, and made drawings, and the sailors busied themselves with their appointed tasks, were matched by Cook's mounting concern over the missing *Adventure*. Little could be done in the way of a search except to take a pinnace to East Bay, climb a hill overlooking the strait where Cook had built a cairn in 1770, and scan the waters of the strait. With no success.

* There follows the shouting of men and the creaking of cables.

This was on 15 November. By 22 November the *Resolution* lay ready for sea: the tents were struck, the observatory, ovens, and forges brought on board. But now comes a darker note, and one which Cook, Forster, Sparrman, and Wales were to discuss in the stern cabin and devote pages to in their journals. Those illustrations on the medieval maps showing the anthropophagi chewing on human flesh were to be reenacted on the *Resolution*'s quarterdeck.

Cook, returning from a shore trip with Forster and Wales to gather fresh greens, had found a scene of utter confusion on the *Resolution*'s quarterdeck. Perched on the taffrail sat the head of a young Maori recently killed in a skirmish between the warring natives. It had been brought on board by Pickersgill, who, along with other officers stretching their legs ashore, had come across a small party of natives and their canoe. A heart, pierced by a forked stick, decorated the canoe's bow. Nearby lay human bones, entrails, and the head. Pickersgill had bought the head—with two nails—and brought it back on board. Here were more natives, and they showed a lively interest in the head. A slice was taken, seared on the galley gridiron—much to the disgust of the cook—and, according to Clerke, eaten by a native "most ravenously" with much sucking of fingers. Cook now arrived from shore to find this extraordinary scene. Cook, a man not given to flights of fancy, had long suspected cannibalism among the Maori. Here he was to be an eyewitness. Stifling his repugnance, he gave orders for another slice to be cooked. It was again eaten with relish. The effect on the gaping sailors was as varied as the men themselves. Some laughed and said the natives had been on a hunting party and got themselves a fine buck; others vomited. Oddidy, a native from Raiatea Island near Tahiti who had shipped aboard the *Resolution,* being "desirous of seeing Brittania," burst into tears and ran into the stern cabin. A dark shadow had fallen across Rousseau's picture of the noble savage.

The day after this gruesome spectacle, Cook wrote a short memorandum. It gave the date of his separation from the *Adventure,* arrival and departure dates from Ship Cove, and the route he proposed to sail. No rendezvous position with Furneaux could be established, as nothing could be depended upon. The letter was sealed into a bottle and buried beneath a large tree at the watering place. And, in the most satisfying tradition of schoolboy adventure stories, LOOK UNDERNEATH was carved into the trunk.

They sailed next day and two days were spent scanning the shores of the strait and firing cannons in a vain search for the *Adventure.* On 27 November Cook arrived at his decision and, taking his departure from Cape Palliser, stood southeast. He was convinced that no harm had come to the *Adventure:* most probably Furneaux had been driven far to leeward by those pernicious northwesterlies and had elected to run for Cape Horn or the Cape of Good Hope.

In fact the ships were but a few miles apart when Cook took his departure for the south. During that night of the separation on 29 October, the
Adventure, a smaller and less weatherly vessel than the *Resolution,* so short
of ballast and water and so tender that all her sails had to be struck in the
squalls, had failed to weather Cape Palliser—renamed Cape Turn-and-be-
damned by the crew—and ran 260 miles north along the east coast of
North Island to Tolaga Bay. Here they wooded and watered. They had left
the bay on 16 November and were off Cape Palliser on 24 November,
beating back and forth trying to weather that anathematized cape. By 30
November they were anchored in Ship Cove and had found the message.
It was perhaps as well for Furneaux that the *Resolution* had sailed: his crew
and ship were in no state to accompany Cook on this second arduous ice
cruise. As he read the message, the *Resolution* was surging south some 360
miles away, rolling in a heavy swell from the southwest under the curious
gaze of soaring albatross.

On 7 December, at eight o'clock in the evening, the Resolutions passed
over the antipodes of London—and drank to the health of their friends
and family on the exact opposite side of the globe. The antipodean Lon-
doners, as Wales noted, were made up of penguins, petrels, seals, and
albatross. A few days later, much to the satisfaction of Sparrman, they
sailed over the antipodes of parts of Sweden. On the same day they crossed
the Convergence into the Antarctic. Air temperatures just north of the
Convergence had hovered in the mid-forties Fahrenheit; the readings now
dropped below freezing, and with the cold came snow and hail. To Oddidy, the Pacific islander, all this was so strange, so new, so incomprehensible—and he knew the trouble he was going to have in describing the
white rain and the white balls to his fellow islanders. On 12 December, in
61°15′S, appeared the first iceberg: 11½ degrees further south than the first
iceberg of the previous year. Oddidy, as an *aide-mémoire,* had tabulated the
islands passed in the Pacific with small wooden pegs. A peg was laid aside
for this first iceberg. Within days he had given up, and just left one single
peg to remember, as he called them the many "white, evil, useless lands."

On 15 December, just north of the Antarctic Circle, one of Oddidy's
white, evil, useless lands came close to bringing a very abrupt end to all the
Resolutions. Even Cook, that most phlegmatic of journal writers, thought
it a near fatal encounter.

It had been a frustrating day—not that day could be much distinguised
from night when so close to the Circle at midsummer—with the pack ice
thickening as they sailed south. Skirting the pack, they were forced east
and then northeast. Suddenly they found themselves embayed by pack and
were forced to tack and stretch back southwest, with the pack to the south
of them and icebergs and pack to the north. The wind veered to the west;
they tacked again and stood north—the only direction open to them—
toward the massed icebergs.

It now became a mist-ridden, slow-motion slalom course between ice-bergs and floes. A situation requiring an analytical mind and good judgment by the officer of the watch. With all hands at dinner, the officer made a near-catastrophic error in estimating speed and leeway, and attempted to weather a large iceberg. He conned the *Resolution* into the impossible position—the iceberg close under his lee, no room to tack or wear, every attempt to squeeze closer to the wind slowing the *Resolution*—which only increased her leeway and drift toward those sheer white cliffs. A call for all hands brought every soul on deck, where they stared with horror at their nemesis. And there, in the graphic words of Elliot, they waited for the "event with awful expectation of distruction, Capt Cook order'd light spars to be got ready to push the ship from the Island if she came so near, but had she comd within their reach, we should have been Overwhelm'd in a Moment and every Soul drown'd; the first stroke would have sent all our Masts overboard, and the next would have knock'd the Ship to pieces, and drown'd us all."

By some miracle, perhaps aided by the concentrated force of over a hundred human wills, the *Resolution* slid round the end of the iceberg in the backsurge of the sea off the sheer cliff face. It was the backsurge that saved them. "According to the old proverb," wrote Cook with a touch of wry humor, "a miss is as good as a mile, but our situation requires more misses than we can expect. . . ."

The next week was spent sailing in an easterly direction through ice floes and icebergs. Fresh water was gathered from the sea, but it came from rotten old ice and took time to drain before being melted. Icicles were beaten off the shrouds and added to the melting boiler. The ship was cleaned and smoked; the ship's bell tolled the passing of the frigid endless hours; ice fell with a thump on deck from spars, stays, and shrouds; the sails froze hard into curved metal-like sheets; the ropes froze into wires; the block sheaves were frozen solid, making any sail trim a titanic effort. The men on deck crackled as they hauled, worked, and walked in their thinning frozen fearnought clothing. But through it all, according to one of the seamen, the sailors were cheerful enough belowdecks, hunched over their grog, with not a man sick "but of old scars." Christmas lay ahead.

Forster, meanwhile, bitterly unburdened his thoughts to his journal. *Omnia pontus erat**—a favorite quotation—described his sorry lot. His cabin was fetid, cold, and drafty (the seamen, he thought, were better housed), with everything moist, moldy, and looking more like a subterranean room for the dead than the living. Grudgingly he admitted Cook's stern cabin little better, with its broken panes, damp sails spread for repair, the air foul with farts of sailmakers fed on pease pudding and salted cabbage. The ship's meat was salted, two years old, and indifferent; the peas,

---

* Everything was sea.

flour, raisins, and biscuit stale and musty. Topsides was no better. The decks were never dry, the sun seldom shone, mist and fogs surrounded them. Only a few birds and the "solitary eremitic whale" chose to live in this wretched summer *sub Jove frigido.**

Adding to the gall and wormwood festering in his soul lay the thought that he had discovered nothing new in the Pacific and New Zealand, that Banks and Solander—the one very rich and the other very skilled in natural history—had by now published their discoveries of the *Endeavour* voyage. And their publication would most certainly make a mockery of his own findings.

The day Forster, plunged in gloom, catalogued his various miseries, the *Resolution* crossed the Antarctic Circle for the second time and reached 67°31′S. A few days later she lay hove-to in calm clear weather, the sea like glass, surrounded by some two hundred icebergs, all larger than the ship. It was Christmas Day again and cause for celebration. The stern cabin and gunroom were full of officers, petty officers, and gentlemen drinking wine, while forward the men dined on a double portion of plum-duff pudding, drank their hoarded grog, joked about the voyage, and swore that they would certainly die happy and content on any one of those vasty icebergs with a rescued keg of brandy in their arms.

The drunkenness, ribaldry, jokes, oaths, and blasphemy—inevitably—offended the Forsters (Sparrman was now getting used to the seamen's habits), and as Forster stared bleakly around the horizon at the icebergs surrounding the ship "like the wrecks of a destroyed world," his ears full of the "oaths & execrations, curses & Dam's," he thought himself in some image of Hell (a cold one to be sure; but then he had heard of a parson in Iceland who represented to his flock the image of Hell as a cold place: on being asked why, he answered that if Hell were hot they would all willingly go to the Devil).

By New Year's Day 1774 the *Resolution* was some four hundred miles north of the Christmas revelry, sailing north, yards braced round, tacks on board, her bluff bows shouldering aside the sea, Cook intent upon eliminating—or finding—land in another section of the Southern Ocean.

Forster took to his bunk sick with a cold and aching joints. Here, dosed with essence of antimony and bark, he remained for a month, scarcely stirring out. It gave him ample opportunity to rail bitterly against Cook and people like him who pursued their obdurate course against all the dictates of humanity and reason. Such people should be sent off to search for the Northwest or Northeast Passages—but woe to the poor crew under them. *Quicquid delirant reges plectuntur Achivi.*† In Forster's opinion the *Resolution* should be heading toward Cape Horn and then the Cape of Good Hope.

* Under a cold sky.

† Whatever mad schemes kings have, the Archaeans are punished.

On 6 January, in 52°S, Cook altered course to a more easterly direction. The change brought an easier motion, a feeling of relief, an anticipatory sense among all the Resolutions, from lieutenants to waisters, of the looming delights of the Cape of Good Hope. On 11 January, in 47°51′S and about two-thirds of the distance between New Zealand and Cape Horn, Cook ordered a further change of course: southeast. Instant consternation among all aboard, much murmurings, much talk and whisperings, all hopes shattered. But the ripples from the stone thrown into the millpond of their misconceptions soon subsided.

The slant southward took them into storm-force winds, huge seas—one wave broke on board, flooded the stern cabin through the skylight, and brought thoughts of death by drowning to George Forster—the decks below covered with a constantly moving film of water. Forster, racked by rheumatic pains in his legs, lay in his sodden bunk and penned more diatribes: on the voyage, Cook, the salt-meat diet, the moldy bread, the cold, the damp. He was not living, not even vegetating—only withering, dwindling away.

On 26 January the *Resolution* crossed south of the Antarctic Circle for the third time. Four days later, at four o'clock in the morning, the sky and clouds to the south showed unmistakable signs of iceblink—the white glare on low clouds from the light reflected off great masses of ice. By eight o'clock they had reached the cause of the iceblink. An immensity of ice stretching across their path: a mile-deep stretch of broken ice floes, but so close-packed as to be impenetrable—and beyond this a solid unbroken pack holding within it close to a hundred icebergs. Except for the quiet voices of the sailors the only living sound came from the mournful croaking of penguins. Unknown to the Resolutions, the coastline of Antarctica lay some ninety miles away; but even if they had seen it they could never have reached it. Cook came to the only decision open to him and gave the order to bring the *Resolution* about and stand away from the barrier of ice. Later he made an entry in his journal that briefly lifts a corner of the cloak of privacy surrounding this enigmatic man of masterly understatement:

I will not say it was impossible anywhere to get in amongst this Ice, but I will assert that the bare attempting of it would be a very dangerous enterprise and what I believe no man in my situation would have thought of. I whose ambition leads me not only farther than any other man has been before me, but as far as I think it possible for man to go, was not sorry at meeting with this interruption, as it in some measure relieved us from the dangers and hardships, inseparable with the Navigation of the Southern Polar regions. Sence therefore we could not proceed one Inch farther South, no other reason need be assigned for our Tacking and stretching back to the North, being at that time in the Latitude of 71°10′South, Longitude 106°54′W.

Cook had taken the Resolutions further south than any humans before them. And of that select group, two claimed to have come closest to the South Pole. The young midshipman George Vancouver, just before the

Resolution tacked away from the ice, scrambled out to the end of the jibboom, lifted his hat, waved it above his head, and cried out, "Ne plus ultra!" Anders Sparrman, however, in a less dramatic fashion, claimed that *he* had been nearer to the Pole. In order to avoid the bustle on deck as the ship tacked, he took himself off to his cabin in the stern and observed the ice through a scuttle. Now when square-rigged ships tack and pass through the eye of the wind, they make considerable sternway. This sternway gave him the prize of the Pole.

The *Resolution* stood north, crossed the Antarctic Circle on 3 February, and three days later, after much thought, Cook arrived at his plans for the remainder of the year. And it is a tightly reasoned exposition that enters his journal.

He was now convinced that no continent was to be found in the Pacific sector of his search—any land must be much further south than the *Resolution* had sailed and probably inaccessible due to ice. As to land in the South Atlantic sector, Dalrymple's or Bouvet's, that would take a complete summer. They could reach the Cape of Good Hope by April of this year, but it would mean the effective end of the expedition. The South Pacific still held many unanswered questions and possibly large islands; he had a healthy crew, an able ship—another season in the Pacific could only be productive for navigation, geography, and science. Therefore the next few months would be spent in a great counterclockwise sweep through the Pacific. First would be the search for the land said to be sighted by Juan Fernandez in 1576 and claimed to be somewhere at 38°S (not the island of Juan Fernandez—that was well known); then Easter Island, which was but poorly situated on the charts; then to Tahiti for any news of the *Adventure;* further west to settle the position of Austrialia del Espiritu Santo—land discovered by Pedro Fernández de Quiros in 1606, rediscovered by Bougainville in 1768 and but vaguely described; then south to between 50° and 60°S latitude to pick up the westerlies for an arrival at Cape Horn in November. They would then have the best part of the summer to explore the South Atlantic sector before heading for the Cape of Good Hope. It was, as Cook admitted, a great undertaking and many impediments could stand in its way.

This grand design, when laid before his officers, met with nods of approval and carefully hidden joy at the thought of the tropics and the delights of Tahiti.

They were now making fast progress to the north, one noon-to-noon run crossing three degrees of latitude under a quartering wind and a prodigious swell from the southwest. By 9 February they had crossed north of the Convergence and the snow and sleet showers changed to rain.

An impediment to the grand design came from a most unexpected quarter. Cook, seemingly impervious to cold heat or sickness, now became dangerously ill. He later dismissed it as a "billious colick and so violent as to confine me to my bed." Treatment consisted of purges, enemas, castor oil, ipecacuanha, chamomile tea, warm plasters on the stomach, and, after twenty-four hours of violent hiccups, opiates. Even Forster feared for Cook's life, and James Patten, the *Resolution*'s competent surgeon, tended Cook day and night. After a week the patient responded to treatment by this "skillful physician and tender nurse"—the patient's own description. When he was able to take food, a Tahitian dog owned by the Forsters was sacrificed to make a broth for the weakened commander. As Cook wryly noted, "thus I received nourishment and strength from food which would have made most people in Europe sick, so true it is that necessity is gov-ern'd by no law."

Some eight months after Cook's supping of dog broth, the *Resolution* sailed into the familiar anchorage in Queen Charlotte Sound. Behind them lay the great sweep through the Pacific: Juan Fernandez's land dismissed as cartographic and geographic fiction; Easter Island visited with its strange statues; the Marquesas Islands with their handsome people; Tahiti—no news of the *Adventure*—where Wales checked the rate of Mr. Kendall's watch; Oddidy returned to Raiatea, where he strained the credulity of his fellow islanders with tales of snow, hail, and icebergs. He was the last to leave the *Resolution* when she sailed. At the harbor mouth he was allowed to fire off cannons in celebration of King George III's birthday and the ship's farewell to the islanders, climbed into his canoe clutching a testimo-nial from Cook, and burst into tears. Oddidy in turn had been a great favorite with the Resolutions. Then on to the Friendly Islands, followed by Quiros's land—renamed by Cook the New Hebrides—which turned out to be a small group of disease-infested islands. Discovery of a large island (New Caledonia) with a small island off the southern tip named the Isle of Pines. This was an island set about with enough reefs and shoals to turn a seaman's hair white overnight. But it brought joy to the heart of Cook. Here were stands of massive pines—*Araucaria columnaris*—ideal for spars, yards, and masts. From the sea these pines had been mistaken by Forster and Sparrman for basaltic columns; the seamen claimed they were trees. Bets were laid—several bottles of wine between Cook and Forster—and great was the glee, particularly from Wales, when the dogmatic "phi-losophers" were confounded upon their own ground. The Isle of Pines was followed by the discovery of Norfolk Island—yet another source of magnificent pines suitable for yards and masts.

At Queen Charlotte Sound the first order of business was to set the seine net for fresh fish and examine the bottle containing Cook's message. The bottle had vanished. But taken by whom? An inspection of the area around Ship Cove showed trees cut down by saw and axe, marks of an observatory. Here, perhaps, was proof of a visit by the *Adventure*.

For the Resolutions the next days were busy ones. Tents, forges, ovens were set up on shore, sails unbent for repair, topmasts struck for modifications; the observatory was set up yet again, the ship scrubbed clean inside and out. Pitch and tar for paying the deck seams had long been finished and an inventive compound—fat scraped from the galley coppers mixed with chalk—used as a substitute. Loads of shingle came aboard as ballast and six guns were struck down into the hold. The *Resolution* was being prepared for the passage around Cape Horn.

The Maoris returned and Cook heard varying tales of a shipwreck followed by a massacre. The stories were all rather confusing and contradictory, and small credence could be put on them. The Forsters and Sparrman botanized, and Wales's observations showed an accumulated error on Mr. Kendall's watch of nineteen minutes and thirty-one seconds. It was, thought Cook, most remarkable proof as to the reliability of this wonderful piece of craftsmanship.

The *Resolution* sailed on 10 November bound east for Cape Horn. But first came a slant southeast to cross an unexplored stretch of ocean. Sixteen days later, satisfied that here was nothing but an empty sea, Cook altered course east for the Pacific end of the Magellan Strait.

The 4,500 mile passage running their easting down in the mid-fifties proved, according to Cook, a most uneventful month. The *Resolution,* no sleek oceangoing greyhound, ran her modest noon-to-noon runs of over a hundred miles with satisfying regularity—including the best day's run of 183 miles. True, as the bluff-bowed ex-collier plowed along in a welter of foam, she showed a tendency to roll in the Southern Ocean swells—about 80 degrees of arc as measured by the inclinometer devised by Wales—and the sailmakers were kept constantly at work repairing much-repaired sails. Over two years of voyaging were taking its toll.

On 17 December they raised their landfall in South America and coasted southeast down the frightful-looking west coast of Tierra del Fuego. At the sight of it Forster trotted out the appropriate Latin quotation: *Pars mundi damnata a rerum natura, et densa mersa caligine.** It was one to be much used in the coming months. The huge flocks of shags, petrels, albatross, and skuas took some of the harshness from the scene and, the glutton overcoming the naturalist, with them came tantalizing thoughts of fresh meat in lieu of the interminable salted diet.

Some 80 miles short of Cape Horn, Cook decided to "take a view of the country" and look for wood and water. A tempting inlet with tall rocky towers—named York Minster by the Yorkshire-born Cook—lay to one side of the inlet, with islands on the other. They steered for the entrance. The wind, contrary to expectations, fell calm: two boats were lowered and started a valiant but vain effort to tow the mother ship clear of the rocks and breakers. Then a light breeze sprang up from the southwest, giving Cook two choices: to stand out to sea or to inspect the inlet. Prudence

*A part of the world cursed by nature and plunged in dense mists.

dictated the first but curiosity won the day, and that night they lay at anchor within sound of the surf thundering on the shores of Tierra del Fuego. Next day, the wind still being light but enough to give steerage way, the *Resolution* moved to a more secure anchorage and one close to ample supplies of wood and water.

The unusually calm weather prompted young George Forster (who, no doubt, had been forced to listen to officers and men detailing the horrors off Cape Horn) to write a pompous passage on this weather, so different from what he had been led to expect: "The destruction of vulgar prejudice is of so much service to science, and to mankind in general, that it cannot fail of giving pleasure, to every one sensible of its benefits."

The Resolutions' third Christmas was now upon them. And a Christmas at anchor rather than one spent in a gale off Cape Horn was probably at the back of Cook's mind when he sought out the land. The names given by Cook to the area still remain on the charts: Christmas Sound, York Minster, Adventure Cove, Devil's Basin, Shag Island, Port Clerke, Point Nativity, Goose Island. The last provided an abundance of geese—one for every three men—and they were served boiled, roasted, and in pies for the Christmas feast. The afterguard and gentlemen washed it down with Madeira wine (much improved by its voyaging) and the lower deck with spirits. It proved a memorable Christmas: so much so that in the aftermath of two days of carousing (like beasts, according to Forster), Cook ordered most of the men ashore to recover in the fresh air.

The Yaghans, the southernmost inhabitants of the world, paddled out in their canoes and flocked aboard the *Resolution*. Perhaps among them were the grandparents of the unborn Fuegia Basket and York Minster (two natives of the area destined to be carried off to England in a burst of evangelical zeal by FitzRoy of the *Beagle*). The Resolutions found these natives but poor specimens of humanity when compared to the islanders of the South Pacific. Small of stature, they stank abominably of rancid seal oil. It was advisable to stand to windward of them. The women, naked except for a scrap of otter skin at the loins, were so unprepossessing as to repel even the most ardent of the sailors. The men's clothing consisted of a small piece of sealskin draped around their shoulders. And Forster, somewhat surprised considering the cold, commented on the length of their scrotums. Young Forster too made some acid comments on the prevailing philosophy of the "noble savage" and its adherents, "who have either had no opportunity of contemplating human nature under all its modifications, or who have not felt what they have seen."

On 28 December, the ship wooded and watered, the crew sober, the *Resolution* stood out of Christmas Sound. Next day they passed the notorious Cape Horn, speeded on their way with a pleasant soldier's breeze from the west-northwest, and passed into the South Atlantic. Cook now laid a course for Le Maire Strait separating Tierra del Fuego from Staten Island:

at Good Success Bay—the *Endeavour*'s anchorage of 1769—on the Tierra del Fuego shore they would look for signs of the *Adventure*. Pickersgill was sent ashore in a boat to investigate the anchorage while the *Resolution* lay offshore surrounded by prodigious numbers of seals and whales—the latter, according to Clerke, "blowing on every point of the compass and frequently taint[ing] the whole atmosphere about us with the most disagreeable effluvia that can be conciev'd." Pickersgill returned after being "courtesly received" by some natives but found no signs of the *Adventure*. He nailed to a conspicuous tree a card bearing the message *Resolution passed the Straights Dec ye 31st 1774*. The bay, according to Pickersgill, was so full of seals and whales that the seamen's oars were striking their backs. The boat being hoisted in, the *Resolution* stood away in thick hazy weather—like sailing in the dark, according to Cook—for the east end of Staten Island.

The next day, on a small island lying along the north shore, they saw such an abundance of seals and penguins—a living larder—that Cook found the temptation too great to pass up and searched for an anchorage to have the opportunity "to taste of what we saw now only at a distance." An anchorage was found a bare mile off the island from where the seals could be heard bellowing like cattle. Boats were hoisted out, the men landed, the slaughter started. The marines with musket and bayonet were perhaps the best armed; but one corporal, wielding a Tahitian war club designed for the caving-in of human skulls, chose an older and cleaner method for the killing of seals. The officers and gentlemen for the most part left the more gory work to the marines, seamen, and young ruffians among the midshipmen: penguins, geese, gulls, ducks, giant petrels, shags, and sheathbills (a new species, to the enormous delight of Forster) fell to their muskets in this massive *battue*.

Within hours the *Resolution*'s decks resembled a slaughterhouse. The blubber was rendered down into oil for ship's use and the meat was butchered for the galley coppers and ovens. However, when it came to the eating, the older sea lions and fur seals—for these were the two species found on the island—proved rather rank, and only the young cubs were found palatable. Shags and penguins went into the galley coppers as dinner for the ship's company. But the conservative nature of the seamen showed itself a few days later with the men tiring of penguins and shags and turning back to their salt beef and pork.

They sailed on 3 January 1775. Cook was now entering upon the last stage of his search for *Terra australis incognita*. Numbered among the *Resolution*'s charts was a 1769 edition of Dalrymple's *"Chart of the Ocean between South America and Africa,"* which showed a huge tract of land, complete with offshore islands and a large bay marked "Gulf of St Sebastian." The western point of this gulf lay in 57½°S latitude and 54½°W longitude. The chart was based, with remarkable ingenuousness by that

choleric Scot, on Ortelius's map of 1587, which was based on Oronce
Finé's 1531 map, which had been copied by Mercator in 1569. Mercator
gave the gulf its name. Dalrymple, however, had buttressed his construction with the track of Halley's *Paramore* in 1700, and that of Antoine de la
Roche, an English merchant sailing from Lima to England in 1675. This
ship had been carried far to the eastward of Staten Island, had sighted a
mountainous snow-covered island, had spent two weeks anchored in a bay
at the southeast end, but, due to appalling weather, made no landing. The
weather clearing, they had seen to the southeast what appeared to be a
small island, distant some thirty miles. They had then sailed north.

In 1756 an island "of frightful aspect" was sighted by the Spanish ship
Leon, under charter to French merchants. She too had been carried far east
of Staten Island. Dalrymple's chart was marked with an island separated
from the hypothetical southern continent by the Straits de la Roche. Dalrymple's position for the island put it at 54°31′S and 45°W. Cook, however,
warily noted that a 1761 French chart by d'Anville marked the *Leon*'s island
(named Isle de St. Pierre by the French) in the same latitude but about 10
degrees further west. Cook, needless to say, had small faith in longitudes
given by merchant ships—or even latitudes, for that matter. Having demolished Dalrymple's grandiose southern continent in the Pacific, he now
harbored reservations about one in the South Atlantic.

A day out from Staten Island the *Resolution* was struck by a vicious
squall that carried away the main topgallant mast, the starboard studding
sail boom, and the fore-studdingsail. Much to Forster's chagrin, it also
carried away three of his precious shirts hung up for drying. By 6 January
the *Resolution* had sailed across the western promontory of Dalrymple's
continent, and Cook hauled north to get into the latitude of de la Roche's
and the *Leon*'s island. By 12 January they were over the supposed island,
and they started sailing east across Dalrymple's continent; the swell came
from the east-southeast—a sure indication that no large land mass lay in
that direction. The sea and air temperature now dropped dramatically;
unknown to the Resolutions they had crossed the Antarctic Convergence
into polar waters. Not, this time, from north to south, but west to east
where the Convergence makes its sweep north.

On 14 January Thomas Willis, Elliot's "wild and drinking" midshipman, sighted either a very large iceberg or land. About the ship were flocks
of petrels, albatross, giant petrels, and one or two snow petrels—sure sign
of ice. Spyglasses were trained on Willis's sighting and bets were laid: ten
to one for ice, five to one for land. A sounding showed 175 fathoms with a
muddy bottom—sure sign of land. And land it was. But the approaching
of it proved difficult. From calm conditions the weather turned vile: snow,
sleet, and a nasty sea combined with vicious squalls—one of them knocking
the *Resolution* over forty-two degrees as measured by Wales. Two days
later they were passing between Willis' Island—so named by Cook—and

another island they named Bird Island* after the vast numbers of albatross, shags, skuas, giant petrels, blue petrels, and penguins.

These two islands lay off the northwest end of a mountainous stretch of land running away to the southeast. Cook decided to explore the northern shore. On 17 January an inviting inlet appeared and the *Resolution* was hove to, a boat was lowered, and the boat's crew with Cook, the Forsters, and Sparrman headed toward the shore. Cook took soundings as they approached the inlet but found no bottom with the boat's 34-fathom lead line. At the head of the bay lay a large glacier—Cook had no word for this and merely described it as a huge mass of ice and snow fronted by a perpendicular ice cliff of great height. Pieces were continually breaking off the cliff face with a noise like cannon fire. The boat party were seeing the birth—the calving—of small icebergs.

Three landings were made in the bay, with the Forsters finding only three plants—tussock grass, wild burnet, and a mosslike plant growing on the rocks. Of trees and shrubs there was not a sign, "not even big enough to make a toothpick." As to wildlife, one young midshipman shot an elephant seal, and the beaches were crowded with fur seals. More birds fell to science and the pot—albatross, shags, gulls, sheathbills, penguins, and a species of duck that made "most delicate eating." In a ritual ceremony the Union flag was unfurled, muskets were fired in volley, and Cook took possession of the new land in the name of "His Brittanic Majesty and his Heirs for ever." The bay, appropriately enough, was named Possession Bay. Loaded with fresh meat, the boat returned to the *Resolution:* Cook—unlike the seamen—was growing heartily tired of salt meat and preferred penguin meat. Its taste, he thought, was close to bullock's liver, with the inestimable value of its also being fresh.

The *Resolution* continued her coasting passage down the shore, with Cook naming prominent geographic features as they came into view: Cape Saunders, Cumberland Bay, Cape Charlotte, Royal Bay, Cape George, Cooper's Isle, Sandwich Bay, and, finally, Cape Disappointment. The last was so named on 20 January, when they discovered that this forbidding-looking land was no continent but only an island some two hundred miles in circuit.

Cook, at Forster's prompting, named the island Georgia. Forster had suggested South Georgia and also suggested inscribing on the map of the island the inevitable Latin quotation, this one from Horace: *Tua sectus orbis nomina ducet.*†

What George III would have made of this if he had cast an eye on an entry in Forster's journal is problematical. According to the irascible naturalist, if a captain, his officers, and crew were convicted of some terrible

---

* Bird Island is now the site of a British Antarctic Survey station.
† Half the world will bear your name.

crime, their punishment should be to explore these inhospitable, cursed, and dreadful regions: the thought of living in them filled his whole soul with horror and despair. Cook would have probably read the entry with a wry smile.

During the coasting passage down the north coast of the island Clerke had sighted the top of a sugarloaf-shaped hill across the sea to the southeast. After the disappointment of finding the supposed continental land to be a mere island, the *Resolution* bore away to investigate this new tempter. After three days of calm, storm, fog, and rain the sugarloaf hill resolved itself to be a collection of rocky islets, the only inhabitants shags. Here was the land sighted by de la Roche and converted by Dalrymple into a continent.

Cook now stood east until close to 30°E longitude and then, on 26 January, changed course for the south. At 60°S, in fog so thick they were unable to see the length of the ship, Cook ordered a change of course to the east. This zigzag course was no arbitary choice, a vague blundering around in the Southern Ocean. They had mistaken the first glimpse of South Georgia for an iceberg. Was it not possible that Bouvet had indeed sighted land at his Cape Circumcision? Cook, until now, had suspected the putative cape to be an iceberg. To 60°S latitude he would go, and then angle northeast toward Bouvet's landfall. And, in a moment of candor, Cook admitted to feeling "now tired of these high Southern latitudes where nothing was to be found but ice and thick fogs."

A few days later, just north of 60°S, the fog clearing, a Dutch seaman named Samuel Freezland sighted a thousand-foot towering pinnacle of rock: it lay close to an elevated coast whose snow-clad summits pierced the clouds. The rock became Freezland Peak and the coastline Cape Bristol. To the south lay more land—the southernmost land so far sighted—and in homage to the ancient voyage of Pytheas into the north and the legendary land of Thule that appeared with such disconcerting ambiguity on medieval maps, the new land was named Southern Thule. What appeared to be a fog-shrouded bay between Southern Thule and Cape Bristol was named Forster's Bay.

The next few days were frustrating ones. Pestered with ice and fog, the Resolutions caught glimpses of more land as they sailed north. But approaching close was out of the question. The sea was choked with ice; the coast—whenever they caught a glimpse through the swirling fog—showed no harbors, the cliff faces presenting an implacable front. The fog cleared sufficiently to show land identifiable as indeed islands: Saunder's Island and Candlemas Island.

On 3 February Candlemas Island vanished in the murk astern. Sandwich Land was the collective name given to this grim-visaged sighting of the last few days. Cook thought it "either a group of Islands or else a point of the Continent, for I firmly believe that there is a tract of land near the

Pole, which is the source of most of the ice which is spread over this vast Southern Ocean." Forty-five years later the Russian expedition under Bellingshausen, in a masterly survey, proved Cook's first supposition correct, and that Sandwich Land was but an arc of islands, volcanic in origin, stretching across three degrees of latitude, their main inhabitants being millions of penguins.

Candlemas Island proved the last land sighted until their landfall at Cape Town seven weeks later. During those weeks the fall of snow became so heavy that the *Resolution* had to be brought into the wind, the sails aback, in order to shake off the accumulation of snow and ice whose weight endangered both sails and ship. The search for Cape Circumcision proved fruitless and Cook returned to his earlier thoughts that Bouvet had mistaken an iceberg for land. The sauerkraut finally ran out and was sorely missed: it had, at least, made the three-year-old salt meat a fraction more edible.

Toward the end of February, having crossed his track of 1772, Cook finally headed toward the Cape of Good Hope. The voyage had effectively ended. And Cook set down his thoughts on what had been accomplished.

I had now made the circuit of the Southern Ocean in a high Latitude and traversed it in such a manner as to leave not the least room for the Possibility of there being a continent, unless near the Pole and out of the reach of Navigation; by twice visiting the Pacific Tropical Sea, I had not only settled the situation of some old discoveries but made there many new ones and left, I conceive, very little more to be done even in that part. Thus I flater myself that the intention of the Voyage has in every respect been fully Answered, the Southern Hemisphere sufficiently explored and a final end put to the searching after a Southern Continent, which has at times ingrossed the attention of some of the Maritime Powers for near two centuries past and the Geographers of all ages. That there may be a Continent or large tract of land near the Pole, I will not deny, on the contrary I am of opinion there is, and it is probable that we have seen part of it. The excessive cold, the many islands and vast floats of ice all tend to prove that there must be land to the South and that this Southern land must lie or extend farthest to the North opposite the Southern Atlantick and Indian Oceans. . . .

As to any land south of his track, he had thoughts on that too:

Lands doomed by nature to everlasting frigidness and never once to feel the warmth of the Suns rays, whose horrible and savage aspect I have no words to describe; such are the lands we have discovered, what may we expect those to be which lie more to the South, for we may reasonably suppose that we have seen the best as lying most to the North, whoever has resolution and perseverance to clear up this point by proceding farther than I have done, I shall not envy him the honour of the discovery but I will be bold to say that the world will not be benefited by it.

For a passing moment Cook toyed with the idea of repeating the search for Kerguelen's land—but dismissed it. Their provisions were moldy and Cook dreaded the thought of scurvy, the plague of the sea, with nothing on board to combat it.

By the end of the first week of March they were well to the north of the Convergence and putting on lighter clothing. On 16 March two vessels were sighted standing to the west, one of them flying Dutch colors. It was an indication they were entering well-ploughed waters. Cook, as ordered by the Admiralty, now collected all the logbooks, journals, and charts made by the officers and petty officers. The men's chests were searched. Poor Elliot mournfully recorded that "everything was given up, and sealed up by Capt. Cook, so that I can safely say that notwithstanding all the pains I had taken, the next day I had not a figure to shew, any more than if I had never been the Voyage." (Elliot, however, was in for a pleasant surprise. Back in England he was invited to breakfast with Cook. "I attended his invitation and did receive my Chart etc., with my Name, *Elliott's Chart and Ship's Track,* written on it in his own hand, and which writing I venerate to this day, and can never look at without feeling the deepest regret at the melancholy loss of so great a Man.") The Forsters, Wales, and Sparrman were allowed to keep their journals but were asked, and gave their word, that nothing would be communicated to England about the voyage until the Admiralty gave permission.

That evening they sighted the South African coast. Two days later, progress being slow, a boat was sent nine miles to the Dutch ship, which proved to be an East Indiaman bound from Bengal. The ship's captain gave the *Resolution* some sugar and arrack, and some English seamen, sailing aboard the Dutchman, gave disturbing news of the *Adventure.* Furneaux had arrived at the Cape twelve months previous and the scuttle-butt running along the waterfront had it that a boat's crew had been murdered and eaten by the native New Zealanders. So those circumstantial stories heard by Cook in New Zealand might have a grain of truth in them; but Cook decided to withhold judgment until he received fuller news at the Cape. He had found the New Zealanders no wickeder than other men; indeed he thought them brave and open—though unlikely to take an insult without resenting it.

The next day Forster and Clerke visited another East Indiaman, this time English, the *True Briton* bound from China to England—but not calling at the Cape. It gave Cook the opportunity to send a letter to the Admiralty Secretary, Forster the opportunity to break his word by sending an account of the voyage to Daines Barrington (Forster expected to gain much from his acquaintance with Barrington, an English lawyer, antiquary, and naturalist), and both Clerke and Forster the opportunity to feast upon Chinese quail and roast goose. They returned with a parcel of old newspapers—which gave much enjoyment in the reading; and a fat pig, some geese, and tea—which gave much pleasure in the eating.

On the morning of 22 March, two years and four months after leaving, the *Resolution* anchored in Table Bay. For the Dutch in their colony it was Tuesday 21 March: the Resolutions had gained a day by sailing around the world west to east. (Indeed, the *Adventure* and the *Resolution* were the first vessels to sail around the world in this direction.) And at the Cape, Cook found a letter from Furneaux awaiting him.

It made melancholy reading. In it Cook learned that Furneaux had found the message in the bottle at Ship Cove in New Zealand, but, like Cook, had to spend some days rebaking moldy bread, wooding, and watering. Ready for sea on 17 December, a boat with ten men was sent to gather fresh greens. As they had not returned by the next morning, a launch under the command of James Burney (he had been promoted to lieutenant and transferred from the *Resolution* at Cape Town), with the boat's crew and ten marines went off in search. At Grass Cove (now Whareunga Bay) they found what was left of the green-gathering party: entrails, roasted human flesh in baskets, the head of Furneaux's Negro servant, two severed hands, both identifiable—one by a scar (an eerie presentiment of the identification of Cook's remains in Hawaii), the other by a tattoo. The evidence of cannibalism was so obvious that Burney, when back in England, only spoke of Grass Cove in a whisper.

The *Adventure* had sailed on 22 December and their Christmas must have been a melancholy one. Furneaux then had run his easting down close to 60°S (further south than Cook's passage to Cape Horn), with albatross, petrels, penguins, whales, and seals their only companions in this vast ocean. They were well south of Cape Horn, close to 61°S, when they entered the South Atlantic. A few miles further south and they would have discovered the South Shetlands forty-five years before William Smith in the *Williams*. As it was, but for thick hazy weather they would have certainly seen Elephant Island and South Georgia—they passed twenty miles to the north of the former and twenty miles south of the latter. A search for the elusive Cape Circumcision proved fruitless and the *Adventure* arrived at the Cape of Good Hope on 17 March 1774.

Poor Furneaux. He seems a man dogged by bad luck. His men massacred, his command a vessel that could sail no closer than eight points to the wind: given clear weather, a famous figure in Antarctic exploration rather than a footnote. The *Adventure* arrived back in England on 14 July 1774. Furneaux's luck did not improve. Appointed captain of the *Syren*, he served in North America until 1777, when his ship was driven ashore and he was taken prisoner. He returned to England in the autumn of 1778 and languished on half-pay until his death in Devon, three years later, at the early age of forty-six.

The *Resolution* spent five weeks at the Cape repairing the wear and tear of sixty thousand miles of sailing: all-new running rigging and sails, hull and deck recaulked, rudder repaired. The Forsters, much to the relief of their shipmates, had left the *Resolution* before she even came to anchor, spirited ashore in an East Indiaman's launch. Here they resided in lodgings (along with Cook and Sparrman) and botanized until the *Resolution* was ready for sea. Sparrman quitted the *Resolution* permanently to continue his studies at the Cape and to entertain his acquaintances with tales of the voyage—it was the talk of the Dutch colony—and the remarkable fact of his achieving the record of being closest to the South Pole.

Cook, too, was busy. An East Indiaman, the *Ceres,* was shortly to sail for England: with her went a package of officer's journals; views and paintings by Hodges, that "indefaticable gentleman"; charts by Cook and "Mr Gilbert my Master whose judgment and asseduity, in this as well as every other branch of his profession is exceeded by none"; and, in the same letter to the Admiralty Secretary, the comment that "Mr Kendals Watch has exceeded the expectations of its most Zealous advocate and by being now and then corrected by Lunar observations has been our faithfull guide through all the vicissitudes of climates." Old John Harrison could not have had a finer accolade—and the watch is still in working condition at the National Maritime Museum in Greenwich.

Less pleasurable than writing paragraphs praising his men and Mr. Kendall's watch was the reading of Dr. Hawkesworth's version of the *Endeavour* voyage. Written in the first person, as if by Cook, it contained much misinformation: Banks and Cook appeared interchangeable, nautical *faux pas* occurred with depressing regularity, and, to make matters worse, the introduction claimed that Cook had read the manuscript and approved it. Which was not the case. Cook was mortified.

More pleasing were meetings with a French East Indiaman commander, Julien Marie Crozet. The two men were of the same age and struck up an instant rapport; when they finally parted it was with feelings of mutual esteem. Both men were cut from the same cloth. Crozet had been second in command to Marion du Fresne on a French expedition that Cook had heard rumors about at the Cape of Good Hope in 1772. They had discovered islands to the southeast of the Cape—the Crozet Islands—and rediscovered what was to become Prince Edward Island and Marion Island (so named by Cook on his third voyage). In New Zealand, Marion du Fresne and some of his men had been massacred by the Maoris—those New Zealanders again—and Crozet had taken command of the expedition. He showed Cook a chart of the French discoveries, including Kerguelen's, and Cook noted it "laid down in the very situation where we searched for it, so that I can no means conceive how both of us and the Adventure missed it." The French were mistaken in their longitude. Cook, twenty months later on his third voyage, was to put the matter to rights.

The *Resolution* sailed on 27 April in the company of the East Indiaman *Dutton*, bound for St. Helena. Cook, "depending on the goodness of Mr Kendal's Watch," was determined to sail direct for the island: the Indiaman, used to finding the island by sailing into its latitude and then running the latitude down, were nervous. And here we have that sparkling vignette described by Elliot where Cook in the gaiety of his heart "laughed at them, and told them he would run their jibboom on the island if they chose."

But St. Helena, which dutifully appeared over their jibbooms on 15 May, proved a source of embarrassment to Cook. Hawkesworth's book had also been read on this insular outpost of the East India Company; and in it the inhabitants read to their amazement that no wheeled vehicles were to be found on the island and that the islanders exercised wanton cruelty toward their slaves. At a dinner for the officers of the *Resolution* and the *Dutton* held at the governor's house, Mrs. Skottowe, wife of Governor John Skottowe,* chafed Cook unmercifully on the subject of wheeled vehicles and slaves. I would like to think that this spirited lady (one who "troubled the naval officers more than many an ocean storm") sent for a copy of the offending book and read out to the company, the candlelight reflecting off the silver, wine ruby red in decanters and glasses, the officers' buttons gleaming, their faces flushed with wine and embarrassment, a passage such as follows—one supposed to have been written by Cook on Tahiti.

It is scarcely possible for those who are acquainted with the athletic sports of remote antiquity not to remark a rude resemblance of them in this wrestling match among the natives of a little island in the midst of the Pacific Ocean. And our female readers may recollect the account given of them by Fénélon in his *Telemachus,* where, though the events are fictitious, the manners of the age are faithfully transcribed from authors by whom they are supposed to have been truly related.

And then the raised quizzical eyebrows as she glanced mischievously at the discomfited Cook. But worse was in store. The embarrassment was not complete. Lodging at the Governor's house, Cook found every contrivance of wheeled vehicle drawn up outside his bedroom window. His only answer to all this was to firmly shift the blame on Hawkesworth and make amends to the islanders in the published journal of the *Resolution*'s voyage. Plus a courteous bow to "the celebrated beauties of St. Helena," for he could "not do my Country women of this island justice if I did not confirm the report of common fame."

But then Cook was no prig, even if he did stay aloof from the readily available carnal delights of the Pacific islands. The memory of his Elizabeth

---

* Here was a family connection for Cook. The Governor's father, a member of the gentry, had employed Cook's father as his farm foreman and also paid the small fee to send young James Cook to the local school where he learned his arithmetic, reading, writing, and catechism.

perhaps held him chaste, or the knowledge that lechery would compromise his effectivness as a commander. No matter; it is said that on Saturday nights at sea he always proposed the toast "to all beautiful women."

They sailed from St. Helena on 21 May, making calls at Ascension Island, Fernando de Noronha "to determine its longitude," and the Azores, made land near Plymouth on Saturday 29 July 1775, and steered up Channel toward Portsmouth.

At five o'clock Sunday morning the ebullient Clerke was writing a letter to his friend Joseph Banks. They were past Portland, had a fine breeze from the northwest, a flood tide under them, and expected to anchor shortly at Spithead from their "Continent hunting expedition." Clerke would not describe the voyage until he saw Banks, but this letter would be sent by "our civil Gentry, who will fly to Town with all the sail thay can possibly make." A postscript is pure Clerke: "Excuse the Paper, its gilt I assure you, but the Cockroaches have piss'd upon it—We're terrible busy—you know a Man of War—my respects & every social wish to the good Doctor [Solander]—I'll write him as soon as possible—here's too much damning of Eyes & Limbs to do any thing now."

A few hours later the *Resolution* anchored at Spithead. The last sentence in Cook's journal of this most remarkable of voyages reads: "Having been absent from England Three Years and Eighteen Days, in which time I lost but four men and one only of these by sickness." The voyage had demolished the two-thousand-year-old idea of a huge inhabited southern continent, redrawn the map of the Pacific, laid the foundation for the coming age of scientific navigation, and, with Forster's work, made the first tentative steps in the gathering of knowledge of Antarctica's natural history.

For Alexander Dalrymple the return of the *Resolution* happened at the worst of all possible times. The year 1775 saw the publication of his *Collection of Voyages, chiefly in the Southern Atlantick Ocean*. Here he suggested colonizing the island discovered by de la Roche and the *Leon*. Food could be grown for the East India ships by West Indian slaves, an industry set up to exploit the whales and seals (an idea ahead of its time), and, finally, the island could be used as a base for exploration of the southern continent of which Cape Circumcision was but a small indication. The true irony, however, lay in the future for Dalrymple. He was invited to sit on the committee supervising the engraving of the charts and views of Cook's last voyage into the northern hemisphere.

Forster, too, was destined to have his hopes destroyed. During the voyage he had harbored the notion that it was he who would write the official narrative. But the lesson of Hawkesworth was still green at the Admiralty. Cook was the one to do it (with polishing by the Reverend John Douglas, canon of Windsor). Which brought bitter and vitriolic correspondence from Forster. And his intransigent behavior over the matter even alienated his friends. But Forster saw a coup de main to confound his perceived enemies—and also make money—by having George write a book (his son, according to Forster, being free of any promise not to publish before the official narrative) based on the father's journals. *A Voyage Round the World* by George Forster was published in March 1777—six weeks before Cook's *Voyage Towards the South Pole*. But by then Cook was back in the South Pacific. During the long, interminable voyage Forster had been haunted by thoughts of Banks and Solander. On *his* return *he* would receive the public acclaim accorded to the English gentlemen and the Swedish naturalist. He was to be sorely disappointed. The positions were reversed. It was Cook who was the talk of the town.

The *Resolution* was ordered up to the Thames and at Gallions Reach, on a beautiful August day, Lord Sandwich with his mistress Martha Ray and a party of ladies and gentlemen inspected the now famous vessel. Solander wrote a letter to Banks describing a day made brighter by the First Lord spreading promotions like confetti. Clerke had some drawings of birds done by a midshipman that were intended for Banks; Anderson, the surgeon's mate, had made a good botanical collection; on board were three Tahiti dogs, "the ugliest most stupid of all the canine tribe"; Forster had brought back a springbok, a suricate, two eagles, and several other birds from the Cape—all intended for the Queen; Pickersgill made the ladies faint and sick by showing them the Maori head, preserved in spirits, that had been sliced and eaten on this very quarterdeck. A most satisfying day. And all on the *Resolution* inquired after Banks.

It would have been natural for Banks to have formed part of that gathering with his friend Sandwich and Solander. But the voyage that he prophesied as having no "prospect but distress and disappointment" had returned in triumph—and he felt the embarrassment. Nevertheless, Banks, being a man too generous and sensible to harbor ill feeling or jealousy, shortly healed the rift with Cook. The Dance portrait of Cook was commissioned and hung in Banks's London house.

Cook sailed from England for the last time in July 1776, his ship again the *Resolution* and his consort, from the Cape of Good Hope onward, the *Discovery*, commanded by the promoted Charles Clerke. Their mission: to search for a Northwest or Northeast passage from the Pacific to the Atlantic. One season was spent by the expedition in the Arctic before returning south to Hawaii for the winter. And here events moved inexorably toward their tragic end. The *Discovery*'s cutter was stolen and on 14 February 1779 Cook rowed ashore with a landing party: a chief would be taken hostage and held until the return of the cutter. In a sudden explosion of violence a fight broke out between the natives and the landing party. Four marines were killed and Cook was hacked to death in the Pacific waters lapping the shores of Kealakekua Bay. He was just fifty years of age.

Clerke, although ailing, now took over command of the expedition.

One of his first orders was that no punitive measures, no vengeance, should be visited upon the Hawaiians. The expedition sailed north for the Arctic and Clerke died at sea from tuberculosis (a disease contracted in the King's Bench prison when this genial, generous, warmhearted man had stood surety for his brother's debts), and was buried at Petropavlovsk on the Kamchatka Peninsula, his grave surrounded by willows planted by his shipmates. He was thirty-eight. One of his last acts had been to dictate— he was too weak to write—a letter to his great friend Joseph Banks. The last paragraph reads:

Now, my dear & honoured friend, I must bid you a final adieu: may you enjoy many happy years in this world, and in the end attain that fame your indefatigable industry so richly deserves. These are most sincerely the warmest and sincerest wishes of your devoted affectionate departing Servant,
Chas Clerke

News of Cook's death was already on its way to England across the wastes of Siberia and Russia. Clerke had sent Cook's journals, his own, and letters to the Admiralty through the good will and help of Magnus von Behm, the Governor of Kamchatka. The news reached England in January 1780, some eight months before the return of the expedition.

For Elizabeth Cook it was a devastating blow. And every year on the anniversary of his death she kept to her room, fasted, and read her husband's Bible. The same day the news of Cook's death arrived at the Admiralty, Sandwich wrote of it to Banks. Next day it was made public in the *London Gazette*. George III is said to have shed tears; the eulogies poured forth. Perhaps, after Elizabeth, seamen mourned him most, for here was a seaman's seaman. And running over the names of the ships under his command they must have realized that here lay the distillation of Cook's character and career: *Endeavour, Resolution, Adventure, Discovery*.

But this skeptical man was more than all those verities and virtues. A telling anecdote is recorded by James Boswell, that most assiduous of conversation recorders (how one wishes that he had sailed with Cook), on Cook's reaction to a remark made by a notable Scottish judge, buttressing his argument on the links between beings of a lower order and man, that Cook had seen a nation of men like monkeys. Not so, said Cook. "I did not say they were like monkeys. I said their faces put me in mind of monkeys." Precision in navigation, survey, geography—and thought.

Cook's second and third voyages laid a powder trail that led south to Antractica. The powder keg at the end of this burning fuse exploded almost forty years to the day after his death. Four hundred miles to the south of Cape Horn, new land was discovered.

VIII

The Continent Discovered

A new land has been discovered off Cape Horn lat.61 long.55
by the ship *William* on a voyage from Montevideo to Valparaiso. The fact is susceptable of no doubt—the same ship was
again dispatched there by Capt. Sherriff, of the *Andromache*
frigate, to survey the coast, which the W. explored for 200
miles: the Captain landed, found it covered with snow, an
abundance of seals and whales—no inhabitants.

New-York Mercantile Advertiser, March 1820

ON A WARM summer's day of 1785 a sober-clothed gentleman
sat in his London lodgings composing a letter. William Rotch,
whale oil merchant, whaleship owner, Quaker, and, as Thomas
Jefferson slyly called them, a "Nantucketois," had news for his
brother Francis in the newly fledged United States of America. Rotch was
in London with an unusual proposition for the British government. The
Revolutionary War had been disastrous for American whaling—Rotch calculated his losses at $60,000—and the peace was no better. The American
market was glutted, prices were low, and the old outlet of colonial days—
Britain—had placed an import duty on whale oil from alien sources.
Rotch's proposal, breathtaking in its audacity, was to move the Nantucket
whaling industry to Britain—Milford Haven in Wales would be an ideal
site—and thus bring American whaling expertise to the benefit of the
British state. The state, of course, would have to pay. And the proposed
amount was sticking fast in the responsible minister's throat. But this letter
concerned more than details of financial fencing.

Rotch had just read Cook's recently published journal of his last voyage
into the Arctic. And an item about furs had caught his attention. It appeared that in China the British seamen had sold fur skins "at the enormous price of $100 per skin." These skins, as far as Rotch could gather,
were sea otter skins—much prized by the Chinese—and had been bought
for mere trifles—nails, buttons, etc.—from the natives along the northwest

coast of North America. Here was an activity where American whalers could make a handsome profit. Competition from the British would be minimal. Their East India Company had a monopoly on trade with China: merchandise, specie—smuggled opium from India—going into China, and tea coming out. The same idea had been proselytized in the United States by John Ledyard, born in Groton, Connecticut, who had sailed as a corporal of marines with Cook. As a result, an American ship had sailed from New York in 1784 with a cargo of ginseng and furs from eastern North American trading posts, and returned with tea, silk, nankeens, chinaware. The American China trade had started.

Francis Rotch had spent most of the Revolutionary War years in the Falklands, heading an American whaling fleet in exile. There, he knew, there were thousands of fur seals. A ship had been dispatched in 1784 to take both fur seals and elephant seals: the ship and cargo returned to New York in 1786, where the thirteen thousand fur seal skins sold for $6,500. The skins were sent to Nantucket and then shipped to China. They sold for $65,000. The China trade in fur sealskins from the southern hemisphere had started.

Word of such an amazing profit soon spread. Leather-bound volumes containing the voyages of Drake, Anson, Byron, Bougainville, and Cook were studied with care; Dampier's *New Voyage Round The World* with particular care. At the Juan Fernandez Islands, according to Dampier, "the seals swarm around the island . . . as if they had no other place in the world to live in; for there is not a bay nor rock that one can get ashore on, but it is full of them. . . ." Over the next few decades the sealers spread from the Falkland Islands to the shores of Patagonia, South Georgia, into the Pacific, and up the coast of Chile. The main onslaught hit the Juan Fernandez Islands in 1797. Edmund Fanning from Stonington, Connecticut, and in command of the brig *Betsey,* sold one hundred thousand fur seal skins to the Chinese: most of the skins had been collected on Juan Fernandez. When the *Betsey* returned in 1799 the China goods yielded a net profit of $52,300 to the ship's owners, with an eighth of that going to Fanning as part owner. Amasa Delano—a sealer and ancestor of Franklin Delano Roosevelt—estimated that more than three million sealskins were taken off the islands in a space of seven years. By 1807 the seals were virtually exterminated. Other islands, closer to the Convergence, were to follow the same pattern: South Georgia, South Sandwich, Crozet, Marion, Prince Edward, Macquarie, Kerguelen. Up until 1796, only the Chinese knew the furrier's craft of taking off the fur seals' long, stiff guard hairs and leaving the soft inner fur. Then Thomas Chapman, a London furrier, discovered a similar process. The market had expanded.

The sealers, having discovered an island rich with fur seals and worked it for one or two seasons, would then talk of the beaches being "almost entirely abandoned by the animals." It is a comment worthy of a modern bureaucrat or businessman trying to disguise an unpalatable truth. The sealers knew well enough that they had only a few seasons before the seals "abandoned" the beaches—and went to extraordinary lengths to keep their discoveries secret. "In the history of the seal trade," said Jeremiah Reynolds, speaking before the U.S. House of Representatives in 1836, "secrecy is what they know has been deemed a part, and a most important part, of their capital."

And the coinage of this capital could show a remarkably rough-milled edge. One old sealing skipper gave the following advice to a friend about to sail for the Bounty Islands near New Zealand:

If you got out there early and saw a great show of seals, I should get as many on board as I could without running any risk of not getting back in time. I would leave on the rocks all the men that I thought would blab; go to the most convenient port, ship my skins, get what I needed and go back to the rocks, and finish up the season and go to Valparaiso without touching at New Zealand, and I should expect to have another season without company. . . .

A subtler approach, and one guaranteed to delight the hearts of all small boys of whatever age, reeking of *Treasure Island*'s Spy Glass Hill and the directions for buried treasure, was practiced by Henry Fanning, brother of Edmund Fanning, when captain of the sealer *Catherine*. Leaving a gang of sealers on Prince Edward Island, Fanning went off in search of the Crozet Islands, rediscovered them, found them full of seals, returned to Prince Edward Island, took off his men, but, as other American sealers were working the island, "waited a day or two so that suspicions that they had discovered any island might not be excited in the minds of the officers and men belonging to two vessels. . . ." But how to pass the message of the Crozets' position to other vessels of the partnership—and without letting the rival sealers into the secret? The partnership had worked out a simple stratagem. A cairn would be built on the northeast point of the island and a message left in a bottle. But not under the cairn. The bottle would be buried thirty feet southwest of the cairn and two feet underground. The partnership vessel did arrive, found the cairn demolished and a large hole dug underneath. But the rival sealers had failed to find the bottle buried thirty feet away.

But then the sealers were living a boy's adventure-story life, the treasure being finding fur seal beaches on strange islands far from civilization. And as a sealer you shared, just like pirates, in the treasure. No pay but a share, a lay, of the profits. And sometimes it was a boy's adventure story complete with shipwreck until rescued—if you were lucky. Now it was *Robinson Crusoe* and living by one's wits on the resources available. Such a story was told by Charles Goodridge sailing aboard the English cutter *Princess of Wales* and wrecked on the Crozet Islands. Goodridge and his shipmates spent close to two years on the island before being rescued:

Sea elephants served us for meat, lodging, firing, shoe leather and sewing thread. We washed in their blood and removed dirt and grease from our clothes. It was just like soap. Sea elephant blubber and a piece of rope yarn made a lamp. The teeth formed pipe bowls, with the leg of waterfowl as stems, and we dried the island grass and smoked it. Sea elephant bones formed our grates. We cooked the hearts and tongues. The brains were often ate raw, and they were as sweet as sugar. Flippers were boiled to make a jelly which tasted good when penguin eggs, pigeons and sea hens were added.

The early years of the nineteenth century provided a rich fund of similar tales. For many of the sealers, their life, following Thomas Hobbes, was solitary, poor, nasty, brutish, and short.

But what of the seals themselves—those unfortunate creatures below the Convergence who were brought close to the edge of extinction? The Antarctic fur seal, *Arctocephalus gazella,* is a gregarious creature whose breeding patterns, like those of all fur seal species, are loaded in favor of exploitation. Half of its life is spent at sea but in late October and November the bulls—"whigs" to the sealers—come ashore to their familiar rocky coasts and sheltered beaches. They have, in the jargon of zoologists, "strong site fidelity." Here the six-foot-long bulls establish territories and wait for the smaller females—the sealers' "clapmatches"—who arrive two to three weeks later to pup. The bulls, parading their territory, collect together about half a dozen females into their harem. After pupping, the female suckles her pup for about a week and then mates. There follows a cycle of going to sea for a week, then returning to suckle her young for three days. By April the breeding months ashore are over and the beaches are empty. But this bare recital of the fur seal's life ashore suggests a bovine, placid, torpid creature: in fact, a fur seal beach is a noisy playground full of sheer energy, exuberance, vitality. Fur seals, with their ability to turn their hind limbs forward and balance on their large foreflippers, can move, gallop, along the shore—often faster than a man can run. The bulls defend their territories, fight; the young males prowl the outskirts; the pups play together in small groups; the females gallop back and forth between shore and sea.

Once discovered, a sealing beach would be worked until no seals were left alive. And the method of killing and skinning was brutal, quick, and effective: a blow on the nose with the sealing club and then, in the words of Amasa Delano, "knives are taken to cut or rip them down on the breast, from the under jaw to the tail, giving them a stab in the breast that will kill them." Then started the skinning, the taking off of all the thin layer of blubber and some of the lean; then the beaming, the final fleshing of the skin; then the stretching out and pegging on the ground to dry; then the salting and stacking, "in the manner of salted dried cod fish." An expert sealer, Delano reckoned, could kill and skin sixty seals an hour.

In contrast to the vigor of a fur seal rookery, an elephant seal beach

A sealing shallop laid up for winter.

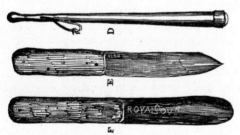

A seal club and knives.

Horse for cutting blubber.

A sealer's scabbard.

A sealer's boat hut.

The dress of shipwrecked sealers.

displays some of the passivity and languor of the fabled Turkish seraglio. And what a seraglio and what a pasha. The male of the southern elephant seal, *Mirounga leonina,* can weigh four tons and measure twenty feet from his pendulous nose to his hind limbs. His harem, which can number sixty to seventy temporary concubines, are much smaller creatures, rarely exceeding twelve feet and weighing less than a ton. These seals also show "site fidelity." The females, gregarious creatures, in September come ashore, where they collect in large groups and are soon joined by the breeding males, the "beachmasters," who, having collected their harem, fight off any intruding male. The pups are born about a week after the mother hauls out. By October the beaches are packed. Both males and females fast when ashore: the females for about thirty days and the males up to ninety days. They live on those reserves of fat, the blubber, which can reach thicknesses of five inches. The blubber, rendered down, tried out, like whale blubber, produced the oil sought by the sealers. A barrel of blubber, according to the sealers, would make a barrel of oil.

The killing was a bloodier business than the killing of fur seals. Females, young males, and pups were clubbed on the snout and then lanced to make them bleed. The larger bulls were prodded to rear up, shot in the palate, and then lanced. And an elephant seal has a prodigious amount of blood. The blubber cut away—it took half a dozen men to turn over a large bull—would be set to soak in water for a day; then minced into smaller chunks; then boiled in the witch's-cauldron-like try-pots. After cooling, the oil went into casks. And it produced an oil equal in quality to that of the best whale oil.

By today's standards all this is quite unforgivable. But in the late eighteenth and early nineteenth century whale and seal oil lubricated machinery, lit town and city streets, lit the lamps of home. This was a society dependent upon whale oil. Future generations, no doubt, will also purse their lips and shake their heads over twentieth-century man's besotted infatuation with the internal combustion engine and petroleum-based plastics—a society held hostage by a fossil oil.

The South Shetland Islands lie some 60 miles off the northwest coast of the Antarctic Peninsula. From Elephant Island in the northeast to Smith Island in the southwest they stretch 250 miles in an inhospitable phalanx of rock, ice, and snow, giving some protection to the coast of the Peninsula from the Southern Ocean swells rolling in from the west. During the winter months the islands are closed in by pack ice.

A vessel sailing from Staten Island at a leisurely five knots and steering a course just west of south—to allow for the east-running set in the Drake Passage—will arrive off the islands in four days. It is not a long passage, although it can be a stormy one. As the sands of the second decade of the nineteenth century trickled to an end, these islands still lay undiscovered. Nearly all the other islands below the Convergence with breeding beaches of fur and elephant seal had been discovered and the animals exploited close to total extermination. The sands were about to start trickling away for the seals of the South Shetlands.

During the month of February 1819, the curiosity of a gliding albatross might have been caught by the sight of a vessel butting south across the white-flecked waters of the Drake Passage. The vessel, with the rather

A collier brig similar to the *Williams*. By E. W. Cooke, 1828.

prosaic name of *Williams*, would have looked more at home in the North Sea carrying coal. Tubby-looking, eighty-two feet overall and twenty-five feet in beam, rigged as a two-masted brig, she had been built in 1812 at the Northumberland coal-shipping town of Blyth. Her master and part owner, William Smith, also hailed from Northumberland, and had celebrated his twenty-eighth birthday four months previous on the passage from England to Buenos Aires. One of the countless master mariners in the world's largest merchant fleet, Smith, like James Cook, had learned his trade in North Sea colliers—with the added experience of Greenland whaling. Smith was also a careful navigator, for the *Williams* carried a chronometer.

This was his fourth voyage to South America carrying merchandise to a very lucrative market—even though the continent was in constant turmoil, with the colonial provinces fighting for independence from Spain. Smith and his ship were now bound round Cape Horn to Valparaiso carrying a mixed cargo of wrought and cast iron, cotton, silk, hats, tools, cutlery, saddles, musical instruments, books, wine. The weather, however, was doing its best to slow the delivery. Constant gale-force westerlies made Smith decide to sail far south to clear the cape and perhaps find a fair wind. After the Greenland whaling the thought of ice held only a few terrors.

Shortly after dawn on 19 February, in gale-force southwest winds and through frequent snow and sleet showers, land was sighted ahead, distant some six miles. Smith estimated their latitude about 62°S and longitude 60°W. A gale-force wind and poor visibility off an unknown coast is no time and place for exploration: Smith wisely hauled off north and waited for the weather to improve. He was not to wait long. Next day, the weather clearing, he doubled back toward the land; and at noon the invaluable chronometer put them at 62°17′S, 60°12′W, with a headland bearing south by west about twelve miles distant.

Smith named the headland after his ship, and today Williams Point forms the northeast tip of Livingston Island. Soon the lookouts were seeing tide-rips and breakers close to this inhospitable-looking coast. Smith was not an explorer but a merchant seaman and part owner. Commerce was his calling, and he was well aware of the clause quietly lurking in his marine insurance policy which spoke of "undue deviation." In short, if he were to damage his vessel and cargo while exploring rather than prosecuting his voyage as quickly and safely as possible, the insurance policy would be null and void. And so, on that clear and now pleasant day, avoiding the scattered ice floes, his ex-whaler's eye keenly noting the vast numbers of whales and seals swimming in the brash-covered sea, Smith set his course northwest for Valparaiso.

They reached port on 11 March and Smith wasted no time in reporting his discovery to William Shirreff, captain of the frigate *Andromache* and senior Royal Navy officer patrolling this long stretch of the South American coast. Shirreff, to give him his due, was a harried man. His responsibility in this time of turmoil was to look after the interests and welfare of the large colony of British merchants in Chile, not to go haring off to chase some will-o'-the-wisp land buried amid the ice of the southern latitudes. In this delicate political atmosphere the activities of another ex–Royal Navy captain, Thomas Cochrane, tenth earl of Dundonald—but simply "el Diablo" to the Spanish—were doing nothing to make his life easier. This buccaneering and great fighting seaman was now vice admiral of Chile and commander in chief of its seven-ship naval force. Even at that moment the febrile brain of this extraordinary man was thinking of ways to free Napoleon Bonaparte, immured on St. Helena like an evil genie in a bottle, and set the ex-Emperor on a South American throne. Nevertheless, Shirreff had the consolation of a twice-weekly cricket game followed by dinner in a marquee. A cricket club had been founded after an inaugural game between the *Andromache* and the frigate *Blossom,* and the game was now played on a convenient stretch of ground at Valparaiso. And Cochrane was away blockading Callao with his set of mercenaries.

Smith had mistaken an iceberg for land, suggested the skeptical Shirreff. Not so, said Smith. He with his Greenland experience could tell icebergs from land. Had Smith taken soundings? Unfortunately not. The British merchants were equally skeptical. But news spreads fast in small communities and this tidbit of information of a possible discovery—and more importantly of vast numbers of whales and seals—came to the ears of Jeremy Robinson, one of a number of agents employed by the U.S. State Department to keep a finger on the pulse of the turbulent happenings in South America and report to Washington. Robinson was to use this gleaning from the waterfront later in the year.

It was the middle of May before Smith had assembled another cargo for the *Williams,* this one destined for Montevideo. North-country men have a reputation in England for being a stubborn breed, and it was soon clear that Smith was realizing the stereotype. Or was it the condescending attitude of the Royal Navy officers and their thinly veiled contempt for the merchant seaman that still rankled? Whatever the reasons, Smith decided, on his return passage around Cape Horn, to sail down into the high southern latitudes and bring back positive proof that land existed. It was perhaps a foolhardy decision: this was the winter season and what Smith was attempting was unusual and unique. Few shipmasters would hazard their lives and ships in a deliberate attempt to sail south during the winter months. The Northumberland determination had overcome the "undue deviation" clause.

It had taken the *Williams* nineteen days to sail from the discovery to Valparaiso. The return passage took eleven days longer. Battered by gales and contrary winds, the brig sailed south across the Convergence into the cold Antarctic waters. On 15 June they had reached 62°12′S—but further west than their previous sighting of land. That day, with a calm sea and gentle breeze, the sea began to freeze. The ice rapidly thickened. Smith and his vessel were totally unprepared for these conditions and the course was changed to the north. And, under reduced sail for fear of damaging the ship, the *Williams* threaded her way through the floes. Within an hour they were in clear water. Prudence now overcame stubbornness and Smith put his vessel on course for Montevideo. No land had been sighted.

At Montevideo Smith found that the ice had extracted a small tribute from the *Williams,* with several sheets of copper torn from the hull. He also found the news of his February discovery common gossip along the waterfront. And a group of American merchants offered Smith large sums of money to take the *Williams* back south; it was not the lure of the land, but those reports of whales and seals. Smith refused.

It was nearly three months before Smith had collected another cargo for Valparaiso, but by the end of September the *Williams* had cleared the river Plata on her third passage around Cape Horn. This time Smith was determined to find his land. Off the cape the wind was fair for a quick passage to Valparaiso, but Smith, untempted by this siren song, laid a course south. On 15 October, in misty weather, land was sighted about nine miles distant. It was an island (Desolation Island) some six miles from his previous landfall. They sailed toward it—this time taking soundings—and with the armed lead found a depth of forty fathoms with a bottom of fine black sand. With night approaching, Smith hauled back north under reduced canvas and waited for the morning. Dawn came fine and clear and the *Williams* stood back toward the land, which, with the improving visibility, Smith saw to stretch off to the northeast. The long day was spent coasting along, making sketches and taking soundings. His objective was a point of land which "we called the North Foreland . . . soundings regular from 35 to 21 fathoms, good bottom, sand and gravel, finding the weather favor us, down boat and succeeded in landing. . . ."

They landed on the shores of what is now Venus Bay, and on that rocky coast planted a board with the Union Jack, gave three cheers, and took possession in the name of King George III. Smith noted that the land was "very high and covered with snow, vast quantities of seals, whales, penguins. . . ." After the return of the landing party Smith stood offshore for the night. The landing had taken place on 16 October 1819—five days after Smith's twenty-ninth birthday.

Until now, Cook's Southern Thule had been the southernmost land found on the globe. Smith's discovery was more than two degrees further south and, inhospitable as it looked, the beaches could be turned to profit with their "seals stowed in bulk." But he was not quite done with his discovery. With the coming of dawn and an easterly wind, the *Williams* sailed back along the coastline and Smith realized they were passing a series of islands rather than one continuous coast. Back at Williams Point, looking through his telescope, Smith thought he saw pine trees—and the scene reminded him of Norway. It was wishful thinking, combined with the strange tricks Antarctica plays with light. The next day at dawn very high land was sighted. It was named Smith's Cape (now Smith Island). And rising 6,900 feet from the sea, the land is indeed the highest point of all the South Shetland Islands.

But the time had come to shape his course for Valparaiso, assume the mantle of a merchant marine master rather than explorer, and deliver his cargo. And report his findings with a certain amount of satisfaction. No one, not even the most skeptical of Royal Navy officers, could doubt the truth and obvious worth of his discoveries.

The *Williams* arrived at Valparaiso on 24 November and Smith wasted no time in reporting his findings to the Royal Navy. This time he was listened to with a great deal more attention by both navy and merchants. John Miers, a British engineer well acquainted with Smith, was particularly intrigued. (Miers had been invited out to Chile by Cochrane—who was then on a reconnaissance voyage to Spanish-held Valdivia, with a buccaneering eye on taking the well-fortified harbor and town.) Miers, an erudite man with a bent for natural history, felt all the collector's excitement, saw the potential for sealing, and also the possible use of the new land as a refuge and base in case the South American situation became untenable. With a group of British merchants, he decided to charter the *Williams* for a voyage south. But the Royal Navy stepped in: Shirreff, all doubts vanishing before Smith's evidence, persuaded Miers and his partners to forgo their plan. The navy would charter the *Williams,* put aboard crew from the *Andromache,* and sail south as soon as possible.

Shirreff's decision was not, perhaps, one taken on the spur of the moment. In a letter dated 15 November 1819 (nine days before the return of the *Williams*), the American agent Jeremy Robinson was writing to the Secretary of State, John Quincy Adams, giving him information on Smith's first sighting. "Sir," wrote Robinson, "I avail myself of an opportunity . . . to notify you of a recent important discovery of land in the South Seas. . . . Captain Sherriff, the commander of the Andromache and other British naval forces in these seas, will dispatch a vessel in a few days to survey this land and report upon it." The letter continues with a suggestion that a U.S. government vessel be sent to explore the southern regions where ". . . new sources of wealth, power and happiness, would be disclosed and science itself be benefited thereby." Adams received another letter on the same subject from his Buenos Aires agent, J. B. Prevost. His letter lacks the rhetoric of Robinson's and dismisses the value of the land; but Prevost is acutely aware that the land offers "a new field to the adventures of our countrymen in the number of seals and whales that abound on its coast."

The same month of Prevost's letter—January 1820—another letter, this one from Sir Thomas Hardy, commander of the Royal Navy's Brazil station, was aboard the frigate *Creole* sailing from Buenos Aires to England. The letter informed the Admiralty that Hardy had received news "by private account" of an island "discovered in Latitude 62°40′S and running from 60° to 63°40′W by Mr Smith master of the merchant vessel Williams . . . he landed . . . and observed a great many seals. . . . I am told that Captain Shirreff has sent to survey it. . . ."

But this is jumping a few weeks ahead of our narrative. With the Royal Navy charter of the *Williams,* Smith, having played his part and directed the course of action for three voyages, retired into the background and a new figure stepped forward to stage center. Shirreff, having hired the *Williams,* Smith, and his crew, put aboard a Mr. Edward Bransfield, master of the *Andromache,* as overall commander. Bransfield, like so many men, had been press-ganged into the Royal Navy. He was considered by Shirreff to be a very competent navigator and able officer.

Sailing with Bransfield were three midshipmen (one with the ability to make drawings of wildlife and scenery) and a surgeon. Along with the Royal Navy personnel went provisions for twelve months—in case they were trapped in the ice—with four bullocks and other livestock. Bransfield's orders were to ascertain if the South Shetlands were indeed islands or part of a continent; to plot latitudes and longitudes of harbors; to observe, collect, and preserve every object of natural science; to keep weather and magnetic records; to observe the characters of the inhabitants—if any; and, finally, to take possession of all discoveries.

With these instructions tucked away in his sea chest, Bransfield and the *Williams,* to the bellowing of the bullocks, weighed anchor and put out to sea from Valparaiso on December 1819. For Smith it was all most gratifying. The dismissive reception of nine months previous had been satisfyingly reversed.

The passage south was without major incident except for torn sails and a sprung boom suffered during one blustery gale. The land was raised on 16 January 1820. Livingston Island—for this was their landfall—rises to thirty-three hundred feet, and the bay into which they sailed—Barclay Bay—is described by the *Antarctic Pilot* as "encumbered with rocks and very dangerous." This uninviting bay was soon abandoned and the course altered to stretch northeast along the north shore of the land. By 22 January they had passed Smith's previous landing site, rounded the North Foreland, coasted down the short east coast of the island, and sailed into a large bay on the south shore. Here they made a landing, Bransfield planted a flagstaff with the Union Jack, coins of the realm were buried in a metal container, and British sovereignty was claimed over the land. The bay was named George's Bay (now King George Bay) and the island King George Island.

Unknown to Bransfield, some one hundred miles to the east on Rugged Island, a Union Jack had been hoisted, the land claimed for King George, and His Majesty's health drunk with glasses of grog. All on Christmas Day 1819—nearly a month before Bransfield's ceremony. British merchants in Buenos Aires had chartered a brig, the *Espirito Santo,* and put aboard some British crew and a master, Joseph Herring—he was to publish an article about the enterprise in the July 1820 edition of the *Imperial Magazine*—to seek out Smith's discovery. They were to stay thirty-three days on the island and take huge numbers of seals. When Bransfield had made the landfall and sailed into Barclay Bay, the *Williams* was but five miles from the sealers.

A day after Bransfield's flag raising, yet another sealer arrived at Rugged Island and anchored in "sandie bottom" close to the *Espirito Santo*. She was the American 131-ton brig *Hersilia*. Built in Mystic, Connecticut, she was sixty-eight feet overall, twenty-two feet eight inches in beam and had a depth in the hold of ten feet. This was her maiden voyage. She had sailed from Stonington in July 1819 under the command of an experienced sealer, James Sheffield, who was also one of her eight owners. Her second mate was the twenty-year-old Nathaniel Palmer, also from Stonington. Not on this voyage, but on later voyages, Palmer's activities were to earn him a place in American polar hagiography. Although fitted out for sealing, the *Hersilia* also carried trade goods for the South American market, insurance against a poor sealing season. Somewhere on the passage south, possibly in Buenos Aires, Montevideo, or the Falkland Islands, Sheffield learned of Smith's discovery. That keen Yankee nose had found the islands and a sealing bonanza. The Americans only spent sixteen days clubbing and skinning seals before they sailed with a cargo of 8,868 skins. More could have been carried, but they had run out of salt.

As the sealers went about their business, Bransfield and the *Williams*, on 27 January, sailed from King George' Bay and set a southwesterly course along the south shores of the islands. On the same day, 1,400 miles to the east and 420 miles closer to the South Pole, two Russian naval vessels, having crossed the Antarctic Circle, were sailing south in cold gloomy weather and snow squalls. The weather cleared sufficiently for the officers to take sun sights that put them at 69°21′S. Ahead of the ships, according to the expedition commander, lay a "solid stretch of ice running east through south to west. Our course was leading us straight into this field, which was covered with ice hillocks." Another officer wrote that "we encountered continental ice of exceptional height and on that magnificent evening, looking from the cross-trees, it extended as far as the eye could see. . . ." The Russians were seeing the ice shelf rimming this section of Antarctica. They were, in fact, seeing Antarctica. The first sighting. But we must leave the Russians eyeing this strange-looking ice front—they were to see it again—and return to the *Williams* sailing along the southern shores of the South Shetlands.

By 29 January the *Williams* had sailed eighty miles along the shores of these bleak-looking islands, had sighted land (Deception Island) soon lost in the fog, and turned south across the strait that now bears Bransfield's name. The next day they sighted Tower Island rising to a thousand feet, with more land lying behind it. Passing to the west and then south of Tower Island, they soon had a better view of the mountain ranges of the Antarctic Peninsula, which rise close to seven thousand feet. It was, as one midshipman recorded in his journal, "a prospect the most gloomy that can be imagined, and the only cheer the sight afforded was the idea that this might be the long-sought Southern Continent. . . ." Bransfield named it and recorded it on his chart as "Trinity Land partly covered with snow." The midshipman was right: they were seeing, a few days after the Russians, part of Antarctica.

They now stretched away to the northeast, the land to starboard, sailing in reef-strewn waters with the added danger of thick fog. It cleared to show the shore lined with icebergs and two high mountains—the present-day Mount Jacquinot and Mount Bransfield. They groped northerly in thick fog, passed and named O'Brien Island, saw land to starboard—Gibbs Island—sighted Elephant Island, and off the north shore, landed on an island they called Seal Island after the "ninety fine fur skins" taken. On 4 February Bransfield landed on the east coast of Clarence Island, "and planted in a small cove, at the foot of a most tremendous precipice, a board with an inscription similar to that which was left on the coast of George's Bay. . . ." Clarence Island—with a peak rising to 6,312 feet—Bransfield marked on his chart as being visible at a distance of one hundred miles. (Seventy-three years later, aboard the *Balaena,* one of a four-ship whaling exploratory voyage from Scotland, Dr. William Bruce recorded seeing Clarence Island from a distance of eighty miles.)

The *Williams* now made a southerly course into the Weddell Sea until stopped by pack ice. They were eighty miles south and two hundred miles east of their plotted position for Trinity Land. Unknown to themselves, they were now on the east side of the Antarctic Peninsula. The return passage was uneventful: north of Elephant Island and back along the north shores of the South Shetland Islands. On 19 March they saw the last of these islands which presented such a "dreary and dismal aspect." The *Hersilia* and the *Espirito Santo* had long since sailed north.

The *Williams* reached Valparaiso on 15 April, discharged from service in the Royal Navy, and Bransfield, the surgeon, and the three midshipmen returned to their ships. And William Smith prepared the *Williams* for a return trip to his discovery. This time for sealing. Smith also heard the story of Cochrane taking the forts guarding Valdivia's harbor, the surrender of the town—and all at the cost of twenty-six casualties by Cochrane's mercenary forces. It was an exploit worthy of that old rogue Francis Drake. But Cochrane, it was rumored, was thinking of resigning in an argument over prize money—the ex-frigate captain was always arguing over money—with the patriot Chilean government of Bernardo O'Higgins.

Bransfield's journal and chart was sent to the Hydrographic Office in England, where the journal was promptly lost. Only the chart remains, and the account of the voyage written by one of the midshipmen that appeared in the *Literary Gazette* of November 1821. Bransfield and his crew had sighted the continent, and also, unknown to themselves, had been the first vessel to sail—albeit only a short distance—into the Weddell Sea.

A few weeks after the *Williams* had arrived back in Valparaiso, the *Hersilia,* on 21 May 1820, sailed into Stonington with her cargo of seal-skins—they sold for $22,146.49—and the electrifying news of the sealing paradise on the islands south of Cape Horn. On the same day, across the globe, the two Russian vessels that had sighted the ice shelf rimming Antarctica were standing out from Sydney bound on a Pacific cruise before returning to the waters below the Convergence.

"Emperor Alexander Pavlovich of glorious memory, desiring to help extend the fields of knowledge, ordered the despatch of two expeditions, each consisting of two vessels, for the exploration of the higher latitudes of the Arctic and Antarctic Oceans." So run the resounding words of the President of the Scientific Committee of the Imperial Naval Staff introducing the first edition of the *Voyage of Captain Bellingshausen to the Antarctic Seas 1818–1821*. The impressive opening is somewhat at variance with the rather late publication date of 1831: two volumes with an atlas—and only six hundred copies. Bellingshausen has been ill served by posterity. St. Petersburg, having digested Bellingshausen's journals, reports, charts, saw little to gain in Antarctica. Central Asia was a more pressing concern.* Bellingshausen's narrative remained in Russian until 1902, when it was translated into German. The first English translation only appeared in 1945 with the Hakluyt Society's volumes, edited by Frank Debenham. Bellingshausen's track did not appear on any British chart until 1837. Only a handful of geographers and fewer seamen knew of his voyage. Nathaniel Palmer, who met Bellingshausen at the South Shetlands in 1821, could not even remember his name. Fifty-five years later Palmer recorded the meeting with "Admiral Krustenstern" and the "Frigate 'Rostok' & a sloop of the name I have forgotten. . . ." Which is a classic example of the faulty memory of old age.

H. R. Mill, in his 1905 *The Siege of the South Pole,* described Bellingshausen's voyage as a "masterly continuation of that of Cook, supplementing it in every particular, competing with it in none." Thaddeus Thaddevich Bellingshausen was born in 1778 (a year before Cook's death) on the Estonian island of Saaremaa. The Bellingshausens were well-established Baltic Germans (the family house, now a mental institution, still

* In 1817 General Sir Robert Wilson published his *Sketch of the Military and Political Power of Russia*. A best-seller, it ran to five editions. Wilson's credentials were impeccable. The official British observer with the Russian armies, he had witnessed the burning of Moscow in 1812 and sent the first news of Napoleon's retreat to Britain. Wilson's book warned the British public of Russia's alarming expansion. During the sixteen years of Alexander's reign, two hundred thousand square miles of territory and thirteen million subjects had been added to the Imperial domain. The Russian army had increased from 80,000 to 640,000. Russia's appetite for more territory and subjects, Wilson warned, had not been sated. The main meal would be British India. The first shots had been fired in the Great Game.

stands) and the young Bellingshausen joined the Imperial Navy in 1789. Most of his career was spent with the Black Sea fleet, but for three years, 1803–6, he served as fifth officer during the Imperial Navy's first circumnavigation commanded by Admiral Krusenstern. This Russian officer had served in the British Royal Navy and attempted to model the Russian navy on the same lines. Both he and Bellingshausen were fervent admirers of James Cook, to the point of worship. He was, for them, the *ne plus ultra* of seamen.

The Emperor's reasons for ordering the two-pronged investigation of both Arctic and Antarctic were twofold. After the defeat of Napoleon, and with Russian troops entering Paris in 1814 (it is said that one Russian legacy in the French language is the word *bistro*—from the Russian *bystro* meaning "quick"), Alexander's sense of manifest destiny, both for himself and Russia, intensified. The unstable Tsar, often awash in floods of religious mania, saw himself as the God-ordained leader of the Christian monarchies. Its concrete expression came with the signing, in 1815, of the "Holy Alliance" between the sovereigns of Russia, Austria, and Prussia. Other European monarchs, with a few exceptions, soon followed. Metternich, the cynical Austrian minister, called the document "a loud-sounding nothing," and Castlereagh, the British Foreign Secretary, damned it as "a piece of sublime mysticism and nonsense." More practical reasons for the expeditions—as opposed to the mystical sense of destiny—were to train a cadre of seamen for the Imperial Navy and to discover lands for "establishing future permanent sea communications or places for the repair of ships."

Russia's empire now stretched across the Bering Strait into North America. Communications to the Russia west of the Urals were long, arduous, and difficult. The government had to maintain an expensive communication and transport system across the monstrous stretches of Siberian forest, steppes, swamps, rivers, and plains. Goods had to be broken down to transportable size; ship's cables cut to fifty-foot lengths; heavy anchors moved in pieces. The furs traveled back at an exorbitant cost to the national treasury. Transportation by ship would be much easier and cheaper. But Russia, unlike France, Britain, Holland, Portugal and Spain, had no possessions scattered across the world's oceans. In the Southern Ocean, perhaps, one could be found.

Bellingshausen heard of his appointment to command the Antarctic expedition in April 1819 while he was stationed on the Black Sea. A month later he was receiving his orders at St. Petersburg, where he learned that the expedition consisted of two ships. the *Vostok* (East), 130 feet overall, 33 feet in beam, and with a 10 foot draft, built the previous year of unseasoned pinewood at St. Petersburg. Lieutenant Commander Ivan Zavodovski, well known to Bellingshausen, was her commander. The consort was the smaller *Mirnyi* (Peaceful), an ex-transport, 120 feet overall and 30 feet in beam, commanded by Lieutenant Mikail Lazarev. The *Mirnyi*, a poor sailer, was to prove a great trial to Bellingshausen over the next two years. The total complement of the expedition came to 190 men and included an astronomer, an artist, and a priest. Two German naturalists were supposed to join the expedition at Copenhagen, but refused at the last moment. Which led Bellingshausen to make some acid comments on the German-dominated Imperial Academy of Science and its refusal to appoint Russian naturalists.

With a munificence not often seen in autocratic governments, the ships' company were paid eight times the normal rate; the officers, astronomer, and artist were given a mess allowance; an entire year's pay was given to all officers and men. Close attention was paid to the victualing, which included salt beef, salt and fresh pork, wheat and rye biscuits, sauerkraut, beef tea in tablet form, clear soups, tea, molasses, sugar, cocoa, spruce essence, cider, and vinegar. The spruce essence and molasses were for the making of beer: "As beer is the healthiest drink at sea, it would seem beneficial to give it frequently to the men."—so ran part of the orders from the Imperial Admiralty Council.

Bellingshausen, scanning the pages of instructions pouring out from the Admiralty Council, the Imperial Admiralty Department, and the Minister of Naval Affairs probably heaved a sigh of relief when he noted a paragraph to the effect that "The Imperial Academy of Science, owing to lack of time, has not prepared instructions for the scientific staff. . . ." No matter, continues the remorseless Minister of Naval Affairs; he was here forwarding some guidelines on the subject. Geodetic, astronomical, pendulum experiments for gravity readings, navigation, lunar distances, flood and ebb tides, compass variation, barometric pressures, atmospheric conditions, wind direction at different altitudes (using small balloons), seawater and salinity observations at different depths, ice conditions and formations, native dyes and substances. Natives themselves should be studied as to color, stature, and constitution, not forgetting their "inner anatomy should it be possible to obtain bodies for dissection." Not to be forgotten either were geology, mineralogy, and botany. The artists were expected to draw "all that may be seen in Nature, and an accurate delineation of any rare and curious things worthy of note will be expected from their efforts." Finally, just in case anything had escaped the Minister's wide-flung net, Bellingshausen "must not neglect any opportunities for making investigations, notes and observations of anything which may help in the advancement of science in general, or in any of those branches in particular."

After six hectic weeks Bellingshausen and his two ships sailed from Kronstadt on 4 July 1819.* After a call at Copenhagen the *Vostok* and

* Russia was still on the old-style Julian calendar; twelve days should be added for the Gregorian calendar.

Mirnyi were anchored at Spithead, off Portsmouth, by 30 July. Next day the officers were posting toward London to buy charts, books, telescopes, transit instruments, sextants, chronometers, and Mr. Donkin's tinned food—And also play the tourist, with visits to St. Paul's, Westminster Abbey, the Tower, Vauxhall Gardens, and the theatres. The seventy-five-year-old Sir Joseph Banks, gout-ridden, ailing, and wheelchair bound—but still President of the Royal Society—was consulted in the hopes of finding naturalists to replace the wayward Germans. But it was all too short notice. And the Russians sailed from Portsmouth on 26 August minus an important part of their scientific staff.

Bellingshausen, following Cook's example, put the ship's company on a three-watch system, paid careful attention to the cleanliness of his men, and gave orders that their linen be changed twice a week and hammocks washed twice a month. As they sailed out into the Atlantic, he had the surgeon inspect the men for venereal diseases. Much to his surprise the *Vostok*'s men were apparently free. "This," as Bellingshausen recorded, "may be regarded as very unusual, as there are more prostitutes in England than anywhere else, particularly in the chief ports."

After a stop to load water, wine, and fresh provisions at Tenerife, they sailed south and crossed the equator on 18 October. Bellingshausen was the only person in the expedition who had previously crossed the legendary line. A bucket of water was drawn from the sea and Bellingshausen sprinkled the officers and cadets ". . . to introduce them, so to speak, to the waters of the southern hemisphere." The introduction for the seamen was a little more drastic: the purser—having been sprinkled by his commander—heaved a full jug of water into their faces. It was still remarkably more decorous than the mayhem practiced by Cook's sailors. Indeed, a reading of Bellingshausen's narrative shows his men, particularly on feast days, behaving with an almost nunlike demureness: but perhaps this is the commander, with an eye cocked for his readers' sensibilities, smoothing the rough corners of his seamen.

"With the exception of Mr Lazarev, Mr Zavodovski and myself, none of the officers in either ship had ever had occasion to make astronomical observations." The sentence leaps off the page in Bellingshausen's narrative, and one suddenly realizes the need for this voyage to train a cadre of officers in the embryonic Russian navy. Each one of the officers had bought a sextant in London or Portsmouth—and by the time they had reached Rio de Janeiro all were familiar with celestial navigation, including lunar distances. The voyage, in fact, was to become noted for its precision in navigation and the prodigious number of sights taken to check their position and rating of the chronometers.

The Russians spent three weeks in Rio de Janeiro—a town, according to Bellingshausen, with a disgustingly dirty appearance. All the summits of the hills were crowded by monasteries where only the men of God had the "benefit of fresh healthy air and the pleasures of fine prospects from the heights." The slave markets, with their cramped masses of wretched Africans, appalled Bellingshausen. Twelve years later it was to be an opinion shared by Charles Darwin—and lead to the argument between Darwin and Captain FitzRoy of the *Beagle*.

The *Vostok* and the *Mirnyi* sailed on 22 November loaded with oxen, sheep, forty large pigs, twenty suckling pigs, ducks, hens, rum, sugar, lemons, pumpkins, onions, garlic, and green vegetables. Last to be loaded were bales of hay for the oxen and sheep. Bellingshausen set a course for South Georgia, some two thousand miles to the south, and the first stage of their polar voyage. On the evening of 12 December, two hundred miles off the island, the air temperature suddenly dropped 5 degrees Fahrenheit. They had crossed south of the Convergence. A day later they had their first snow. On 15 December, surrounded by blue petrels, snow petrels, albatross, "pestrushki,"* penguins, and whales, they sighted Willis Island and South Georgia.

Cook had surveyed the north shore of South Georgia. Bellingshausen would do the same for the south shore. As they sailed along the coast, out from one of the bays sailed a small boat flying British colors. It was soon hove to under the lee of the *Vostok*. Three men were aboard—one of them a Russian who had deserted a Russian warship at an English port. The deserter explained they were off two British whalers anchored in one of the bays. They had been on the island for four months taking elephant seals for their oil. The sealers, said the Russian, moved along the shores in their boats, found a seal beach, landed, went about their business, all the while living under their upturned boat and using penguin skins and blubber scraps to fire the try-pots and cook their food. Bellingshausen gave them a much welcomed present of grog, sugar, and butter, and the sealers sped back toward the grim-looking island.

By 18 December, amid frequent snow and sleet squalls, Bellingshausen decided to end his running survey of an island "frozen and, so to say, dead. . . ." Waiting for better weather could only shorten his voyage into the high latitudes. His next investigation would be the Sandwich Land or Sandwich Islands discovered by James Cook. On 20 December they sailed by their first iceberg—which "made a great impression upon us." Two days later a small unknown island was sighted and named by Bellingshausen after the third lieutenant of the *Vostok*—Lyskov. Next day another island was sighted and named Visokoi Island (High Island). Soon a third island was seen. This one was more unusual, for from it "a thick stinking vapour was continually rising." They named it Zavodovski Island; they were seeing the tip of an active volcano.

On 24 December Zavodovski made a landing on his island and found

---

* Cape pigeons, or pintado petrels.

huge numbers of penguins incubating eggs. The landing party climbed halfway up the volcano, swinging sticks to clear a path through the penguins; they found the ground hot beneath their feet and were forced to return by the combined smell of warm penguin guano and fumes from the crater. (A glance at a modern map of the island leaves the reader with the distinct feeling that nothing has changed. The island's circumference is about nine miles; the highest point is Mount Asphyxia, at 1,805 feet. The features of the coast bear such names as Acrid Point, Stench Point, Fume Point, Reek Point, Pungent Point, and Noxious Bluff. The author landed on the island in 1983 and scrambled up a gully dug by snowmelt. The bottom of the steep-sided gully was carpeted with dead penguin chicks—pushed there by adult penguins.)

That evening, the clothing of some of them rich with the island's pungent smells, the Vostoks and Mirnyis celebrated Christmas Eve and "the anniversary of the deliverance of Russia from the invasion of the French. . . ." It was favorite Russian fare: cabbage soup with pickled cabbage, fresh pork, pie of rice and minced meat. For drink each man had half a tankard of beer followed by a glass of rum punch with lemon and sugar.

It was 5 January before Bellingshausen had completed his survey of Sandwich Land. It had been carried out under vile conditions in seemingly perpetual gales, snow, rain, sleet, fog, and amidst ice floes and icebergs. The weather would clear for an instant; the officers would scramble to take their sights, plot the islands, and Paul Mikhailov, the artist, would make elegant sketches of the grim-looking clumps of rock, snow, and ice. The sketches still appear in the *Antarctic Pilot*. Their painstaking efforts showed that Sandwich Land—including their own discoveries—was but a stretch of islands, volcanic in origin, with no connection to any southern continent.

Having settled the matter, the two vessels stood east. Following Cook's example they collected ice for fresh water—the large amount of livestock also had to have their water. Penguins standing on ice floes were captured and ended up in the cook's boilers—the men making caps from the skins and using the oil to grease their leather boots. Some of the birds were kept alive, put in the chicken runs, and fed on pork. They soon died.

Just west of the Greenwich meridian, Bellingshausen made his dive south. On 15 January they crossed the Antarctic Circle and a day later were stopped by *materik* (continental) ice. In all probability they were seeing the edge of the present-day Finibul Ice Shelf, which rims the Crown Princess Martha Coast of Antarctica. Ice shelf fronts advance and retreat, and it is probable that the front in 1820 was further north than it is today. Ice shelves can be considered an integral part of the continent—not quite so obvious as the Trinity Land sighted by Bransfield a few days later, but still Antarctica.

A few days later, farther east, they were once more stopped by the same type of ice: the "materik" ice once again. Bellingshausen turned north and then east. On 2 February they altered course to the south. It was snowing heavily when they crossed the Antarctic Circle for the third time. On 5 February they reached 69°07′S, close to 15°W longitude. Across their path stretched another strange ice front: "A continent of ice, whose edges are broken off perpendicularly . . . ice islands near that continent show clearly that pieces are broken off this continent, because they have edges and

Bellingshausen's *Vostok* and *Mirnyi*. Sketch by Paul Mikhailov.
Courtesy of the Scott Polar Research Institute

surfaces similar to the continent." So wrote Bellingshausen in a letter to the Minister of Naval Affairs. In his narrative Bellingshausen wrote, "Its edge was perpendicular and formed into little coves, whilst the surface sloped upwards towards the south to a distance so far that its end was out of sight even from the mast-head." The Russians were seeing the ice shelf that rims the Princess Astrid Coast.

Bellingshausen now attempted to sail south, near to the longitude where Cook had first crossed the Antarctic Circle—not in an attempt to beat Cook's record, but to compare the ice conditions forty-seven years later. The pack ice stopped them sixteen miles north of Cook's most southerly position. They had now been thirteen weeks at sea since leaving Rio de Janeiro. In order to bolster his men's morale in the grim sailing conditions, Bellingshausen made sure that all Russian feast days and festivals were kept with punctilious regard. It meant welcome additions to their standard rations and extra issues of punch, grog, and wine, which perhaps compensated for the inconvenience of having to dress in full uniform. The *Vostok* and *Mirnyi* now sailed east, below 60°S latitude, across the unexplored section of the Southern Ocean where Cook had made his northerly sweep to search for Kerguelen Island. By the first week in March Bellingshausen decided it was time to leave these high southern latitudes, where the temperature hovered 8 degrees Fahrenheit below freezing, where snow and spray froze an inch thick on sails, rigging, tackles, hull, and deck. Where in these "dark, harsh climes it seems as if men's hearts grow cold in sympathy with the surrounding objects, men become gloomy, depressed, harsh and to a certain extent indifferent to everything. . . ."

It was decided that two vessels would separate, with the *Mirnyi* taking a more northerly course for Australia—but a course some 150 miles south of that taken by Furneaux and the *Adventure*. The *Vostok* would hold a more southerly track. But even sailing in lower latitudes brought small relief. For over a week the *Vostok* labored under storm-force winds, riding it out under bare poles, with hammocks lashed to the mizzen shrouds to give windage aft and keep her head closer to the wind and seas—no sail was strong enough to be set without being ripped to shreds.

At the end of March the *Vostok* sailed into Sydney harbor and anchored off the town. They had been 131 days at sea, and the surgeon reported that only two men showed signs of scurvy. The sheep and pigs were far worse off: every single one of them showed signs of the disease. Lazarev and the *Mirnyi* sailed into Sydney a week later. And found that their countrymen had set up tents ashore and made themselves at home, with one of the tents acting as a steam bath: the steam coming from red-hot cannonballs doused with water.

After refitting, the ships set off on a four-month circuit of the South Pacific. First they sailed to New Zealand, where at Queen Charlotte Sound they ate descendants of potatoes planted by Cook's expedition. A call was made at Tahiti to rate the chronometers at Point Venus. The island remained the same, but neither Cook or Banks would have recognized the islanders. Missionaries from the London Missionary Society had landed in force on the island in 1797 and immediately set about destroying the islanders' culture with puritanical zeal. The easygoing natives proved no match for the artisan warriors of the Lord: gone were the long tresses of the women and the native dress. The hair was cropped short and European calico prints primly covered the women's bodies. Gone too were the ancient games, dances, and amusements. The Sabbath day was sacred to the Lord. Although liquor was banned, it soon became obvious to the Russians that bottles of grog had replaced nails as the unit of currency when dealing with European ships. King Pomare asked Bellingshausen to write him a note in Russian asking that the bearer of the note be given a bottle of rum. "I wrote," recorded the warmhearted Bellingshausen—perhaps to outmaneuver Mr. Nott, the English missionary—"to the effect that he should be given three bottles of rum and six bottles of Teneriffe wine." The South Sea Garden of Eden, Bougainville's "New Cythera," had turned into a "New Jerusalem": English lower-middle-class Protestant version.

The South Pacific voyage ended back at Sydney on 9 September. The ships were unrigged, all the running rigging was replaced, strengthening was added to the hulls, pens were built for the pigs—Bellingshausen had found that "these animals require an absolutely quiet place protected against damp and cold."

The Russian minister in Rio de Janeiro had sent a dispatch to Bellingshausen in Sydney giving word of William Smith's discovery of the South Shetlands. Here, then, were more islands for the Russians to survey on the next stage of the polar voyage. But this news was not confined to the Russians alone. The word had also reached the sealers sailing out of Sydney. The Sydney-owned brig *Lynx* sailed a few days after the Russians, bound for the South Shetlands and the new sealing grounds.

The Russians sailed on 31 October. On board were pigs, sheep, and eighty-four birds, including cockatoos, parrots, doves, a lory, and a parakeet. And they all made a great deal of noise: screeching, whistling, and with the parrots squawking their few words of English. A small kangaroo romped loose about the deck, destined to become the sailors' favorite pet. Adding to the noise of the departure were the guns fired in salute to the fort and returned by the fort. And Mr. Piper, the port captain, fired his own personal farewell salute from his house on the promontory overlooking the harbor. The Russians had been freely welcomed by this small colonial town and felt pangs of regret at departing. Ahead of them, as they well knew, lay uncomfortable months.

Bellingshausen, in order to explore waters untouched by Cook, set course for Macquarie Island, 1,230 miles to the south of Sydney. From here they would sail into the unknown. A week out, the *Vostok* sprang a leak near the bow—a leak so serious and gushing in with such force that it could be heard. Its position made it impossible to repair; but to return to Sydney for repairs would eat into the short season. They would sail on under shortened sail, nursing the *Vostok*. Carronades were struck down into the hold and carpenters fitted internal stanchions and braces to stiffen the working hull. A few days later, in gale-force winds and a vile cross-sea, the *Vostok* was laboring so badly that the noise of the creaking hull, beams, and bulkheads drove the officers from their cabins to huddle on the quarterdeck in wet misery. It was not an auspicious start for their second polar venture.

Macquarie, however, proved a pleasant surprise. They had seen the grim snow- and ice-covered bastions of South Georgia and expected the same from Macquarie: both islands were set in the same latitude. This new landfall proved to be beautifully green, snow and ice free. Admittedly, the weather stayed wet and windy—but this was only to be expected from any outcrop of rock set in the Southern Ocean.

Sealers came out to greet them, and, after being lubricated by offerings of butter, grog and biscuits, became eager to help these strange visitors. The Russians learned that two gangs of sealers were working on the island, one of thirteen men and the other of twenty-seven. Some had been on the island for nine months—one man had spent six years without leaving—and all were elephant sealing for oil. The fur seals had been totally exterminated. The Russians were shown the sealers' crude living quarters—they had to be led in by hand, as the hovels were so dark—with their seal bladder windows and blubber fires. The sealers, over their mugs of grog, told the Russians how they lived: the killing of the seals, the cutting off of the blubber, the rendering into oil in the try-pots. All to be shipped to Sydney and Britain. For food they had penguins and penguin eggs—in season—elephant seal flippers, sea birds, and an antiscorbutic cabbage. The sealers scraped the stalks and roots, cut them up fine, and made a soup of it. Bellingshausen, realizing the value of this wild cabbage, had loads of it brought aboard to make *shtshi*—the Russian cabbage soup. Later in the voyage he wished that more had been brought on board.

On 20 November, having given the sealers more rum and provisions, the Russians made their farewells and watched Macquarie vanish in the murk astern. Nearly two months were to pass before they saw land again. And those weeks were filled with storms, danger, discomfort and near disastrous collisions with fog-shrouded icebergs as they skirted the pack ice lying to the south. The *Vostok*'s pumps worked continuously, swirling water across the deck. It is one of the ironies of this voyage that if Bellingshausen had returned to make repairs at Sydney, the later sailing into the waters south of Macquarie would have found the band of pack ice guarding the gateway to the Ross Sea vanished. It was to be twenty years before James Clark Ross with the *Erebus* and *Terror* found the gateway—but that was two months later in the season. Such are the fortunes of discovery.

With the pack ice to the south of them, the Russians sailed east, below 60°S latitude and close to the Antarctic Circle, avoiding Cook's track wherever possible. Two inches of ice encased the spars, rigging, and sails; it had to be beaten off with hammers and clubs. Feast days and festivals were observed with proper ritual. St. Nicholas's Day—Nicholas being the patron saint of Russia and protector of sailors—on 6 December, with Macquarie cabbage soup, fresh pork, pickled cabbage, lemon juice, wine, spruce beer. The Tsar's birthday on 12 December, with prayers of thanksgiving and a twenty-one-gun salute. Christmas Day with more prayers of thanksgiving on the delivery of their country from Napoleon's invasion. New Year's Day 1821 celebrated with a glass of hot punch; after dinner Bellingshausen ordered each man to have a large glass of coffee with rum instead of cream. "This new drink," noted Bellingshausen, "greatly pleased the men and the whole of the day until evening passed very gaily."

During that first week of the New Year the Russians had virtually given up hope of sighting land in the bleakness of the icescape. Suddenly, on 10 January, with no early warning signs of seaweed—there were, however, terns and skuas flying around the ships—land was sighted, showing black in shafts of sunlight coming from behind the clouds. Bellingshausen recorded the moment: "Words cannot describe the delight which appeared on all our faces at the cry of 'Land! Land!' Our joy was not surprising after our monotonous voyage, amidst unceasing dangers from ice, snow, rain, sleet and fog." The next day they managed to sail within fourteen miles of its shores before being stopped by pack ice. But, to their great disappointment, the land proved to be only a small island and no part of a continent. No matter; Bellingshausen gave orders that a glass of hot punch be served to all hands and they drank to the health of the Tsar. The officers busied themselves with measurements of the island's height, which ranged from 4,390 feet to 3,961 feet—the *Antarctic Pilot* gives it as 5,750 feet—and its position by celestial observation: 68°57'S and 90°46'W—very close to its true position. Bellingshausen named it Peter I Island in honor "of the founder of the fleet of the Russian Empire. . . ."*

A week later, still below the Antarctic Circle, on a clear cold day of outstanding beauty, more land was sighted. One of the headlands stretched to the north and ended in a high mountain. Another mountain chain stretched away to the southwest. Pack ice prevented any approach closer than forty miles. Bellingshausen named the new discovery Alexander I Land, adding that he called "this discovery 'land' because its southern extent disappeared beyond the range of our vision. . . ." The discovery remains on modern maps as Alexander Island—it is a large island separated from the continent by a narrow ice-covered sound.

Bellingshausen now set a course for the South Shetlands. On the morning of 24 January a hail came from the lookout: "Land in sight above the clouds!" Poking through the clouds were the 6,900-foot-high peaks of

---

*The first landing on the island was not made until 1929, when Norwegian whalers from the *Norvegia* made a rough survey.

Smith Island. The Russians now sailed northeast along the south shores of the islands, making a running survey as they went. The islands were given Russian names—most of them battle victories over the hated Napoleon: Borodino (Smith Island), Little Yaroslavetz (Snow Island), Smolensk (Livingston Island), Beresina (Greenwich Island), Polotsk (Roberts Island), Leipzig (Nelson Island), Waterloo (King George Island). The last was landed on close to William Smith's North Foreland and the landing party brought back some rocks, moss, seaweed, three live seals, and some penguins. By 29 January they were off the north shore of Elephant Island. Sailing conditions now worsened: in gale force winds and blinding snow the island vanished from sight. It seemed a fitting end for their last sight of land in the Antarctic.

By now the *Vostok*'s structural condition and the health of his men worried Bellingshausen. They had pumped their way to the South Shetlands, and the fourteen weeks of damp cold living were showing on all their faces. It was time to steer north for Rio de Janeiro and a much needed overhaul for both men and ships. On 1 February, in 56°35′S, they saw the last of those constant companions—an iceberg. On 8 February, in milder conditions and well north of the Convergence, they opened all hatchways to air the lower decks.

Many of the birds brought on board at Sydney had died, but the hardier survivors were brought on deck, where they "set up a many-voiced chorus." One parrot flew ahead of the *Vostok* and fell into the water. Quickwitted sailors thrust a long pole into the sea and the drowning bird clutched at it in sheer terror. Back on board, such was its fright, hours passed before it unclasped the pole. By 27 February the *Vostok* and *Mirnyi* were anchored in Rio de Janeiro's harbor. They sailed on 23 May and after a call at Lisbon were saluting the forts at Kronstadt on 24 July 1821. They had been away from the anchorage 751 days and sailed 57,073 miles—and no man had been lost to scurvy. It was indeed a voyage to rival Cook's. But the results were very different. The reports of the voyage dropped into the bureaucratic black hole of the Russian administration: all Bellingshausen's efforts might never have happened. Alexander I's fevered mind seemed more concerned with secret societies, military colonies, and repression of dissent. Central Asia, not the Antarctic, was to become St. Petersburg's concern.

The expedition, like all good expeditions, was one without major catastrophic incident. But a minor incident—which concerns this narrative— did occur during the days spent surveying the South Shetlands. On 25 January 1821 the Russians spotted eight British and American sealers anchored close to the shore. A few hours later, when between Deception and Livingston Islands, the Russians encountered a "small American sealing boat." It was the *Hero* and Nathaniel Palmer out of Stonington. Let Bellingshausen take up the story:

I lay to, despatched a boat, and waited for the Captain of the American boat. The lead did not touch bottom at 115 fathoms. Soon after Mr Palmer arrived in our boat and informed us that he had been here for four months' sealing in partnership with three American ships. They were engaged in killing and skinning seals, whose numbers were perceptibly diminishing. There were as many as eighteen vessels about at various points, and not infrequently differences arose amongst the sealers, but so far it had not yet come to a fight. Mr Palmer told me that the above-mentioned Captain Smith, the discoverer of New Shetland, was on the brig *Williams,* that he had succeeded in killing as many as 60,000 seals, whilst the whole fleet of sealers had killed 80,000. As other sealers also were round the South Shetland Islands just as at South Georgia and Macquarie Islands the numbers of these sea animals will rapidly decrease. Sea elephants, of which there also had been many, had already moved from these shores farther out to sea. . . . Mr Palmer soon returned to his ship, and we proceeded along the shore.

Bellingshausen's comment on the fate of the fur seals was to prove accurate. This was the second—and most bloody—of the South Shetland Islands' sealing seasons. And one in which the Stonington sealers took a major part.

The *Atlantic Coast Pilot,* published by the U.S. Coast Survey Office in 1878, had this to say of Stonington:

The village of Stonington is of some importance, especially during the summer—being in the vicinity of the hotels at Watch Hill, and also the terminus of the New York and Stonington line of steamers—a favorite route to Boston during the summer. Above the village the eastern shore of the harbor is composed of low, level lands, almost entirely cleared, dotted with handsome houses, surrounded by ornamental grounds.

Which sounds more like a publicity leaflet from the local chamber of commerce than sailing directions. Except for the "line of steamers" the *Pilot*'s description, over a hundred years later, still fits this pleasant Connecticut town. And during the summer months, as with other shoreside villages, the summer crowds still take over: the *thonk* of tennis balls from the yacht club courts mixes with the clanking of wire halyards from the moored yachts, the whine of outboard motors, the more subdued rattle of ice cubes in the endless round of summer socializing. The casual summer visitor taking an evening stroll along the pleasant tree-lined streets might perhaps tingle to a surge of patriotic pride at seeing the cannons which fought off British warships commanded by Commodore Sir Thomas Hardy during August of 1814. Eyeing the lovely Greek Revival and Federal buildings, the same visitor, if the patriotism were diluted with conservation concerns, would perhaps suffer a bout of middle class angst when the thought strikes home that these buildings were built on money from sealing. Such concerns would have bewildered the inhabitants of Stonington in 1820.

The news of Smith's discovery appeared in the marine columns of New England papers during late March and early April of 1820. Its potential as a new sealing ground sent ripples of excitement along the waterfronts.

Only five sealers had sailed from United States ports in 1819. The old sealing grounds for fur seals appeared to be exhausted, the voyages long, the profits slim. The return of the *Hersilia* to Stonington with a cargo of skins gathered in a few days—and sold at a handsome profit—turned the ripples of excitement into a tidal wave. The *Hersilia*'s crew, it was said, had seen three hundred thousand seals at one view. Here indeed were rich pickings.

Edmund Fanning, the old sealer from earlier days, set about organizing a fleet to sail from Stonington. The brig *Frederick*, commanded by Benjamin Pendleton, had sailed from Stonington intent upon a sealing voyage just a few days before the return of the *Hersilia*. Her consort, however, the schooner *Free Gift*, commanded by Thomas Dunbar, still lay at Stonington. It was all quickly organized. The *Free Gift*, due to rendezvous with the *Frederick*, would carry *Hersilia*'s news and sailing instructions for the South Shetlands. Three other vessels would follow and all would work together. Young Nathaniel Palmer with his share of the *Hersilia*'s skins now became part owner of the schooner *Express* and commander and part owner of the sloop *Hero*. Built at Groton, the flush-decked sloop, only some forty-seven feet overall but beamy at close to seventeen feet, with a shallow draft of just under seven feet, would search for new sealing beaches and transfer skins from shore to the larger vessels anchored in a protected harbor. The last vessel in the fleet was the *Hersilia*. But this was not the only fleet fitting out in Stonington—the *Clothier*, the *Emeline*, the *Catherine*, and the small *Spark*, serving the same function as the *Hero*, were all readying themselves for the passage south.

Over fifty men had shares in the ownership of the nine Stonington vessels. And the names have a sonorous, New England biblical ring: Elisha Faxon, Jedediah Randall, Peleg Denison, Enoch Burrows, Nathan Smith, Asa Lee, Ephriam Williams, Zebenton Hancox, Jeremiah Holmes, Cyrus Williams, Jedediah Perkins, Nathan Sanborn, Nathaniel Palmer, Issac Williams. All names, one likes to think, that were carefully inked onto the flyleaf of the large family Bible at their baptism.

As the supplies went aboard the Stonington vessels the same frantic activity was taking place in New York, Boston, Salem, Nantucket, New Bedford, and Fairhaven. Hogsheads of navy bread, barrels of salt beef, salt pork, salt cod, white beans, peas, molasses, sugar, mustard, vinegar, corn meal, potatoes, dried apples, flour, rice, coffee, tea, rum, gin, Teneriffe wine, candles, wicks, lumber, spikes, nails, paint, copper sheets, spare oars, boat anchors, tar, whale line, fish lines, hooks, guns, ammunition, seal clubs, skinning knives, beaming knives, mincing knives, sharpening steels, try-pots, ladles: all went aboard and found a stowage place.

In New York, James Byers, a merchant, a shipowner, and a man familiar with the sealing business, was busy putting together a four-vessel fleet. On another front he was lobbying the U.S. government to send a warship to take possession of the islands and protect the American sealers who were prepared—his men at least—to make a permanent settlement on the islands. Possession was essential, as "the new islands or Continent may prove as profitable to our country as Nootka Sound trade to England. Depend upon it, this business is well worth the serious attention of Govt." This in one of a series of letters to General Daniel Parker, Adjutant and Inspector General of the U.S. Army. Parker sent the letters to Secretary of State John Quincy Adams—a man keenly aware of the tune played by mercantile, fishing, and whaling interests. Adams in turn passed the letters and those from the U.S. agents in South America to President James Monroe.

Adams, in a covering letter, urged action by sending a frigate to take possession and thought the idea of a settlement "a very good expedient for protecting the real objects—to catch seals and whales. . . ." London, no doubt, would be very annoyed: "Just now they have their hands so full of Coronations and Adulteries, Liturgy, prayers and Italian Sopranos, Bergamis and Pergamis, High Treasons and Petty Treasons, Pains, Penalties and Paupers, that they will seize the first opportunity they can to shake them all off, and if they can make a question of national honour about a foot-hold . . . upon something between Rock and Ice-Berg, as this discovery must be, and especially a question with us, they will not let it escape them."* Nevertheless, Adams rather relished the thought of tweaking the nose of Lord Castlereagh, his opposite number in London. It was a prospect "Quite fascinating," in fact.

Monroe, a little hazy as to his geography—like other Presidents—thought that the "discovery of land in the Pacific, of great extent, is an important event, and there are strong reasons in favor of your suggestion to aim at its occupancy on our part." It was now up to the Secretary of the navy to find a frigate and, a sudden prudent thought crossing the President's mind, "strengthen our force along the American coast."

Byers, meanwhile, was redoubling his efforts to sway the U.S. government. His vessels had sailed and were equipped to build huts, the men to

* Adams's obviously delighted remarks on "Coronations and Adulteries etc." refer to the tribulations of the British monarchy and government. Queen Caroline, George IV's estranged wife, had been living abroad since 1813 and, it was hinted, had had many lovers, including her majordomo, an Italian named Bartolomeo Bergami. She had returned in 1820 to claim her rights as queen on the death of George III. The London mob had taken her cause to its rough-and-ready heart: anything to wipe the eye of the despised George, who had persuaded his ministers to put her on trial in the House of Lords for adultery. And adultery by a queen consort, under a fourteenth-century law, could be accounted high treason. Italian witnesses gave evidence before the goggling peers, the mobs rioted, broadsheets were distributed, petitions gathered, verses composed—all in support of Caroline. It was the greatest scandal of the year—and the most entertaining. Fear of a revolution forced the King's ministers to abandon the trial. The law on adultery by a consort of the monarch being accounted high treason still remains.

settle the islands, and they had been ordered to be on the sealing grounds by 1 October. "Some think that the 1st of Dec. is as early as we ought to venture in that high latitude—but I know better." Byers, as astute a New York merchant as any, did not know better. He knew nothing of the conditions below the Convergence. In fact his vessels did not arrive on the sealing grounds until December. But Byers, in September, was still fighting from his corner in New York: "If the British Govt. send any armed vessels, they will not, I think, like to approach the high latitudes till about Dec. We Yankees you know, do not fear cold Weather. There is not the least doubt in my mind that but the British will attempt to Drive our Vessels from the Islands. Not by open hostility & blows but by blustering & threats. The vessels from this quarter all went out armed for their own safety against pirates or robbers of any other description, and we will make a bold defence over against John Bull." Poor Byers: by this time it was all too late. The navy had no vessels available . . . dangers of unexplored coast in high latitudes . . . fears of collision with British . . . bringing back American mutineers from West Indies more important . . . etc., etc. So ran the circumspect replies of the Navy Department.

By the time Byers retired, defeated in his efforts to prod the U.S. government into action, his vessels were spread across the Atlantic—some in the Falklands, some still sailing toward the Falklands. The islands were to become the springboard for the South Shetlands. And by October the Yankee sealers were swinging at anchor, shooting geese, collecting eggs, swapping stories, readying themselves for the short passage south. Here too were British sealers, intent upon the same purpose.

Commodore Sir Thomas Hardy's letter of January 1820, informing the Admiralty of William Smith's discovery of the South Shetland Islands, arrived at Spithead on Saturday 29 April, was received at the Admiralty on Sunday, noted by the Secretary and passed on to Captain Thomas Hurd, the Hydrographer, on Monday—and the news became public on Tuesday in the London evening newspaper the *Courier*. Provincial newspapers soon carried the same item, with the last sentence carrying the important bait: "Abundance of seals and whales were found in its neighbourhood." The *Courier*, a few months later, carried further news of the discovery: fifteen thousand skins had been taken—all in a very short time—and sold in Buenos Aires. To men in the sealskin trade—the skinning business, as they called it—stories of fifteen thousand skins collected in a short time were of serious interest. (Thirteen thousand skins from southern sources had been the total brought into England during 1819.)

The effect of these news items and rumors along the waterfronts resulted in the same activity as that taking place in New England's seaports. Vessels were readied, crews collected, masters appointed. During the summer and early autumn months of 1820 the sealing vessels from both countries were sailing south, some in company, some alone, down the long lonely stretches of the North and South Atlantic. For many of them the passage included a call at the Cape Verde Islands to load salt and brackish water; then on to the Falklands for more water, wild fowl, eggs, and beef from the feral cattle. Then a last call at Staten Island for wood and water.

The *Hero* and the *Express* sailed into the Falklands on 16 October to find other American sealers and two British: James Weddell aboard the *Jane* and George Powell aboard the *Eliza*. Palmer, Weddell, and Powell were all to play a significant part in Antarctic exploration. The Stonington men sailed from the Falklands at the end of October. After a stop at Staten Island for wooding, watering, and making some repairs—the *Hero* and the *Express* had collided during the short passage from the Falklands—they sailed for the South Shetlands and the sealing grounds.

Four days later Palmer was "anxiously looking for land. Plenty of penguins, whales and gulls about us." Next day they sighted Smith Island; but they were too far west, and it took them two days to beat up to the *Hersilia*'s old anchorage at Rugged Island. Here they found the *Hersilia*— she had been at the islands for twelve days—with the *Frederick* and the *Free Gift* anchored about two miles away at New Plymouth. The *Antarctic Pilot* has few good things to say about New Plymouth: open to northwest gales and with poor holding ground, it had only one advantage—for sealers, that is: a nearby long, rocky shore much liked by fur seals as a breeding area. By 13 November five vessels of the Stonington fleet were anchored together in the harbor, little better than an open roadstead, and were unloading wood, casks, canvas, and spars to make crude shelters. The seals were "not yet up." But when they did appear they were met by the waiting sealing gangs.

The sealers, following the pattern of male fur seals, established territories—and drove off latecomers and intruders. The skins represented money and sealing gangs from other vessels meant fewer skins for their own vessel. Here were market forces at work in their ugliest guise. One British sealer from the *Hetty* recorded her men being driven off a beach by fellow countrymen wielding sealing clubs and flensing knives. One beach close to New Plymouth is ominously named Robbery Beach. Another incident, a sealing version of a Hollywood cowboy movie, has a group of grim-faced New Englanders hunched together in the cramped oil-lit cabin of a sealer at anchor, in yes, Yankee Harbor, organizing a raiding party to wrest back from the British some stolen sealskins. The Americans had been driven off the beaches along the north shore of Livingston Island: the British regarded this as their territory. The animosities of two wars were being revived. The Yankee skippers thought they could muster 120 men in a sealing posse. The *Huntress*'s log records that "they would have to land and by the best information we can git the English have but about 80 men there." The expedition set off but returned empty-handed. No reason is given in the *Huntress*'s log. But a clue appears in the log of the *Huron*. A boat had been sent ashore but soon returned. They had been met by 60 to 75 English sealers, who were "all armed with Guns, Pistoles, & Swords and appeared in a hostile manner. . . ." The sealers might come to each other's aid when disaster struck and ships were wrecked—five vessels were lost during this 1820–21 season—but they drew the line at sharing seals.

One is appalled at the holocaust visited upon the seals of the South Shetlands during these few months. James Weddell estimated that 320,000 skins were taken off the islands in two seasons, along with 940 tons of elephant seal oil. As the slaughter was so indiscriminate, he also estimated another 100,000 seal pups died with the death of their mothers. As a conservation measure he advocated a limit of 100,000 seals each season. A pious hope: any conservation method would have been unenforceable. The seals, in short, as one English sealer put it, were being murdered "merely for the covering of the animal for the gratification of our pride." Over 200,000 sealskins came on the London market after the 1820–21 season—and this from less than half the sealing fleet. A conservative estimate would put the total seal deaths at over half a million. A century later, L. Harrison Matthews, studying whales at South Georgia, and going out with Norwegians on elephant sealing expeditions, wrote, "Slaughtering seals always degrades and brutalises those who do it. . . ."

Contrasted with this ugly picture of greed and ruthlessness is the seamanship and courage of the sealers—particularly those aboard the small shallops who brought the skins off the exposed beaches to the mother ship anchored in safe harbors. For these men were sailing in dangerous, uncharted waters, making their own sailing directions and rough charts as they slipped along the islands and through the straits. Today's *Antarctic Pilot* still carries ominous warnings and chilling names given to these dangerous waters: Neck-or-Nothing Passage, through which a vessel, on parting her cable in an easterly gale, can run to sea; Hell Gates, where many "lives and boats have been lost"; Turmoil Rock lying close to Chaos Reef, places to be avoided; Cape Danger on Desolation Island, with a nearby anchorage at Blythe Bay where fish may readily be caught on hooks baited with penguin meat. The unwary mariner, however, can also be readily caught. Fine weather is an indication of a coming easterly gale, as is the gathering of large flocks of Cape pigeons in the bay. The mariner is advised to slip his cable and seek shelter elsewhere. Here are the authentic voices of the sealers carried down across the years.

One such voice is that of Robert Fildes from the Liverpool sealer *Cora*. The *Antarctic Pilot* still carries his description of the tidal streams along the north shores of the islands. "Later accounts," says the *Pilot*, tipping its peaked hat in salute, "have not improved on this early description." With their tidal streams running fast, some with whirlpools, through rock- and

reef-strewn straits; with their sudden gales, fogs, and ice, the South Shetlands were—and still remain—no place for the fainthearted.

Two days after the Stonington vessels had collected together at New
Plymouth, Palmer and the *Hero* were sent off by Pendleton to look for
new sealing rookeries and, if possible, a better anchorage. Part of the entry
for Palmer's log on 15 November reads: "Got underweigh on a cruise
stood over for Deception. . . ." Deception Island lies some twenty miles
from New Plymouth (it was the land sighted by Bransfield and "lost in
thick fog"). The question is: how did Palmer know it was called Deception?
Had Pendleton given him the information—garnered from other sealers—
or did Palmer, working from rough notes, later write his log in the quiet of
an anchorage and give the island its name? It is a question—like so many
concerning the sealers' activities—that will never be answered.

The island is an unusual one and boasts a checkered history. About
eight miles across, it is the tip of a collapsed volcanic cone—a caldera—
whose walls have been breached. Only one narrow entrance gives access
from the sea to the water-filled crater—and the entrance is hard to find.
Hence the name Deception. It lies some sixty miles off the Antarctic Peninsula and, on one of the rare clear days, from the high caldera rim, it is
possible to see the mountainous backbone of the Peninsula. Sealers came
to use its protected anchorage, as did whalers a century later—the wrecked
machinery and oil tanks still line the shores—and it was from here that Sir
Hubert Wilkins, in 1928, made the first Antarctic flight.

Today Deception is a cruise ship island where tourists take a dip in the
hot waters of Pendulum Cove—an exercise which, for many of them and
for some unfathomable reason, is the highlight of their Antarctic cruise.
The hot waters are a reminder that Deception is not dead: the last major
eruptions, of 1967, 1969, and 1970, destroyed Chilean and British scientific bases.

Palmer found the entrance to Deception Island, Neptune's Bellows,
and about a mile inside the harbor came upon a good anchorage; then
"went on shore and got some eggs." After he had explored the crater and
found it "an excellent harbor secure from all winds," the *Hero* slipped back
out through Neptune's Bellows and set a southerly course. Ten hours later,
after a pleasant sail with a southwest wind, the *Hero* was close to land
(probably Trinity Island), the sea around them filled with icebergs. At
midnight they hove to under jib and waited for dawn. At four o'clock in
the morning the mainsail rattled up and they started a cautious wending
course through the icebergs. Soon they found a strait which, because it
was "Literally filled with Ice and the shore inaccessible we thought it not
Prudent to venture in. . . ." Unknown to Palmer, he had sailed a course a
few miles to the west of the track sailed by Bransfield in January. The
inaccessible shore was probably a westerly section of Bransfield's Trinity

Land. Nothing, obviously, could be done in this ice-choked sea, and Palmer bore away to the north. He estimated—no sights were taken—the mouth of the strait to be 63°45'S: close to the mouth of today's Orleans Strait. The northerly course took them back to Livingston Island, where they laid off, under jib alone, for the short night. Early in the morning they stood north-northeast along the shore and found a strait (McFarlane Strait) and two excellent anchorages (Half Moon Island and Yankee Harbor on Greenwich Island). By 21 November Palmer was back with his companions at New Plymouth. The weather, having been fine, had turned ominous, with frequent hail squalls. But Palmer brought the good news of some "fine sealing beaches" and the two good anchorages. The hail squalls were a portent of dirty weather—and it soon arrived. The *Frederick* began to drag her anchors, Pendleton made a decision to move the fleet to the new anchorage, and all, as Palmer recorded, were "anxiously waiting for a time to get underweigh as the holding ground is very bad." The weather did moderate and by 24 November all five of the Stonington fleet were anchored in Yankee Harbor. Here they remained for the rest of the season.

Palmer's short exploratory voyage records the second sighting of the Antarctic Peninsula—although no claim is made in the log that this might have been continental land. It is quite possible, even probable, that other sealers had seen the coast before Palmer. But no logs or diaries survive; all is hearsay. Palmer's log does survive. As does a record of the first landing on the continent.

John Davis of the New Haven ship *Huron* and Christopher Burdick of the Nantucket schooner *Huntress* met in the Falklands, that crossroads of sealers, whalers, and privateers, in November 1820. Burdick had sailed from Nantucket in August, bound for the South Shetlands. At West Point Island he found "two ships and there shallops, one from New Haven, bound east'd, and the other from Salem had been lying hear two years past and with a part load of a load of oil and a few skins." The discovery of the South Shetlands was obviously news to Davis—he had sailed from New Haven in March—and the information was tempting. The two skippers came to an agreement to work together at the new sealing grounds. Davis also had the inestimable value of a tiny schooner-rigged shallop, the *Cecilia*, brought down on board "knocked down," now assembled and riding at anchor nearby. The three vessels sailed in company on 22 November. The South Shetlands were sighted on 30 November but the weather, a mix of rain, snow, and fog, combined with the lack of charts, made any close approach dangerous. Three days later, the weather clearing, they closed the dismal-looking coast to less than a mile. Suddenly thick fog rolled in again. It was now that the little *Cecilia* showed her worth and the New Englanders their seamanship. The two larger vessels hauled offshore and the *Cecilia* vanished in the fog to search for a suitable anchorage. They were anxious days for the men aboard the *Huntress* and the *Huron* as they tacked back and forth in the thick fog. It was not until 7 December that they sighted the *Cecilia* again. But she brought good news of an anchorage—Yankee Harbor—that held four Stonington vessels. The *Cecilia* leading, by 8 December the three newcomers were anchored close to their fellow countrymen. In the two weeks that the Stonington vessels had swung at anchor in Yankee Harbor, the *Hero* had brought in over twelve thousand prime skins.

For Davis and Burdick no time was to be lost. Next day the *Cecilia* sailed off with men, stores, canvas, wood, clubs, knives. All would be landed on likely-looking beaches. But unoccupied beaches were hard to find. The islands now held some sixty vessels and a thousand men. In a month, during which the *Cecilia* made four cruises, she collected only five thousand skins. The *Hero,* in the same period, brought in thirty-five thousand skins.

It was time for the *Cecilia* to sail further afield and look for untouched beaches. During the last week of January, Davis came to his decision: to "go on a cruise to find new lands, as the seal is done here. . . ." On 30 January, after picking up skins from the three sealing gangs on Livingston Island, Davis and the *Cecilia* set a course toward Smith Island. The island proved a sore disappointment, for here they found a sealing gang of seventeen men and two whaleboats from the Sydney brig *Lynx.* Davis moved over to Low Island some twenty miles to the southeast. This proved more satisfactory. There were no other sealers, and in four days they had a thousand skins on board. Away to the southeast lay another island (Hoseason Island): by seven o'clock of the evening of 6 February the *Cecilia* was heading toward it. And passed it. Ahead of them they could see a more tempting—and much larger—stretch of land. By ten o'clock the next morning the *Cecilia* was close in. The whaleboat was hoisted out and the boat's crew headed for shore. An hour later they were back, having "found no signs of seal." The weather being clear, Davis took a noon latitude sight that put them at 64°01′S. The *Cecilia* then gently nosed her way into a large bay with "the land high and covered intirely with snow."

The wind now swung into the northeast and began to pick up. By afternoon it was blowing a gale with thick, plastering snow. It was time to shorten sail. The mainsail reefed, the bonnet taken off the foresail, snugged down, the little schooner headed back toward Yankee Harbor some 110 miles away. The last entry in the log for this day reads, "I think this Southern Land to be a Continent." It was an inspired guess by Davis—and a correct one. The *Cecilia* had sailed into Hughes Bay and, for less than an hour, the boat's crew had been the first men to walk the shores of Antarctica. The coast is now the Davis Coast. But the names of the men who jumped ashore are unknown. By 9 February the *Cecilia* was sailing between Deception and Livingston Islands where, just a few days previous,

Palmer and Bellingshausen had had their meeting. By 10 February the *Cecilia* was anchored in Yankee Harbor. On board were 1,670 skins.

Both season and seals were now running out. And the vessels, one by one, began quitting the islands—some, with only half a cargo, to winter in the Falklands; others, with full holds, to sail north to New England—the Stonington men with 88,000 skins—and London. By the end of March the bloodstained beaches were deserted, except for those bloated vultures of the islands, the giant petrels—the "stinkers"—squabbling over the thousands of carcases. But not quite deserted by humans. On King George Island, an officer and ten men from the London *Lord Melville* were to spend a most uncomfortable winter after their ship had been driven off-shore and failed to return. They were picked up the following summer.

The next summer, the 1821–22 season, only saw some forty sealers back in the South Shetlands. It was the final blow to the fur seals and virtually exterminated them from the islands. The Stonington men had made a fine profit from their first onslaught and, even though it must have been obvious that another season's killing would not produce the same fat returns, Edmund Fanning and his son William, along with Pendleton, organized a six-vessel fleet—one more ship than the previous year. Palmer took command of a larger vessel, the sloop *James Monroe*, the *Hero* this time being skippered by Harris Pendleton. Both vessels, according to their orders, were to "act as a tender or shallop to the vessels of this concern." By 6 November the fleet lay at anchor in Deception Island. Yankee Harbor had been choked with ice. It proved a poor season. By 27 January a disap-pointed William Fanning, aboard the *Alabama Packet* in Deception, was writing a letter to his father telling him that the fleet had only collected some one thousand fur seal skins and eleven hundred barrels of elephant seal oil. The *Express,* the *Free Gift,* and the *James Monroe* would sail in a few days for Stonington. The *Frederick,* the *Alabama Packet,* and the *Hero* would try their luck along the Chilean coast for sea lion skins. The *Hero* was later sold at Coquimbo in Chile, and the Stonington men returned to New England with forty-seven thousand inferior sea lion skins.

But before his return to Stonington, Palmer, on one of his early explor-atory cruises for sealing beaches, had taken the *James Monroe* to Elephant Island. Here, on 30 November, he had met a small English vessel, the *Dove,* built as a North Sea fishing smack and commanded by George Powell. A Londoner, Powell was about the same age as Palmer; this was his third voyage as a sealing captain. Indeed he had met Palmer in the Falklands just the previous year—he in the *Eliza* and Palmer in the *Hero*. Powell was a well-educated man and, unusual for a sealer, showed a keen interest in discovery and natural science. A meteorological log was kept, seawater temperatures taken, magnetic variations noted, soil samples brought back for the Royal Society. Powell also carried a chronometer.

The Englishman suggested to Palmer that they should sail in company on an exploratory cruise to the east. After skirting north of Elephant Island and then south of Clarence Island, the two vessels headed east in a nasty cross-sea, fresh winds, and the usual interminable fog. The fog became thicker and, being much pestered with ice and for fear of missing land, the two vessels hove to and waited in the dreary, gray, heaving sea for the visibility to clear. As they lay there the *Dove* passed 120 gallons of fresh water to the Americans, who were running short. A day later, in the afternoon, the fog began to lift, and soon the two sloops were under easy sail heading east. The sun suddenly appearing, Powell took a sight that put them at 60°10′S and 49°07′W. Early the next morning, after skirting some pack ice, the lookout at the *Dove*'s masthead sighted land. The *James Monroe* was about four miles astern and Powell shortened sail for the Americans to catch up. Palmer, recorded Powell, "doubted whether it was land or ice; but, at all events, he said he would follow me. . . ."

Land it proved to be. But, wrote Powell, only "three spiral rocks quite inaccessible, without the least sign of vegetation." The sun was up, the horizon clear, the chronometer ticking away. Powell took sights for longitude and latitude that put the islands at 46°52′W and 60°32′S. And named them Inaccessible Islands. Away to the east lay more land. But, according to Powell, they encountered "great difficulty in getting up with it, owing to the vast quantity of ice that was drifting about in every direction." By the afternoon of 7 December Powell had landed on the new discovery, claimed it for King George IV, named it Coronation Island, and left a bottle with a note of the discovery. The Americans did not land, saying to Powell "it would not be worthwhile, for they could see no prospect whatever of any seals." The two vessels sailed along the north shore of what was turning out to be a group of islands, with Powell making a rough running survey. An anchorage was found on the east end of Coronation Island and whaleboats went out in search of seals, and crossed to other islands, making a rough survey. Powell started a rough draft of his chart of what is now the South Orkneys.

Palmer, Powell hints, was little interested in charting and was scornful of these islands with no fur seals—only a few leopard seals. After 11 December the *James Monroe* drops out of Powell's narrative. The Englishman sailed south from his discovery but was stopped by pack ice at 63°20′S. Short of provisions, the *Dove* sailed back to Clothier Harbour in the South Shetlands. Palmer returned to Deception Island.

Powell sailed into the Thames in August of 1822. By November, from R. H. Lauries, the London chart sellers, any interested person could buy the *Chart of South Shetland, including Coronation Island* and *Notes on South Shetland, &c, Printed to Accompany the Chart of These Newly Discov-*

ered Lands, which has been Constructed from the Explorations of the sloop Dove. It was one of the first published charts, complete with sailing directions, for part of the Antarctic.

We know the fate of the fur seals. But what of the men whose tracks crossed during those few months in the Antarctic? William Smith died in an almshouse, poverty-stricken, forgotten, obscure. The *Williams* outlived him by thirty-five years, working as a collier brig in the North Sea before being broken up in 1882. Bransfield and Bellingshausen, the two navy men, both died in 1852: the former in comfortable circumstances, leaving his wife an annual pension of £50; the Russian an admiral and Governor of Kronstadt. John Davis sank into obscurity until the 1950s, when his log resurfaced and he entered Antarctic history. George Powell, that rather unusual sealing master, was killed by natives on the South Pacific island of Vavau less than three years after his discovery of the South Orkneys. Nathaniel Palmer made one more South Shetland voyage, a chaotic, privately funded combined sealing and exploratory expedition, riven by mutiny, that achieved nothing in the way of discoveries and little in the way of seals. Its finest achievement was that of Dr. James Eights of Albany, who sailed as the expedition's naturalist. Both Eights and his five papers published after the voyage sank into obscurity, even though he can be considered the first Antarctic scientist, with his discovery of fossil wood and descriptions of the ten-legged "sea spider." He also predated Charles Darwin by six years in suggesting the transportation of rocks by icebergs.

I hold two images of Palmer in my mind's eye. One is a portrait painted as a young man, the other a portrait photograph taken later in life. The painting shows a pleasant-faced young man with a hint of a smile on his lips, formally dressed. The photograph is of an elderly man sitting down, arm resting on a table with his hand clutching a pair of gloves. The formal coat is stretched tight across a well-filled belly. The face is whiskered, but the easy open countenance has been replaced by a touch of ruthlessness. Here is the prosperous businessman, shipowner, skipper, designer of fast sailing vessels, member of New York Yacht Club, yacht owner. Oddly enough I prefer the younger man: the sealer who took his small *Hero* below the Convergence, who started his sailing as a small boy aboard the blockade runners during the War of 1812 with men, it was said, "who could smell their way from Hell Gate to Providence with their eyes shut."

And around Palmer swirls a rather heated, unedifying whirlwind of controversy on who first sighted Antarctica. The Palmer adherents claim the honor for him. And are then gently reminded that Bransfield in the *Williams* sighted the Antarctic Peninsula ten months before their claims for the young sealer. The Palmerites' move is to hint darkly at the sinister fact of the strange disappearance of Bransfield's log—and conveniently forget the chart and accounts published in the magazines of the day. The

Russians counter with a checkmate move and claim the game won with Bellingshausen's sighting of the Finibul Ice Shelf a few days before Bransfield's sighting of Trinity Land. The game is just as sterile and barren as the polar ice cap. But it is no game to the people of Stonington. To them it as an established fact that Nathaniel Palmer, their local hero, wears the laurels. So be it. Anything else, even the truth, would be a blow to civic and national pride. In this game only the seals are losers.

IX

Weddell and Brisbane
Sail South

WEDDELL SEA: great ice-filled sea which indents Antarctica between Palmer Pen. and Coats Land; centering in about 73°S, 45°W. This sea was disc. in 1823 by James Weddell, Master, RN, who named it George IV Sea. The present name, honoring the discoverer, was proposed by Dr. Karl Fricker in 1900, and it has been universally accepted. Not adopted: George IV Sea.

United States Board on Geographic Names, *Gazetteer No. 14,* 1956

CURSORY GLANCE at the map of Antarctica shows two seas indenting the continent and bringing the sea's edge to within seven hundred miles of the South Pole. They are the Weddell Sea and the Ross Sea. Give another cursory glance at a list of the seals that forage the waters surrounding Antarctica, and the eye will alight on the Weddell seal and the Ross seal. Both sea and seals are named after two nineteenth-century seamen who explored the waters of the Southern Ocean. Both men were of Scottish ancestry and both men served in the Royal Navy. Here the resemblance ends.

James Clark Ross was a navy man from the top of his romantically tousled head of hair to the tips of his well-polished boots. The handsomest man in the Royal Navy, it was claimed (along with the profile went a certain amount of amour propre), Ross was the very *beau idéal* of every Victorian maiden's dream of a Royal Navy captain. Besides having made his fame in the Arctic, Ross was also a member of that exclusive club of Southern Ocean explorers, navy men all, made up of the Englishman James Cook, the Russian Thaddeus Bellingshausen, the Frenchman Dumont d'Urville, and the American Charles Wilkes. Of that pantheon of polar worthies James Weddell would have been most comfortable with Cook. But Cook had been dead eight years when Weddell was born in 1787, and the seaman who comes to mind with the closest affinity to Weddell is William Scoresby.

A contemporary of Weddell, the Yorkshire-born Scoresby first sailed into the Arctic seas aboard his father's whaling ship at the tender age of ten and had his first experience of being beset by the Arctic pack ice. By the age of twenty-one he had his own command—the aptly named *Resolution*—and, contrary to all wharfside opinions about one so young, brought back thirty whales to the port of Whitby. Over the next decade Scoresby proved to be one of the most successful of the Arctic whaling captains. But he was more than an uncommonly good whaler and seaman. Equipped with an inquiring, observant, and analytical mind—sharpened by winter education at Edinburgh University; summers were for whaling—he made the Arctic seas and their surroundings his study. Snowflakes, formation of ice (he even fashioned lenses from ice, and with the aid of the sun's rays burned wood, fired gunpowder, and lit the tobacco pipes of his astonished whaling companions), meteorology, magnetism, hydrology, and polar atmospherics all came under his eager scrutiny. In 1815 his paper on the formation of polar ice was read before the Wernerian Society. It was the first of its kind and included suggestions and recommendations for reaching the North Pole across the pack ice. Scoresby advocated light flexible sledges that could be made amphibious by a covering of waterproof skin. The sledges should be drawn by reindeer or dogs—Scoresby favored dogs—and the sledge drivers should have specialized knowledge learned from the Eskimos. Sledging should start early in the year, before the end of April and the soft summer snow—for "soft snow would diminish the speed and augment the fatigue of the animal." All this was sage advice: and all of it was to be rigidly ignored by the Royal Navy in its nineteenth-century assault on the Northwest Passage and North Pole. In 1820 Scoresby published his classic *An Account Of The Arctic Regions,* a book destined to lay the foundation stone of Arctic science.

It is possible that Weddell and Scoresby met—both were members of the Royal Edinburgh Society—but even if not, Weddell was well acquainted with Scoresby's writings, and frequent reference is made to Scoresby in Weddell's own classic *A Voyage Towards the South Pole . . . Containing An Examination Of The Antarctic Sea,* published in 1827.

Weddell's parents, unlike Scoresby's, had no connection with the sea. His father, an upholsterer by trade, had moved south to London from Dalserf in Scotland. His mother, Sarah Pease, was a member of the Society of Friends and came from the well-known Quaker family (Edward Pease backed George Stephenson in the building of a pioneer passenger railway from Stockton to Darlington and worked for the Peace and Anti-Slavery Societies). Such a combination of Scottish Presbyterianism and English Quakerism could have produced an inflexible and obdurate mind. That it did not is most certainly due to Weddell's mother, who combined all the sensible, kindly, and attractive aspects of the Quakers. Weddell was devoted to her. The father died with young James barely out of rompers and Sarah Weddell was left in genteel poverty. Quaker scruples on fighting wars had obviously been overcome, for the elder son Charles joined the Royal Navy. The young James joined him aboard the fourteen-gun sloop *Swan,* signing on as a boy, first class, aged nine. In an age of ever-extending adolescence one is constantly amazed at an era where children were pitchforked with such insouciance into the hurly-burly and responsibilities of adult life. Nevertheless the child survived, even though it must have been a harrowing experience: for the *Swan* was commanded by a tyrannical officer whose idea of discipline was based on the lash. With such a commander it is little wonder that the boy was discharged at his own request after six months' service.

Until 1818 Weddell's life was bound and circumscribed by the twenty years of war fought by Great Britain against Revolutionary and Napoleonic France. Weddell, even after those unhappy months in the Royal Navy, was wedded to the sea—first in the mercantile service, where he rose to be a chief mate, and then, surprisingly, while in Jamaica, volunteering into the Royal Navy as an able seaman.

It would appear that Weddell was making a deliberate choice to follow in Cook's footsteps. A story is told, however, that he was forced to join the navy after knocking his skipper to the deck during a fight. In a merchant service where disputes were settled by the fist or belaying pin, the anecdote is quite plausible. No matter; within six months the A.B. had rocketed to warrant officer and by the December of 1810 Weddell was an acting master.

Contrary to that genre of Napoleonic naval-war sagas brimming with daring, cutting-out expeditions, flashing cutlasses, cannons' roar, gunsmoke, and blood, Weddell's only action came in 1813 when, while he was master of the ten-gun brig *Hope,* the patriotically named *True Blooded Yankee,* an American privateer, was captured in the English Channel.

Two years later, in the early hours of 19 June, as the cold moonlight shone on the Belgium countryside and the looters prowled like wolves among some ten thousand dead and dying horses and forty thousand dead and dying soldiers, Napoleon Bonaparte stood warming his hands before a flickering fire and contemplated the total disintegration of his army. The Emperor of France—or Corsican Tyrant, depending upon your nationality—had fought, and lost, his last battle.

When James Weddell heard the news of Waterloo is unknown. In that June of 1815 he was master of the *Espoir* and sailing from the West Indies toward Halifax, Nova Scotia. For nearly six years he had served in a navy that numbered over one thousand ships manned by 130,000 men. The long war ended, the navy was rapidly axed to one hundred vessels and 23,000 men. Of the men involved in this drastic reduction, the commissioned officers—due to political interests, power, and privilege—remained virtually untouched. And the navy found itself in the absurd position of having one officer on the payroll for every three seamen.

For Weddell, now in his early thirties, vigorous, intelligent, and ambitious, there was patently little future in staying in a service where the chance of a commission had been reduced to practically zero and promotion was slothlike, with the upper rungs of the ladder clogged by ageing captains, commodores, and admirals. This was a navy where seniorority ruled the promotion list and the old toast of "a bloody war and quick

Portrait of James Weddell.
Courtesy of the Royal Scottish Geographical Society

promotion" held a great deal of macabre truth. And the bloody war had ended. The choice was obvious and the navy lost a very capable master, an able commander of men, a navigator of unusual distinction well versed with the newfangled chronometers and with an unusual aptitude for the older method of lunar distances. The gainer was the merchant service, and, for Weddell, his own command on a round-trip voyage to the West Indies.

In an age when news from overseas traveled at the same speed as a sailing ship, the waterfront taverns and the countinghouses formed an informal news bureau. Here would gather the seamen, mates, and skippers, and here the gossip would circulate in a fug of tobacco smoke and over pots of ale and glasses of rum or brandy. Now the rumor of William Smith's discovery of land south of Cape Horn was circulating along the water-fronts of Valparaiso and Montevideo during the early months of 1819. Weddell could have listened to these tales in the West Indies before they became public knowledge in the newspapers of the USA and Great Britain. Even if the rumors were false, mere tavern scuttlebutt, the seals of the Falkland Islands, South Georgia, and the Patagonian coast were fact—and the new manufactories required oil for lubrication and lighting, while the rapidly increasing population demanded more leather, felt, and fur.

Whatever the reason, toward the end of 1819 Weddell was sailing south across the equator with a new command and intent upon a new enterprise. His vessel was the two-masted American-built brig *Jane,* some seventy-five feet overall and twenty feet in beam and outfitted for the taking of fur seal, elephant seal, and whale. Taken as a prize in the War of 1812, the *Jane* was about thirty years old but had the advantage of being an ideal size for sealing. The owners were new to sealing but no strangers to the world of ships: one was James Strachan of the Leith shipbuilding company of Strachan & Gavin, and the other James Mitchell, a London insurance broker.

This first voyage of Weddell's aboard the *Jane* gives a hint of his inclination for exploration combined with his care as a navigator. In 1762, on a voyage from Lima to Cadiz, the Spanish ship *Aurora* had sighted what were thought to be islands to the east of Cape Horn at 53°S and 48°W. Further reports of sightings came trickling into the Spanish authorities, and in 1794 the Spanish corvette *Atrevida* was sent to investigate. They confirmed the islands' position and the Aurora Islands dutifully appeared on Spanish charts. Weddell, however, remained skeptical. Of course the chance remained that the islands did exist—in which case they might harbor seals. Weddell set about the search with care. Unusual for a common sealer, the *Jane* carried chronometers (most sealing-vessel owners and captains had a penny-pinching attitude to navigation: dead reckoning and latitude sights sufficed); and the rates of these were checked in the harbor of St. John's on Staten Island some five hundred miles to the west of the charted position of the Aurora Islands. The chronometers checked, the *Jane* wooded and watered, the brig sailed from Staten Island on 27 January 1820. An exhaustive and thorough search yielded no islands and Weddell, much to the evident relief of his crew, who were here for seals, which represented money, set course for the Falkland Islands.

As a careful and very professional navigator, Weddell was "led to consider in what way those Spanish officers could have fallen into so great a mistake." More so as they had been equipped with chronometers and sailed from the Falkland Islands (about three days' sail from the alleged Auroras) on a voyage whose sole purpose had been to find the truth in a mass of conjecture. Over Weddell's shoulder hovered the shade of the exemplary James Cook, who would also have deplored the bungling of the

Atrevida's officers. If they had seen islands, the only possible ones were the sheer faces of the Shag Rocks 210 miles further east than their reported Aurora Islands; if this was the case their navigational sins were heinous. Putting the matter in a more charitable light, the officers, being probably "men unaccustomed to traversing cold and tempestuous seas encumbered with ice," had mistaken icebergs for land.

Unknown to Weddell another sealer had been searching for the Aurora Islands just a few weeks prior to the *Jane*. This was the American brig *Hersilia* out of Stonington, Connecticut, commanded by Captain James Sheffield, with William Fanning as supercargo: according to Edmund Fanning, the supercargo's father, both men possessed "nautical talents and both able lunarians." The *Hersilia* carried a Spanish chart showing the position of the Aurora Islands, and these the Americans found close to their charted position. Sheffield's description, however, indicates that the Americans, like the Spanish, were wildly off in their reckoning of longitude, for the description tallies with the appearance of the Shag Rocks. These pinnacles of rock have no landing place and no seals. The disappointed Americans turned about and set course for Staten Island. Now when Sheffield had sailed from Stonington in July 1819 he knew nothing of William Smith's discoveries south of Cape Horn; but somewhere on his passage south, perhaps in Buenos Aires (for he carried trade goods for the South American market), or in the Falkland Islands he learned of Smith's newly discovered land rich with seals. The *Hersilia* sailed south from Staten Island on 11 January 1820 to be the first—and only—American sealer to arrive at the South Shetlands and the new bonanza sealing grounds.

If any single month of a specific year can stake a claim to significance in the historiography of the Antarctic, this month of January 1820 would be high on the list. Any interested extraterrestrial observer idly scanning Antarctica's coastline would have seen two or three sealing vessels at the South Shetlands: the *Williams*—now under charter to the Royal Navy—surveying the islands and sighting the Antarctic Peninsula; and, further east, the Russian *Vostok* and *Mirnyi* sailing to within thirty miles of the continent.

Weddell and his crew, blissfully unaware of all this activity in the south, sailed to the Falklands, where they spent the winter. For three decades these islands had been the haunt of American, British, and French whalers and sealers. Sheltered harbors with fresh water were plentiful; for the marketplace in their home countries were skins and oil, and for their own consumption were penguin eggs, albatross eggs, fish, geese, and, on East Falkland, wild cattle to be turned into hides, tallow, fresh beef, and salt beef. And to make the sealers' cup of happiness brimful—for these men had scant regard for the niceties of any government's bureaucratic rulings—the islands had been free for a decade from any pettifogging authority. The only disadvantage was the lack of timber for fuel; but in lieu of this peat could be cut and the turf dried for the cooking fires.

Weddell, the Royal Navy master coming to the fore, spent the winter months collecting information on the safe anchorages, watering places, hazards, dangers, and tidal currents around the islands. During these same months, in the northern hemisphere, American and British sealers were furiously preparing their vessels for the massive attack on the sealing grounds of the South Shetlands. The word was now out and public, and it was a question of first come first served. Some called in at the Falklands on their way south (including the small Stonington sloop *Hero,* under the command of the young Nathaniel Palmer) and in November the *Jane* sailed from her winter anchorage and headed south to take her share of skins.

By January 1821 the *Jane*'s hold was full and Weddell set sail on the long voyage back to England. With him he carried news of the shipwreck of four sealers: the American *Clothier* and the British *Hannah, Lady Trou-bridge,* and *Ann.* Weddell also acted as postman, for he carried letters from men and officers on other sealers. One of them, from an officer on the ninety-foot brig *George,* perhaps speaks for the feelings of them all:

We left the Falklands on the 25th of November and made this detestable place on the 1st of December; *detestable,* I say, because I am certain it was the last place that ever God Almighty made . . . as the snow never quits this place, even now in midsummer . . . the weather is as cold as you have it at Christmas. We are constantly wet, and overhead in blood and blubber. The seals are not as plentiful as they were represented to be before we left Liverpool, so we must put up with a moderate quantity. We have now on board nine thousand skins and I am still in hopes that we shall procure about two thousand weekly. . . .

The *George* returned to London with eighteen thousand skins.

The *Jane*'s voyage also showed a handsome profit—enough for Weddell and Strachan to buy a smaller vessel to act as consort for the *Jane.* This was the *Beaufoy,* a flush-decked fore-and-aft-rigged cutter with a plumb stem and long widow-making bowsprit. No time was lost and both vessels were fitted and provisioned for another sealing voyage into the Southern Ocean—including stronger iron cables to replace hemp ones—and three months after arriving at London from his first voyage, Weddell and the *Jane,* in the company of the *Beaufoy* commanded by Michael McLeod, were sailing down Channel. By August 1821 they were in Madeira taking aboard stores and the island wine, then at the Cape Verde Islands for salt, and then, a few weeks later, making a final stop at New Island in the Falklands, where they found themselves in the company of the American brig *Charity,* owned and commanded by Charles H. Barnard.

In the soft light of the cabin oil lamps, and with the decanter of Madeira circulating, Weddell heard Barnard's story. It was one that Weddell "greedily devoured," and he devotes four pages to it in his *A Voyage Towards the South Pole*. Those four pages are briskly introduced: "New Island is remarkable for having been for two years the solitary residence of a Captain J. Barnard, an American, whose vessel was run away with in the year 1814 by the crew of an English ship which, on her passage from Port Jackson, had been wrecked on the south side of these islands. I met with Captain Barnard in 1821 at the place of his exile, and his conversation naturally turned to that subject. . . ."

Barnard wrote of his experiences in a book published eight years after his talk with Weddell. Not for him the pithy titles of today, but *A Narrative Of The Sufferings And Adventures Of Capt. Charles H. Barnard, In A Voyage Round The World, During The Years 1812, 1813, 1814, 1815, & 1816; Embracing An Account Of The Seizure Of His Vessel At The Falkland Islands, By An English Crew Whom He Had Rescued From The Horrors Of A Shipwreck; And Of Their Abandoning Him On An Uninhabited Island, Where He Resided Nearly Two Years.* It is a most satisfyingly melodramatic tale of treachery, avarice, and deceit on the part of the English, who comprise a cast of characters straight from *Moll Flanders, The Beggar's Opera, Tom Jones,* and *The School for Scandal* (complete with a bold bad knight, ladies of easy virtue, sottish captains, intemperate soldiers, and helpless children). This picaresque tale is combined with a Robinson Crusoe survival story—with the added satisfaction that an enlarged version of the small stone hut built by Barnard on New Island still stands at the head of a small sandy inlet, making it one of the Falkland Islands' oldest existing buildings.

It was perhaps at Weddell's prompting that Barnard wrote his narrative, for Weddell is mentioned in it as being "my particular friend." It was a friendship cemented by their common bond of a Quaker background, a mutual admiration for each other's seamanship, and a loose working partnership.

The *Jane,* the *Beaufoy* and the *Charity* sailed for the South Shetlands, arriving late in October. This was now the third season of sealing among the islands and the seals were getting harder to find. Nearly a thousand men and some forty-five American and British sealers were now working the beaches. Desperate to find new breeding grounds, the smaller vessels of the sealing fleet were sent off on scouting expeditions. Such a one was the *Beaufoy;* and three days before the Christmas of 1821 the *Beaufoy* sailed into Yankee Harbor on Greenwich Island and anchored among the moored American sealers. On board were three captains: McLeod, Weddell, and Barnard, returning from a scouting trip to Elephant Island. On 11 December, when some 240 miles to the east of Elephant Island, the *Beaufoy* had sighted land even further to the east. Unkown to the Beaufoys, this land—the South Orkney Islands—had been discovered on 7 December by the Englishman George Powell in the tiny *Dove* and Nathaniel Palmer aboard the *James Monroe,* both vessels sailing in company and on a similar scouting expedition as the *Beaufoy.*

Here at the South Shetlands occurred a small incident that graphically illustrates the enduring myth of mermaids, mermen, and the magic ability of seals to take on human form. It is an ability encapsulated in the old Orkney song "The Grey Selchie of Sule Skerry," with its line running "I am a man upon the land, I am a selchie in the sea." Any Irish or Scots sealer of the time would have been familiar with the song or similar songs and the legends concerning seals. Was it not true that the McCodrums of the Western Isles and the Kenealys from Ireland were descended from seals?

One of Weddell's men, probably Irish or Scots, was left alone on one side of an island to guard sealskins while his companions searched another shore. He had gone to sleep but was woken by a noise resembling human cries. A search revealed nothing and he returned to his lonely vigil. The noise came again and this time he made a longer search in case a boat's crew were in trouble and calling for help. The cries grew louder and this time came with a musical strain. Let Weddell take up the story:

On searching around, he saw an object lying on a rock, a dozen yards from the shore, at which he was somewhat frightened. The face and shoulders appeared of human form, and of a reddish colour; over the shoulders hung long green hair; the tail resembled that of the seal, but the extremities of the arms he could not see distinctly. The creature continued to make a musical noise while he gazed about two minutes, and on perceiving him it disappeared in an instant. Immediately when the man saw his officer, he told this wild tale, the truth of which was, of course, doubted; but to add weight to his testimony (being a Catholic), he made a cross on the sand, which he kissed in form of making oath to the truth of his statement.

Weddell, exceedingly diverted by this tale, sent for the visionary sailor. In the *Jane*'s cabin the seaman repeated his story and repeated his oath as to the truth of it. Weddell could only conclude that the story was true, or—the pragmatic and skeptical Quaker mind opposing the Celtic mists— "that it must have been the effects of a disturbed imagination." Now this writer once came upon a seaweed-draped seal (long green hair?) lying on a beach in the South Shetlands—and the seal was making what, with a dollop of disturbed imagination, could be called musical noises. It was a Weddell seal, which makes noises underwater for either echolocation or communication. It is a pleasing fancy then, to surmise that the seal of Weddell's account (he called it a "non-descript") was in all likelihood the type of seal to be named after him: *Leptonychotes weddellii.*

Seals were now scarce in the South Shetlands, and by February of 1822 the *Jane* was at the newly discovered South Orkneys. Here Weddell could satisfy two urges: one for skins and the other his liking for survey work. The latter had to be cursory as the season was ending and he had no second vessel, the *Beaufoy* having sailed for South Georgia where other sealers were scraping the beaches of their meager offerings. Here the *Jane* rejoined the *Beaufoy* and both vessels sailed for England at the end of March. By July they were unloading their mixed cargo of skins and oil for the London market.

The next two months were busy ones for Weddell. The second voyage had turned a small profit and the three owners decided on a third voyage south. And so, as the shipwrights and carpenters hammered and caulked the leaky seams of the two vessels, Weddell set about ordering and checking the now familiar items of his trade: barrel staves and iron hoops for casking up the oil; lances, clubs, harpoons (for the chance whale); flensing, beaming, and skinning knives; grindstones and whetstones; axes, saws; and the big iron try-pots made by that most excellent company of Johnson & Son, Wapping Docks, London. For the two vessels—they had to be totally self-sufficient—were bolts of canvas, spare spars, cordage, tallow, Stockholm tar, needles and thread, palms, cobbler's wax, marlin, anvils, bellows, lengths of iron, hammers, iron and copper nails, spare planking for the whaleboats, spare oars, leather for pumps and oar looms, coal, candles, lamp wicks and oil, gunpowder, cartridge and ball for the side arms, fowling pieces, and small cannon.

Dear to Weddell's heart, and a sign of his mastery of his trade, were the three chronometers: one of eight days, made by James Murray, one of two days, by Murray & Strachan, and one of one day, also by James Murray. All these had to be rated and checked. Then came the compasses, barometers, and thermometers to be checked, the latest charts purchased, and latest news gleaned of news from the south.

Supplies of paper were needed, and logbooks, journal books, ink, and perhaps the newly fashionable steel pens, which were replacing the old goose-quill pens that needed constant sharpening. For chart work were the excellent new pencils invented by the Frenchman Nicholas-Jacques Conté and the Austrian Josef Hardtmuth. Like the quills, they had to be sharpened, but the graphite-clay mixture encased in the softwood sheath was excellent for drawing and writing and could be erased.

Weddell was later to regret—not expecting to reach such a high southern latitude—that "I had not supplied myself with instruments which would have enabled me to extend my observations." But no matter; he could console himself with the knowledge that those he had were "of the best construction."

Next to be considered was the matter of victualing. Perhaps the partners toyed with the idea of trying out the new Donkin & Hall canned meats and vegetables, which were receiving some attention in maritime circles. This after the wide publicity and heroes' welcome given to Lieutenant Edward Parry and the Royal Navy ships *Hecla* and *Griper* on their return from the Canadian Arctic. The expedition had wintered at Melville Island at 74°47′ N and Parry had been loud in his praise of the Donkin &

Hall products. Even now, as the *Jane* and the *Beaufoy* were being readied for their voyage south, the intrepid Parry with the *Hecla* and the *Fury* were searching in the Arctic for that elusive Northwest Passage, and with them were more of Messrs. Donkin & Hall's products. It was, however, most surely a fleeting consideration: the canned food was expensive, and only liberal-pocketed government departments, with an eye cocked for national prestige, could afford the indulgence. Sealing was a business dangerously balanced between profit and loss. Cold economic facts, not national prestige, were the overriding concerns. Weddell, the pragmatic and knowledgeable seaman, would also have been aware of the conservative nature of his deck crew, wedded to their plum duffs, salt pork, salt beef, and pease pudding. Anything new was usually considered by the crew as a canny subterfuge by the owners to deprive them of their rights. And so the barrels of victuals were trundled aboard: salt pork, salt beef, hard cheese, dried pease, barley, flour, oatmeal, and rum.

By the middle of September, two months after their return, Weddell's two vessels lay ready and waiting among the thousands that lay in the docks and along the reaches of the river Thames as it flowed in a great U bend along the shores of the queerly named Isle of Dogs. The two sealers were stored, victualed, ballasted, and with the crew on board. With a touch worthy of Robert Louis Stevenson, Weddell opens the story of this, his third sealing voyage.

Our adventure was for procuring Fur-Seal skins, and our vessels were the brig *Jane,* of Leith, of 160 tons, and the cutter *Beaufoy,* of London, of 65 tons, both fitted out in the ordinary way, and provisioned for two years. The former, with a crew of twenty-two officers and men was under my command; the latter, with a crew of thirteen, was commanded by Mr. Matthew Brisbane.

Now Matthew Brisbane is a new name. This thirty-five-year-old Scot had replaced his fellow countryman Michael McLeod as commander of the *Beaufoy.* Brisbane came from a seafaring family and was to prove a tough, resourceful, and very capable commander: the two men were destined to get on well with each other and Brisbane received nothing but praise from Weddell. But Brisbane was obviously one of those men dogged by misfortune: in his future lay three shipwrecks and a brutal murderous death in the Falklands.

It had been a fine summer, this one of 1822, the seventh anniversary of the Battle of Waterloo. The harvest was in early; the root crops were plentiful, still waiting to be lifted; the fall fruit ripe and abundant, apples heavy on the trees and the essential hops for beer making of excellent quality. Even grapes grown out of doors were as good as those raised under glass.

But this halcyon summer stood in stark contrast to the tempestuous years since Weddell had quit the Royal Navy. During those years three hundred thousand soldiers and seamen had been cast adrift to join the growing ranks of destitute and unemployed. And this, in a country whose population was doubling in half a lifetime, looked set to produce anarchy in an economy wildly swinging between boom and bust. The Reverend Thomas Malthus's doomsday prediction that the population was growing faster than its means of subsistence appeared frighteningly true. Riot, anger, discontent, and hunger were the lot of the voteless majority. And the established church, aristocracy, gentry, and nouveau riche manufactory owners fearfully watched the embers of those atheistic French Revolutionary ideas—long thought smothered—being fanned into flames by the demagogue radicals.

Amidst all this turbulence Great Britain was increasing her wealth at bewildering speed: and the props of that wealth rested on King Cotton and King Coal. For the Janes and Beaufoys, both industries provided a reason for their calling as seamen and sealers. The enormous import of raw cotton and the export of finished goods required ships and seamen, as did the movement of coal along the coast and export abroad. Coal in its turn drove the steam-powered looms of the northern mills; coal was turned into coke for the smelting of iron to be turned into more machines. Machines and looms for cotton and wool required whale and seal oil for lubrication and the processing of coarse linen and wool fabrics. And the mills and manufactories required lighting with oil, as did the streets of the expanding cities and towns. A worrying thought, however, and one that seemed insoluble to the oil-importing merchants, was the rapidly increasing use of coal gas for street lighting. Gasworks were being built in all the major towns and London—in less than ten years—had increased its gasometers from one to forty-seven. The only way for the embattled oil merchants to fight back was to promote the use of gas from oil. As to the sealskins, they were always in demand for their fur or as leather.

The other prop to the country—a symbolic one—was monstrous, large, albeit weak, and rotten. Only two years previous, the Duke of Bedford had been convinced that the monarchy was doomed to collapse. That obese voluptuary, the Prince Regent, had finally claimed his inheritance from his old, mad, blind father and now reigned as King George IV— Byron's "fourth of the fools and oppressors called George." Behind the bulky figure of His Majesty loomed the figures of his ducal brothers: some comic, some sinister, some stupid, but all of them appearing to lack even the glimmerings of common sense. "The damnedest millstones about the neck of any government that can be imagined," snapped an irate Duke of Wellington. The poet Shelley's opinion, couched a little more elegantly in verse, was equally pointed:

Princes, the dregs of their dull race, who flow
Through public scorn—mud from a muddy spring—
Rulers who neither see nor feel nor know
But leech-like to their failing country cling.

A King such as this was loathed and despised in his capital city, where his public appearances were met with jeers, hisses, catcalls, and hurled cobblestones. (The London mob have never been respecters of persons.) However, royal visits to Dublin, Hanover, and Edinburgh met with rapturous receptions, providing soothing balm to the royal ego. Indeed, the Edinburgh visit—orchestrated by Sir Walter Scott—of this summer of 1822 saw the King wrapped in tartan riding up Princes Street, with the cheers of the loyal Scots loud in his ears. It must have set up some royal musings on the different receptions given him by his more disrespectful subjects in London. So much so that he commissioned a portrait of himself—bonneted, sporraned, and kilted in acres of tartan—to be painted by Sir David Wilkie. The Scottish tourist industry, the tartan industry, and the mythologizing of Scotland were off and running.

But probably the closest that any of the crew of the *Jane* and the *Beaufoy* had come to royalty was to slap their thighs and guffaw at the shop windows where hung the wickedly satirical and scurrilous colored cartoons of James Gillray, Thomas Rowlandson, and George Cruikshank, lampooning the more egregious follies of the monarchy. Also as remote to the crew would have been the genteel world of Jane Austen: the world of the gentry and upper bourgeoisie, where disagreements were settled verbally and decorously, and where the the latest offerings from the pen of Scott, Keats, Shelley, and Byron were awaited with bated breath. The heroes of the Janes and Beaufoys were John Gully, Tom Cribb, Jem Belcher, and Tom Spring, bare-knuckle fighters every one—with the unbeaten Tom Cribb the doyen of them all. Cribb was now retired and owned a public house in London; here they could have gone, drunk pots of ale or bowls of hot punch, and talked to the great man himself.

This was an England where arguments among the commonfolk were settled with fists, and where the most popular spectator sport—next to horse racing—was the bare-knuckle prize fight. When a fight was announced, thousands would drive, ride, and walk to the designated place of the "mill." The patrons were the sprigs of the aristocracy, and the spectators a geological cross-section of the layered society of England. In its way these crowds were a truly democratic gathering of the country. Other sports collected crowds, cricket being one of them—but others would make the modern spectator blanch with horror: badger baiting, dogfighting, cockfighting, bull baiting, and rat catching. This was a robuster age and the people were equipped with stronger stomachs.

Leaving behind these entertainments, on Friday 13 September—an unlucky day for any superstitious crew member—the *Jane* and the *Beaufoy* sailed with a fair wind and tide down the reaches of the river Thames to the Downs. This is a roadstead lying along the southeast coast between the North Foreland and the South Foreland, with the treacherous Goodwin Sands offshore affording a little shelter. Here the pilots for the Thames would be picked up or dropped off, and here would gather great fleets of vessels waiting for a fair wind to take them down Channel. If the wait was long, the roadstead would fill with hundreds of vessels, a floating forest of masts. The fair wind would arrive and the forest would vanish in clouds of canvas.

The *Jane* and the *Beaufoy* spent less than a week anchored in the Downs, but the superstitious seaman would have had the gratification of being proved right. Another vessel, badly mishandled, ran across the *Jane*'s bow, carrying away her bowsprit cap, jibboom, and spritsail yard, and ripped the furled jibs. Here in the Downs these sorts of accidents were meat and potatoes to the seamen crewing the famous Deal luggers. These open boats, launched off the beach, flitted between the anchored vessels like seabirds and ferryed stores, provisions, passengers, crew, captains, and pilots. And in storm conditions provided a lucrative, but dangerous, salvage and rescue service. They were also the bane of the Revenue Service, for these three-masted luggers were built for speed, salvage, smuggling, pilotage, and fishing, in that order. The ferrying of passengers to and from the beach was also carried on by the smaller galley punts setting a single lugsail and the even smaller, lightly built, black-painted four-oared galleys. And even these cheeky blackbirds of the smuggling trade were the despair of the Revenue cutters as they derisively pulled away upwind in light airs.

Weddell makes no mention of being ferryed ashore to Deal in one of these hoveling boats, but a year later Deal was described by the radical William Cobbett, that writer of muscular English prose performing the verbal equivalent of Gillray's and Rowlandson's visual art. The village to him was "a most villainous place. It is full of filthy looking people . . . I was glad to hurry along through it, and to leave its inns and public-houses to be occupied by the tarred, and trowsered, and blue-and-buff crew whose very vicinage I always detest." Cobbett, needless to say, was a born and bred countryman with not a drop of salt water running in his veins: he looked upon seaports as alien excrescences rimming a land that should be devoted to the growing of wheat, barley, and hops and the raising of cows and pigs.

If Weddell had entered one of those anathematized inns of Cobbett's, he would no doubt have struck up a conversation with some fellow seaman and the talk would have drifted to the topic of these new steam-powered vessels—some with iron hulls—that were appearing on the rivers and canals. Even as they talked, was there not a steam-engined ferry with its rumbling paddlewheels and ridiculous stovepipe funnel belching smoke and smuts crossing the Channel between Dover and Calais? For the con-

servative-minded these developments were either disconcerting or a passing fad, of little account; for the farsighted they represented a new future
for overseas trade and a change in tactics for war at sea.

On 17 September, the wind having swung into the northeast, the
massed vessels in the Downs, including the *Jane* and the *Beaufoy,* weighed
anchor and with the freshening favorable wind headed down Channel for
the open Atlantic. At the approaches to the Channel, the two vessels parted
company: the *Jane* steering for Madeira and the *Beaufoy* for the Cape
Verde Islands. The *Jane* spent but one day at Madeira, taking on board the
casks of the island wine, Weddell's agent being Mr. John Blandy. (A hundred years later, Sir Ernest Shackleton aboard the *Quest,* on the explorer's
last voyage into the Southern Ocean, used the same company for the same
purpose.) By 14 October the *Jane* had rejoined the *Beaufoy* at Bonavista in
the Cape Verde Islands, and both vessels started taking on board thirty-six
tons of salt for the curing of sealskins.

Here at the islands Weddell, a keen and meticulous observer of Southern Ocean natural phenomena, cast his ironic eye on the behavior of his
fellow man. At Bonavista he had cause to dine several times with the
Bishop of the islands, a prelate, Weddell noted, "of forbearance, suavity of
manners and rigid clerical discipline." But the clerical discipline, Weddell
drily noted, did not extend to his priestly retinue; away from the prelate's
censorious eye they were, "like the laity, fond of the society of ladies and
open to their attractions."

After taking aboard the salt and some rather scrawny livestock, the *Jane*
and the *Beaufoy* sailed on 20 October. A day out from the islands the *Jane*
was discovered to have a serious leak in the counter. She was hove to and
every movable item shifted forward to bring her down by the head and
raise the stern out of the water. In this undignified attitude the counter
was patched with a temporary repair, followed by the tedious business of
shifting everything back to return the *Jane* to her sailing lines. Weddell was
now going to be delayed by a stop at an anchorage in the Falkland Islands
or along the South American coast, where a more satisfactory repair could
be made.

On 7 November the two vessels crossed the equator and a week later,
off the coast of Brazil, they sighted a Portuguese schooner. Weddell knew
a slaver when he saw one, and closing with the schooner he forced her to
heave to. With the *Jane* and *Beaufoy* close alongside and within cannon
shot, Weddell, with officers and a boat's crew, boarded the slaver. On
board were 250 slaves destined for the Bahia market. All the men were
crammed below in the hold like fish in a barrel, and the women and
children were shackled on deck. Weddell, with his Quaker background,
was appalled. And frustrated. Slavery had been abolished in Great Britain
some fourteen years previous, but it still flourished in the Americas. But
Weddell was only too aware that any action taken against the slaver—his

officers were all for taking her as a prize—would lay him open to charges of piracy. Reluctantly he reboarded his own vessel, and the slaver with its cargo of humanity continued her interrupted course to Bahia.

Weddell's most pressing problem was now the curing of the leak—a cure that would withstand the battering of the Southern Ocean. The Falklands were too far away and Weddell decided upon finding a sheltered bay along the coast of Patagonia for the repairs. The beaches of this desolate bleak coast would also provide seals. By 10 December they were off the Valdes Peninsula; but the entrance to Port Valdes proved shoal, and with a strongly running current the decision was made to look further south for a harbor of refuge. On 19 December the *Jane* and *Beaufoy* came to anchor in the well-sheltered bay of Port St. Elena. Brisbane and the *Beaufoy* only stayed for a day before sailing south along the shores of St. George's Bay in search of seals. The two captains arranged to rendezvous some two hundred miles further south at Penguin Island off the Patagonian coast.

The *Jane,* alone now, was brought down by the head by two feet and the rudder unshipped. With the stern and counter now free of any obstruction, the carpenter and his men set about repairing the planking. Weddell, as the work progressed, used his talents as a surveyor and worked up a chart of the protected bay. Any harbor of refuge on this desolate, windswept, treeless coast was to be valued: and this one could provide fresh water some half mile from the shore, and fresh meat in the shape of hare and guanaco. One of these deerlike animals was shot and provided 120 pounds of meat. Christmas Day, the repairs completed, was spent in the bay, where they feasted on the guanaco, which tasted like well-fed mutton. They sailed the next day.

By New Year's Day of 1823 the two vessels were back in company, sailing south midway between the Falklands and the Patagonian coast. It was now late in the season, a month late for any chance of finding any quantity of seal in the South Shetlands—and both captains were well aware that four seasons of intensive slaughter had stripped the beaches clean. The alternative was to look for new shores. First, however, were those beaches of the South Orkneys discovered by Powell and Palmer and briefly visited by Weddell during the previous season. After that Weddell was determined to search in areas never before investigated—south, if possible; but Weddell, being a pragmatic man, knew that everything depended upon the ice conditions.

But before all this a matter had to be investigated close to where they were sailing. In 1819 a Captain Bristow had reported shoals with breaking seas midway between the Falklands and the Patagonian coast at 50°55'S and 65°7'W. Another whaler, Captain Robert Poole of the *Aigle,* had reported shoals close to Bristow's reported position. Here was another opportunity for Weddell to pinpoint another danger to seamen. The search, with men scanning the seas from the masthead, proved fruitless.

And Weddell, showing a degree of tetchiness, wrote: "Had it been accurately laid down I ought to have found it." But the Aigle Reef still has a tenuous life on Admiralty charts, where it is marked as ED (Existence Doubtful).

Now no more time could be lost on their passage to the South Orkneys. And the passage proved rough. On 6 January, in freezing conditions, they were hit by storm-force winds combined with an irregular and dangerous sea. The breaking waves swept clear the decks, stove in two boats, and washed away parts of the *Jane*'s bulwarks. And then, as is the way of things at sea, they were suddenly left windless, rolling brutally in the swells. A few days later they were past the Antarctic Convergence, the surface temperature having dropped from 49 to 33 degrees Fahrenheit. In sight were icebergs, and flirting with the *Jane* and the *Beaufoy* were those cheeky birds of the Southern Ocean, the Cape pigeons.

On 12 January they had their first sight of the South Orkney peaks. But, in light airs constantly shifting in direction and in a heavy groundswell, it took them another two days before closing the land. Weddell found these bleak and desolate islands, with their towering craggy peaks like the mountaintops of sunken land, more imposing than the South Shetlands. Fogs were now appearing with unsettling frequency, and the landscape when glimpsed through the dank and swirling mists, imposing as it might be, harbored few seals. On 15 January only a half dozen seals were brought aboard the *Jane*. These were not fur seals but of a different species, slightly puzzling to Weddell, and he called them sea leopards. Here he made a mistake. They were curious enough for Weddell to have them skinned and stowed safely away with their skulls, separate from the fur seal skins.*

The shallops of the *Jane* and *Beaufoy* set off to make a closer examina-

* Two years later, the *Jane* and the *Beaufoy* safely back from their voyaging, these skins were sent by Weddell to Professor Robert Jameson, who held the chair in natural history at Edinburgh University. Jameson was no stranger to receiving offerings from the polar regions. A few years before, he had been given a live polar bear by William Scoresby, which had put the professor in something of a quandary as to its housing and feeding. Scoresby dedicated his *Account Of The Arctic Regions* to the perplexed professor, who had given much encouragement and advice to the Arctic whaler and scientist. The inspiration to Scoresby found no echo in the young Charles Darwin, who attended Jameson's lectures on geology and zoology: he found them so unbearably dull that the young Darwin determined never to read a book on geology or in any way study the science. However, at Cambridge Darwin changed his notions when he came under the wing of the noted geologist Adam Sedgewick, and later in life Darwin was to describe geology as the "noble science."

Professor Jameson, after careful inspection of the skin, teeth, and skull of the specimen presented to him by Weddell, declared it a new species of seal. The French naturalist R. P. Lesson, after studying Jameson's description and a drawing by Weddell, named the seal after the man who brought it back from the South Orkneys.

Today the skin of that seal killed in the South Orkneys described by Jameson and destined to become the type specimen for *Leptonychotes weddelli* rests in the basement of Edinburgh's Royal Scottish Museum, wrapped in plastic. The skull, crushed by the sealer's club, sits in a cardboard box. The skin itself is still in remarkably good condition and shows the needle holes suggesting that the specimen was at one time stuffed and on display.

tion of the South Orkney shores—but a fifty-mile stretch of beach offered up only one fur seal. The parent vessels were between Saddle Island and Laurie Island (Weddell's Melville Island) at the eastern end of the South Orkneys. Saddle Island had been very accurately positioned by Weddell as to latitude and longitude, and he decided to sail west, for the twofold purpose of extending the search for the elusive seals and plotting the westernmost end of the island group. No seals were found but the cape was positioned and then the vessels stretched back to the east to plot the easternmost point of the island group. By 22 January they were off Cape Dundas and two boats were sent ashore to look for seals while Weddell busied himself with sextant and chronometers.

That evening the boats returned with a dozen seals—but only two fur seals. The South Orkneys were proving a grave disappointment. Nevertheless some of the officers, on climbing a hill, had seen a distant range of peaks off to the southeast. Here, perhaps, lay a more lucrative hunting ground. The two vessels sailed that night with a fair wind toward the beckoning peaks.

Sunrise is early in these latitudes, and as the twilight faded with the coming of the sun the chagrined crew saw the land turn into a substantial line of immense icebergs. They were, as Weddell succinctly put it, "unde-ceived." The vessels weaved their way south through the chain of icebergs and came into clearer water. And with the wind from the north Weddell decided to stay on this southerly course. It was, however, but slow prog-ress, with frequent fogs, snow squalls, and the necessity to heave to at night to avoid damaging collisions with growlers and ice floes. The *Beaufoy* kept station close to the *Jane*'s weather quarter, like a faithful terrier. Imagined dangers loomed out of the fog when the nervous second mate called Weddell from his cabin with the shout that breakers were close under their lee. Weddell scrambled on deck and ordered the *Jane* brought on the wind; but the danger evaporated with the clearing fog and no signs of breakers. Weddell could only surmise that the surfacing and breathing of whales had startled the mate.

By 27 January they had reached 64°58′S—well to the south of the South Shetlands. Here Weddell made a decision that would come back to haunt him. At the time it seemed a sensible one, backed by careful reason-ing. The reasoning went thus: the summer season was now well advanced and it seemed prudent to stand north and look for land between the South Orkneys and Cook's Sandwich Land while the nights were comparatively short—for darkness added to fog made navigation in an icy sea even more dangerous.

The decision taken, the vessels' heads were set to the north. It was a passage where they were constantly surrounded by icebergs; but these had become so familiar that the two small craft, dwarfed by the floating islands, weaved between them with a certain degree of insouciance. But caution,

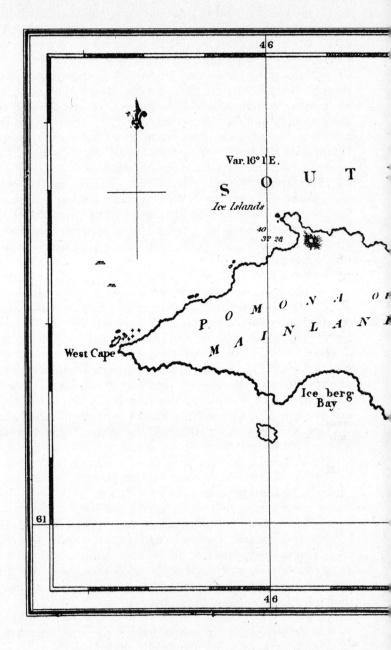

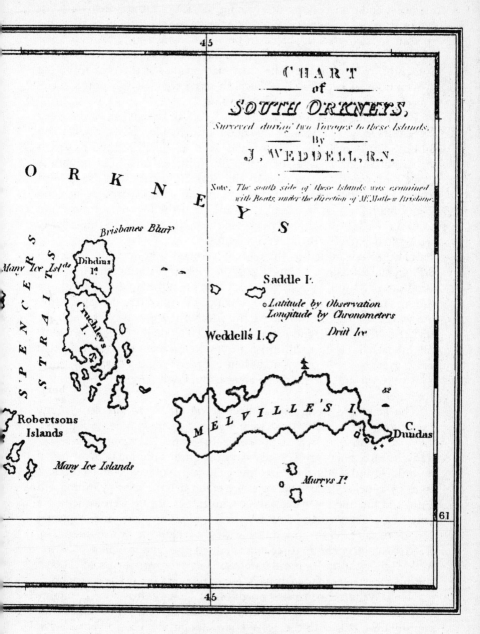

Chart of the South Orkneys.

From *A Voyage Towards the South Pole*, London, 1827

vigilance, and eyes constantly scanning the seas are the watchwords for sailing in an ice-strewn sea. One night the *Jane* abruptly hove to as the lookout spotted what appeared to be a rock dangerously close on their course. A sounding with the lead line found no bottom, but the two vessels prudently lay hove-to until the chief mate made out the rock to be the swollen body of a dead whale. "Such objects," Weddell drily noted, "seen imperfectly in the night, are often alarming."

By 1 February they were in latitude 58°50′S and about halfway between the South Orkneys and Sandwich Land (South Sandwich Islands), with no land in sight or any indication of land. Here Weddell changed course to the southeast, quartering the sea in his fruitless search. Ten pounds— about nine months' wages for an able seaman in the Royal Navy—was offered by Weddell as a prize to the first man to sight a coastline—an echo of Columbus's offer of a similar reward. (But the lookout of the *Pinta* never received it—Columbus pocketed the prize, blandly claiming that *he* had sighted land during the previous night.)

The £10 reward led to the dashing of many a hope as the *Jane* and *Beaufoy* altered course to investigate the lookout's triumphal—if prema- ture—cry of "Land!" By 4 February Cook's Sandwich Land lay within a hundred miles and the search had convinced Weddell that no new discov- eries would be made in this part of the Southern Ocean. Any land must lie further to the south—and it was south that Weddell now determined to sail. He talked this over with Brisbane and found that imperturbable man just as eager to press southward as himself, even though the sailing condi- tions were vile and the southerly course could only lengthen their collec- tive miseries.

The Janes and Beaufoys had been living for weeks in cold, clammy discomfort. The vessels' decks were constantly wet with dense fog, rain, snow, sleet, spray, and seas at 36 degrees Fahrenheit. Air temperature hov- ered at the freezing level. The men were obviously suffering in these dismal conditions, and Weddell ordered the galley stove moved from its caboose on deck to belowdecks where the fire could dry the men's clothing. To warm and fuel the inner man, three wineglasses of rum were issued on a daily basis. The victuals, however, were rationed to one and a quarter pounds of salt beef or pork a day, with a weekly issue of five pounds of bread, two pints of flour, three pints of dried peas, and two pints of barley. Weddell thought these rations barely sufficient for work in a cold climate, but the uncertainty of the voyage's length required the strictest economy.

When Weddell had turned north on 27 January their course roughly followed the 40°W line of longitude. On this second probe south they were following close to the 30°W line of longitude. On 10 February, in 66°S latitude, their frustrating search appeared to be rewarded. In the early light of dawn the chief mate made out land to the south, dark colored and shaped like a sugarloaf. Weddell, peering through his spyglass, could only agree. The bitter wind was blowing from the south and the two vessels were jammed hard on the wind to reach the tantalizing cliff face. The rest of the morning watch, marked off by the half-hourly tolling of the ship's bell, slowly passed. Near midday the sacred instruments of chronometer and sextant were brought on deck and the hieratic noon sight ceremony was performed, followed by the sounding of the bell and the start of another nautical day. Throughout all this the dark cliff face drew closer and the air of excitement on deck reached fever pitch.

Halfway through the afternoon watch, as the four strokes of the bell faded in the cold air, with all the crew on deck, the island's rocky shore lay visible a quarter mile distant. Before the next bell was struck they had halved the distance. And the island's rocky cliff face had mutated into an iceberg with its north face thickly encrusted with black earth, stones, and rocks. It was another savage blow to the hopes of the crew, a blow that could only lower their fast-sinking morale.

Weddell, equally discouraged, sought consolation in the hope that the earth-encrusted iceberg had broken away from land—and that the land was close. With the wind southerly, it would have been an easy decision to wear ship and steer north to more temperate latitudes. Weddell, however, held on to the wind and stood southwest. For nearly a week they struggled south against the prevailing wind. During one frustrating twenty-four hours they won only sixteen miles southing. Not only was the wind against them, but on that same day they had to fight their way through a massed phalanx of sixty-six icebergs.

And then suddenly, on 16 February, their fortunes changed. It was as if those ever fickle deities of the Antarctic had finally relented: the Janes and Beaufoys had proved their worth, and, having passed through the magic citadel ramparts of icebergs, were now set free on a halcyon sea. The wind swung into the west and felt almost warm, the sea became gentle, few icebergs were in sight, flocks of seabirds wheeled about the vessels, and the smooth surface of the sea was broken only by surfacing fin and humpback whales. Under these idyllic conditions the *Beaufoy* left her usual position on the *Jane*'s weather quarter and sailed wide to extend their range of view.

The noon position on 17 February put them at 71°34'S and 30°12'W. They were the southernmost ships and humans in the world. Cook had reached 71°10'S in 1774 aboard the *Resolution*. Now the smaller *Jane* and even smaller *Beaufoy* had joined that elite handful of polar exploration vessels. The ideal sailing conditions lasted throughout the next day. Let Weddell take up the story:

In the evening we had many whales about the ship, and the sea was literally covered with birds of the blue peterel kind. NOT A PARTICLE OF ICE OF ANY DESCRIPTION WAS TO BE SEEN. The evening was mild and serene, and had it not been for the reflection that probably we should have obstacles to contend with in our passage northward, through the ice, our situation might have been envied. The wind was light and easterly during the night, and we carried all sail.

These benign and unusual conditions continued. The next day saw the carpenter repairing one of the boats while the crew wielded palms, needles, cobbler's wax, thread, serving mallets, marline, tallow, and tar, servicing spars, sails and rigging—activities close to the hearts of chief mates and boatswains worldwide.

The *Jane* and the *Beaufoy* in 68° S, February 1823.

On 20 February the wind shifted into the south and blew fresh. Away to the southeast lay a clouded horizon and flocks of birds. Toward these portents the two vessels thrashed their way, now hard on the wind. Just before noon the sky cleared, and under the midday sun the two vessels sparkled like jewels with spray-wet decks and rigging. The horizon lay clear all around them, their only companions being three icebergs, one of them crowded with penguins. The noon sight put them at 74°15′S and 34°16′ 45″W. No indication of land lay to the south and from the south came that cold, frustrating, and freshening wind.

It was the wind direction that forced a decision upon Weddell. For the last few days he had been in the position of a gambler calculating the odds and pressured by time to make a critical wager. If he won, he would gain an enigmatic parcel containing either new sealing grounds, a passing profit, and fame as an explorer, or possibly—the ultimate macabre joke—nothing. If he lost, it meant the probable death of himself and his men. Cook on all his deep probes south had been halted by the ice. Weddell, 185 miles further south than Cook—but one month later—had a clear sea in front of him. But the south wind had dramatically changed the odds. They could sail southeasterly or southwesterly, but not to the south. Land could lie in any direction. But even if land and seals were found, the season was ending and astern lay over a thousand miles of ice-strewn sea, fogs, and lengthening nights. If they were caught by the ice the hopes of survival were nil. His position was similar to that of Ernest Shackleton, who eighty-six years later marched to within 97 miles of the South Pole. Shackleton knew that he and his companions could reach the Pole but that the odds of a safe return to their winter quarters at Cape Royds were nil. Shackleton turned back. Weddell, reluctantly, arrived at the same conclusion. Better a prudent mariner than a dead one. And just as Shackleton would hold a small ceremony at his furthest south amidst the terrible wastes of the polar plateau, so did Weddell in the sparkling sea that he named George The Fourth Sea.

Weddell made a signal to the *Beaufoy* to bear away and steer northwest. He then gathered his crew, told them his decision, and, knowing that the men would be sorely disappointed—for this was a sealing voyage and their share depended upon the cargo—put some heart into them with the information that they had penetrated further south than any previous seamen, including the great Captain James Cook. To mark the occasion and to put on a brave show, their colors were hoisted, the cannon was fired, an extra allowance of rum was issued, and the crew gave three hurrahs.

That evening as the *Jane* and the *Beaufoy* stood northward carrying all possible sail, Weddell ruminated on his decision to turn north on 27 January. Those days wasted could have been more profitably spent in these higher latitudes making for an even deeper probe to the south—perhaps even to the South Pole itself. It was as well for Weddell's equanimity that, unknown to him, the Antarctic coastline of Coat's Land lay but two days' sail to the southeast and the Filchner Ice Shelf three days' sail to the south of that noon position of 20 February.

The coast and the ice shelf were to wait until the early years of the twentieth century before being discovered by W. S. Bruce's Scottish National Antarctic Expedition aboard the *Scotia* and Dr. Wilhelm Filchner's German expedition aboard the *Deutschland*. Both ships had auxiliary engines and both were ice reinforced—but the *Scotia* barely escaped being beset and the *Deutschland* lay trapped by the ice for nine months. Unluckier were Dr. Otto Nordenskjold's Swedish expeditionary ship the *Antarctic* and Sir Ernest Shackleton's *Endurance*: both were beset, held, crushed, and sunk by the Weddell Sea pack ice.

Closer to Weddell's time, three national naval expeditions were to fail in even penetrating the outer ramparts of the Weddell Sea pack ice. In 1838 Dumont d'Urville and his two French navy vessels, the *Astrolabe* and the *Zélée,* only reached 63°23'S. The French commander dismissed Weddell with Gallic disdain as a "simple seal hunter" and considered him a liar. But this was d'Urville's first experience of the ice; his temperament was always more attuned to the civilized ambiance of the Mediterranean and felt uneasy amidst the raw and basic elements offered by the Antarctic.*

The next attempt to better Weddell's farthest south would be made by the Americans in their woefully equipped vessels of the United States Exploring Expedition led by Lieutenant Charles Wilkes. As with d'Urville, Wilkes's orders bid him follow "the track of Weddell as closely as practicable, endeavoring to reach a high southern latitude." Toward the end of February 1839, far too late in the season, Wilkes sailed from Tierra del Fuego and headed for the Weddell Sea with the *Porpoise* and the *Sea Gull.* Two other vessels, the *Peacock* and the *Flying Fish,* sailed the same day and headed further west, following U.S. Navy Department orders to "stretch towards the southwards and westwards as far as the Ne Plus Ultra of Cook or longitude 105°W'." Cook and Weddell were again the measure in this chauvinistic game of national prestige as to which country could sail closest to the South Pole.

Wilkes failed miserably in the Weddell Sea, only reaching the tip of the Antarctic Peninsula and the South Shetlands. The ice conditions and the weather they found appalling. The clothing of the men was totally inadequate for these severe conditions, and Wilkes darkly hinted that it was the fault of both suppliers and government inspectors, of whom "I hesitate to give their names publicity. The deception is in my opinion to be attributed to both." More seriously—and here the blame can be attributed to

---

* It was in the Mediterranean that the younger d'Urville, serving as an *enseigne* aboard the *Chevrette,* had found a modicum of fame. On the island of Melos he realized the extraordinary grace and beauty of a statue hidden away in a Greek peasant's cowshed. The marble sculpture was of a partially naked woman holding in her raised left hand an apple; over the right arm a draped sash fell from her hips to her feet. It was obvious to d'Urville that this statue represented Venus of the Judgment of Paris. Events now move with the melodramatic brevity of a subtitled silent movie:

The ignorant peasant is willing to sell the statue.
The captain refuses to have the sculpture aboard his ship.
The *Chevrette* sails to Constantinople.
The statue is described by d'Urville to the French ambassador.
A French ship is ordered to Melos to buy the statue for France.
But a grasping priest now owns the statue.
The avaricious cleric sells the statue to the French—but at a much higher price.
Greek brigands attack the French sailors as they carry the statue to their ship.
The statue looses her arms in the struggle.
The statue is installed in the Louvre.
The Legion d'Honneur is awarded to d'Urville.
Which accounts for the Venus de Milo's having no arms.

Wilkes—both vessels were overcrowded (the *Vincennes* and the *Relief* had been left at Tierra del Fuego) and the men, surprisingly for such a short passage, showed signs of scurvy. The attempt to best Weddell was abandoned. The vessels sent to beat Cook's record also failed.

Nevertheless, both American and French expeditions would recoup the reverses to their national self-esteem and pride in 1840 with discoveries on the opposite side of the Antarctic continent.

The third national naval expedition, a British one, was commanded by Captain James Clark Ross in his two ships the *Erebus* and *Terror*. It had the advantage over the French and American expeditions, not only in the quality of the ships and provisioning, but also in that those expeditions' excursions into the Antarctic were auxiliary to their major area of activity in the Pacific. The British expedition was organized for the sole purpose of making magnetic studies in the high southern latitudes and locating the south magnetic pole. The opening sentences of the Admiralty orders to Ross, with their magisterial cadences, contain the essence of the voyage's purpose:

Whereas it has been represented to us that the science of magnetism may be essentially improved by an extensive series of observations made in the high southern latitudes, and by a comparison of such observations with others made at certain fixed stations, and whereas practical navigation must eventually derive important benefit from every improvement in that science; we have, in consideration of these objects, caused Her Majesty's ships *Erebus* and *Terror* to be in all respects prepared for a voyage for carrying into complete execution the purposes above mentioned.

The orders continue in their stately, measured tones. After magnetic observations at St. Helena, the Cape of Good Hope, and Kerguelen Island, Ross should sail to Van Diemen's Land (Tasmania), where another magnetic observatory should be established. The Lieutenant Governor, Sir John Franklin, had been instructed to prepare instruments, and Ross was to establish the observatory in the most advantageous position, leaving an officer and assistants in charge, "making such provisions for their victualling and lodging as appear to be most convenient, and not inconsistent with the Naval Regulations." The orders now warm to their work:

In the following summer, your provisions having been completed and your crews refreshed, you will proceed direct to the southward, in order to determine the position of the magnetic pole, and even to attain it if possible, which it is hoped will be one of the remarkable and creditable results of the expedition.

Ross's attempt to sail to the south magnetic pole—an impossible feat, as the pole was then located on land—had been rewarded by his sailing south close to the 180-degree meridian into the sea that bears his name. They passed Weddell's furthest south on 23 January 1841 and celebrated, as the Janes and Beaufoys had done, with an extra allowance of grog. It being a Saturday night, the grog was drunk with the seaman's favorite

212

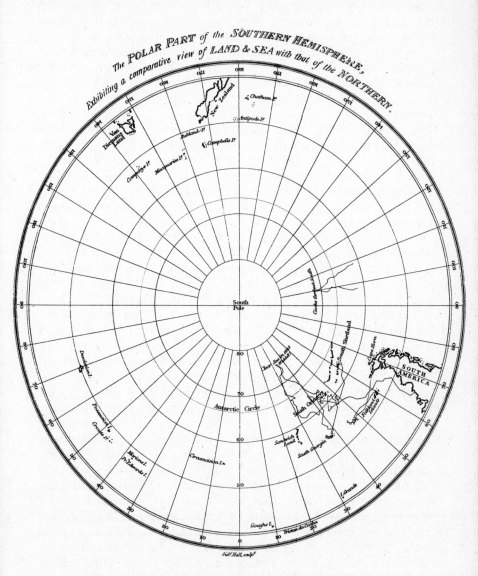

Polar part of the northern hemisphere and polar part of the southern hemisphere.
From Weddell's *A Voyage Towards the South Pole*, London, 1827

toast of "Sweethearts and wives"; and no doubt, as always when no ladies present, the toast was followed by a sotto voce "may they never meet." A few days later the ships reached the impenetrable ice shelf that Ross named the Icy Barrier—now the Ross Ice Shelf—and a furthest south of 78°04'S.

After wintering in Tasmania and Sydney, Ross spent the second Antarctic summer in the Ross Sea and then sailed east to spend the third winter in the Falkland Islands. Their last joust with the Antarctic ice started in January 1843. It was a hard struggle with the Weddell Sea pack, and their furthest south of 71°30'S was not reached until March. Unknown to Ross, Cape Norvegia on the eastern shores of the Weddell Sea lay but fifty miles away. Not until 1930 would the cape be discovered—from the air by Riiser-Larsen flying in a seaplane from the small Norwegian whaler *Norvegia.*

Ross, after his interminable struggle with the pack ice, could only conclude that Weddell "was favoured by an unusually fine season, and we may rejoice that there was a brave man and daring seaman on the spot to profit by the opportunity." It was a more generous and correct appreciation of Weddell's voyage than the snide comments of d'Urville and the patriotic rodomantade of the youthful Lieutenant Reynolds aboard one of the vessels of the U.S. Exploring Expedition. On their second tussle with the polar seas the Americans had sailed from Sydney on 26 December 1839 and reached 65°25'S with no ice in sight. "We would pass 70°," wrote the excited lieutenant, "eclipse Cook and distance the pretender Weddell." The shades of generations of sealers would have looked over the shoulder of that hubristic young man as he wrote those words and wagged their heads in amazement. But, in order to place those comments in perspective, Reynolds's first sight of an iceberg had happened only a few days before.

A true appreciation of Weddell's achievement has to be seen in the context of the Weddell Sea ice conditions. A glance at a map of Antarctica shows the Antarctic Peninsula rising like a splinted thumb from the clenched fist of the continent. Close to the rim of the continent the prevailing winds blow counterclockwise, herding the sea ice, shelf ice, and icebergs into the bight of the Weddell Sea. Here the ice is stopped by the Peninsula and the southwest and western areas of the sea become virtually impassable for ships. The ice plates ride over and under each other, forming pressure ridges, hummocks, above the surface and ridges below the surface. The only relief from this monstrous pressure is for the ice to grind slowly northward along the immovable barrier of the Peninsula until it eventually spins off into the waters of the Southern Ocean at the Peninsula's tip. Here at the tip the surface currents are under the thrall of the prevailing westerly winds and the ice now streams away in an easterly direction like a plume of smoke from a chimney. And this plume of ice makes a very effective barrier for any ship that attempts to enter the Weddell Sea near the Peninsula.

The breakup of the winter sea ice starts in the eastern portion of the

Weddell Sea. But even in winter, polynyas—open stretches of water—occur along the eastern shoreline as the sea is broken away from the fast ice by the strong easterly winds. An even larger polynya than the normal coastal ones appeared in the 1970s on satellite images: a huge open ice-free lake, some 116,000 square miles in area, surrounded by pack ice.

The sealers in the South Shetlands learned very rapidly that ice conditions varied wildly from summer to summer. One season would have little ice and the next a dangerous amount. Ross's assessment that Weddell had been favored by an unusually fine ice-free season is the correct one. Fortune, in short, smiled on Weddell during that summer of 1823.

X

Weddell and the Fuegians

There is no reason to believe that the Fuegians decrease in
number; therefore we must suppose that they enjoy a sufficient share of happiness, of whatever kind it may be, to render
life worth having. Nature by making habit omnipotent, and
its effects hereditary, has fitted the Fuegian to the climate and
the productions of his miserable country.

Charles Darwin, *The Voyage of The Beagle,* 1839

FTER THAT deep penetration of the Weddell Sea in February
of 1823, the nearest land where James Weddell could refresh his
men and refurbish his vessels lay some twelve hundred miles to
the north. And South Georgia, uninhabited but with a wealth
of wildlife and anchorages, was the island to which the two vessels now set
their course. The passage was relatively uneventful—if sailing amidst fog,
ice, and lengthening nights plus frequent gales can be called carefree.
During the night of 5 March, in thick fog, the two vessels lost touch with
each other. The separation worried Weddell; his concern was not only for
the smaller *Beaufoy* but also for his own vessel, as the *Jane,* two days later,
was running at over ten knots before a southwest gale through icebergs
and broken ice. The chief mate was stationed high in the foretop and
shouted alterations in course to the helmsman as ice floes were spotted
lying low in the hollow of the racing seas. And these were frigid seas that
swept the decks clear of every moveable item. But Weddell was determined
to make the most of this favorable storm and the *Jane* roared through the
days and nights with all the watch on deck scanning the seas for ice.

By the morning of 9 March the wind had moderated and shifted to the
northwest. The noon position put them some one hundred miles away
from South Georgia, which, much to Weddell's relief, was far enough
north to lessen the chances of their falling in with more ice. Instead they
were bedeviled with thick fog and light variable winds. But, much to their
joy, at eight o'clock in the morning of 12 March, the weather having

cleared with an increasing wind, they sighted a familiar sail to the northwest. Within an hour they were alongside the *Beaufoy* and with shouted
exchanges found all well with Brisbane and his crew. An hour later they
sighted the peaks of South Georgia. Weddell's relief is apparent from this
extract from his *Voyage Towards the South Pole:*

Notwithstanding the forbidding appearance of this land, every one, I believe, in
the two vessels, feasted his eyes upon it; and at 3 in the afternoon both ships came
to anchor in Adventure Bay [Undine Harbour] in 7 fathoms water, over a bottom
of strong clay.

Our arrival here, though it was not a country the most indulgent, we considered to be a very happy event. Our sailors had suffered much from cold fogs and
wet during the two months they had been navigating the south; and as we had
been nearly 5 months under sail, the appearance of scurvy (that disease so fatally
attendant on long voyages) was to be dreaded. Our vessels, too, were so much
weather-beaten, that they greatly needed refitting; so that taking into account our
many pressing wants, this island, though inhospitable, was capable of affording us
great relief.

Our crews here fed plenteously on greens which, although bitter, are very
salutary, being an excellent antiscorbutic: with regard to meat, we were supplied
with young albatrosses, that is to say, about a year old: the flesh of these is sweet,
but not sufficiently firm to be compared with that of any domestic fowl.

Our harbour duties, and a search upon the island for animals for our cargo,
were immediately commenced and carried on with zeal, although we experienced
frequent interruptions from heavy gales which were now prevalent; it being near
the time of the autumnal equinox of this hemisphere.

Weddell, following in the footsteps of Cook, was using the natural
resources of the land, no matter how strange, to combat scurvy. The greens
he refers to were probably the burnets that grow on the island and which
he would have recognized. Indeed, according to the seventeenth-century
herbalist Nicholas Culpeper, a few stalks and leaves of the "Great Burnet
. . . put into a cup of wine, especially claret, are known to quicken the
spirits, refresh and cheer the heart and drive away melancholy." As to the
wildlife, nearly a century later, in 1916, and some twenty miles from where
Weddell's men feasted on year-old albatross chicks, another group of men
would gather round a driftwood fire and watch with salivating impatience
a gently simmering pot. One man would later scribble into his diary remarks on the contents of that pot: "All hands have been gathering dry
tussock grass for the floor of the cave the Boss & skipper have fixed sails at
the mouth & there is a good wood fire going & our wet clothes drying.
We have not been as comfortable for the last 5 weeks. We had 3 young & 1
old albatross for lunch. With 1 pint of gravy which beats all the chicken
soup I ever tasted."

The other men—obviously sharing the epicurean diarist's opinions—
lay around after their meals, stomachs confortably full, and discussed making enough money to start another expedition by taking hundreds of these

albatross chicks and selling them to epicures, gourmets, gourmands, and gluttons of Europe and New York at £50 apiece. The diarist was Harry McNiece and the two gastronomic entrepreneurs—the Boss & skipper— were Sir Ernest Shackleton and Captain Frank Worsley. With three other men they had just made their landing on South Georgia after the epic seven-hundred-mile winter voyage from Elephant Island in the twenty-foot *James Caird*.

In his *Voyage Towards The South Pole* Weddell apologizes to his readers for the descriptions of the wildlife on South Georgia, fearing he has been tedious and the remarks of little importance. His fear was misplaced. All the books published about the island and its wildlife contain references to Weddell. Indeed, a most graceful compliment comes from Robert Cushman Murphy, the first curator of oceanic birds at the American Museum of Natural History and author of the classic *Oceanic Birds of South America*. Murphy spent the summer of 1912–13 at the Bay of Isles near a large king penguin colony and in his story of that summer, *Logbook for Grace,* writes that Weddell's account of the bird's life history could not be bettered and that he, Murphy, would not change a word of it.

Weddell was obviously enchanted by these elegant, dignified, and stately birds: "In pride, these birds are perhaps not surpassed even by the peacock, to which in beauty of plumage they are indeed little inferior . . . their frequently looking down their front and sides in order to contemplate the perfection of their exterior brilliancy, and to remove any speck which might sully it, is truly amusing to an observer." The smaller, urchinlike penguins are described, with their regrettable thievish habits of stealing stones from their neighbor's nests; the aristocratic wandering albatross is chronicled with its twelve-foot wingspan, stately courtship ritual, and ability to "defend [itself] for half an hour against an active dog" with its powerful beak; the plebeian giant petrel—the sailor's Nelley or Stinker, with its unlovely looks and gross eating habits—for a flock of six hundred of these voracious birds "has been known to devour 10 tons of the sea-elephant fat in six or eight hours." Even the strong-stomached sealers found the flesh of these Southern Ocean harpies quite uneatable. As to the fur seals and elephant seals, Weddell estimated that thirty years of sealing had seen twenty thousand tons of elephant seal oil sold on the London market and at least 1.2 million fur seal skins taken by American and British sealers.

For over a month the *Jane* and the *Beaufoy* lay at anchor in Undine Harbor. The men searched the shores for seals, clambering and dragging their whaleboats across the half mile of tussock and bog that separates Undine Harbor on the south shore of the island from Elsehul on the north shore. And finding few seals. Today the beaches of Elsehul during the breeding season are so crammed with fur seals that it is not only danger-

ous—the bull is a violently aggressive and disconcertingly speedy creature—but virtually impossible to cross. Fur seals are very mobile on land
and, perhaps to escape the crush on the beaches, can be found among the
tussocks of that narrow neck of land between Undine and Elsehul trodden
by Weddell's men and all the other sealers.

One day, as his men continued the search for the elusive seal, Weddell
took himself, his chronometers, sextant, and a pan of mercury to the top
of a hill near this pathway. The passion for precision survey work was to
the fore again. The day, a rare one for South Georgia, was windless, cloud-
less, and the snow-covered mountains and sea glittered like a jumbled heap
of precious stones in the brilliant sunlight. Ideal conditions for taking the
Sun's altitude from a stable platform rather than a heaving deck, with
the pan of mercury acting as an artificial horizon. After setting up the
equipment, Weddell was astonished to see the surface of the mercury
agitated and ruffled by some unseen force. He could only assume that the
shaking was caused by infinitesimal earth tremors. The altitude sight had
to be abandoned. Two years previous to this strange experience Weddell
had passed within two hundred yards of Bridgeman Island in the South
Shetlands and had noted an odd phenomenon. The island is small, in the
shape of a truncated pyramid rising to nearly a thousand feet and is virtually
snow free. On sailing past he had noted smoke pouring from fissures in the
cliff face. This, plus the evidence of earth tremors in South Georgia and
the similarity of rocks from the South Shetlands, South Georgia, and Tierra
del Fuego, caused Weddell to surmise—he was the first person to do so—
that a geological kinship existed between South America and the Antarctic
islands.

On 17 April the *Jane* and the *Beaufoy* sailed from South Georgia bound
for the Falkland Islands. The nine-hundred-mile passage took three weeks.
Shifting headwinds plagued them, forcing the crew to tack the vessels like
racing yachts on the wind shifts. The *Jane* came close to losing her mast
when backstays and shrouds parted in a wild and irregular sea; but Weddell,
the prudent seaman, had rigged extra shrouds and stays for just such an
eventuality. During one storm the heavy seas swept away the *Beaufoy*'s
bowsprit; but the *Jane* carried a suitable spar for a replacement. On 11 May
the two worn and battered vessels dropped anchor at New Island. A few
days later they were anchored some twelve miles away in the protected
Quaker Harbor of Swan Island—the present-day Weddell Island. Here the
Jane's topmasts were struck down and all made snug for the winter. The
smaller and handier *Beaufoy* was kept ready for sealing. It was also another
opportunity for Weddell to collect more information on the anchorages,
currents, tides, and dangers of the islands. The information proved easier
to collect than cargo. Another season would have to be spent in the south
in order to fill their woefully empty holds. On 7 October the *Jane* and

Beaufoy sailed from the Falklands and set course for the South Shetlands, the two vessels, as Weddell ruefully observed, "having prepared, but with scanty means, for a southern navigation."

A week later, only a hundred miles south of Cape Horn, they sighted their first iceberg. It was an ominous portent. On the morning of 16 October they sailed past a two-mile-long tabular iceberg and later that twilit night slipped like ghosts through seven more. Icebergs so far north came as a surprise to Weddell, but worse was over the horizon to the south. Ninety-five miles from the South Shetlands, in thick fog, they ran into impenetrable pack ice. Thinking it only a small local patch, the *Jane* and the *Beaufoy* ran before the wind in an easterly direction, skirting the edge of the ice for twenty miles. For the whole of that distance the ice presented a silent implacable front heaving slowly in the swells. Night coming on, they hauled to the north, away from this sinister and sinuous barrier, and waited for daylight.

Ice so far north at this time of year was most unusual. William Smith, the discoverer of the South Shetlands, had reached further south in the middle of the 1819 winter. It was all very disconcerting. Weddell was now akin to an army commander searching for a weak point along the defensive perimeter of ice guarding the citadel of the South Shetlands. The dank and gray dawn of 17 October found them sailing south for another probe along the massed ice floes of the islands' defenses. First of all Weddell tried an outflanking maneuver. He had noticed a strong easterly current and reasoned that the ice might be doubled on its left flank. He signaled to the *Beaufoy* and the two vessels worked their way west along the edge of the pack. This opening tactic failed, for the ice presented no weakly defended flank. Fortunately for the Janes and Beaufoys, they had no foreknowledge that this opening move was only the first in a monthlong battle with the ice.

It was to be a campaign stamped with all the classic hallmarks of encounters between sailing ships and pack ice. Leads would lure them south and the ice would close astern of them in a pincerlike movement, leaving them helpless in a shrinking lagoon, their only escape to batter their way northward through the weakest section of the cordon closing around them. Bitter storm-force winds joined forces with the ice. "I was glad," wrote Weddell, "to see the *Beaufoy* was prepared for the worst, and by the advantage which a cutter possesses over a square-rigged vessel, in having fore and aft sails, with comparative little bulk aloft, she seemed to lie much easier than we did. Our main topsail was storm-reefed, which requiring the sheets to be eased off several feet, reduced the sail to the size of a mere napkin." The violent seas swept the decks clear, taking with them one of the whaleboats and leaving rapidly accumulating ice in its place. Weddell thought the mantle of ice on hull and deck helped in holding the vessel's structure together under the constant pounding of the seas. The disadvantage, however, was the increasing sluggishness of the craft under the extra weight of ice. To make matters worse, the *Jane*'s rudder-stock froze in the trunk, making her a virtual hulk battered by the seas.

Conditions for the men were now appalling. They were frozen above deck and they were frozen below deck. Their clothes, after twelve months of wear, were paper thin and for many of them the wet rags they wore were the only clothes they owned. Weddell gave away his spare clothing, blankets were cut up for stockings, old canvas sewn to make jackets, and pump leather was put into service to repair boots. Weddell had nothing but praise for his companions: "I never, during my experience at sea, have seen an equal degree of patience and firmness as was exhibited by these seamen. No dastardly request to reach a better climate was ever hinted at, but they continued in the strictest obedience and determination to make light of difficulties."

During this terrible month their most terrifying experience came with an iceberg. Finding a weakness in the pack ice, the *Jane* and the *Beaufoy* penetrated into the floes for about eight miles before both vessels became immoveable. The *Jane* had been leading, using her heavier weight to force a passage through the floes, and the *Beaufoy* came alongside in the looser ice displaced by the *Jane*. Around them in the pack lay some forty icebergs; but nothing is static in this seemingly frozen world and some of these icebergs were moving west under the impetus of a deepwater current while the windblown pack, holding fast the two vessels, moved east. One particular iceberg, surging through the pack and moving inexorably toward them on a collision course, was watched with horror. About 180 feet high, this brutal mass of ice sported a projecting and fissured overhang high and large enough for the two vessels to be swept under. All on board could see with dreadful clarity what the outcome would be. First the masts would be sheared off and then the weakened overhang would break away and tons of ice would thunder down on the decks. All their frantic efforts failed to move the two vessels out from the course of the charging iceberg and their rapidly approaching death. Only when the glittering mass of this frozen sword of Damocles overhung the *Jane*'s quarterdeck did the fates relent. A large and thick floe acted as a fender between the *Jane* and the iceberg's side, keeping the spars and masts clear of the overhang. Within minutes the vessels were swept down the sides of the iceberg and into clearer water swirling in the behemoth's wake.

Four days later, after battering their way back north, they sailed into open water. Not without damage however. The monthlong battle with the ice had taken its toll. Stove-in planking that had been crudely patched,

OVERLEAF
Chart of the South Shetlands.
From *A Voyage Towards The South Pole*, London, 1827

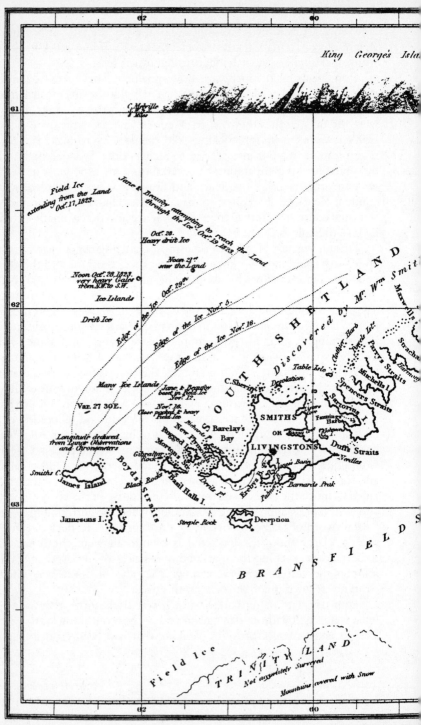

King George's Islar

C. Melville
Inlet

61

Field Ice
extending from the Land
Oct: 17, 1823.

Jane & Beaufoy attempting to reach the Land
through the Ice Oct: 29 1823.

Oct: 28.
Heavy drift Ice

Noon 27th
saw the Land

Noon Oct: 28, 1823.
very heavy Gales
from N.W. to S.W.

Oct: 29th

Ice Islands

62

Drift Ice

Edge of the Ice Nov: 5.

Edge of the Ice Nov: 16.

Many Ice Islands

Jane & Beaufoy
beset in Field Ice
Nov: 12.

Var. 27 30 E.

Nov: 16.
Close packed & heavy
Field Ice

Longitude deduced
from Lunar Observations
and Chronometers

Smiths C.

James Island

Boyd's Straits

Black Rocks

Ragged I.

New Plymth

Gibraltar
Rock

Morton Str.

Basil Halls I.

Richards I.

Devils Pt.

S. O U T H   S H E T L A N D

Discovered by Mr. Wm. Smith

Maxwells

C. Sheriff.

Decolation

Table Isle

Clothier Harb.

Boyds Islt.

Parry's Straits

Strachan

Harmony

Mitchells I.

Spencers Straits

Santorins I.

Barclay's
Bay

SMITHS
OR
LIVINGSTONS
I.

Fanning
Harb.

Elephant

Dorsler

Dutn Straits

Verdler

Joness Basin

Barnards Peak

Palmes

63

Jamesons I.

Steeple Rock

Deception

B R A N S F I E L D S   S

Field Ice

T R I N I T Y   L A N D

Not accurately Surveyed

Mountains covered with Snow

London, Published by Longm

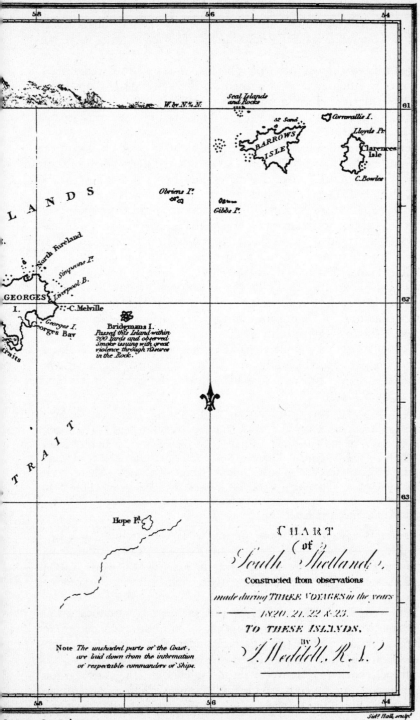

torn-away bulwarks, main guard-board ripped away, and damaged stem could be counted among the major items. They were lucky to be still afloat.

Weddell, worn down with worry, his men tired and dispirited, his vessels battered, admitted defeat, signaled the *Beaufoy*, and stood northwest on a course for Cape Horn. In sight astern of them lay the South Shetlands: they had fought to within twenty miles of the islands but the pack ice had triumphed and held the field.

On 23 November the *Jane* and the *Beaufoy* dropped anchor in the small sheltered harbor of Wigwam Cove some ten miles north of Cape Horn. Within hours the boats and men were ashore collecting wood and water while Weddell and the carpenter inspected the vessels and made a list of the damages caused by the ice. They were to spend three months in Tierra del Fuego, moving from anchorage to anchorage in search of seals and with one extended period moored in Indian Cove with the *Jane* hove down by the stern as the carpenter worked on the damaged stem and planking. During December Brisbane and the *Beaufoy* made a fruitless passage back across the Drake Passage in another attempt to reach the South Shetlands. The islands were still locked in ice. After the remarkable ice-free conditions of the previous summer, the pack had returned with a vengeance for this summer of 1823–24.

Weddell devotes a complete chapter in his book to Tierra del Fuego and an extensive appendix on the weather at Cape Horn. The superscription for this chapter betrays his fascination with the natives of this bleak and inhospitable land:

Voyage to Tierra Del Fuego.—Cape Horn.—The Natives; Their Visit, Manners, &c.—Punishment of a Thief, and Its Good Effect.—Native Dogs.—The Habits, Behaviour, &c. of the Fuegians.—Islands of St. Francis.—Change of Anchorage.—Other Tribes.—Canoe.—State of Society, &c.—Islands of Diego Ramirez.—Language of the Fuegians and Curious Hebrew Analogies.—Music and Its Effects.—New Clay Clothing.—Necklaces, Baskets, Bows.—Arrival of the Beaufoy.—Feugian Settlement.—Vessels Separate.—Face of the Country.—Effect of Climate on the Fuegian Character.

Now this nascent anthropology might have been motivated by a shrewd appreciation of his readers' appetite for tales of naked savages living along wild and desolate shores at the uttermost part of the world. All this would make for most exciting reading when contrasted with the comforts of a home set in the tamed and pleasing English countryside.

But his comments show an interest and generosity toward these primitive people living their waterborne nomadic life in crude canoes and cruder shelters. True, along with Cook's Pacific islanders, they held most regrettable views on the sanctity of property—views totally opposite to those held by European societies. And, with surprising cunning, the natives would pilfer belaying pins, tin cups, iron hoops, and sealskins from the *Jane* and the *Beaufoy*. One of these thieves was so adroit that Weddell, his patience wearing thin, had him placed in the rigging and given one stroke with the lash. If the thieving lessened in blatancy, it only increased in circumspection.

As well as thieving, all the natives possessed extraordinary powers of mimicry. Weddell tells a tale with great relish of an incident aboard the *Beaufoy* illustrating cunning in pilfering and ability in mimicry.

A sailor had given a Fuegian a tin pot full of coffee, which he drank, and was using all his art to steal the pot. The sailor, however, recollecting, after a while, that the pot had not been returned, applied for it, but whatever words he made use of were always repeated in imitation by the Fuegian. At length, he became enraged at hearing his requests reiterated, and placing himself in a threatening attitude, in an angry tone, he said, "You copper-coloured rascal, where is my tin pot?" The Fuegian, assuming the same attitude, with his eyes fixed on the sailor, called out, "You copper-coloured rascal, where is my tin pot?" The imitation was so perfect, that everyone laughed, except the sailor, who proceeded to search him, and under his arm he found the article missing. For this audacious theft, he would have punished the mimic, but Mr. Brisbane interposing, sent him into his canoe, and forbade his being allowed to come on board again.

Dealing with natives who unknowingly broke the Eighth Commandment was one thing. Dealing with natives who were unaware of the First Commandment—"Thou shalt have none other gods but me"—was quite another. Weddell's Quaker background places him firmly in the ranks of the nineteenth-century evangelical movement—that middle-class, influential, and proselytizing form of Christianity rooted in the nonconformist sects and caring more for the salvation of souls than for High Church ceremonial. But the saving of souls requires some means of verbal communication, and during his three months of contact with the Fuegians Weddell attempted a small study of their language. He thought it close to the Hebrew and thus "certainly a question of some interest to philologists." Extracts from the Bible were read to them: "not," Weddell hastens to add, "that they were expected to understand what was read, but it was proper to show them the Bible, and to read it, in connection with making signs of death, resurrection, and supplication to heaven." Alas, the only reaction of the copper-colored pagans was to mimic Weddell's words and gestures. One of them put his ear to the Bible "believing that it spoke" and another—that regrettable urge surfacing again—tried to sneak the Good Book into his canoe. Weddell sadly adds that if they "could have made proper use of it I would willingly have given it them." After three months Weddell had to admit that they had "nothing like a form of worship among them." Souls indeed ripe for the plucking. Weddell's evangelical conclusions, springing as they did from the kindest and most paternalistic of motives, are worth repeating:

I would willingly, for the honour of human nature, raise these neglected people somewhat higher in the scale of intellectual estimation than they have reached; but I must acknowledge their condition to be that of the lowest of mankind. At this age of the world, it appears almost incredible, and certainly disgraceful, that there should still exist such a tractable people in almost pristine ignorance. . . .

The philanthropic principle which these people exhibit towards one another, and their innoffensive behaviour to strangers, surely entitles them to this observation in their favour, that though they are the most distant from civilised life, owing pricipally to local circumstances, they are the most docile and tractable of any savages we are acquainted with, and no doubt might, therefore, be instructed in those arts which raise man above the brute.

Weddell, in these two paragraphs, is preparing his readers for the chapter's ending and conclusion; "tractable people in almost pristine ignorance" and natives to be "instructed in those arts which raise man above the brute" are but clarion notes of the trumpet to pawing evangelistic warhorses. With the final two paragraphs Weddell unmasks his batteries and sounds the charge:

I have only now to recommend these people, in whom I have taken a lively interest, to the philanthropic part of the world, as presenting an untouched field for their exertions to ameliorate the condition of their fellow men.

True humane and religious charity is best bestowed on those who most need our help, and are willing to receive it; and this is certainly the case with these Fuegians, who, of all uncivilised tribes with whom we are acquainted, seem most destitute of every thing which tends to rouse the human mind to exertion.

Nine years after the Janes and Beaufoys had entertained and kept a wary eye cocked upon the Fuegians and Weddell had held his Bible readings, another vessel would drop anchor in the sand and mud of Wigwam Cove. Crammed aboard the hundred-foot-length of the ten-gun brig HMS *Beagle,* commander Captain Robert FitzRoy R.N., were over seventy remarkably disparate people and in the hold a medley of rather bizarre items rarely found aboard a Royal Navy vessel.

The *Beagle* had sailed from England in December of 1831, and now, a year later, was fulfilling one of the purposes of her voyage. FitzRoy and the *Beagle* were no strangers to Tierra del Fuego, for in 1828 the twenty-three-year old FitzRoy had taken over command of the *Beagle,* then engaged in surveying the horrendous maze of islands and channels at South America's tip, after the suicide of her commander, Captain Pringle Stokes. FitzRoy spent two years in the Fuegian channels and proved his worth as both a commander and a surveyor. It was, for such a young man, an outstanding achievement. But FitzRoy had all the self-assurance and confidence of an aristocrat descended from a liaison between King Charles II and his mistress Barbara Villiers (the amorous and delectable Lady Castlemaine of Samuel Pepys's erotic dream, "which I think the best that ever was dreamt").

Hand in hand with that aristocratic aplomb bordering on arrogance went FitzRoy's religious fundamentalist evangelical beliefs, all rooted in a rigid belief in the Bible's literal truth.

FitzRoy had read Weddell's book and heard the call to raise the Fuegians from their savage state. Acting on his own initiative, he made the decision to bring four young Fuegians to England, where they would be given a Christian education and then returned to their native land to spread the good word. In a letter written at sea aboard the *Beagle* on 12 September 1830, he justified his action to his superior officer Captain Philip Parker King. The final paragraph reads:

Should not his Majesty's Government direct otherwise, I shall procure for these people a suitable education, and, after two or three years, shall send or take back to their country, with as large a stock as I can collect of those articles most useful to them, and most likely to improve the condition of their countrymen, who are scarcely superior to the brute creation.

The reply from the Admiralty—King had forwarded the letter to *his* superiors—stated that "their Lordships will not interfere with Commander FitzRoy's personal superintendence of, or benevolent intentions towards these four people, but will afford him any facilities towards maintaining and educating them in England, and will give them a passage home again."

And now here, at Wigwam Cove, were three returning natives (one had died of smallpox in England) accompanied by an inexperienced young missionary and some most unsuitable stores donated by well-meaning but naive charitable organizations. Stowed aboard the *Beagle* were wineglasses, tea trays, soup tureens, mahogany dressing-cases, white linen, beaver hats, plates, cups, saucers, and—much to the ribald comments of the sailors— chamber pots. It was some weeks later and in another anchorage when a pleasant-faced, snub-nosed young man scribbled some caustic comments into his diary on these rather bizarre items' being landed on the shores of Tierra del Fuego. To his mind it all showed the most culpable folly and negligence. The diarist, some three years younger than FitzRoy, was the civilian naturalist aboard the *Beagle*—he had paid £500 for the privilege— and, coming from a suitable social background, shared the captain's table at mealtime. In short, he was playing the combined role of naturalist and social companion. Over the five years of this seminal voyage, Charles Darwin was to play both parts with superb acumen and skill.

But Weddell's "docile and tractable" natives were not Darwin's. "Stunted," "miserable," "abject," "hideous," "filthy," "greasy"—these are Darwin's adjectives. For the nascent clergyman, fresh from the sherry-sipping atmosphere of Anglican Cambridge, the shocking difference between savage and civilized man was almost incomprehensible. The gulf yawned wider than that between wild and domesticated animals. All that Darwin could conclude was that nature had "fitted" the Fuegians to the climate and the "productions of his miserable country." The Fuegians and their, to him, almost bestial state of life were to haunt him and his thinking for the rest of his life. Within a few months of his return from the five-year *Beagle* voyage, Darwin opened his first notebook on "transmutation."

Twenty-two years later *The Origin Of Species By Means Of Natural Selection or The Preservation Of Favoured Races In The Struggle For Life* was published by John Murray, price 15 shillings. Printed on heavy cream paper and bound in green cloth covers, the original print run of 1,250 copies was oversubscribed. Since 1859 the book has never been out of print. And the idea that it contains still sticks like a bone in the throat of Christian fundamentalists and creationists.

Sigmund Freud suggested that science has dealt two great blows to our naive self-esteem. The first by the realization that the Earth is not the center of the universe, but a mere speck in a system of extraordinary magnitude; and the second that we have been robbed of our conceit of special creation by divine providence, and relegated to descent from the animal world.

In the introduction to the *Origin of Species* Darwin acknowledges his debt to the five years spent aboard the *Beagle*. Without those years it is doubtful if the book that revolutionized our view of the living world would have ever been written—at least by Darwin. The young man scolded by his father as caring "for nothing but shooting, dogs and rat-catching, and [destined to] be a disgrace to yourself and all your family" and the later beetle-collecting ordinand at Cambridge would have evolved into the Reverend Charles Darwin of independent income and country parish. Natural history and the display of collections showing the Creator's divine purpose was an approved clerical hobby in the early nineteenth century, and Darwin might have turned into a Victorian counterpart of Gilbert White, that gentle curate of the parish church of St. Mary in Selborne and the author of *The Natural History Of Selborne*—another book that has never been out of print since its publication in 1789.

To ascribe Darwinian mechanisms to historical, social, and political events is to enter a philosophical minefield. Communists, fascists, and capitalists have all embraced "social Darwinism" to bolster their power-oriented materialistic dogmas. Karl Marx wrote to Engels that Darwin's book "contains the basis in natural history for our view"—even though it was developed "in the crude English style." German militarists thought warfare "a biological necessity." And to the American economist and sociologist William Sumner the robber baron Rockefellers, Morgans, and Carnegies proved that "millionaires are the product of natural selection." Nevertheless—and stepping very gingerly—it is tempting to use the Darwinian mechanism of the cumulative effect of small changes and suggest that, from the moment in the cabin of the *Beagle* when Captain Pringle Stokes lifted the pistol to his head and shot himself, the following thirty-one years be seen as the story of a nonrandom series of events whose cumulative effect led to the publishing of *The Origin of Species*.

One of those events was the stoking of FitzRoy's evangelical fires by his reading of Weddell's plea to the "philanthropic part of the world" that "humane and religious charity is best bestowed on those who need our help. . . ." Namely the Fuegians. And without the Fuegians' being spirited away to England, the second voyage of the *Beagle* would never have happened. And so, in such a fashion, did Dumont d'Urville's "simple sealer" unknowingly play a small part in altering the human species' view of itself.

During the first week of 1824 the captains of the *Jane* and the *Beaufoy* sat down and worked out a campaign to fill their cargo holds. Brisbane and his men would stay in Tierra del Fuego until 20 January and then sail for the Falklands and South Georgia. Weddell would cruise east along the Fuegian and Patagonian coasts before crossing over to the Falklands. During the last week in March the two vessels would rendezvous off Point Lobos on the Patagonian coast and sail in company back to the London markets.

Weddell's passage to the Falklands was uneventful. The shores supplied fur seals and offshore were welcome pods of pilot whales. The latter creatures were a welcome bonus for Weddell and his men, not only for the normal grade oil rendered from the blubber, but also for the very fine grade oil found in the adipose tissues of the bulging forehead: an oil that fetched a premium price and one used in the lubrication of precision instruments.

It perhaps made up for the disappointment of being unable to land at Good Success Bay when the strong current swept the *Jane* into the Le Maire Straits before they had a chance of anchoring. The natives had appeared on the shore and "shouted at the full stretch of their lungs, inviting us to land," but alas, to no avail. The evangelical in Weddell had been eager to meet with this tribe, as this was the bay where James Cook and the *Endeavour* had spent five days in 1769. And where the two Negro servants of the young Joseph Banks had died from the combined effects of rum and exposure when caught in a blizzard. As to the Fuegians, Weddell thought "it would have been agreeable to have ascertained whether, from his intercourse with them, they had derived permanent improvement, though his stay amongst them was too short to produce any great result."

The *Jane* cruised as far north as the Santa Cruz River, taking whales in the coastal waters and seals off the beaches. In the calm of the river's protected anchorage they converted the blubber to oil and casked it up, restowed the hold for the passage back to England, and made an unsuccessful attempt to shoot guanaco—the creatures proved too timid to come within range of their muskets—and Weddell sent men to gather the blue-black berries of the box-leafed barberry, "which when ripe is pleasant to the taste, and highly beneficial as an antiscorbutic, of which we took advantage, and eat great quantities of them."

They sailed from these pleasant surroundings on 17 February and by 2 March were anchored at the Falklands in the now familiar Ship Harbour of New Island. Here they took on water and peat for the galley fire. By 12 March, having called at West Point Island, they were anchored at Port Egmont near the site of the old British settlement of 1765. All that remained were the ruins. A few days later Weddell, much to his surprise, saw two warships round the headland and make their way cautiously into the harbor. One of the whaleboats was alongside the *Jane,* and Weddell with some of his crew scrambled into the boat and rowed out to meet the visitors.

They proved to be the Spanish seventy-gun *Asia* and the twenty-gun *Achilles.* Weddell boarded the *Asia,* where he was "politely received," and then pointed out to the Spaniards the best and safest anchorage. It was advice they chose to ignore and in so doing, as Weddell succinctly put it, "caused themselves a great deal of trouble," when they dragged their anchors on the following day in a hard gale from the northwest.

The officers from the *Asia* claimed they had sailed from Lima and were bound home to Spain. Weddell, however, suspected that this was a subterfuge, as they appeared unduly eager to glean information on the navigation around Cape Horn and through the Le Maire Straits. His suspicions were confirmed when he learned from his boat's crew that the *Asia*'s seamen had told them that they were but ten weeks out from Cadiz.

The Spanish officers' dissembling can be traced to their inbred suspicion that all English seamen were cut from the same cloth as the terrible *corsario* Drake. Such a one, "el Diablo," Lord Cochrane, had made a name for himself ravaging the Spanish coast and shipping during the Napoleonic wars. For the last few years, acting as admiral of the tiny Chilean navy and aided by mercenary American and British sailors and marines in Chile's struggle for independence from Spain, el Diablo had, with a cheek, audacity, and brilliance equal to Drake's, captured Valdivia, terrorized the loyal Spanish, cut out the Spanish frigate *Esmeralda* from Callao harbor with extraordinary impudence and daring, and generally wreaked havoc with schoolboy glee along the coasts of Chile and Peru. No wonder the Spanish were playing this one close to the chest.

Weddell meanwhile, his patriotic Royal Navy master's eye cocked, noted the complement, condition, and morale of the two ships: "they appeared in all respects effective, and though they were not so expeditious in their movements, as is the practice in our navy, they were indefatigable and secure in their operations." High praise indeed from a consummate seaman. It was also no small satisfaction to Weddell to point out to the Spanish officers that their charts were incorrect as to the existence of the Aurora Islands.

On 19 March, the weather being settled and the wind fair for the

rendezvous with the *Beaufoy* off the Patagonian coast, the *Jane* made her
farewells to the Spanish ships and sailed from Port Egmont. The passage
to Point Lobos was stormy, with a howling, southerly gale and seas that
swept away two of their boats. The *Beaufoy* failed to appear and Weddell
could only conclude—and hope—that their small consort had been driven
north by the gales and was now making her own way back to London. The
Jane was also being driven north and, off the river Plata, developed a leak,
forcing her into Montevideo.

Here in this war-torn city where "many of the streets are so broken up
as to be almost impassable" and "the whole together, at this time, presents
the accumulated wreck of a series of years, agitated by almost perpetual
civil and foreign contests," Weddell met with Sir Murray Maxwell, commodore of the South American station and commander of H.M.S. *Briton*.
Maxwell had heard of the arrival of warships at the Falklands and suspected
tricks from the old Gallic enemy. Weddell was able to allay his fears and
described them as Spanish, which did away with a conjecture of their being
"French in the character of Spaniards, as some *finesse* of that kind was
possible."

Weddell's timely information was repaid by the loan of carpenters from
the *Briton;* within three weeks the *Jane* had been repaired and Weddell was
pitched into a social round of dinners with British merchants celebrating
King George IV's birthday and an improbable dinner with local Spanish
and Portuguese that turned into a fracas between the antipathetic factions.
It was all very different from entertaining the Fuegians.

In their turn the Montevideans, like the Fuegians, came under Weddell's scrutiny. Of the different inhabitants of this strife-torn city founded
by the Portuguese and taken by the Spanish, Weddell found "the rich, as
may be expected, live in ease and authority" while the "labouring class of
people are not remarkable for industry being rather addicted to idleness
and inebriety." The ladies of the city Weddell found to be small of stature,
attractive, and "lusty." The visiting gauchos, the pampas cowboys, "are
not considered the most honest class of men, and they have perhaps,
committed more assassinations than any other." It was a comment to have
a sad relevance for Matthew Brisbane.

On 4 May, the *Jane,* repaired courtesy of the Royal Navy, ran down the
river Plata with a fair wind bound on the last leg of the long voyage. The
passage was uneventful and in fifty-nine days they were off Falmouth,
arriving before the packet from Montevideo that had sailed two days before the smaller *Jane.*

On 9 July the *Jane* sailed up the Thames to Gravesend: they were finally
home after a voyage of nearly two years. Here among the packed shipping
Weddell found that Brisbane and the *Beaufoy* were also safe and sound,
having arrived on 20 June.

The first order of business for Weddell was to substantiate and legiti-
mize the record south latitude of the *Jane* and the *Beaufoy*. Three degrees
further south than the exemplary James Cook was bound to be met with
raised eyebrows in certain naval quarters. This record, after all, had been
accomplished by two small ordinary sealing vessels and not by a well-
equipped naval expedition. Weddell had his chief officer and two seamen
swear under oath before the Commissioner of His Majesty's Customs as
to the truth of the story told by the ship's logbooks.

Weddell was now thirty-seven years old; five of those years had been
spent in the Southern Ocean, and his own personal journals carried much
more than the stark facts of the ship's log. That inquiring mind of his
had collected information on harbors and anchorages, tides and currents,
magnetic variations, ice conditions, flora and fauna. Months had been
spent in the immediate neighborhood of Cape Horn, and his knowledge
of the sailing conditions, weather, and safe anchorages near this legendary
and fearsome cape was unsurpassed. To complement the written information there were rough drafts of his survey work of harbors, anchorages,
and islands. All this Weddell intended to incorporate in an official letter to
the Commissioners of His Majesty's Navy; but he was persuaded by friends
and his co-owners James Strachan and James Mitchell to publish a book of
his voyages. The book, merely by being published, would also add credence to the furthest-south record. But the main motive is contained in a
final paragraph of the book.

The most patient and diligent research is always necessary to the attaining a correct
knowledge of those parts of science of which I have treated in the foregoing
pages: and if I have contributed, by my private adventure, to the advancement of
hydrography, I conceive that I have only done that which every man would ende-
vour to accomplish, who, in the pursuit of wealth, is at the same time zealous
enough in the cause of science to lose no opportunity of collecting information
for the benefit of mankind.

Two months after his return Weddell had sent his charts to the Admiralty, and a year later appeared his *A Voyage Towards The South Pole,* with a
second edition appearing in 1827. It is more than a plain narrative of his
voyages, for it also contains an Appendix with "Observations On The
Navigation Round Cape Horn"; "Observations On The State Of The
Poles," and "Observations For Finding The Longitude By Chronometers," charts of anchorages and harbors, and sketches showing views of
headlands and approaches to land. In short, it is a volume of sailing directions for a part of the Southern Ocean.

Even though Weddell had been part of the massacre of the fur and
elephant seals of the South Shetlands, his economical nature had seen the
folly of the greedy mass slaughter. In his book he advocated conservation

methods if any new sealing grounds were to be discovered. It is one of the earliest conservation proposals applicable for the Southern Ocean.*

The quantity of seals taken off these islands, by the vessels from different parts, during the years 1821 and 1822, may be computed at 320,000, and the quantity of sea-elephant oil, at 940 tons. This valuable animal, the fur seal, might, by a law similar to that which restrains fishermen in the size of the mesh of their net, have been spared to render annually 100,000 furs, for many years to come. This would have followed from not killing the mothers till the young were able to take the water; and even then, only those which appeared to be old, together with a proportion of the males, thereby diminishing their total number, but in slow progression. This system is practised at the river of Plata. The island of Lobos, in the mouth of that river, contains a quantity of seals, and is farmed by the Governor of Monte Video, under certain restrictions, that the hunters shall not take them but at stated periods, in order to prevent the animals from being exterminated. The system of extermination was practised, however, at Shetland; for whenever a seal reached the beach, of whatever denomination, he was immediately killed, and his skin taken; and by this means, at the end of the second year, the animals became nearly extinct; the young having lost their mothers when only three or four days old, of course all died, which, at the lowest calculation, exceeded 100,000.

While Weddell worked on his charts and book, Matthew Brisbane and the *Beaufoy* were outfitting for another voyage south. Two months after returning from the voyage with the *Jane,* the *Beaufoy,* sailing alone this time, slipped down the Thames bound for Patagonia, the Falkland Islands, and Tierra del Fuego. The Fuegians still captivated Weddell and he gave specific orders to Brisbane that the *Beaufoy* revisit the natives they had met in 1823 and—that evangelical strain surfacing again—see if any benefit had been gained by the Fuegians from their contact with the Janes and Beaufoys. Brisbane returned to England on 14 April 1826 and Weddell added a short account of the voyage, mainly concerning the Fuegians, to the second edition of his book.

According to Brisbane, although two years had passed the natives recognized the *Beaufoy,* Brisbane, and some of the seamen. It is not surprising that Brisbane was recognized, for he had amazed the Fuegians on the previous voyage with his ability at killing game with the native slingshot made from seal or otter skin. Medals were produced that had been given to them by Weddell on the previous voyage and then quickly hidden away again, "probably from fear of having them reclaimed." Pilfering, alas, was still performed with its usual dexterity. But friendly relationships were still maintained and "their sick applied regularly for medical aid, and the women even presented their afflicted children for assistance."

Weddell concluded that the natives had indeed benefited by exposure

---

* In 1788 another master in the Royal Navy, John Leard, had proposed similar conservation methods for the Patagonian coast, South Georgia, and the Falkland Islands.

to the "arts and intelligence possessed by us" and that the "humane disposition possessed by the Fuegians merits our attention." It is another plea
from an evangelistic heart. Nevertheless, they still showed signs of that
native improvidence. Weddell had left an iron try-pot at Indian Cove in
the hope that the Fuegians would render oil from the blubber of "dead
whales which are sometimes thrown upon their shores." The try-pot had
merely been beaten with rocks and stones in a fruitless attempt to break it
up.

The other beneficiary of the *Beaufoy*'s voyage was Professor Jameson
in Edinburgh, who was sent the skin and skull of a South American puma
killed by Brisbane on the Patagonian coast. This beast, just before its own
death, had killed the *Beaufoy*'s pet bulldog.

A month after Brisbane's return two Royal Navy ships, HMS *Adventure,* commanded by Captain Philip Parker King, and HMS *Beagle,* commanded by Captain Pringle Stokes, sailed from Plymouth Sound bound
for South America and the mammoth task of making an accurate survey of
the coasts of South America from the mouth of the river Plata in the
Atlantic to Chiloe Island in the Pacific—including the maze of islands and
channels of Tierra del Fuego. A month later, in London, Matthew Brisbane was appointed master of the *Prince of Saxe Coburg,* a sixty-five-foot
schooner owned by Mr. John Pirie, and outfitting for a sealing voyage to
the South Shetlands. Unknown to Brisbane, he and the crew of the schooner were destined to have an appointment with the *Beagle* along the desolate shores of Tierra del Fuego.

The same year that Brisbane took command of his new vessel, Weddell
offered his services to the Admiralty with a proposal for an expedition into
the high southern latitudes, either in an appointed position or in the form
of financial help to defray the costs of two vessels fitted out under his own
command.

Weddell's proposal met with short shrift from John Barrow, the influential, devious, and coldly calculating Second Secretary (the equivalent of
today's Permanent Secretary) at the Admiralty. This powerful and serpen-
tine civil servant (it was Barrow's suggestion to isolate Napoleon on St.
Helena) reigned forty years at the Admiralty and, with a short whaling
voyage as a youth into the Greenland seas, and never having seen an iceberg, draped himself with the mantle of the Sage of the Arctic. His was the
driving force behind the Royal Navy's futile attempts at grappling with the
Arctic pack ice, and throughout his long tenure he steadfastly refused to
acknowledge the vast experience of men such as William Scoresby and
James Weddell. For Barrow, jealously protective of the Royal Navy, it
was that service's inalienable right and duty to explore and discover—
certainly not the right of common whalers and sealers, no matter how
experienced.

The Admiralty's refusal and the uncertainties of the sealing trade led

Weddell and the *Jane*—he was still part owner—into the more humdrum aspects of the seaman's life in the mercantile service, with voyages to the Mediterranean, Madeira, and South America.

In 1829 the links, financial and emotional, that bound Weddell to his small vessel were finally severed. The faithful *Jane,* now growing old and suffering for those years amidst the ice, on a passage from Buenos Aires to Gibralter and leaking so badly through the seams in her tired planking that the pumps were constantly manned, in near foundering condition limped into Horta in the Azores. Her cargo was quickly unloaded and after a survey the *Jane* was condemned. But Weddell's misfortunes continued, for the ship he boarded to take passage back to England was promptly wrecked on the nearby island of Pico and he barely escaped drowning. The loss of the *Jane* was financially crippling and Weddell was forced to take employment as a paid ship's master. In September 1830 he sailed from England as master of the *Eliza* bound for the Swan River on the west coast of Australia.

A few weeks previous to his departure the *Tula* and *Lively,* two sealing vessels owned by the Enderby brothers and commanded by John Biscoe sailed from London bound for the waters of Antarctica. In May 1831, along the shores of the Derwent River in Tasmania, Weddell and the *Eliza*'s crew were to help moor the *Tula* and carry ashore Biscoe's scurvy-enfeebled crew to hospital. Five months later a group of men, including Weddell, breakfasted aboard the *Tula* before Biscoe set off again in his search for seals in Antarctica. The two men had much in common. Both were extremely competent seamen and navigators, both had served in the Royal Navy as masters, and both had made significant voyages into the high southern latitudes. One would have liked to be part of that company at breakfast.

The *Eliza* sailed for England in January 1832 and six months later was taking the flood tide up the Thames to London. It was Weddell's last voyage. He was living at lodgings in London and being supported by a Miss Rosanna Johnstone when he died on 9 September 1834 at the early age of forty-seven. Like many other whalers and sealers, he died in poverty. But his voyages south and his book had brought him a modicum of fame and his death was reported in newspapers and periodicals that included the *Times* and, as due to a Fellow of the Royal Society of Edinburgh, the *Edinburgh Evening Courant.*

Somewhere in the northwest corner of the churchyard of St. Clement Danes in London lie the remains of James Weddell F.R.S.E. Time and weather have eroded any inscription on the headstone or slab that mark the spot where his coffin was carried by friends and fellow seamen. His true memorial is the sea named after him—King George the Fourth Sea failed to take hold—and the name carried by Antarctica's second most populous seal.

Matthew Brisbane's life after his voyages in the *Beaufoy* was made of the stuff of countless boys' adventure stories—full of shipwrecks, rescues, and adventure, one following fast upon the other.

After sailing from England in 1826 the *Prince of Saxe Coburg*, beset and damaged by ice off the South Shetlands, sought shelter in Tierra del Fuego. Any port in a storm is a seafaring clinché and the ominously named Fury Bay, Fury Island, set along the malevolent coast that stretches northwest from Cape Horn, was the inhospitable and dangerous anchorage forced upon Brisbane. A few years later Charles Darwin described this stretch of coast as "enough to make a landsman dream for a week about shipwrecks, peril and death." It is an apposite comment, for Fury Bay has poor holding ground and Brisbane's schooner was driven ashore by the violent "williwaws"* that lash the Fuegian anchorages. Three of the ship's boats were saved from the wreck, along with most of their provisions. Improvised tents were made from sail canvas and the castaways—some of them turning mutinous—took stock of their precarious situation. With Brisbane's consent seven of the crew set off in one of the whaleboats in an attempt to reach the mouth of the Rio Negro, some five hundred miles south of Buenos Aires and the nearest outpost of civilization. Such a voyage in an open boat through the hundreds of miles of uncharted waterways that constitute the maze of the Fuegian channels, followed by a thousand-mile passage along the bleak Patagonian coast, appeared foolhardy and doomed to failure. Against all odds the men survived and reached the Rio Negro and eventually Buenos Aires.

The two other boats were sent by Brisbane on scouting expeditions to scour the channels in the hope of sighting a passing ship. He and a few men remained on the beach at Fury Bay and set about building a small decked boat from the wreck of the schooner. On 3 March 1827, three months after their shipwreck, one of the searching boats, now about a hundred miles from Fury Bay, sighted the *Beagle* in the Magellan Strait. Captain Stokes took the *Beagle* further down the Strait and then set off with two ten-oared boats to the rescue of the Fury Bay party and the sealskin cargo.

Brisbane took passage back to England, and John Pirie, holding nothing against him for the loss of the *Prince of Saxe Coburg*, made him master of the *Hope*, another Pirie-owned schooner outfitted for sealing. On 23 April 1829 the *Hope* was driven ashore at South Georgia. Again the wreck was used to build a small shallop, and Brisbane with two other crew members sailed the makeshift craft the fifteen hundred miles across the South Atlantic to Montevideo. A year later Brisbane was shipwrecked yet again on the eastern tip of Tierra del Fuego. The wreck was cannibalized and a boat sailed to the Falkland Islands.

---

* Sudden squalls that can reach one hundred knots.

A few months after this third shipwreck, Brisbane had his second encounter with the *Beagle,* now commanded by FitzRoy and on her way back to England with the Fuegians. Brisbane was now working ashore in the Falkland Islands for Louis Vernet in an attempt to set up a viable cattle and fishing colony that could supply produce to South America and visiting ships. Brisbane was in charge of the fisheries. FitzRoy dined ashore with a company that included Vernet, his wife, and Brisbane—and painted a remarkably domestic scene of a thick-walled stone house complete with a good library of Spanish, German, and English books, lively conversation at dinner, followed by music and dancing. FitzRoy found it all very agreeable and "not a little strange at the Falkland Islands where we expected to find only a few sealers."

This cozy domestic scene was not to last. In 1831 the small settlement on Berkeley Sound was totally destroyed and sacked by the U.S. corvette *Lexington* in reprisal for the seizing by Vernet of the American sealer *Harriet* for poaching. Some of the leading settlers, Brisbane among them, were hauled aboard the *Lexington* and clapped in irons; Brisbane was singled out for particular abuse. After this demonstration of *schrecklichkeit* the settlers were taken to Montevideo and released, with the U.S. government justifying its action "as the United States had been in actual use of the islands as a fishery for fifty years."

The *Lexington*'s rampage set in motion a chain of events that eventually led to part of the Falkland Islands' historiography: the Port Louis murders.

In March 1833 the *Beagle* sailed once more into Berkeley Sound and the settlement at Port Louis. FitzRoy was again in command, and with him was the young naturalist Charles Darwin. Both were appalled at what they saw, particularly FitzRoy. His memories had been pleasant ones after that civilized evening with the Vernets and Brisbane. Gone were the low stone-built houses and well-tended gardens. All that remained were ruined walls and some turf-built huts with a few cabbages and potatoes struggling for existence in waste-looking ground. The inhabitants were few and furtive. The Union Jack flew over this sorry settlement—but with no authority to back it up. The British, worried that the United States might occupy the islands with a naval base to protect the North American sealers, had reasserted their claim to the islands and, in Darwin's cutting phrase, "dog in the manger fashion . . . [left] to protect it a Union Jack."

Into this chaotic and anarchic scene, with ex-convict Indians and gauchos slaughtering cattle to sell to the sealers, Brisbane (Vernet was still in South America) returned in an attempt to salvage some of Vernet's investment and property. It was the third meeting of the *Beagle* and Brisbane.

Five months later Brisbane and four other settlers were killed by a gang of murderous Indians and gauchos. Thomas Helsby, who had been brought to Port Louis by Brisbane to act as a clerk and only narrowly escaped being cut down by the gauchos, described the scene of Brisbane's death: "I was then ordered by them into Captain Brisbane's house, and then first saw his body lying dead upon the floor, he appeared to have been making towards his pistols before he fell, and there was a smile of contempt or disdain very strongly marked on his countenance. They dragged his body with a horse to a considerable distance, and plundered the house."

It is a scene strangely similar to that of the famous Victorian painting of General Gordon, disdainful smile on his face, standing at the head of the Residency stairs in Khartoum, facing down the sword- and spear-brandishing hordes of yelling dervishes before he is cut down, decapitated, and the grisly trophy presented to the Mahdi. It is a painting that canonized Gordon and marks the apotheosis of the comfortable Victorian ideal of the lone Briton dying in the face of crude barbarism.

The *Beagle* returned to Port Louis in March 1834. FitzRoy, who had greatly liked Brisbane, was deeply affected when he heard of the manner of his death.

At two hundred yards distance from the house in which he had lived, I found to my horror the feet of poor Brisbane protruding from the ground. So shallow was his grave that dogs had disturbed his mortal remains, and fed upon the corpse. This was the fate of an honest, industrious and most faithful man: of a man who feared no danger, and despised hardships. He was murdered by villains, because he defended the property of his friend; he was mangled by them to satisfy their hellish spite; dragged by a lasso at a horse's heels, away from the houses, and left to be eaten by dogs.

Other Royal Navy men also paid their own form of homage to Brisbane when Captain James Clark Ross with his two ships the *Erebus* and *Terror* spent the winter of 1842 in the Falkland Islands. Brisbane's roughly buried body was disinterred and decently reburied with a wooden grave marker:

TO THE
MEMORY
OF
MR. MATTHEW BRISBANE
who was barbarously
murdered on the
26th August 1833

In the command of the
Beaufoy Cutter he was
the Zealous and able
Companion of Captn
James Weddell during
his enterprising Voyage

to beyond the 74th Degree of
South Latitude
in February 1823

———

His remains were removed to
this spot by the crews of H.B.M.
ships "Erebus" and "Terror"
on the 25th August, 1842

Weddell probably heard of the tragic death of his old friend and sailing companion a few months before his own death. The two men had seen and suffered much together and were bound, not by rigid naval discipline, but by the looser—and stronger—ties of mutual respect. Both had come from similar backgrounds and both had retained their humanity in a brutalizing business. Brisbane had a footloose and tough pioneering quality about him and one can easily see him at home on any of those nineteenth-century frontiers—the Americas, Australia, New Zealand, Africa, or Asia. Weddell presented a different persona from that of the frontier Brisbane. Here was a more subtle and complex temperament: an evangelical scientist manqué with a questioning and adventurous spirit finding its outlet in exploration. His obvious concern for the Fuegians stood in contrast to that of Charles Darwin—a kindly and gentle man who could hardly contain his distaste. But perhaps, coming from a tougher and harder world than Darwin's, Weddell had a built-in tolerance.

Brisbane's wooden grave marker now stands in the museum at Port Stanley, his grave being marked by a more durable marble slab. Five years after Weddell's funeral service, Sir John Barrow—he had been made a baronet in 1835—presented a portrait of Weddell to the Royal Geographical Society. It was a generous gesture honoring an unofficial explorer.

As to the fur seals that fell in such prodigious numbers to the sealers' clubs and knives, they have returned to the shores of South Georgia and their numbers are estimated to be close to 1.5 million. The Fuegians proved less resilient. Having adapted to survive in a harsh and unforgiving environment which brought death to many Europeans, their fragile existence was doomed with the arrival of settlers bringing Western diseases and the darker methods of genocide. As a people and a culture they can be considered extinct.

XI

John Biscoe: The Third Circumnavigation

And courage never to submit or yield: and what is else not to
be overcome?

John Milton, *Paradise Lost*

THE RRS *John Biscoe,* built in 1956, was a homely-looking vessel, her profile crenellated and uncompromising as a fortress, sprouting a zareba of masts, derricks, gantrys, and antennae. And a sheer line so remarkable it looked as if hewn with an axe by a palsied, cross-eyed, demented naval architect. As a Royal Research Ship, she spent most of her thirty-five years amidst the icebergs and pack ice of Antarctica supplying British scientific bases and carrying out biological and oceanographic research. Sixty people or more could be crammed into her 220 feet, twenty-six of them scientists and support staff. Tucked away among the scientific paraphernalia was a messroom where you could drink draft beer in the ripe smoky atmosphere of a Glasgow pub. A few decks higher, in an airier and lighter wardroom, the bulkheads hung with paintings and photographs, you could sip pink gins either standing before a fireplace or lounging comfortably in faded chintz-covered armchairs. The *John Biscoe,* being a good British hostelry, had a saloon bar and a lounge bar. American ships tend toward the plastic, formica, vinyl, and stainless steel—materials with a hose-down-wipe-clean touch to them. Americans take their bathrooms when they travel; the British take their pubs.

Robert Graves defined the Arabic word *baraka* as the Moslem sense of blessedness that attaches itself to buildings or objects after years of loving use by noble-hearted people. RRS *John Biscoe* had *baraka* by the bucketful.

This noble little vessel was named after John Biscoe, master in the Royal Navy, merchant mariner, sealer, and discoverer of Enderby Land in Antarctica. No portrait of Biscoe hung on the bulkhead of his namesake ship, nor does he gaze down, fixed in oil paint, framed in gilt, on members of learned societies. No portrait of Biscoe exists and little is known of his life except for the three years when, in his mid-thirties, he commanded an expedition of two small vessels and made the third circumnavigation of Antarctica. Ten years after his voyage, poverty-stricken and in ill health, Biscoe died at sea. The RRS *John Biscoe* made a fitting tribute.

When, in 1830, John Biscoe and his two small vessels, the *Tula* and the *Lively,* slipped down the Thames on a favorable tide, they were following in the wake of James Cook and Thaddeus Bellingshausen. However, unlike Cook's and Bellingshausen's, this was no national expedition with navy ships and navy men, but a small commercial venture in search of seals and equipped for two years at a cost of £6,147 by the English whaling company of Enderby Brothers.

Herman Melville has preserved this company, like a fly in literary amber, in *Moby Dick.* Captain Ahab and the *Pequod,* in quest of the great white whale, meet up with another whaling vessel on the whaling grounds. This is the English *Samuel Enderby,* with a captain who has also lost a limb to the white whale—and who is fitted out with an ivory arm to match Ahab's ivory leg. "'Ere the English ship fades from sight," wrote Melville, "be it set down here, that she hailed from London, and was named after the late Samuel Enderby, merchant of that city, the original of the famous whaling house of Enderby & Sons; a house which in my poor whaleman's opinion, comes not far behind the united royal houses of the Tudors and Bourbons, in point of real historical interest."

The founding father, Samuel Enderby, had died in 1797, leaving behind him a prosperous and thriving business and, as an indication of his wealth and position in society, a family coat of arms and crest. All defined as a "shield Azure, bearing a ship's topmast in pale proper with a topsail set and dexter pendant flottant between two mullets of six points impaling, Azure a lion rampant Sable, Crest a Harpooner also proper in the act of throwing or striking." Whaling was a respectable business and had received the imprimatur of the Heralds' College.

By 1830 the company, now being run by Samuel Enderby's grandsons Charles, Henry, and George, was on the decline—as was the English whaling industry in general. Coal gas, not whale oil, now lit city streets and factories (the Gas Light & Coke Company had been founded in 1809 to sell coal gas in London); rapeseed oil was being used for textiles; but most importantly, the competition from Australian and American whaling was proving formidable.

Samuel Enderby had started a tradition in the company continued by his sons and grandsons. All masters of Enderby whalers were instructed to bring back natural-history specimens collected on their voyages—and the grandsons extended this to include geographical exploration. It was a dangerous policy for an ailing business. But Charles and George were founding members of the Royal Geographical Society and when Charles came aboard the *Tula* on 10 July 1830 to bid farewell and give Biscoe his final orders, they contained special instructions "to endeavour to make discoveries in a high southern latitide."

Biscoe was used to receiving orders. Born in 1794, he had entered the Royal Navy as a volunteer at seventeen, served on the North American and West Indian stations as midshipman and acting master, and at twenty-one, with the ending of the Napoleonic wars, left the service. His only training being for the sea, he turned toward the merchant service: another member of that faceless company of seamen who served in the Royal Navy during its endless wars and who were beached on half-pay or dismissed with the coming of peace.

During those few years in the Royal Navy, Biscoe had come to the attention of one of his commanders. Captain Moberly of the *Moselle* recommended him for promotion with the following words: "Is an active lad, keeps a good reckoning, is attentive and promises to make a good officer." And he must have come just as highly recommended to the notice of the Enderbys—for he knew nothing of sealing or whaling.

Biscoe's command consisted of a brace of craft: the *Tula* and the *Lively* with a complement of twenty-seven men and two boys. Both vessels were small, the *Tula* of 157 tons, seventy-four feet overall, and rigged as a brigantine. She was bluff-bowed and square-sterned, her only concession to the graceful being a figurehead of a woman under the standing bowsprit. Biscoe made a small sketch of the *Tula* in his journal. She is shown with a forestaysail and a scrap of spanker set and a big sea running. Underneath, in Biscoe's hand, is written: "Tula bearing up for an iceberg."

The *Lively* was even smaller: built as a Cowes pilot boat, only fifty-two feet overall, cutter-rigged with a single mast. Her advantage was having a shallow draft of only eight feet—useful for close inshore sailing. The diminutive *Lively* was no stranger to the Southern Ocean. She had just returned from a sealing trip to Kerguelen Island in the company of the Enderby-owned seventy-two-foot cutter *Sprightly*, where she had rescued a party of British sealers who had been stranded on that bleak outpost for two years.

Compared to the victualing, clothing, and equipment of Cook's and Bellingshausen's expeditions, Biscoe's was woefully spartan and lean. Three chronometers were provided by the company, but, as was the custom, the master had to provide his own charts. Bellingshausen's voyage was unknown to Biscoe, but he must have been aware of Weddell's book and charts and also of the charts of the South Shetlands and South Orkneys by George Powell. But even with these, this was still going to be a voyage into the unknown. As to the crew, they had to clothe themselves: indeed, a kindly and generous merchant captain, on hearing of their destination, gave all the crew a pair of sea boots.

Whaling, particularly the southern whaling, rated low on the British seaman's social scale—and sealers even lower. Whaling at least had the skill of the chase and a hierarchy based on those skills. Sealing was considered plain butchery, with the sealers, for the most part, living ashore in a squalor worse than any whaler's fo'c's'le. Anyone prepared to sign on for this voyage was either foolhardy or desperate for a berth, or held a suicidal thirst for hardship and adventure.

The cutter *Lively.*

Nautical terminology and sailing-ship nomenclature can prove an irritating obstacle course for the landsman—and a glorious nitpicking field for the marine pedant. Stephen Leacock, in one of his *Nonsense Novels,* has parodied the sailing-ship story with such deft and wicked hilarity that, once read, it makes all sea stories read like *Soaked in Seaweed: or, Upset in the Ocean.* At the risk of sounding like Leacock, where men nail up masts, hang bowsprits over the side, and varnish lee-scuppers, it should be mentioned that the *Tula,* although classified as a brigantine, could also be described as a "hermaphrodite brig"—square-rigged on the foremast and fore-and-aft-rigged on the main. An ugly name and the bisexual connotations did nothing for *Tula*'s steering and sailing qualities. As Biscoe, to his chagrin, was soon to find out.

After dropping down the Thames Biscoe picked up his small whaleboats at Deal on the English Channel coast and made his final departure on 21 July 1830. Destination, Cape Verde Islands to provision and water. Progress was agonizingly slow; it took them a month to reach the islands at an ambling rate of three knots. The *Tula* proved difficult to steer in light winds, and in calms her motion was diabolical, with a quick, snappy, jerky roll—tiring for the crew and hard on the ship's running and standing rigging. Two weeks were spent at the Cape Verde Islands provisioning, watering, and fitting extra shrouds on the mainmast to ease the strain on the existing rigging in the pious hope it could save them a dismasting. Their next port of call was to be the Falkland Islands, a passage of over six thousand miles across the equator and into the far reaches of the South Atlantic.

Stretched across the oceans of the world are invisible thalassic equivalents of mountain ranges, passes, valleys, swamps, and swift-running rivers. All these can help or hinder a sailing vessel on her passage across the apparent plains of the ocean. Areas of prevailing winds (trade winds) are avoided or sought after, depending on the direction of the passage. Areas of calm and light variable winds (doldrums) are the equivalent of a morass to a land traveler. Finally there are the currents of the world's oceans, which a sailing ship can ride to her advantage or buck to her disadvantage.

Hard-won knowledge of this invisible seascape had been collected over the centuries by countless seamen. Biscoe had used—to the best of his abilities—the northeast trades and the south-flowing Canary current on his passage to the Cape Verde Islands. From here, on his passage to the Falklands, he would be forced to cross the morass of the equatorial doldrums: a band of calms, thunderstorms, squalls, and light variable winds close to the equator between the northeast and southeast trade winds. The *Tula*'s recalcitrant and vile handling qualities in these conditions foreboded a slow and uncomfortable passage across this stretch of perverse ocean.

The ideal crossing point of the doldrums is somewhere between 24°W and 29°W, where the band of light winds and calms is at its narrowest. Biscoe, due to the weather and the poor sailing qualities of the *Tula,* was forced to cross at 17°W. And it proved another slow passage before the Falklands were finally raised on 8 November and, three days later, they came to anchor at Port Louis on Berkeley Sound. The passage had taken over two months.

Port Louis lies at the head of Berkeley Sound and the Carenage makes a perfect landlocked harbor, surrounded by the gentle, rolling, treeless hills. Winds can still be a problem even in such surroundings. And the Falklands provide local winds of remarkable strength. Biscoe, even though he had trouble watering due to gales, recommended Berkeley Sound and wrote approvingly: "Fish, bullock, and fresh water can be easily procured, with a variety of anti-scorbutic herbs to use as vegetables: the entrance being also clear, the anchorage good, and the depth of water considerable close to the beach. A refitting yard here, could be very easily established, and would be both a great public and private benefit."*

On the passage from England the *Lively*'s master had been a Mr. Smith. At the Falklands, for reasons unknown, he deserted. It could have been second thoughts on the advisability of taking the pint-size *Lively* into the high southern latitudes. A Mr. Avery replaced him. In the coming months he too would have second thoughts on his choice.

The two vessels sailed from Berkeley Sound on 27 November. They were now starting on the essence of their voyage: sailing into the inhospitable regions of the high latitudes on a combined commercial and exploratory venture. For many of the crew, as the *Tula* and *Lively* ran down the sound, those green rolling hills were to be their last view of an ice-free land.

Biscoe's instructions ordered him to search for the Aurora Islands—those mythic islands vainly searched for by Weddell—and then make his way to Cook's "Sandwich Land." Biscoe, like Weddell, found no islands and also consigned them to the scrap heap of cartographic misinformation. "They must," wrote Biscoe, "be either considered henceforward as not existing or looked for in some other position." Biscoe now bore away east, passing north of South Georgia. No reason for landing here—the seals had been well nigh exterminated from the island. By 10 December they were sailing past their first icebergs.

Their introduction to the Antarctic proved a typical one—the next day they were blanketed by fog. Fog is disliked and feared by seamen at any time, but never more so when sailing amidst icebergs and growlers. To add to Biscoe's worries the two vessels now lost touch with each other; his concerns were compounded by the knowledge that his chart showed them to be in the region of the northern islands of the South Sandwich group. Sailing over an awash growler—it made a horrendous noise as it ground along the planking—must have added to all their fears. And as a final malignant piece of sheer devilry, the barometer, that most important indicator to seamen of changing weather conditions, "burst of itself."

On 14 December, much to Biscoe's relief—it eased their "mutual great anxiety"—the *Lively* was sighted and they shaped their course south. It

---

* Nothing remains of that old settlement except for the foundations of buildings and the outlines of an embankment. But the sound, once the haunt of whalers and sealers, is active again as a refuge anchorage for the multinational fishing fleet that works the waters surrounding the islands.

soon became apparent to Biscoe that his chart was inaccurate, and on 17 December, reasoning that the islands were to the west, he altered course and began to battle against the prevailing westerlies. Two days later, in poor visibility, they noted an "appearance of land" to the west-southwest. On 21 December Biscoe's decision to claw west was vindicated. "The land," wrote Biscoe, "has a most terrific appearance being nothing more than a complete rock of about 6 or 7 miles in length . . . and covered with ice and snows so much that it was hardly possible to distinguish the rock, the snow and the clouds above them one from the other, and there being no appearance of a landing place after standing in within 5 or 6 miles it was the opinion of most on board that nothing of consequence could be got which agreeing with my own ideas on the subject I hauled off to the southward in hopes to find a better chance elsewhere."

The remaining days of 1830 were to prove frustrating ones. The cutter and small boats were ordered in to examine the steep faces of the islands— but always returned with disappointing news. No landing places, no fur seals, no elephant seals. The penguins alone seemed to be the only creatures adapted to these forbidding islands: "nothing to be seen on shore but penguins which were in great numbers."

By Christmas Day they were to the southeast of the islands, having been forced there by the wind and drifting pack ice. The only consolation, even though the winds were strong westerlies, came from the smoothness of the sea. This, they thought, was an encouraging sign: it could be an indication of a large body of land to the west. They were mistaken, and the benefit they were receiving was the dampening effect of what must have been a large area of pack ice to windward. But every benefit was gratefully received. "Independent of the small seas of field-ice," noted Biscoe, "the whole space was completely covered with drift pieces, some swimming very deep in the water, which a vessel striking upon would most likely knock a hole in her bottom, so that from the 26th to the 29th forenoon, we were utterly prevented from steering on any course for more than a few minutes at a time . . . and never at any time had we less than fifty or a hundred ice-islands round us."

Biscoe now showed that tenacious and determined spirit that was to characterize him during the coming months: he resolved to force his way back to the islands and continue the search for seals. By 30 December they were among the islands and the whaleboats made another fruitless search for the elusive creatures. The lack of seals and landing places, together with the weather conditions, now prompted Biscoe to make a New Year's resolution to quit these fog-bound, grim, and inhospitable islands, and bear away to the southeast in search of new land. And to keep as close as possible to the edge of the pack ice in hope of making more southing.

A week later they found themselves in a large bay of ice. From the masthead Biscoe noted that "to the southward, the ice appeared so smooth and firm, that any might have walked on it." The visibility was sparkling clear after the gloomy fogs of the South Sandwich Islands and Biscoe was convinced that "any land of any considerable elevation might have been seen eighty or ninety miles." Adding to the sterility of the scene, its blue skies and expanse of smooth white ice, was the remarkable absence of wildlife. The vessels had normally been accompanied by petrels and porpoising penguins. Now there was nothing. Wildlife or not, Biscoe noted with obvious relief that "the water continued very smooth."

From 7 to 16 January—the last a memorable day: fifty-eight icebergs in view, water temperature 34 degrees Fahrenheit, air temperature 45 degrees in the shade and 77 degrees in the sun, "with a corresponding genial warmth to the feelings of the crew"—their course, dictated by wind and ice, had been almost due east. The next day they turned the corner of the solid pack, and with a westerly wind wormed their way through the floes, heading southeast. By 21 January the sea was clear and the following day they crossed the Antarctic Circle. Such are the vagaries of pack ice.

But the ice-free waters and favorable winds were not to last. The seabirds were back but so was the ice, and more ominously, the wind settled into an easterly—the direct opposite of their desires and hopes. On 28 January, at 10°43′E they reached their farthest south of 69°S. Any further progress southward lay blocked by pack ice. Unseen and unknown to Biscoe, only sixty miles away lay the edge of the ice shelf fronting what is now the Princess Astrid Coast—a coastline to be discovered a century later by a Norwegian whaling expedition.

For the next two months the two vessels struggled, and not only against the ice. Those damnable easterly winds that had come as such an unwelcome surprise to Biscoe were giving him what he called "a beating passage of it, which with the frequent calm, now and then a strong blow from the S.E., with generally a heavy swell from the quarter for some time before and after, together with the thick weather, incommode me very much." It was not the only aggravation. The cutter was also a nagging worry. The aptly named *Lively* was constantly being lost in the fog and frequent changes of course were forced on them by the pack ice. At one point the exasperated Biscoe was forced to leash the errant cutter, like a straying puppy, to the *Tula:* "At midnight the weather became so thick that, although I could speak the cutter, I could not see her, and as we were completely surrounded by broken ice and obliged to use the sweeps, I made a line fast to her to prevent our separation; the weather quite calm and sea smooth."

But even with the constant activity, Biscoe's inquiring mind was pondering on the question of the formation of this huge area of pack ice and thousands of icebergs. At 68°S he had observed sea ice forming to a half-inch thickness overnight—and this in summer. What, he reasoned, might it form during the middle of winter? Icebergs were another matter. Biscoe

knew that Weddell had observed an iceberg with so much black earth
embedded in it that he first thought it to be land. He also knew that most
navigators thought icebergs were formed "contiguous to land." Biscoe
had other ideas. He was convinced, having now seen hundreds of icebergs
and no sign of collected earth, that they "originated from a vast body of
ice, frozen on the surface of the water, and accumulating with time."

Indeed, he was convinced that from their present latitude to the South
Pole itself lay nothing but a solid mass of floating ice, with perhaps in-
tervening islands. This was the spawning ground of icebergs. Biscoe was
right in a certain way—not that icebergs are formed from the sea, for if
they had managed to sail those sixty miles and reached the shoreline, he
could then have walked on solid ice to the South Pole. But ice of such a
thickness that would have dumbfounded Biscoe, being on the order of ten
thousand feet in depth.

One particular iceberg, well weathered, and sculpted with arches and
caverns, attracted Biscoe's attention. As they admired this architectural
effort of nature, a large mass fell off with a tremendous noise. Inspired by
this and in a spirit of scientific inquiry—or more probably as a means of
providing entertainment to the crew—Biscoe ordered round shot and
powder broken out. With the two vessels rolling gently in the swell, a
cannon was loaded and trained on the iceberg. The first shot, due to the
roll of the *Tula,* went high; but the sound sent flocks of screaming gulls
wheeling into the air. The second round was a hit—but it had no more
effect than knocking off some ice shards. Biscoe then launched the whaleboat and rowed round the iceberg and satisfied himself that it bore no
signs of earth.

It is certain the crew must have enjoyed this divertissement from the
usual tense and nerve-wracking passage through the ice. Diversions were
few and Biscoe had missed one on 20 February. While he was sleeping
below, the crew on deck had been entertained by a spectacular display of
the aurora australis, and the officer of the watch had been so entranced
that he forgot his standing orders and failed to wake his captain—causing
Biscoe to make some rather acid comments in his journal.

Five days after this heavenly display came a tantalizing "appearance of
land" to the south. From the masthead Biscoe could see a large cliff of ice
"as high or nearly so, as the North Foreland" which stretched for some
thirty or forty miles. Some ice-domed humps indicated the possibility of
land. Only very narrow leads zigzagged their way through the pack ice—
too narrow for the *Tula* and *Lively.* A whaleboat was lowered and Biscoe
with the boat's crew threaded his way through the narrow channels toward
the ice cliff. But nearly an hour's pulling convinced them of the impossibil-
ity of getting through the ice. The vessels being hull down, the weather
taking on an ominous look, Biscoe prudently made his way back. He was

convinced that the ice cliff was nothing more than a massive, solid body of ice. In fact, what they were seeing was the continental ice sheet near the Tange Promontory.

For two days after this little excursion the visibility stayed poor, with frequent snow squalls. The wind still remained obstinately from an easterly direction, and adding to their discomfort was a vile, lumpy sea which threw both vessels around to such an extent they were forced to reduce canvas to ease the strain on spars and rigging.

By the morning of 28 February, however, the seas became more regular and tolerable. They were now at 47°20′E and 66°S and steering south through broken pack ice. At 4 P.M. they sighted "several hummocks to the southward, which resembled tops of mountains." Off-duty crew crowded the rigging and with the officers' telescopes trained south, the watch worked the vessels through the leads. After two hours it was hearteningly apparent that something more positive than the usual "appearance of land" could be entered in the ship's log.

The hummocks were now standing clear, definite and discernible, as the tops of black mountains thrusting their flanks through the ice and snow. Those mountaintops must have caused great excitement and jubilation among the crew. It made bearable the months of damp and freezing misery. Biscoe's journal mentions nothing of this. A laconic "great satisfaction" is all that he recorded.

For two days Biscoe forced and jammed his two vessels through the pack—receiving some heavy blows from the ice in the process—toward those tantalizing mountaintops. It was impossible. The wind was light and fickle; overnight an inch of ice was forming in the open leads. They were trying to sail through porridge. It was all very frustrating. Since leaving the South Sandwich Islands they had spent two months struggling south in an effort to discover land. They had found it, and it was unreachable. But if the last two months had been trying ones, the next two were to prove harrowing.

Their ordeal, as if staged by a cunningly malevolent director, opened seductively on 3 March with a brilliant and spectacular display of the aurora australis. This time Biscoe was to see it. But again, with a certain ironic touch, the deck crew were to catch the rough edge of his tongue. Let Biscoe describe the scene:

Nearly the whole night, the Aurora Australis showed the most brilliant appearance, at times rolling itself over our heads in beautiful columns, then suddenly forming itself as the unrolled fringe of a curtain, and again suddenly shooting to the form of a serpent, and at times appearing not more than a yard above us; it was decidedly transacted in our own atmosphere, and was without exception the grandest phenomenon of nature of its kind I ever witnessed. At this time we were completely beset with broken ice, and although the vessels were in considerable danger in running through it with a smart breeze, which had now sprung up, I could hardly restrain the people from looking at the Aurora Australis instead of the vessel's course.

After the light show the *Tula* and the *Lively* were led, with devilish directorial trickery, into a three-mile-wide open channel flanked by icebergs to starboard and pack ice to port, leading them toward the land. It proved a cul-de-sac. Biscoe sailed back into clear water and searched along the ice edge for another passage to the headland, which had been named Cape Ann. Other mountains were named after the Enderby brothers and one, Mount Gordon, after one of the Enderbys' sisters.* By the afternoon of 5 March the wind had increased to gale force from the southeast, accompanied with blinding snow. In these blizzard conditions the *Lively* was lost to sight. By midnight the wind had increased to hurricane force.

The *Tula* was now virtually unmanageable and she was driven willy-nilly, a mass of ice and snow, to the northwest. Monstrous seas broke over her, washing away one whaleboat and stoving in the other; rails and bulwarks were carried away; the ice thickened on hull, deck, masts, spars, and rigging. The men could barely function in the bitter cold, their hands and fingers reduced to frozen claws. These conditions lasted until the morning of 8 March, leaving the *Tula,* as Biscoe succinctly noted, "almost a wreck." The horizon was empty of any signs of the *Lively.*

The hurricane-force winds had driven the *Tula* 120 miles to the north. But as soon as the winds had moderated, Biscoe wore his battered craft around and headed southward once again. Several men had been injured during the hurricane and five were "under cure": scurvy, that dread disease of seamen, was making its appearance. As they headed back to Cape Ann the weather settled into a malignant cycle: a southeast gale every twenty-four hours broken by a short calm, all this with constant snow and sleet squalls. On 16 March, with the air temperature at 22 degrees Fahrenheit, they sighted Cape Ann again.

It was Biscoe's hope that the pack ice skirting the land had been blown away by the hurricane winds—but the barrier still remained. Even Biscoe was weary now, and he had his men to consider. The carpenter and two other men had lost the use of their legs, and scurvy was obviously making its deadly inroads into the others. With no other sail breaking the horizon it could only be assumed that the *Lively* was sunk. With all these considerations it is no wonder that the entry for 16 March is a doleful one:

I feel myself absolutely obliged to give up all further pursuit in this part. The land inaccessible, heavy gales frequent every day, some of the people getting sick . . . the vessel is very uncomfortable . . . ships a great deal of water and is now on the outside, both hull and ropes, where the spray can reach, one mass of ice.

* Elizabeth Enderby married Lieutenant General Gordon and bore him a son—Major General Charles Gordon (1833–85) who was killed during the ten-month siege of Khartoum.

But the "in this part" indicates this was to be no total capitulation. Defeated at Cape Ann, Biscoe was still determined to win on another front. But time was short, winter was closing in, the health of his men was deteriorating. For another three weeks the *Tula* hunted along the edge of the pack ice searching for a passage through to land. On 6 April Biscoe finally capitulated. The *Tula*, still a mass of ice, had only three crew who could stand, let alone work. Biscoe was now convinced that any land to the south was inaccessible and found himself "obliged although very reluctantly to give up any further pursuit this season. . . . I consider it most prudent to proceed to New Zealand in prosecution of my voyage and to get into a climate more settled as soon as possible. . . ."

The *Tula*, battered and weather-beaten, carrying her crew of invalids, made her slow way east. On 23 April the carpenter died and he was soon followed by another crewman. The *Tula* was now being sailed by one seaman, one boy, the two mates, and Biscoe. Pitifully weak, they were forced to heave to at sunset and make sail again at dawn, waiting out nights now long and dark and only brightened by an occasional and derisory aurora.

As the noon-to-noon positions crept across the chart it became obvious that a haven had to be reached before New Zealand. His men had to be put ashore as soon as possible. Hobart in Tasmania was his closest refuge and although without charts of the area, Biscoe altered course to close with the land. Toward his companions he put on a brave front—but his journal reveals his true feelings: "I endeavoured all in my power to keep up the spirits of those on board, and often had a smile on my face, with very different feelings within."

Early in May Biscoe navigated his floating lazar house up the Derwent River to Hobart. James Weddell, who was there commanding the *Eliza*, sent over men to help moor the *Tula*. Then the sick were carried ashore to hospital. This meeting between Weddell and Biscoe is intriguing. Here were two men, much of the same age, both seamen and navigators above the common ruck; both had served in the Royal Navy; both had inquiring minds. Weddell's book and charts were certainly stowed aboard the *Tula*. What did they talk of, these two men with so much in common? Formation of icebergs? Religion? The sealing trade? Mutual acquaintances from navy days? Antiscorbutics? Chronometers? Shipowners and their foibles? Rigging? Politics? The convicts of Hobart? The problems of steam engines for seagoing vessels? Did Biscoe tell Weddell of his discoveries? (The Enderbys had ordered Biscoe to remain silent on any new sealing ground discoveries. Keeping the seamen silent was another matter. Sailors in shoreside taverns are not noted for taciturnity: rum will also loosen the closest of mouths.) Whatever their talk, nothing is known. The past is silent. What is certain is that a bond of friendship, of camaraderie, as will be seen, must have sprung up between them.

The next few months were spent in Hobart repairing the *Tula* and recovering their health. During those months nothing was heard of the *Lively*. At the start of September the *Tula* sailed down the Derwent on the second stage of her voyage. At the river mouth, sailing toward them, the Tulas sighted a familiar little vessel. It was the *Lively* sailing up to Hobart. They met, exchanged news, and sailed back in company to Hobart.

The tale that Avery had to tell was extraordinary. After being driven apart during the March storm, the *Lively* had suffered infinitely worse—if that was possible—than the *Tula*. Avery, described by a reporter on the *Tasmanian* as a "plain sailor-like man, but extremely intelligent and well informed," had lost all his crew except for one seaman and a boy with a broken hand. Two of the men had died below decks and, in a macabre scene straight from the Grand Guignol, Avery, the only one with enough strength, had performed the grisly task of tying a line around each body and hauling them through the hatchway by block and tackle, before, in the melodramatic words of the reporter, "launching them into the deep."

Avery had also, like Biscoe, decided to make for Tasmania; but only managed to reach Port Phillip (near present-day Melbourne) about a month before Biscoe arrived at Hobart. Terribly weak, the three spectral figures, two men and one boy, "in the very utmost state of distress," managed to anchor the *Lively* and stagger ashore to forage for water and provisions. When they returned the *Lively* had vanished—either taken by natives or broken free from her mooring. For two weeks the castaways searched along the shores and inlets of the bay. They found her aground in one of the inlets; managed, after much effort, to refloat her; and then eventually sailed for Hobart and the timely meeting with the *Tula* at the mouth of the Derwent.

Back at Hobart the *Lively* was refitted and the two men and small boy recovered their health. On 8 October 1831 James Weddell and other friends of Biscoe breakfasted in the small cabin of the *Tula*. After the final farewells the *Tula* and *Lively* weighed anchor and sailed for New Zealand. Here they wooded and watered, then they left for the Chatham Islands off the east coast of New Zealand to try their luck with the fur seals. The seals, however, had been virtually exterminated and only twenty-three skins were stowed in the hold when they sailed for the Bounty Islands a little further south. The Bounty Islands produced nothing.

Biscoe now set his course to a spot on the ocean about a third of the distance between New Zealand and Cape Horn. This was to be yet another search for more reported islands—the Nimrod Islands. After sailing over their supposed position, Biscoe consigned these, like the Aurora Islands, to the cartographic junk pile. They were now headed for the South Shetland Islands to try and add to that paltry number of sealskins.

Sailing east with a touch of south in it, Biscoe decided to cross south of James Cook's track of 1774 in the hope of finding land—unaware that Bellingshausen had preceded him by eleven years. Not too far south, however. After the previous year's experience he wanted to arrive on the sealing grounds with seaworthy vessels and a healthy crew.

The passage they were making, compared to the horrors off Enderby Land, was pleasant enough. They sighted their first iceberg on 24 January and a few days later were treated to the sight of another one suddenly collapsing with a noise like a thunderclap, leaving only a small nucleus bobbing among the shattered fragments. On one day of good visibility they counted 250 icebergs in sight from the deck. The accompanying wildlife was a perpetual source of encouragement. Friendly escorts of Cape pigeons wheeled around the two vessels; at a further distance glided the aloof albatross; petrels skimmed the seas, which were plumed with spouts of whales and splash of porpoising penguins. The barometer had been replaced and caused a certain amount of worry when it dropped to an ominous 27.3 inches, but the storm-force winds that this would have predicted in the northern hemisphere failed to arrive. The *Lively*, again, was producing the usual crop of headaches: she had run short of water and had to be supplied with six hogsheads from the *Tula*. Biscoe thought drinking melted iceberg water brought on dysentery. The condition of the cutter's canvas also caused concern. But all in all, except for the constant danger from growlers and icebergs, the passage across this section of the Southern Ocean was proving relatively undemanding.

On 15 February 1832, five weeks after they had left the Bounty Islands, land was seen at a great distance to the east-southeast. Biscoe altered course to close it and the next day they lay some miles off. To Biscoe, unaware of Bellingshausen's discoveries of Peter I Island and Alexander Island, this new discovery represented a prize—the southernmost land yet found on the globe. He named his prize after Queen Adelaide, wife of William IV. Biscoe described the new land as follows:

This island, being the farthest known land to the southward, I have honoured it with the name of H.M.G. Majesty Queen Adelaide. It has a most imposing and beautiful appearance, having one very high peak running up into the clouds, and occasionally appears both above and below them; about one-third of the mountains, which are about 4 miles in extent from north to south, have only a thin scattering of snow over their summits. Towards the base the other two-thirds are buried in a field of snow and ice of the most dazzling brightness. This bed of snow and ice is about 4 miles in extent, sloping gradually down to its termination; a cliff, ten or twelve feet high, which is split in every direction for at least two or three hundred yards from its edge inwards, and which appears to form icebergs only waiting for some severe gales or other cause to break them adrift and put them in motion. From the great depth of water, I consider this island to have been originally a cluster of perpendicular rocks, and I am thoroughly of opinion that the land I before saw last year, could I have got to it, would have proved to be in the same state as this, and likewise all land found in high southern latitudes.

Biscoe was riding his hobbyhorse again. And Adelaide Island, very satisfyingly, appeared to confirm his faulty premise that icebergs were formed from seawater freezing between clusters of perpendicular rocks.

The following day was particularly clear: one of those days, not all that rare, when Antarctica seems to burst with extra oxygen and the air is of such diamond clarity that mountain ranges stretch into the far distance as if painted by an exuberant stage designer. To the south they saw more land, which Biscoe estimated to be ninety miles away. It was a remarkably accurate estimate—these were the peaks at the northern end of Alexander Island some one hundred miles distant.

The next day their view of the stage scenery was masked by fog. As they sailed cautiously northwest the fog suddenly cleared and they found themselves sailing past a group of islands—the Biscoe Islands—not as mountainous as Adelaide Island but covered with a shield of snow and ice, perfectly smooth except at the shores. Behind these islands lay a backdrop of a mountain range "which had a grand appearance." They were looking at the mountains of the Antarctic Peninsula. On 19 February a boat was sent to investigate an island in the hopes of finding seals—but returned with the usual negative report. Biscoe named it Pitt's Island, as a nearby iceberg put him in mind of the statesman in "a sitting posture."

A definite ritual appears in the giving of names by the early explorers to Antarctica's major features. Cast an eye at a map of Antarctica and note the royalty, politicians, and millionaires jostling for prime position: royalty and politicians for their possible future patronage, millionaires for their signature on a check. Biscoe's naming of Pitt's Island was pure fancy and perhaps admiration—the politician had been dead many years. Over a hundred years later the islands and outlying rocks making up the Pitt Islands were all given names. And what a relief from the predictable. Here are Trundle, Jinks, Snubbin, Nupkins, Sawyer, Pickwick (the largest of the group), Winkle, Fizking, Snodgrass, Weller, and Jingle Islands. A small harbor is entered through Wardle Entrance and the outlying rocks are Bardell, Buzfuz, and finally, Dickens Rock.

The Pitt Islands lie just over two hundred miles from New Plymouth in the South Shetlands. Two weeks later, having suffered the usual mix of fog, gales, and calm, the *Tula* and *Lively*'s anchors splashed down into the waters of the sealers' old harbor. On one of those days of the long two weeks, Biscoe had pulled into a bay (about five miles from the present-day Palmer Station on Anvers Island) where, as Biscoe noted with some regret, "the water was so still, that could any seals have been found, the vessels could have been easily loaded, as they might have been laid alongside the rocks for that purpose . . . and the sun was so warm that the snow was melted off all the rocks along the waterline." Thinking, incorrectly, that this land formed part of the mainland, he took formal possession of it and named the two highest mountains: one after William IV and the other after Captain Moberly—the same Moberly who had written recommending the young Biscoe for promotion.

Biscoe had now spent nineteen months on a commercial venture that had made significant discoveries—but had failed to find skins or oil to justify the voyage's cost. Here at New Plymouth the enterprise's fortunes might change. Now it was elephant seals, not fur seals, that Biscoe hoped to find. A countryman, Adam Kellock, and his seventy-six-foot schooner the *Exquisite* also lay at anchor in New Plymouth. And he was encouraging—plenty of elephant seals, according to Kellock. Biscoe sent out two boats and accounted for thirty seals. On 17 March the *Exquisite* weighed anchor, leaving the *Tula* and *Lively* alone in the anchorage. Next day Biscoe, leaving a skeleton crew aboard the *Tula*, sailed in the cutter to search for more seals to add to their meager haul. By 2 April they had returned, having seen only eleven elephant seal pups.

Back aboard the *Tula* Biscoe heard of a vicious swell that had swept into the anchorage during the cutter's absence, a swell so large that it caused the skeleton crew some anxious hours. It was time to depart. The *Lively* would return to England and the *Tula* would sail to the nearest whaling grounds and try to fill with oil.

In the cabin of the *Tula* Biscoe wrote his dispatches of the voyage and a letter to Captain Beaufort, the navy Hydrographer, in London. Biscoe was convinced that the land he had taken possession of in February—he called it "William the 4th Promontory"—and the land he had discovered the previous year "forms the headlands of a Southern Continent. . . . I submit to you there is a great field for Discovery in these Southern Regions, which would much benefit Science and Navigation."

The Southern Continent, however, was not quite finished with the Tulas and Livelys. By 10 April, with both vessels ready for sea, they were struck by storm-force winds and heavy seas sweeping into their anchorage. Any chance of sailing out was impossible. The *Tula*, with her deeper draft, was striking bottom in the troughs and her rudder was smashed. All hands left her and boarded the *Lively*, where the combined crews watched helplessly as the *Tula* reared and plunged in the breakers and the seas swept clear across her deck. Recalcitrant and unhandy at times though she might be, *Tula*, with her woman's figurehead buried in the welter of water, represented life hanging on the strength of an anchor cable. It held.

The storm passed and with the seas easing down—Biscoe estimated the highest breakers at seventeen feet—the relieved sailors pulled back to the *Tula* and, with that genius for extempore makeshift so characteristic of seamen, jury-rigged an emergency rudder. Of the seven hundred miles to the Falklands, Biscoe's journal is brief. "We arrived at Berkeley Sound after a very rough passage."

It was 29 April 1832 and Biscoe and his crew, with their two unsuitable vessels, had completed the third circumnavigation of Antarctica. A month was spent in Berkeley Sound recovering their health and setting up a smithy on shore to forge the ironwork for a new rudder. The repairs completed, the search for seals continued. New Island on the west side of the Falklands was their first destination. But the season was late, the seals scarce. More worrying was the fact that the errant *Lively* had gone astray on the passage from Berkeley Sound.

A month after leaving the sound, with no seals and no *Lively*, Biscoe set sail to search the islands for his missing consort. Toward the end of July he was back in Berkeley Sound, to be greeted with bad news. The small *Lively*, ex–Cowes pilot boat that had sailed in waters undreamed of by her builders, had found her last resting place in the South Atlantic. "Mr. Avery," wrote Biscoe, "the commander of the *Lively* came on board with part of the crew having been taken off Mackay's Island by the *Unicorn* commanded by Captain Couzens under the Monte Video colours, the *Lively* being wrecked on that island and was a total loss."

At Berkeley Sound Biscoe waited for news from England. The arrangement had been for the Enderbys to send out the *Rose* with stores and provisions for Biscoe to continue another season in the Southern Ocean. Biscoe, with the extra mouths to feed from the *Lively*, reduced the rations to three and one-half pounds of bread a week and considered this "with fresh soup and other necessaries . . . quite sufficient; the whole of the crew however refused to work and I was oblig'd altogether to give them 5 lbs bread per week each and promise to go into some port for further supply of provisions. . . . But they are quite out of heart with the voyage, and are dropping off one after another as they find chance and indeed I can hardly blame them."

The slow erosion of his crew and the nonappearance of the *Rose* decided Biscoe to sail—with a supply of fresh beef to bolster the five pounds of bread—for Santa Catarina in Brazil. They arrived on 20 September and found supplies that included poultry, pigs, fish, and firewood. That same month, a thousand miles south near the fortress settlement of Bahia Blanca, Charles Darwin was being taught the use of the bolas—with no great success—by guachos, and eating armadillo cooked in its case—it tasted like duck—and "ostrich" (rhea) egg dumplings. More exciting was the finding of colossal fossil bones of extinct animals in a low cliff face. They were discoveries destined to set off that inquiring mind into new and uncharted waters.

As Darwin burrowed at the cliff face, loaded the packhorses with fossilized bones, and speculated on their significance, Biscoe—on a much smaller scale—speculated on a sealing voyage to the desolate Diego Ramirez Islands off Cape Horn. But if Biscoe was still game for another attempt at the Southern Ocean, his officers and crew had other ideas. Seduced by the delights of Brazil, all but four men and three boys deserted. Short-handed and penniless—he had had to sell ship's property and some of his personal belongings—Biscoe came to the inevitable decision to sail for England.

On 8 February 1833, after a voyage of two and a half years, the weather-worn *Tula* entered the London docks with a cargo of thirty sealskins. It was a commercial disaster for the Enderbys. But Charles Enderby could at least salvage some national and geographic prestige. Within three days he was presenting a paper enitled "Recent Discoveries in the Antarctic Ocean" to the Royal Geographical Society. The same paper was reprinted in the United States in the *Naval Magazine*. The Society presented Biscoe with their gold medal—he was the second recipient—and made him a member without payment of dues. It was, perhaps, some small recompense for the hardships of the voyage. By any standards it had been a remarkable expedition. With two small and unsuitable vessels, a crew inadequately clothed and poorly provisioned, Biscoe, with bulldog tenacity, had struggled to reach those tantalizing mountaintops of Enderby Land. Few other men would have spent five such grim weeks to reach so desolate a Pisgah.

The third circumnavigator of Antarctica, Biscoe was the first to realize his discoveries were "the headlands of a Southern Continent" and make the fact known to the Hydrographer in London. The sealer John Davis's note in his log was an inspired guess—nothing more. He had nothing like Biscoe's experience of sighting such similar and such widely separated Antarctic land masses. Biscoe's other hard-won contribution to the unveiling of the continent was to advise that any future voyages in the high southern latitudes be sailed from east to west. In the next decade it was advice noted, heeded, and followed by national expeditions from the United States, France, and Great Britain.

The gold medal from the Royal Geographical Society was soon followed by one from the Paris Geographical Society. And in a letter acknowledging the award Biscoe reaffirmed his interest in further Antarctic exploration: "Allow me to express my very hearty and sincere thanks to the Society, and to assure you that if an opportunity to revisit those latitudes again presents itself, neither difficulty nor danger will prevent me from resuming the exploration of a part of the world still almost unknown and now so interesting."

The opportunity for more exploration came a few years later. But before the return to the cold seductions of the Antarctic came marriage, a command of a brig trading between Liverpool and the West Indies, and then, in 1837, as master of the barque *Superb*, sailing with his family to Australia. Here they made a new home.

In December 1838 Biscoe, in command of the sixty-seven-foot *Emma* and outfitted for whaling, sailed from Sydney. By May 1839 the *Emma* was back in port and a rather piqued *Sydney Herald* reporter wrote that "we were unable to obtain any particulars further than she went as far as 75°S. We heard from one on board of their having fallen in with a schooner and a cutter on a voyage of discovery. . . ." If Biscoe had reached 75°S it would have been a remarkable achievment—further south than Cook or Weddell, and deep into either the Ross or Weddell Sea. But newspaper reports are hardly models of veracity. Biscoe met Dumont d'Urville at Hobart in December 1839 and the commander of the French expedition reported that "he told me that he had lately tried to get further south along the meridian of New Zealand, but that ice had stopped him at 63°S latitude. . . ." As to the schooner and cutter, these were the *Eliza Scott* and the *Sabrina,* commanded by John Balleny—and shortly to make discoveries which would add to those of Biscoe.

The last few years remaining to Biscoe were spent commanding passenger and cargo vessels sailing between Sydney, Port Philip, and Hobart. But his health was failing. On 21 October there appeared a small notice in the Hobart newspapers:

To the PUBLIC—The Charitable Donations of the public are earnestly solicited on behalf of Captain John Biscoe, late of the *Marian Watson,* and formerly of the schooner *Tula,* of about 120 tons, in which vessel, accompanied by the cutter *Lively* of 46 tons only, he explored the Southern Regions, generally for the space of three years; whose unexampled intrepidity on that occasion, in the search of scientific knowledge, is admitted by public testimonials from British and foreign governments, and whose tract is marked on the present Admiralty charts: the hardships and privations of that voyage gave a blow to his constitution, which, after a long series of illness, has at last incapacitated him from following his profession.

His friends now seek the means to enable him to return with his family to England, and confidently appeal to the benevolence of the Van Diemen's Land public to effect it.

Subscriptions received at all the Banks, and by Mr. William Carter, Treasurer.
Subscriptions already advertised £109 12 0

The lieutenant governor of Van Diemen's Land, Sir John Franklin—no stranger to the ice of the Arctic—contributed ten guineas. And a few months after this notice appeared, Biscoe with his wife and children sailed as passengers on the barque *Janet Izat.* It proved John Biscoe's final voyage; he died on the passage back to England. It is not recorded in what latitudes the funeral was held. But it would be pleasing to think that, after the service had been read, the grating tipped, and the weighted canvas-shrouded form slipped from under the Union Jack, it was taken by the waters of the Southern Ocean. And close to one of those icebergs which caused Biscoe so much speculative thought. A harmless hobbyhorse is entitled to every man during his lifetime.

In 1990 Queen Elizabeth II launched a new vessel to replace the ageing *John Biscoe.* Named the RRS *James Clark Ross,* she continues the same tradition of naming British Antarctic Survey vessels after those early Antarctic explorers. One hopes she will take on as much *baraka* as her pugnacious forebear.

XII

Kemp and Balleny: The Last Discoveries by Sealers

Notwithstanding the length of time which has elapsed since the discovery of the western continent, and the consequent impulse given to the spirit of discovery, it is a remarkable fact that the most interesting section of this terraqueous globe still remains unexplored, and almost totally unknown. It is a reproach to every civilized country, that the people of this enlightened age possess so little accurate knowledge of the seas, islands, and perhaps continents which exist in the polar regions of the southern hemisphere.

Benjamin Morrell, *A Narrative of Four Voyages 1822–1831*, 1832

THE ENDERBY BROTHERS, flushed by the heady delights of Biscoe's geographical discoveries and undeterred by their financial losses, sent off another sealing expedition to the Antarctic with the schooner *Hopefull* and the yawl *Rose*. It proved a complete disaster with the *Rose* crushed and sunk by the pack ice off the South Shetlands, the *Rose*'s crew being taken off by the *Hopefull*. The deficit on the Enderbys' balance sheet was somewhat mitigated by the curious fact that the Treasury Department paid out £2,539 to them. It was an instance of canny astuteness by the merchants: the Admiralty had guaranteed to make good a proportion of any losses provided they had a representative aboard in the person of a Lieutenant Rea. The perplexed officer, used to Royal Navy discipline, found the rough-and-ready ways of the sealers little to his liking and described them as a "most mutinous set of dogs."

The Enderbys were now headed down the slippery slopes of financial disaster. And their path to it is a cautionary tale of enterprises mounted

on misinformation, poor planning, misdirected energies, and a cavalier
attitude regarding brutal facts. It was all to end with their financial ruin in
the self-inflicted fiasco of the Southern Whale Fishery Company and an
abortive attempt to settle the remote Auckland Islands south of New
Zealand. But this was all in the future for Charles, Ienry, and George
Enderby. In 1833 they were buoyant with the geographical prizes brought
back by John Biscoe: with these they entered into the hagiography of
Antarctic exploration.

The Enderbys, however, had a rival company in the shape of Daniel
Bennett & Sons of London. Like the Enderbys', their social aspirations
were to be sanctified by the Heralds' College and they would proudly
display a crest and coat of arms. The changing fortunes and ambitions of
this prudent and hardworking family can be measured by the descriptions
of their occupations in the directories. The humble "brazier" changes to
"ship owner" to "merchant" to "South Seas ship owner." Unlike the
Enderbys, this astute family company had little truck with geographical
discoveries. Any reports of such from their captains were studied with
care and regarded with caution. They were not members of the Royal
Geographical Society. Nevertheless it had been a Bennett vessel and captain, the *Dove* and George Powell, who had discovered the South Orkneys
in 1821. And it was Powell who had prepared for publication the best chart
and sailing directions for the South Shetlands then available.

In July 1833, a few months after Biscoe's return to the Thames, a small
Bennett-owned snow, the seventy-two-foot *Magnet,* cleared from London
bound for the Southern Ocean. Aboard were eighteen men all under the
command of Peter Kemp. Little is known about Kemp. He steps forward
from that mass of anonymous merchant navy masters, is spotlighted for a
second by an Antarctic discovery, and steps off stage. Before he took command of the *Magnet* he had been master aboard seven other vessels and
had made at least a dozen voyages into the Southern Ocean, bringing back
train oil, sperm oil, and sealskins. This was an experienced and capable
commander.

Kemp sailed with full knowledge of Biscoe's discoveries and, stowed
carefully in his cabin, two Arnold & Kent chronometers; no. 173 and no.
279. This admirable company had just started a price war by reducing the
cost of reliable chronometers from 80 guineas (about £4,000, or $6,000 in
1996 prices) to 40 guineas. Nevertheless, the purchase by the Bennetts still
represented a considerable investment in a high-risk business.

Kemp now took the *Magnet* on a nonstop passage to Kerguelen Island—a long voyage of eleven thousand miles to the other side of the
globe, denoting an urgency of purpose combined with adequate provisioning. Kerguelen Island, that grim volcanic outcropping set in the
Southern Ocean between Africa and Australia, had been first sighted by
the Breton Yves Joseph de Kerguelen-Tremarec in 1772 and visited by
James Cook on his third circumnavigation in 1774. Even the normally

impassive Cook felt the lowering presence of the island and named it Island of Desolation. The name was apt, for lying as it does on the edge of the Antarctic Convergence and between two weather systems, the island has a climate that can only be described as vile: wind, snow, sleet, and rain form its main components.

American whalers and sealers, their Yankee tongues finding the name Kerguelen troublesome, followed Cook's example and knew it as Desolation Island. And it was the American whalers and sealers who arrived first in the wake of Cook's *Resolution* and *Discovery* and made the island a major center for their operations.

In the December of 1792, the *Asia,* the *Alliance,* and the *Hunter* from Nantucket, after whaling in the Indian Ocean, sought out the island for elephant sealing. Captain Bartlett Coffin of the *Asia* died during their three-month stay and his shipmates "bewryed him in a Deasent Manner" on the bleak shores of an island far from his own island home. It was to be the first of many graves. The news of Coffin's death reached Nantucket in August of 1793 and Zenia Fanning, an indefatigable diarist, wrote in her journal that "the 3rd of the month letters came from Andrew Pinkham . . . Bartlett Coffin's second mate; he writes that Bartlett died 7th Feb., overstrained and hurt himself in January, died in great agony. Poor Cousin Judith is left a Disconsolate widow."

Seventeen years later another widow heard of her husband's death after Captain John Matley of the Bennett-owned *Duke of Portland* died on the island. On the ship's next voyage to Kerguelen she carried a gravestone, suitably inscribed, from Matley's widow. The bleakness of the burial place is strangely alien for a headstone more at home rising from a grass-covered English village churchyard.

Many Bennett company masters, as well as the Americans, were familiar with the Island of Desolation. In the 1799–1800 season Captain Robert Rhodes of the *Hillsborough* spent eight months whaling and sealing in the island's bays and along its shores. He also spent time making a magnificent chart of the north and northeast coast, complete with sailing directions. Forty years later Captain James Clark Ross and the *Erebus* and *Terror* expedition used this valuable information during their three-month stay on the island and the setting up of magnetic observatories. As a compliment to Rhodes, Ross named a bay after this "diligent investigator." Of the sixty-eight days spent at one anchorage, gale-force winds blew for forty-five days and only three days were free from snow or rain. Ross tersely described their stay as "dreary and disagreeable."

This then was the unprepossessing island to which Kemp set his course after rounding the tip of Africa and running his easting down in the huge seas of the Southern Ocean. The island, dismal and bleak as it was, had certain advantages. It could supply ample fresh water after the long voyage as well as fresh meat for the pot in the way of duck, penguin, and seal, plus penguin eggs for the makings of the sailors' favorite boiled duff puddings.

Most importantly the island boasted a fresh vegetable in the globe-artichoke shape of the Kerguelen cabbage. Cook's surgeon, William Anderson, had noticed this valuable plant and named it after Sir John Pringle, the President of the Royal Society. The *Resolution*'s crew, knowing well their captain's strange proclivities, ate it raw and Anderson thought it a valuable antiscorbutic; and *Pringlea antiscorbutica* became a staple for the whalers and sealers who followed after Cook.

The other advantage to Kemp was the island's position, some twelve hundred miles north of Biscoe's Antarctic discoveries and slightly to the east. From Kerguelen Kemp could reach down across the Southern Ocean in the prevailing westerlies to the latitude of Enderby Land and then sail west—following Biscoe's advice that in the high latitudes close to the Antarctic Circle the prevailing winds are easterly.

During the last week of November, having watered and revived his crew after the long haul from England, Kemp and the *Magnet* headed south. It was fast sailing for the first week and during that week, on the morning of 27 November, about 180 miles south of Kerguelen, land was sighted. On Kemp's chart of the *Magnet*'s course appears the terse notation "Saw Land"; and it is on this rather flimsy evidence that the British have claimed the first sighting of Heard Island—yet another bleak outpost set in the Southern Ocean. As the *Magnet* was about 120 miles away from the island it is highly improbable that the sighting was of land and more than probable that it was another of those clouds that have fooled and bedeviled seamen over the centuries.

It was not until 1853 that Captain John J. Heard of the American barque *Oriental*, sailing from Boston to Melbourne and following a great circle course in the Southern Ocean advocated by Lieutenant Matthew Fontaine Maury, Director of the U.S. Naval Observatory, would sail by the island and plot its position.

A rather comforting domestic touch is given to this discovery, as Heard sailed with his wife, Mrs. Fidelia Heard, who kept a diary during the voyage. On 25 November 1853 Heard saw what he thought to be an immense iceberg and, the weather being wet and cold, called to his wife to dress in her "chicken fixing" clothes and come on deck to see the monster berg. Mrs. Heard peered through a telescope at the supposed iceberg, hoping to make a sketch, but the outline was indistinct. Then, as they sailed closer and the visibility improved, her husband declared the iceberg to be land—and land not marked on any known chart. They sailed by their new discovery at a distance of twenty miles and Heard made a reasonably accurate observation of its position and estimated its height at five thousand feet.* It was a classic reversal of the usual Antarctic sightings where icebergs are mistaken for land. Mrs. Heard was overjoyed at this brooding apparition on the northern horizon: "as we are perhaps the discoverers, if

---

* The highest point on the island is in fact 9,005 feet.

so the Capt. will have the privilige of endowing it with a name."

The news of the discovery was made public in the 24 December 1853 edition of the Melbourne *Argus*. A week later Heard wrote to Maury enclosing an abstract of his log describing the passage from Boston and claimed the privilege of naming the island after himself. And then, much to Heard's consternation, he read in the *Argus* that a certain Captain William McDonald of the British ship *Samarang* had discovered islands— plural—on 4 January 1854 close to that island which Heard now considered his own. This was a call to arms in the defense of his discovery. Heard unsheathed his pen on 6 February and dashed off a letter to the *Argus* pointing out the notice of *his* discovery in *their* newspaper and claimed priority of discovery by two months. The same day he wrote another letter to Maury regarding McDonald's sighting and repeated his claim to right of first sighting, and claimed the island or islands and also the naming of them for the United States.

Heard was no fool. As a shrewd, God-fearing, money-conscious New Englander, he was motivated by both patriotic and pecuniary sentiments, and the island—which he was never to see again—represented both. Also, and not to be discounted, for it is the hidden mainspring of many an explorer, was the thrill of being first in discovery and the rather tenuous fame and sense of immortality that it brings. It is an explosive mixture that has led to many vituperative wranglings between explorers and their claques.

The captain was aware that his discovery might be an ideal haven for elephant seals and fur seals, and, by the large quantity of seabirds in the area, a possible source of guano, that most admirable of fertilizers. The United States, reasoned Heard, should claim the island, establish jurisdiction, and exploit its resources for the benefit of the country. And for discovering this source of wealth Heard thought himself entitled to a bounty payment. The Navy Department and the Department of State thought otherwise. In a remarkably brusque brush-off, George L. Marcy of the State Department replied to a letter from Heard. It is a reply, classic in its own way, of a weary and harried bureaucrat burdened by his grave responsibilities and impatient of the piffling demands from the public.

DEPARTMENT OF STATE

To John J. Heard Esq.
Boston,   Washington 10th Nov. 1856
Massachusetts.

SIR: Your letter of the 7th instant relative to an alleged discovery of Islands by you, has been received. In reply, I have to acquaint you, that no reward is promised by the Government for any such discovery. It is, however, authorized to protect the discoverer of deposits of guano upon the conditions prescribed in the Act of Congress, a copy of which is herewith enclosed.

I am Sir, Your obedient Servant

Geo. L. Marcy

That contemptuous "alleged discovery" must have lanced into Heard's vitals as a harpoon into a whale.

In the event—and nothing is more galling for the unheeded prophet than to be proved right—Heard Island did indeed become a source of great wealth for the United States.

The first landing on the island was made in 1855 by Captain Erasmus Darwin Rogers (were his parents admirers of Charles Darwin's dissenting grandfather and supporter of the American and French Revolutions?) from the whaler *Corinthian*. This vessel hailed from New London and the island soon became a virtual outport for sealers from that Connecticut town. Over the next quarter of a century more than one hundred thousand barrels* of elephant seal oil were shipped off Heard Island, a process that employed a fleet of ships and thousands of men.

In 1874, on her world-girdling oceanographic voyage, HMS *Challenger* called at Heard Island. Captain Georges Warcs and the expedition members found about forty American sealers living year-round on the island in dark, odorous, smoke-filled huts let into the ground. Their provisions were limited to flour, dried beans, molasses, sugar, coffee, salt, salt pork, and the island's produce of penguins, penguin eggs, and elephant seal tongues. Cooking and heating were by coal, penguin skins, and scraps from the try-pots. The sealers would live three years in this crude troglodyte fashion, little removed from their Stone Age ancestors, butchering seals by the thousand and rendering the blubber into oil. And earned about $500 each.

In these isolated and barbarous surroundings it is not surprising that sometimes a man's mind would become unhinged. Gripped in an Antarctic *cafard,* he would run amok armed with the lethal weapons of his trade, and his companions, in self-defense, would cut him down like a mad dog.

As to Captains Heard and McDonald, both their names appear on the world's charts and atlases: Heard for the larger island and McDonald for a much smaller group of islands set twenty-eight miles farther west. In the U.S. National Archives lies a beautifully drawn manuscript chart of Heard Island. Probably drawn by a trained draftsman and based on sealers' information, it is titled, alas, Hurds Island: but sealers were notoriously cavalier in their attitude to polite society's conventions—including spelling.

But in November of 1833 all this lay in the future for Heard Island and its elephant-seal-crowded beaches. Kemp chose not to alter course and investigate but held on toward the south. A week later, at 60°S they came upon icebergs and pack ice; but also, an encouraging sign, swimming fur seals. By 14 December, after ten days of frustrating sailing that is represented on the chart like the zigzag wanderings of a bemused drunk, they

---

* About four million U.S. gallons. A gallon of oil fetched 55 cents.

eventually managed to break through the pack and came on clear water. The only encouraging sign had been the sightings of swimming fur seals. The *Magnet* was now booming southwest in clear water. On 19 December they ran into more pack ice and were forced to skirt it and sail west along its edge. Three days later they turned its corner and resumed their southerly course. They were now just west of the 60°E meridian and closing fast to the east of Biscoe's discoveries. Kemp was just where he wanted to be. On Christmas Day, just north of the Antarctic Circle, they ran into impenetrable pack ice. Next day, the visibility clearing, they saw land to the south— but they had as much chance of reaching it as of sailing to the moon. On 29 December, the land still in sight to the south, Kemp ended his futile efforts and headed the *Magnet* north. Biscoe's experience had convinced him that the chances of reaching the coast were so remote as to be virtually impossible. The filling of casks with oil was of greater importance than weeks wasted in unrewarded effort.

Nearly a hundred years were to pass before this stretch of Antarctica's coastline would be seen again be human eyes. On 12 January 1930, Sir Douglas Mawson aboard the *Discovery*,* and very close to Kemp's position, described the land as ice slopes with protruding rocky peaks rising to three thousand feet. The slopes were heavily crevassed and ended in high ice cliffs at the edge of the ice-covered sea: and with that consolidated pack the *Discovery* has as much chance of reaching the land as had the *Magnet*.

Kemp left this frigid and sterile coast and sailed back to Kerguelen, where the men went about their business of killing elephant seals and rendering the blubber into oil. Toward the end of March the *Magnet* sailed for Simonstown in South Africa, and during the passage on 21 April, Kemp fell overboard and drowned.

The *Magnet*, with a new master, returned to England in January 1835. Her log, so the story goes, was lost in a London cab and the only record of Kemp's passage from Kerguelen to the Antarctic coast is the *Magnet*'s track, marked in red, on a chart in the Hydrographic Department. Also shown is a shaded portion for land with the notation "Land seen by Capt. Kemp Dec 26 & 27 1833." The same chart shows Biscoe's track and the coast seen from the *Tula* and marked "Enderby's Land."

George Enderby gave a brief account of Kemp's voyage to the Royal Geographical Society—leaving the impression that the *Magnet* was one of his vessels. The Admiralty were obviously taken in by this subtle innuendo, and on their 1847 chart showing the tracks and discoveries of James Clark Ross and the *Erebus* and *Terror*, Enderby Land and Kemp Land are shown but marked as discovered by Biscoe. The sealer, lost at sea, had even lost his discovery.

---

* This was during the 1929–31 voyages of the British, Australia & New Zealand Antarctic Research Expedition (B.A.N.Z.A.R.E.) led by Sir Douglas Mawson.

Far south of New Zealand and 170 miles off the Antarctic coast, a necklace of five ice-covered volcanic outcroppings stretches for 105 miles across the Antarctic Circle. Known as the Balleny Islands, they are named, separately, after five London merchants and collectively after a sealing captain.

Girded and guarded by pack ice, shrouded in fogs, virtually inaccessible to any landing from the sea, they present an impregnable fortress face to the Southern Ocean. If Antarctica had a mythology, these bleak and unwelcoming islands would be the home of evil-spirited trolls, wicked goblins, hunchbacked warlocks, and malignant dwarves. There is no joy in them.

The merchants after whom these grim islands are named were all solid men of standing—members of that fast-growing class, the middle class, some of whom relished the laissez-faire economic policies of a wealthy and rapidly changing Great Britain. Thomas Sturge was a sperm oil refiner; George Young a whaling ship owner; John Buckle a merchant and connected with the East India Company; James Row another oil merchant and broker; and William Borradaile a merchant and shipping agent. These men, with a William Beale and William Brown—no islands named after them—were all joined together in a partnership and shared fifty-six of the sixty-four shares in each of two vessels. The remaining eleven shares were owned by the Enderbys. It is perhaps a mark of Charles Enderby's persuasiveness—even after the debacle of the voyages by the *Hopefull* and the *Rose*—that these prosperous men would join a questionable and high-risk venture. Particularly when the British whaling industry was on the decline.

In the nineteen years since William Smith's discovery of the South Shetlands, the economic face of Great Britain had changed. These, the 1830s, were now the years when the Industrial Revolution was literally building up steam. Gone for the sealers were those few bonanza years of fur sealing. Now it was oil, either from whales or from elephant seals, that interested this group of merchants. Or was it? Perhaps the lure dangled by Charles Enderby was the more tenuous one of social recognition for geographic discoveries.

George Young, six years after entering into the Enderby-orchestrated partnership, when testifying before a Parliamentary Select Committee investigating the state of British shipping, spoke for many British whaling men when he mournfully remarked that "no consideration would induce me voluntarily to embark £1,000 in the whale fishery, for a conviction that we never can, by any change or diminution of the cost which it is in the power of the Legislature to effect, be enabled to meet the competition to which we are exposed in those trades."

The competition came from coal gas, from American and Australian whaling, and—the Board of Trade having caught the free trade spirit with a vengeance—from the removal of the rapeseed oil duty and the partial removal of the duty on imported whale oil. It was all, concluded Young gloomily and pointing an accusing finger at the free traders on the committee, going to end in disaster: "If you will follow out the policy which has for its object solely the benefit of the consumer, as far as that is connected with the subjects of maritime commerce, you will destroy British navigation."

The owners had invested in the seventy-six-foot schooner *Eliza Scott* commanded by John Balleny and the fifty-six-foot cutter *Sabrina* (another Solent-built cutter akin to Biscoe's *Lively*), commanded by Thomas Freeman. Now neither Balleny or Freeman had any experience in sealing or whaling—making them an odd choice for an ostensible sealing and whaling voyage—and Balleny was an older man, in his sixties, who had spent most of his time in the North Sea and Baltic trade. But this was seafaring that honed seamanship and navigation skills, and Balleny was a very capable celestial navigator, versed in the mysteries of both lunar sights and chronometers. A pious man given to holding divine services—which probably attracted him to the evangelical Enderbys—Balleny was plagued with a hard-drinking and insubordinate chief mate. The rest of the hard-case crew aboard the *Eliza Scott* were little better, and after two months the sorely tried skipper gave up on his Sunday service and attempts to save their unrepentant souls.

On 18 July 1838 the schooner and the cutter sailed from the Downs, and four days later Balleny was taking his departure from England with a position off the Scilly Islands. On board were two chronometers, an azimuth compass, and, for the information of the Hydrographic Office, a mercury barometer. Such was the violently jerky motion of the two vessels, however, that the mercury shot up and down the barometer tube, causing Balleny to give up taking any pressure readings.

After dropping the Scilly Islands below the horizon, Balleny, like Kemp, was now set on a long passage halfway round the world. His course took him down the Atlantic and around the Cape of Good Hope into the Southern Ocean and a run with the prevailing westerlies to a first landfall at Amsterdam Island.

The landfall was unintentional—Balleny had intended to pass north of the island. This clump of volcanic rock rising from the ocean's floor had first been sighted in 1522 from the deck of the *Victoria* during that horrifying passage from the East Indies to Spain and the completion of the world's first circumnavigation. Lying seven hundred miles north of Kerguelen, Amsterdam Island has a milder climate and for Balleny it had the inestimable value of being home to fur and elephant seals. Such an opportunity was not to be missed. In the early morning hours of 4 November, while the *Eliza Scott* and the *Sabrina* lay hove-to off the north shore, Balleny went ashore in one of the whaleboats. Four hours later the boat returned. All that Balleny had seen were the remains of a sealer's hut and a whale carcass. But some fish had been caught, which made a welcome change to their salt meat diet.

A month later the two vessels sailed into Chalky Bay on the southwest coast of New Zealand's South Island. The passage from England had taken five months and the crew were in a state of near mutiny. One of the perennial problems aboard whaling and sealing vessels was the likelihood of the crew's jumping ship to run.

Isolated Chalky Bay, to Balleny, seemed an ideal anchorage to lessen this possibility. He was proved wrong. Some of the crew did run—probably to another whaler anchored in the bay—and his reduced and grumbling crew were set to work catching fish, shooting game, wooding and watering. The precious chronometers were also checked for their rating. On 7 January 1839 the two vessels weighed anchor and Balleny set course for Campbell Island four hundred miles to the south of New Zealand.

This island, much used by whalers and sealers, had been discovered in 1810 by Frederick Hasselborough of the sealing vessel *Perseverance*. Hasselborough was drowned in the island's Perseverance Harbour when a small boat he was sailing capsized in a vicious squall. Also drowned was an Elizabeth Farr from Norfolk Island, and hers was the first grave on the island. Women appear out of place in the aggressively male world of sealing; but in 1838 the Reverend J. Wilkinson testified that Maori women—most of them afflicted with venereal disease—would ship aboard sealers for a payment as high as £100. Convict women from Sydney, Hobart, and Norfolk Island would also willingly exchange their harsh penal life for the dubious pleasures of a sealing vessel's fo'c's'le.

The most enduring legend of Campbell Island concerns "the lady of the heather." It reeks with the romantic haze that surrounds most stories concerning Bonnie Prince Charlie, the last of the Stuarts. However, it is not the dastardly English who receive the usual opprobrium but some subtle and sly Jacobites.

The story concerns a lone woman living on Campbell Island, dressed in a Royal Stuart tartan and a Glengarry bonnet decorated with a sprig of heather. This woman was surmised to be the granddaughter of Prince Charles from his liaison with Clementina Walkinshaw. Even after Charles's death, suspicious Jacobites, seeing informers in every quarter and fearing the granddaughter could harm their forlorn cause, had her kidnapped by a Captain Stewart. Choosing exile to death, she was then taken to Campbell Island, where a crude sod hut was built for her before she was abandoned. A sprig of heather was said to grow next to this crude building. Such then was the tale of "the lady with the heather" that circulated, probably with cruder embellishments, in the fo'c's'les of whalers.

Less than a week was spent by the *Eliza Scott* and the *Sabrina* at Campbell Island. But, with appropriate symmetry, Freeman on going ashore to search for seals found instead three men and a woman living in a squalid sod hut who had spent four years on the island in a vain attempt at sealing. During those same few days Balleny, seeing another vessel, went aboard and found the master to be John Biscoe and the *Emma* out of Sydney. "I find Capt Biscoe is in Search of Land as well as ourselves," noted Balleny in his log. The link between James Weddell, John Biscoe, and John Balleny, the sealing explorers, was completed.

Balleny's two vessels sailed from Campbell Island on 17 January. They were now entering upon the main purpose of their voyage—the discovery of land. The *Sabrina*'s orders were to stay within a half mile of the *Eliza Scott* and, in the event of their being separated by bad weather, to rendezvous at 170°E and 66°S. The weather stayed fair, however, and ten days later they sighted their first iceberg at 63°37′S and 176°30′E and the same day crossed south of Bellingshausen's track of 1820. The Russians, in that same latitude, had found impenetrable pack ice and been forced to alter course to the eastward: but the Russians had been sailing in these waters six weeks earlier in the season. Balleny's timing was working in his favor even if the lone iceberg was a hint of things to come. Two days later they crossed the Antarctic Circle and were soon sailing amidst icebergs and loose pack ice—but not enough to stop their southerly progress. On 1 February, the weather clearing, Balleny took a Sun sight that put them at 68°45′S. They were in clear water and no ice was in sight from the masthead. This was all very encouraging and the two vessels stood south with a favorable wind.

But these ideal conditions lasted but a few hours. Later that day, appearing as if by magic, came a solid line of pack ice. Its seaward edge, slowly heaving in the swells, presented a silent and hostile barrier and from the masthead the gray-white expanse stretched to the horizon. They had reached 69°S at 172°11′E—about 250 miles further south than Bellingshausen had managed to reach in the same meridian. Hidden over the horizon, a mere good day's sail in a clear sea, lay the Antarctic coastline. But they were not to know this.

Blocked from any advance further south, Balleny was now forced by wind and pack ice to sail in a northwesterly direction. For the next week the Antarctic produced its usual mix of weather, with strong winds alternating with calms and fogs. It was bitterly cold and the only encouraging signs were the large number of seals, penguins, and whales.

On 9 February, the fog clearing, they found themselves surrounded by many icebergs and porpoising penguins. More significant was a darkish appearance on the horizon to the southwest. Within an hour the sun was shining brightly and a noon latitude sight put them at 66°37′S—just south of the Antarctic Circle—and the dark patch had changed to what appeared to be land. In the bright sun and with a favorable breeze the two vessels ran across the sparkling sea toward the loom of the land.

By eight o'clock that evening they were an estimated five miles off the land, which could be made out to be three separate islands of considerable height. That night they lay hove-to off the middle of the three and waited for dawn. In the early morning light, with their world drained of all color, the two vessels got under way and attempted to run between the islands, only to find the passage blocked by ice. The weather had now taken on a threatening look, and with the sudden return of fog Balleny, the prudent mariner, hauled off the islands and lay hove-to until it cleared.

During this waiting period in the fog, with not a breath of wind and no steerage way, the only sounds being the slatting of the dank flax sails, the clatter of blocks, and creaking of rigging, an iceberg loomed out of the mists. The situation was very similar to that of Weddell's *Jane* and *Beaufoy*, except here the *Eliza Scott* was not held fast in pack ice. A boat was quickly lowered and the schooner towed out of the path of the threatening mass of ice. In these southern oceans, dangers lurked even in calms.

The fog lifted briefly on 11 February and they saw the islands bearing west-southwest and "of a tremendous height, I should suppose at least 12,000 feet and covered with snow." This is something of an exaggeration as the highest point of any of the islands is only forty-four hundred feet. But the Antarctic light can play tricks on estimates of distance and height— as future explorers were to find out, to their cost and reputation. The next day, with the fog fitfully swirling around them, the two vessels stood in toward the land for another investigation. At six o'clock that evening the *Sabrina*'s boat was hoisted out and the two captains with some crew members made for a likely-looking landing place. But it was a disappointment, for "when we got close with the boat it proved only the drawback of the sea, leaving a beach of 3 or 4 feet at most. Captain Freeman jumped out and got a few stones, but was up to the middle in water. There is no landing or beach on this land; in fact, but for the bare rocks where the icebergs had broken from, we should scarce have known it for land at first, but, as we stood in for it, we plainly perceived smoke arising from the mountain tops. It is evidently volcanic, as the specimans of stones, or cinders, will prove. The cliffs are perpendicular, and what would in all probability have been valleys and beaches are occupied by solid blocks of ice. I could not see a beach or harbour or anything like one."

Balleny's terse description of the islands reflects their grim and somber sterility. Only the waters seemed rich in life, with their abundance of whales, penguins, seals, and seabirds. But no matter; that short and wet landing of Freeman's was a historical one, for until this date no landing had been recorded at such a high southern latitude. Indeed, it can be considered the first landing below the Antarctic Circle.

It was obvious that nothing was to be gained by looking for and attempting more landings, and the two vessels stood to the northwest with that small collection of rocks (they proved to be scoria and basalt, with crystals of olivine) and a sketch of the islands drawn by John MacNab, the second mate of the *Eliza Scott*, showing the two plumes of smoke rising from Buckle Island.

Balleny had now named the islands and peaks after Messrs. Young, Borradaile, Buckle, Sturge, Brown, Row, and Beale, those "spirited merchants who united with Mr. Enderby in sending out the expedition." Captain Beaufort, the Admiralty hydrographer, was later to give them the collective name of Balleny Islands. And in a few years' time these islands became the center of some rather acerbic and acrimonious squabbling between the leaders of British and American naval expeditions.

The remaining days of February were spent sailing on a westerly course between 65°S and 63°S, skirting the pack ice. To the south, behind this barrier of ice, Balleny caught tantalizing glimpses of clear sea, but their chances of reaching it were the same as their chances of sailing through a mountain range. And if an opening did present itself, what were the chances of sailing back? Conditions alternated between snow, sleet, and fog. They had now been sailing below the Antarctic Convergence, with the air and sea temperature close to freezing for five weeks. The watch on deck were chilled to the bone with the ceaseless lookout for icebergs and growlers. Even the activity of the trick at the tiller was attended with problems, for the magnetic compass, so close to the south magnetic pole, gyrated wildly and Balleny, when the conditions served, found compass variations between 50 and 30 degrees. The only heartening sights were the immense flocks of seabirds, pods of whales, porpoising penguins, and swimming seals to enliven the dreary monotony.

This course of theirs, sixty-six years after James Cook's, and sailing in the same quadrant of Antarctica, was an almost parallel track to that of the *Resolution* but three hundred miles further south. And like a twin-track railway, their courses were opposite, with Cook sailing east and Balleny west. The *Eliza Scott*'s master was following John Biscoe's advice as to the prevailing winds in these higher latitudes.

On 2 March, at 64°58'S and 121°08'E, a day of snow and sleet squalls from the southeast and with the temperature just above freezing, the sea suddenly became very smooth and they quickly shortened sail and hove to. As they lay there in this strangely smooth sea, surrounded by drifting ice floes, the visibility suddenly cleared and they saw land to the south. The visibility closed in again and by midnight it was snowing. The next morning, in the ghostly light of dawn, with the decks still covered with snow, they sailed slowly south through the thickening pack ice. Soon they were surrounded by icebergs and then came upon the inevitable consolidated pack. Behind it loomed that tantalizing land. But now the weather was manufacturing its interminable fog and Balleny was forced to skirt the pack in a northerly direction. The land they had seen is now laid down on the charts as the Sabrina Coast. It was their first and last sighting of the continent.

Their course now took them in a northwesterly direction, their constant companions being icebergs seen dimly through the snow and sleet squalls. At midnight on 10 March the crew were entertained by a magnificent display of the aurora australis. Three days later they sailed past an iceberg with a large rock, estimated to be twelve feet by six feet, embedded in the ice. John MacNab, the sketcher of the Balleny Islands, brought out his sketching block and made a drawing of this unusual sight.

Up to this date the cause and origin of Antarctica's unique icebergs had puzzled all of the explorers. Cook, Bellingshausen, Weddell, and Biscoe had all speculated on this phenomenon. And ones with rocks and earth in them were the most puzzling of all.

It was just the sort of problem to engage the questioning mind of Charles Darwin. Coral reefs, pigeons, barnacles, climbing plants, worms. Why not rocks in icebergs?

The three-volume edition of *Voyages of His Majesty's Ships Adventure and Beagle*, the official narrative by FitzRoy and King, had appeared in 1839. Darwin's contribution came in volume 3. The first two volumes, like most official narratives, lay untouched on the library shelves, but Darwin's was an instant success and went through two printings in the first year. Darwin, in short, was now a name.

On the return of the *Eliza Scott* to England, Darwin met with John MacNab—through Charles Enderby—and conjured with the problem of the rock in the iceberg. Unlikely as it might seem, the problem of stones and rocks with no generic relationship to those around them—"erratic boulders"—was a puzzling one to geologists. And here was a classic case of transportation by ice. This case of boulders in icebergs was only the second that Darwin had heard of (Darwin had obviously not read Weddell). Biscoe in all his Antarctic travels had not seen any, but the boatswain of the *Beagle*, a former sealer, had seen a large boulder on the top of an iceberg to the east of the South Shetlands. Darwin then pointed out that all the Antarctic voyagers had remarked on the drift of many icebergs to the low latitudes. "If then," concluded Darwin "but one iceberg in a thousand, or in ten thousand, transports its fragment, the bottom of the Antarctic Sea, and the shores of its islands, must already be scattered with masses of foreign rock—the counterpart of the 'erratic boulders' of the northern hemisphere."

Forty-six years later Darwin's prediction was proved correct when Sir John Murray, that influential and catalytic figure of the 1872–76 HMS *Challenger* expedition (the first steamship to cross the Antarctic Circle) wrote that "The *Challenger* has dredged up fragments of mica schists, quartzites, sandstones, compact limestones, and earthy shales, which leave little doubt that within the Antarctic Circle there is a mass of continental land quite similar in structure to other continents." His conjectural map of the shape of this unknown land mass, based on the findings from the dredges and what was known from the explorers' limited discoveries, was remarkably close to the true shape.

But if that iceberg of Wednesday 13 March 1839 was to engage the attention of one of the nineteenth-century's great men, it was also to prove a decisive day for two young men aboard the schooner and cutter. "This morning," reads the *Eliza Scott*'s log, "Capt Freeman came on board and brought the boy Smith with him and took the boy Juggins on board the cutter." No reason is given for this change of crew, but for poor Juggins it was to prove a fatal move.

The schooner and the cutter were now angling up toward Cook's track of 1773, and a few days after the boy Juggins had changed to the cutter they crossed the 60-degree parallel. Since Freeman had made his wet landing on the Balleny Islands the men had spent over a month sailing 2,250 miles in miserable conditions, and the stresses of the voyage were obviously making themselves felt. One of the conventions of ships at sea is the very sensible one of the helmsman's repeating any orders for alterations of course given him by the officer of the watch. This way the officer knows if his order has been correctly understood.

One sullen helmsman, taking his trick at the tiller, failed to acknowledge Balleny's orders as the captain brought the schooner closer to the cutter. Balleny asked the man if he heard the orders or not. At this the helmsman let out a torrent of abuse and then lashed at Balleny with the tiller rope. The older man, forgetting any pious biblical injunction to turn the other cheek, grabbed the man by the neck and manhandled him forward, remembering this time another biblical injunction about "eye for eye, tooth for tooth, stripe for stripe," and gave him a beating. Among crew like this it was probably the only language that worked.

Just north of the Antarctic Convergence at 50°S and 95°E, the two vessels ran into storm conditions. On the night of 24 March the *Sabrina* was seen to burn a blue distress flare, a lone flickering ghostly light amidst the welter of white water and the howling of the gale. The *Eliza Scott*, however, had troubles of her own in coping with the huge seas that were running. One heavy sea broke on board, smashed her two boats, swept the decks clean, and finally rolled her over on her beam ends, where she stayed for ten minutes, wallowing like a stuck pig. All appeared lost, but the little schooner eventually righted herself and became a living ship again. But the *Sabrina* had vanished. The small cutter, Freeman, and the crew, including the boy Juggins, had found their last resting place in the stormy waters of the Southern Ocean.

Balleny now took the *Eliza Scott* north across the prevailing westerlies into the easterly winds of the southern Indian Ocean and, running before these warm and gentle trades, made a landfall at the southern end of

Madagascar. The island, although under the bloody-minded rule of the dreadful Queen Ranavalona I, proved a welcome respite after the Antarctic. Here was a tropical climate with fresh water and fresh provisions for an ailing and sick crew who had lived for nine months on salt rations. The *Eliza Scott* also needed attention, and over a month was spent at the island while the crew recovered their strength and made repairs on the ice- and weather-beaten schooner.

Balleny sailed from Madagascar in the first week of June, bound for St. Helena in the company of two whalers. A fortnight was spent at the island, and then the schooner left on the last stage of her passage back to England. Balleny was now a sick man and had to hail a passing American whaler, just out from Providence, Rhode Island, for medical supplies. On 18 September 1839 the Custom House officer and Thames River pilot boarded the *Eliza Scott* for her short journey up the Thames to the West India Docks. On board were fewer than two hundred sealskins: gone were the days when a sealer's hold would be packed with thousands of skins.

The indefatigable Charles Enderby, outwardly unfazed by the financial loss, was soon informing the members of the Royal Geographical Society of the facts of John Balleny's voyage and the new discoveries. An extract based on the *Eliza Scott*'s log book, "Discoveries In The Antarctic Ocean In February 1839," appeared in the *Geographical Journal*. In it the subject of the iceberg again surfaced, and Charles Enderby speculated that "this iceberg was distant 1400 miles from the nearest *certainly known* land namely Enderby Land, which bore WSW of it. But it is highly probable, from the compact nature of the ice etc., that land extends between parallels of 66°S and 68°S, in which case the iceberg would not be distant above 300 miles from this supposed land. . . ." It was an intelligent and prescient estimate by Charles Enderby: the land in this sector does lie between 66°S and 68°S, and the three-hundred-mile estimate was a palpable bull's-eye.

Balleny, like so many of his kind, vanished into oblivion. His memorials are the islands named after him and his logbook held by the Royal Geographical Society. Attached to the logbook is a letter written in 1856 by the Arctic explorer Admiral Sir George Back in reply to an inquiry by the Society as to the genuineness of the logbook. To doubt it, in the opinion of Back, would be "an injustice to the memory and labours of this adventurous seaman."

By one of those serendipitous quirks of fortune, the *Eliza Scott*, in sailing up the Thames in the September of 1839, passed two Royal Navy ships outfitting in Chatham Docks for an Antarctic expedition. HMS *Erebus* and HMS *Terror* sailed ten days later, and with them Captain James Clark Ross carried a copy of Balleny's chart and logbook. More importantly, Ross had noted the invaluable information that between the 180° and 170°E meridian lay a possible passageway through the ice to even higher latitudes than those sailed by Balleny. The old seaman had pointed the way for Ross to discover the classic route into the heart of the Antarctic. It was one to be followed, sixty years later, by the ships of the almost mythic figures of Antarctic exploration: Borchgrevink's *Southern Cross;* Scott's *Discovery* and *Terra Nova;* Shackleton's *Nimrod* and *Aurora;* and, the most extraordinary vessel of them all, Amundsen's *Fram.*

Epilogue

URING THE WEEK that the *Eliza Scott* unloaded her paltry cargo of sealskins and the logbook was being copied for Captain James Clark Ross, two French expeditionary ships, the *Astrolabe* and the *Zélée,* with their commander Captain Dumont d'Urville lying in a tub of hot water to ease the agonies of gout, were sailing between Borneo and Java en route to Tasmania. The French, who had made a rather unsatisfactory probe into the Weddell Sea in 1838, were now bound south, rather reluctantly, for another tussle with the ice.

As Dumont d'Urville lay in his tub, six thousand miles to the east, anchored at Tahiti, lay the vessels of the United States Exploring Expedition. Lieutenant Charles Wilkes, although not afflicted with gout, displaying an irascible and gouty temperament, had passed orders to his men that all had to be back aboard their ships by sunset. On Saturdays—the Pacific missionaries' Sabbath—all the officers and men were solemnly paraded on the beach, to the huge enjoyment of the natives, before being marched to the missionary church for the service. And this on the island that since its discovery in 1767 had captivated Western philosophizing gentlemen's thoughts as the home of the "noble savage"—and the thoughts of baser common seamen as the island of unlimited carnal delights. The American squadron, like the French, had also made a most unsatisfactory joust with the Weddell Sea pack ice, and were now bound south for Sydney and another bout with the Antarctic.

The French, American, and British expeditions were to add thousands of miles to the emerging coastline of the Antarctic continent. And in the process, Wilkes, whose prickly disposition acted as a lightning rod for controversy and argument, managed to engage himself in acrimonious disputes with Ross, d'Urville, his own officers, scientific staff, and his superiors in Washington.

Balleny's voyage marks a watershed in Antarctic exploration. In the twenty years from William Smith's discovery of the South Shetlands to Balleny's discoveries of 1839, the sealers and Bellingshausen's Russian expedition had built on Cook's great voyage and limned in parts of a new continent. Cook's and Bellingshausen's expeditions had been government sponsored and, as such, the main elements were the usual mix of nationalistic self-interest and altruism. The sealers' imperative was simpler: profit. For most of them the Antarctic and its islands represented a singularly dangerous and disagreeable place but one which, for a brief moment, offered enourmous financial rewards. In short, it was a place to be plundered and exploited, and they did it with deadly and bloody efficiency. Some, a minority, tempered the butchery with scientific and geographic exploration. Men such as Weddell and Biscoe can be seen as representative of a new spirit of inquiry seeping into a rapidly changing world.

The three national expeditions heading toward Antarctica represented the dawning of this new age. Gone was the brassiness of the Regency period, the peacock clothing, the gentlemen dilettante naturalists and scientists. The evangelical ethos had permeated upward from its dissenting roots into all strata of society and a new soberness, seriousness, and, dare one say it, hypocrisy, were padding with rectitudinous step into all aspects of national life.

In 1774, the year that James Cook and the *Resolution* made the record south latitude, two men joined their combined talents to form an engineering company in the midlands of England. The Soho Engineering Works, with its partners James Watt and Matthew Boulton, was about to change the face of Britain and the world. The steam engines they produced—dramatic improvements on the Newcomen steam engine used to pump water from mines—and Watt's seemingly endless advances in steam engine technology were soon installed in boats. The first working steamboat was built in 1783 by the French Marquis Jouffroy d'Abbas and by the first decade of the nineteenth century a 30-foot paddle wheeler, the *Charlotte Dundas,* was working commercially on Scotland's Forth and Clyde Canal. In America the Robert Fulton–designed and Boulton and Watt–engined 150 foot *Clermont* was churning up the Hudson River from New York to Albany in thirty-two hours and making the return trip in thirty hours. A few years later, in 1817, a lone protesting letter appeared in the English *Colchester Gazette*. It concerned the disaster aboard the steamboat *Courier* after the overeager engineer had hung a fourteen-pound weight on the safety valve and eight passengers had died in the inevitable boiler explosion:

Of all the purposes to which the steam engine has been applied, that of navigating boats and vessels seems the most preposterous; especially as this mode of navigation is chiefly adopted for passage boats. Many persons there are who venture their lives upon the water in any case; how then, any such persons can hazard their lives in a steam-boat, and actually place themselves between fire and water, is not easily accounted for. . . . It is to be wished that the calamitous accidents which have lately taken place may check the rage for steam engines.

The writer might as well have tried stopping the flowing of the tides along the shores of his native East Anglia.

By 1835, W. R. M'Phun of Glasgow saw sufficient reason to publish *The Scottish Tourist's Steam Boat Pocket Guide to the Western Highlands and Islands:* a convenient-sized book for the traveler, being of "snuff box dimensions." The same year, ideas of a larger proportion were being mooted at a board meeting of the Great Western Railway. One of the directors complained to Isambard Brunel, the company engineer, that the projected railway line from London to Bristol was too long. The irrepressible Brunel, thinking big as usual, immediately replied, "Why not make it longer? Build a steamship to go to New York and call it the *Great Western.*" The sheer audacity of the idea was pure Brunel—from London to New York on the company train and ship. The 212-foot steam-engined *Great Western* was launched in July 1837 and made her first transatlantic run from Bristol on 8 April 1838, arriving in New York on 23 April. It was the first of ninety crossings. A steamboat passenger service across the Atlantic had been inaugurated.

Steam-driven locomotives running on iron wheels, steam-driven ships with paddle wheels. The age-old transportation by horse-drawn wagon and sailing ship was rapidly changing.

The first monthly installment of *The Posthumous Papers of the Pickwick Club,* bound in light green covers, price 1 shilling, appeared in London on 31 March 1836. The print run was four hundred copies. The last installment appeared in November 1837 with a print run of over forty thousand copies. It is arguably Charles Dickens's most popular book and its cast of characters (the ungenerous will call them caricatures) have entered the halls of the immortals of fiction. The extraordinary popularity of the monthly issues cut across all social layers: judges surreptitiously read the latest issue while the lawyers droned on, and gatherings of poorer folk listened as one of the group read an installment rented from the circulating library. Say *Pickwick Papers* and the probable image projected on the mind's screen is, of course, one of the benevolent Mr. Pickwick himself, Sam Weller's "angel in tights and gaiters," but also of stagecoaches and stagecoach inns.

To the readers of the 1830s that world was fast disappearing. In its place were the new railways that were laying down iron tracks, building bridges, digging tunnels, and carving out cuttings with bewildering speed. It was all prosecuted with an almost evangelical zeal. When Mr. Pickwick, Sam Weller, and Mr. Jingle stepped onto the world's stage, Great Britain dug 60 percent of Europe's coal and produced nearly 50 percent of its iron. These dispiriting statistics come to life in Alexander Kinglake's travel book

Eothen. Kinglake conjures up an imaginary Turkish pasha whose un-bounded admiration for the new technical marvels resulting from all this coal and iron is summed up by the pasha's repeated "whirr! whirr! all by wheels—whiz! whiz! all by steam!"

The sealers had sailed into the uncharted and hostile ice-strewn waters of the Antarctic aboard vessels but little removed from the fishing, coast-ing, and passage-making craft of their sixteenth-century ancestors—they would have been at ease sailing aboard the hoys, busses, cogs, trows, colliers, bawleys, caravels, luggers, carracks, smacks, tartans, and pinks. And the clothing and provisions were held in the same time warp.

The sailing ship can be considered the most technically advanced man-made artifact before the age of steam and iron. And in order to grapple with the complexities of running and standing rigging, masts and spars, knots and splices, blocks and tackles, sails and steering, the men had to learn a strange language totally divorced from that of their landsmen cous-ins: a language thought by Joseph Conrad to be a flawless thing for its purpose. Once they had learned the ropes they became good hands. And the sailing and killing were all done by hand.

The pasha's steam came late to the Antarctic, but when it came it came with a vengeance. In 1864 a ninety-five-foot steam-powered whale catcher, the *Spes et Fides* (Hope and Faith) slid down the ways from her builder's yard in Oslo. Fitted with grenade harpoons, the ship and weaponry were the brainchild of the Norwegian Svend Foyn. The birth of modern whaling had started. Forty years later another Norwegian-built steam catcher, the *Fortuna*, took the first whale—a humpback—on 22 December 1904 off South Georgia. In fourteen months 236 whales, most of them humpback, were converted into oil at Grytviken. In the 1909–10 season, with South Georgia and Deception Island as the main whaling bases, thirty-seven whale catchers were scouring the Antarctic and took over 6,000 whales. Svend Foyn, an upright and God-fearing man, the Norwegian equivalent of the Puritan whalers from New England, has entered the demonology of modern-day antiwhaling activists.

What of the Enderbys, who have run like a thread through the early explorations in the Southern Ocean? The downfall of Charles, Henry, and George reads like a cautionary tale for businessmen. It was old Samuel Enderby, their grandfather, who founded the company and in 1789 it was one of his ships, the *Amelia*, which rounded Cape Horn and took the first sperm whale in the Pacific. The officers and crew were almost all Nantucket men and the mate, Archaelus Hammond, the man who struck the whale, lies buried in the Old North graveyard on Nantucket. The *Amelia* re-turned to London fully loaded and the floodgates were opened to turn the Pacific and Indian Oceans into a whalers' paradise and a virtual American lake.

Old Samuel died in 1797, leaving a prosperous shipping and whaling company to his three sons. One of them, Samuel Enderby Jr., proved as prolific in fathering children as his father had been in importing barrels of whale oil, and on his death in 1829 the company came into the hands of three of his eight children, Charles, Henry, and George. Charles and George were both founding members of the Royal Geographical Society and served on the council. In this they continued a family tradition, as their grandfather and father displayed a keen interest in natural history and instructed their masters to bring back specimens for Sir Joseph Banks, Cook's old shipmate and now President of the Royal Society. That old Samuel had the ear of men of influence is plain. In 1792 he bought out from the Royal Navy the sloop *Rattler* and sent her into the Pacific on an exploratory voyage with the financial backing of the Treasury and a half-pay navy officer, Captain James Colnett. It was a useful precedent, to be used later by the grandsons for the disastrous voyage of the *Hopefull* and *Rose*. The brothers were to try it again after Balleny's voyage; but the Treasury, having been twice bitten, were by this time wary of any Enderby-proposed schemes, and firmly refused.

Enderby ships also carried convicts out to the penal settlements in New South Wales, and in the 1830s they were bringing back wool. But the plummeting fortunes of the Enderbys can be seen in dry statistics. In 1821 they owned fourteen ships. By 1836 they had but one, the *Samuel Enderby*, built at Cowes in 1834. Her timbers had been saturated in a coal tar derivative to act as a preservative (Charles, an investing butterfly, was a Director of the company promoting this specific). Herman Melville wrote affectionately of their lone remaining ship: "I boarded her once at midnight somewhere off the Patagonian coast and drank good flip down in the forecastle . . . a jolly ship; of good fare and plenty; fine flip and strong; crack fellows all, and capital from boot heels to hat-band." It's as good a valedictory as any.

Within a few years Charles, Henry, and George were living in reduced circumstances—middle-class code for poverty—as a result of a disastrous involvement in a pet scheme of the financially irresponsible Charles: an attempt to colonize the Auckland Islands south of New Zealand and export whale oil. Surrounding Charles is a whiff of the con man. Plausible, persuasive, a gentleman—but not one to trust where money was concerned.

The Enderby connection with the Royal Geographical Society has kept their memory green, unlike that of Daniel Bennett and his sons. This company prospered, but not being self-promoters in fields alien to their business, their name has faded from the rolls of Antarctic exploration. Cape Bennett, on Coronation Island in the South Orkneys, named after them by George Powell in the *Dove*, is their only Antarctic memorial. Nevertheless, a motorist driving along an Oxfordshire road near Faringdon might be puzzled on seeing large black iron cauldrons marking the entrance to a private driveway. The image that springs to mind is a cartoon one: topee-hatted, mustached, safari-jacketed Colonel Blimps being boiled by naked savages. The cauldrons are try-pots marking the old residence of the Bennett family.

Antarctica's atmosphere plays fiendishly clever optical illusions. Mountain ranges loom dramatically close when many miles distant; penguins walking across the ice are mistaken for people and people for penguins; small ripples of sastrugi seen from eye level appear like deep troughs and waves of ice. It is all very disorienting. The continent's history also plays the same strange and rather disturbing tricks. It appears to repeat itself, but the lineaments are subtly changed in the fun house mirror of history. James Cook's voyages brought the sealers south for Antarctica's first exploitation. James Clark Ross's voyages brought the whalers south for the second exploitation. The Enderby family in its role of exploring whaling merchants is repeated a hundred years later by the Christensen family of Norway, whose ships, aided by seaplanes, discovered new stretches of Antarctica's coastline.

Perhaps King George Island in the South Shetlands can be taken as reflecting, in miniature, Antarctica's history. First discovered in 1819, its shores were soon swept clean of fur and elephant seals. Eleven men from the London snow *Lord Melville* spent the first recorded Antarctic winter on the island in 1821. Nearly a hundred years later its beaches were again invaded by whalers and the bleached vertebrae, jaw bones, and skulls, the lichens creeping across their weathered surfaces, still litter the shores. Then came the governments with scientific bases, bulldozers, and an airstrip. Eight nations have their rather superfluous bases on the island: China, Chile, Russia, Uruguay, Korea, Argentina, Poland, and Brazil. Bearded and embryonic Ph.D.s solemnly measure the distance between the pebble nests of penguins. Parka-clad tourists, looking like scarlet Michelin men, waddle the shores, peering at Antarctica through the eyepieces of camcorders and muttering into microphones. One wonders what those bearded, greasy, bloodstained sealers and whalers would have made of all this. Probably shook their heads in disbelief, spat, given the flensing knife a few more strokes on the steel, and carried on working.

The seals and whales are returning, but the work of the bulldozers is irreversible.

Maps

The Southern Ocean

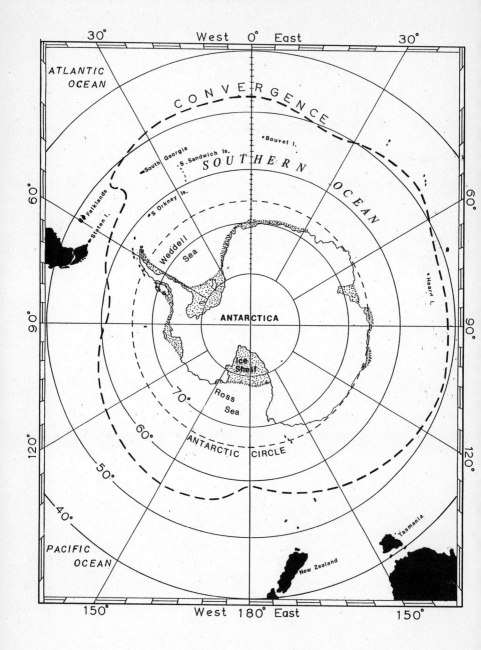

ATLANTIC
OCEAN

30° West 0° East 30°

CONVERGENCE

•Bouvet I.

South Georgia
•S. Sandwich Is.

SOUTHERN

•Falklands
•S Orkney Is.

OCEAN

Staten I.

Weddell

Sea

•Heard I.

90°

ANTARCTICA

Ice
Shelf

Ross
Sea

70°

60°

ANTARCTIC CIRCLE

50°

40°

PACIFIC
OCEAN

Tasmania

New Zealand

150° West 180° East 150°

120°

60°

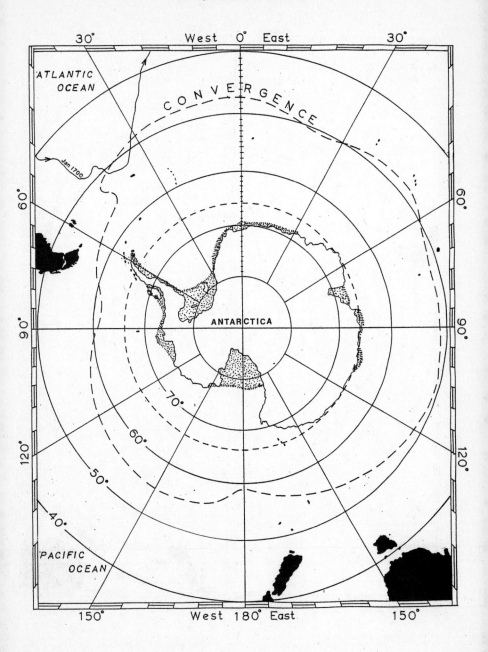

Halley's South, 1699–1700

ATLANTIC
OCEAN

CONVERGENCE

Jan 1700

ANTARCTICA

PACIFIC
OCEAN

Cook's South, 1772–1775

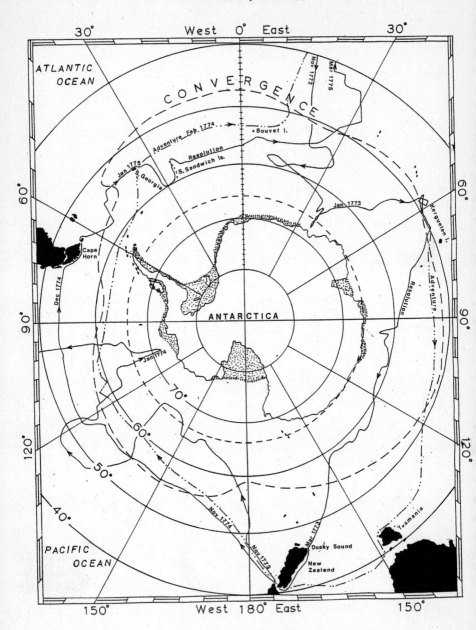

Bellingshausen's South, 1819–1821

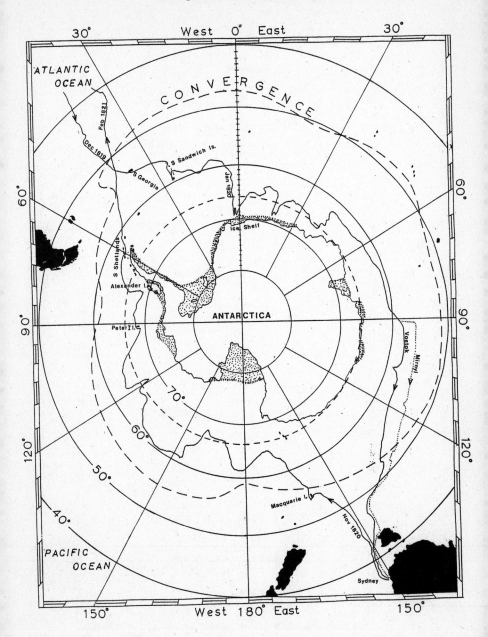

South Sandwich Islands

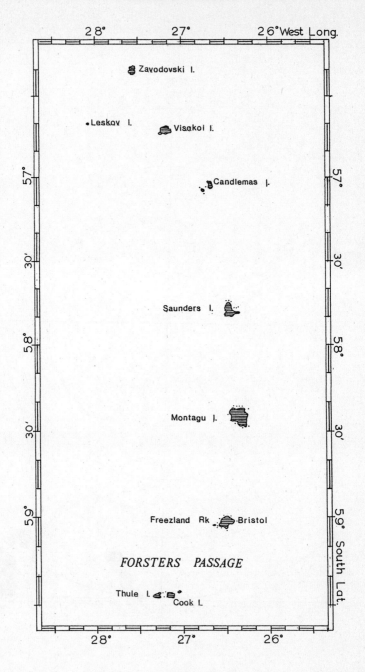

28° 27° 26° West Long.

Zavodovski I.

Leskov I. Visokoi I.

Candlemas I.

57° 57°

30' 30'

Saunders I.

58° 58°

Montagu I.

30' 30'

Freezland Rk Bristol

59° 59° South Lat.

FORSTERS PASSAGE

Thule I.
Cook I.

28° 27° 26°

The Sealer's South, 1820–1823

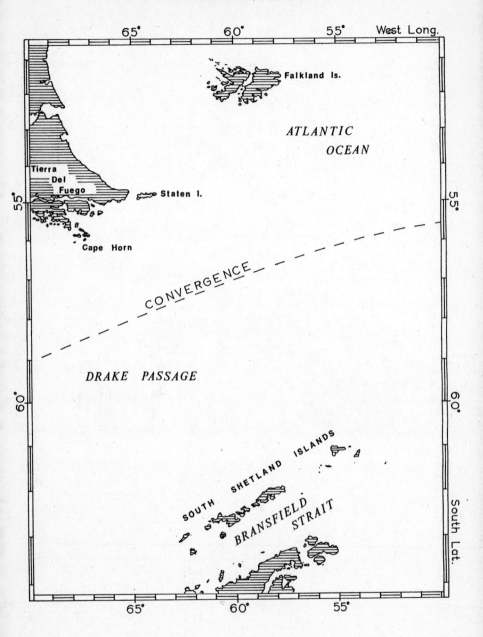

South Shetland Islands

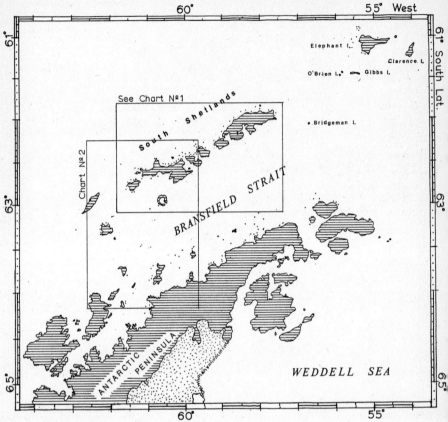

South Shetland Islands

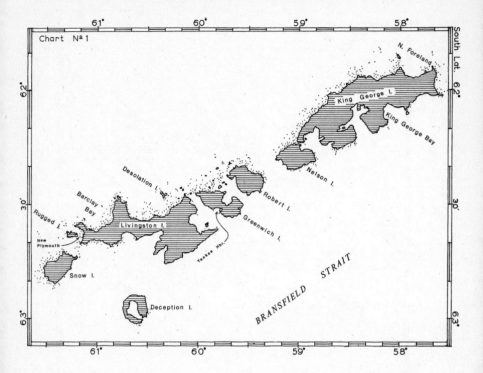

Chart Nº 1

61°   60°   59°   58°

South Lat. 62°

N. Foreland

62°

King George I.

King George Bay

30'

Desolation I.

Robert I.

Nelson I.

Barclay Bay

Rugged I.

Livingston I.

Greenwich I.

New Plymouth

Yankee Hbr.

Snow I.

30'

63°

Deception I.

BRANSFIELD STRAIT

63°

61°   60°   59°   58°

South Shetland Islands

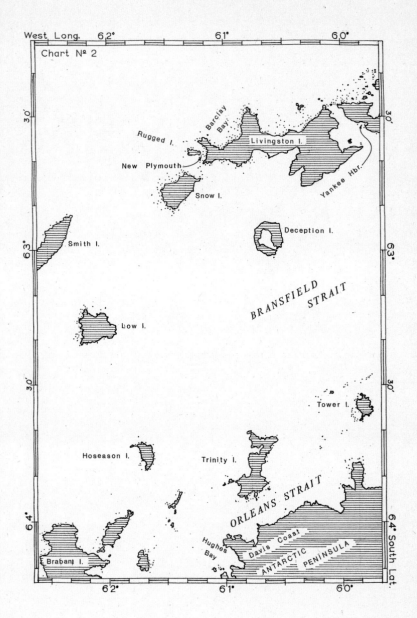

West Long. 62° 61° 60°

Chart Nº 2

30'

Barclay
Bay

Rugged I.

New Plymouth

Livingston I.

Yankee Hbr.

Snow I.

30'

Smith I.

63°

Deception I.

63°

BRANSFIELD STRAIT

Low I.

30'

30'

Tower I.

Hoseason I.

Trinity I.

ORLEANS STRAIT

64°

Hughes
Bay

Davis Coast

64° South Lat.

Brabant I.

ANTARCTIC PENINSULA

62° 61° 60°

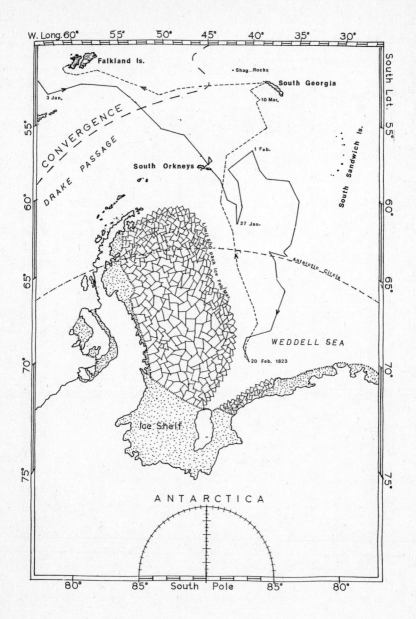

South Georgia

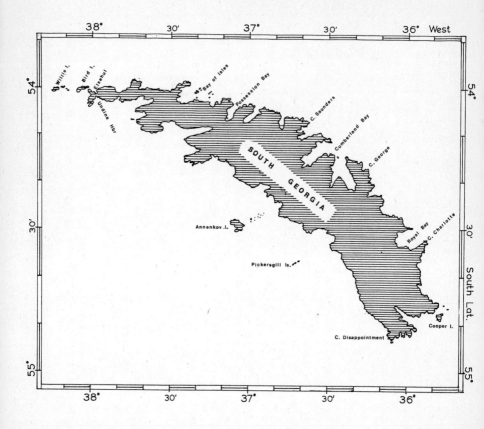

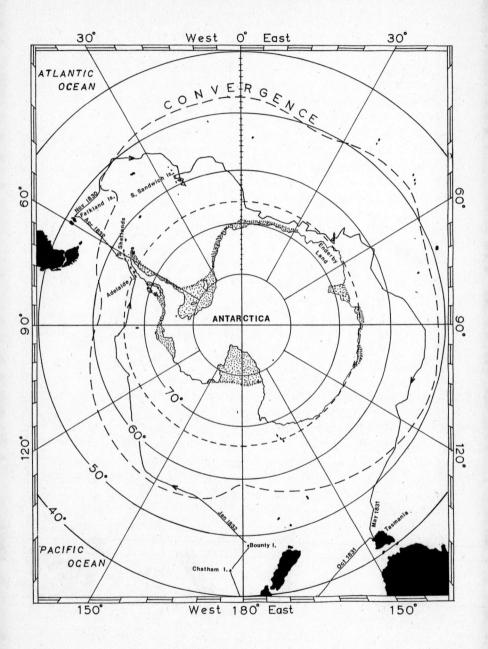

Biscoe's South, 1830–1832

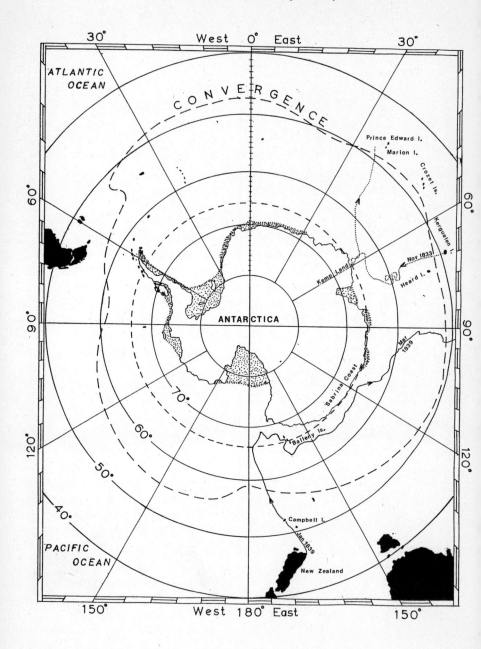

Kemp's South, 1833 and Balleny's South, 1839

Balleny Islands

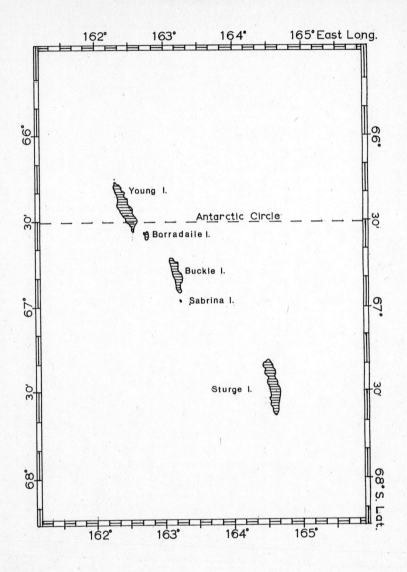

Bibliography

Chapter I • Terra Australis Incognita

Beaglehole, J. C. *The Exploration of the Pacific*. London, 1975.
———. *The Life of Captain James Cook*. London, 1974.
Beazley, C. R. *The Dawn of Modern Geography*. London, 1897.
Burney, J. *A Chronological History of the Discoveries in the South Sea or Pacific Ocean*. London, 1803–17.
Dalrymple, A. *An Historical Collection of the Several Voyages and Discoveries in the South Pacific*. London, 1770–71.
———. *A Collection of Voyages, chiefly in the Southern Atlantick Ocean*. London, 1775.
Dampier, W. *Voyages*. Edited by John Masefield. London, 1906.
———. *A New Voyage Round the World*. Edited by A. Gray, London, 1927.
Debenham, F. *Discovery and Exploration*. London, 1960.
The Encyclopedia of Discovery and Exploration. *The Glorious Age of Exploration*. New York, 1973.
Fernandez-Armesto, F. *Columbus*. Oxford, 1992.
Gibbon, E. *The Decline and Fall of the Roman Empire*. London, 1776.
Gould, R. T. *Captain Cook*. London, 1935.
Hakluyt, R. *The Principal Navigations, Voyages and Discoveries of the English Nation*. London, 1908.
Hogben, L. *Astronomer Priest & Ancient Mariner*. New York, 1973.
———. *Maps, Mirrors & Mechanics*. New York, 1973.
McLaren, M. *The Highland Jaunt*. London, 1954.
Mill, H. R. *The Siege of the South Pole*. London, 1905.
Mitchell, M. *Elcano: The First Circumnavigator*. London, 1958.
Moorehead, A. *The Fatal Impact*. New York, 1966.
Morison, S. E. *Admiral of the Ocean Sea: A Life of Christopher Columbus*. Boston, 1942.
———. *The European Discovery of America: The Northern Voyages 500–1600*. New York, 1971.
———. *The European Discovery of America: The Southern Voyages 1492–1616*. New York, 1974.
Nansen, F. *In Northern Mists*. London, 1911.
The Oxford History of the Classical World. Oxford, 1986.
Skelton, R. A. *Explorer's Maps*. London, 1958.
Slocum, J. *Sailing Alone Around the World*. New York, 1900.
Swift, J. *A Tale of a Tub*. London, 1704.
Toynbee, A. J. *A Study of History*. Edited by D. C. Somervell. Oxford, 1946.
Wilford, J. N. *The Mapmakers*. New York, 1982.

Chapter II • The Haven-Finding Art

Cook, J. *The Journals of Captain James Cook on his Voyages of Discovery*. Vol. 2. Edited by J. C. Beaglehole. Cambridge, England, 1969 (Hakluyt Society).
Forbes, E. G. *The Birth of Navigational Science*. London, 1980.
Gould, T. T. *The Marine Chronometer: Its History and Development*. London, 1923.

Stackpole, E. A. *The Sea Hunters.* New York, 1953.
Wilford, J. N. *The Mapmakers.* New York, 1982.

Chapter III • The Plague of the Sea

Brillat-Savarin, J. A. *The Physiology of Taste.* Translated by M. F. K. Fisher. New York, 1971.
Drummond, J. C., and Wilbraham, A. *The Englishman's Food.* London, 1991.
Gerard, J. *The Herball.* Edited by B. D. Jackson. London, 1876.
Hakluyt, R. *The Principal Navigations . . . of the English Nation.* London, 1908.
Hartley, D. *Food in England.* London, 1954.
Hickey, W. *Memoirs of William Hickey.* Edited by Peter Quennell. London, 1975.
Johnson, S. *Letters of Samuel Johnson.* Edited by R. W. Chapman. Oxford, 1952.
Labat, Père. *The Memoirs of Père Labat.* Edited by J. Eaden. London, 1931.
Lind, J. *A Treatise of the Scurvey.* Edinburgh, 1753.
Lloyd, C. *The British Seaman.* London, 1968.
Masefield, J. *Sea Life in Nelson's Time.* London, 1905.
Morison, S. E. *The Great Explorers.* New York, 1978.
Pigafetta, A. *First Voyage Round the World by Magellan.* London, 1874 (Hakluyt Society).
Veer, G de. *The Three Voyages of William Barents to the Arctic Regions.* London, 1876 (Hakluyt Society).
Walter, R. *A Voyage Round the World In the Year 1740, 1, 2, 3, 4.* London, 1748.
Watt, J., Freeman, E. J., and Bynum, W. F., eds. *Starving Sailors.* London, 1981.

Chapter IV • The Southern Ocean

Belloc, H. *The Cruise of the Nona.* New York, 1925.
Bonner, W. N. *Seals and Man.* Washington, D.C., 1982.
Bonner, W. N., and Walton, D. W. H., eds. *Antarctica.* Oxford, 1985.
Campbell, V. *The Wicked Mate.* Edited by H. G. R. King. Harleston, England, 1988.
Deacon, G. *The Antarctic Circumpolar Ocean.* Cambridge, England, 1984.
Debenham, F. *Antarctica.* New York, 1961.
Hardy, A. *Great Waters.* New York, 1967.
Hydrographic Center. *Sailing Directions for Antarctica.* Washington, D.C. 1976.
Hydrographic Department. *Antarctic Pilot.* Taunton, England, 1974.
Martin, R. M. *Mammals of the Oceans.* New York, 1977.
Ponting, H. G. *The Great White South.* London, 1921.
Ross, J. C. *A Voyage of Discovery and Research in the Southern and Antarctic Regions 1839–43.* London, 1847.
Simpson, G. G. *Penguins.* New Haven, Connecticut, 1976.
Stonehouse, B. *Animals of the Antarctic.* New York, 1972.
Watson, G. E. *Birds of the Antarctic and Sub-Antarctic.* Washington, D.C., 1975.
Watson, L. *Whales of the World.* New York, 1981.
Wilson, E. *Diary of the "Terra Nova" Expedition to the Antarctic 1910–1912.* New York, 1972.

Chapter V • Edmond Halley and the Pink "Paramore"

Armitage, A. *Edmond Halley.* London, 1966.
Aubrey, J. *Brief Lives.* Oxford, 1898.
Evelyn, J. *The Diary of John Evelyn.* Edited by A. Dobson. London, 1908.
Halley, E. *The Three Voyages of Edmond Halley in the Paramore 1698–1701.* Edited by N. J. W. Thrower. London, 1981 (Hakluyt Society).
Ronan, C. A. *Edmond Halley: Genius in Eclipse.* London, 1969.

Chapter VI • Mr. James Cook

Beaglehole, J. C. *The Life of Captain James Cook.* Stamford, 1974.
Benham, H. *Once Upon a Tide.* London, 1955.
Besant, W. *Captain Cook.* London, 1890.

Boswell, J. *The Life of Samuel Johnson.* London, 1791.

Cook, J. *The Journals of Captain James Cook on his Voyages of Discovery.* Vols. 1–4. Edited by J. C. Beaglehole. Cambridge, England, 1955–1969 (Hakluyt Society).

Elliot, J. *Captain Cook's Second Voyage.* Edited by C. Holmes. London, 1984.

Forster, J. G. A. *A Voyage round the World in his Brittanic Majesty's Sloop Resolution . . . during the Years 1772, 3, 4, & 5.* London, 1777.

Forster, J. R. *The Resolution Journal of Johann Reinhold Forster 1772–1775.* Edited by M. E. Hoare. London, 1982 (Hakluyt Society).

Gould, R. T. *Captain Cook.* London, 1935.

Hoare, M. E. *The Tactless Philosopher.* Melbourne, Australia, 1976.

Kippis, A. *A Narrative of the Voyages Round the World by James Cook.* London, 1788.

Knox, J. *An Historical Journal of the Campaigns in North America for the years 1757, 1758, 1759, and 1760.* London, 1769.

O'Brian, P. *Joseph Banks.* London, 1987.

Skelton, R. A. *James Cook: Surveyor of Newfoundland.* San Francisco, 1965.

Taylor, H. *Memoirs of the Principal Events in the Life of Henry Taylor.* North Shields, 1811.

Villiers, A. J. *Captain Cook.* London, 1967.

Chapter VII • The Voyage of the "Resolution" and "Adventure"

Beaglehole, J. C. *The Life of Captain James Cook.*

Boswell, J. *The Private Papers of James Boswell.* Edited by G. Scott and F. A. Pottle. New York, 1928–37.

Burney, J. *The Private Journal of James Burney.* Edited by B. Hooper. Canberra, Australia, 1975.

Cook, J. *Journals.*

Dalrymple, A. *An Historical Collection of Voyages in the South Pacific.*

———. *A Collection of Voyages in the South Atlantick.*

Elliot, J. *Captain Cook's Second Voyage.*

Forster, J. G. A. *A Voyage round the World.*

Forster, J. R. *The Resolution Journal.*

Furneaux, R. *Tobias Furneaux, Circumnavigator.* London, 1960.

Gould, R. T. *Captain Cook.*

Hawkesworth, J. *An Account of the Voyages undertaken . . . for making Discoveries in the Southern Hemisphere.* London, 1773.

Kippis, A. *A Narrative of the Voyages by James Cook.*

Hoare, M. E. *The Tactless Philosopher.*

Migot, A. *The Lonely South.* London, 1957.

O'Brian, P. *Joseph Banks.*

Sparrman, A. *A Voyage Round the World.* London, 1953.

Villers, A. J. *Captain Cook.*

Chapter VIII • The Continent Discovered

Adams, J. C. *The Writings of John Quincy Adams.* Edited by W. C. Ford. New York, 1917.

Auger, H. *Passage to Glory: John Ledyard's America.* New York, 1946.

Balch, E. S. *Antarctica.* Philadelphia, 1902.

Bellingshausen, T. T. *Voyage of Captain Bellingshausen to the Antarctic Seas 1818–1821.* Edited by Frank Debenham. London, 1945 (Hakluyt Society).

Bertrand, K. J. *Americans in Antarctica, 1775–1945.* American Geographical Society, Special Bulletin No. 39. 1971.

Bonner, W. N. *Seals and Man.*

Bonner and Walton, eds. *Antarctica.*

Clark, A. H. *The Fisheries and Fishery Industries of the United States.* Washington, D.C., 1887.

Delano, A. *Narrative of Voyages and Travels in the Northern and Southern Hemisphere.* Boston, 1817.

"Edward Bransfield's Antarctic Voyage, 1819–20, and the Discovery of The Antarctic Continent," *Polar Record.* Cambridge, England, July 1946.

Fanning, E. *Voyages Round the World.* New York, 1833.

Goodridge, C. M. *Narrative of a Voyage to the South Seas.* London, 1832.

Gould, R. T. "The First Sighting of the Antarctic Continent." *Geographical Journal.* London, March 1925.

———. "The Charting of the South Shetlands 1819–1828." *Mariners Mirror.* London, July 1941.

Hobbs, W. H. "Discoveries of Antarctica Within the American Sector, As Revealed by Maps and Documents." *Transactions of the American Philosophical Society.* Philadelphia, January 1939.

Jackson, G. *The British Whaling Trade.* London, 1978.

Jones, A. G. E. *Antarctica Observed.* Whitby, England, 1982.

———. *Polar Portraits.* Whitby, England, 1992.

Kirwan, L. P. *The White Road.* London, 1959.

Ledyard, J. *A Journal of Captain Cook's Last Voyage to the Pacific Ocean.* Hartford, England, 1783.

Martin, L. "Antarctica Discovered by a Connecticut Yankee, Captain Nathaniel Brown Palmer." *Geographical Review.* October 1940.

Matthews, L. H. *Sea Elephant.* London, 1952.

Miers, J. *Travels in Chile and La Plata.* London, 1826.

———. "An Account of the Discovery of New South Shetland." *Edinburgh Philosophical Journal,* 1820.

Mill, H. R. *The Siege of the South Pole.*

Mitterling, P. I. *America in the Antarctic to 1840.* Urbana, Illinois, 1959.

"Notice of the Voyage of Edward Bransfield, master of his Majesty's Ship Andromache, to New South Shetland." *Edinburgh Philosophical Journal,* 1820.

Nunn, J. *Wreck of the Favorite.* London, 1850.

Palmer, N. B. *Logbook of the Hero.* Washington, D.C., Library of Congress.

Spears, J. R. *Captain Nathaniel Brown Palmer.* New York, 1922.

Stackpole, E. A. *The Voyage of the Huron and the Huntress.* Mystic, Connecticut, 1955.

———. *The Sea Hunters.*

Thomas, D. *Cochrane.* London, 1978.

Weddell, J. *A Voyage Towards the South Pole Performed in the Years, 1822–24.* London, 1825.

Chapter IX • Weddell and Brisbane Sail South

Barnard, C. H. *A Narrative of the Sufferings And Adventures, etc.* New York, 1829.

Bertrand, K. J. *Americans.*

Cobbett, W. *Rural Rides.* London, 1830.

Darwin, C. *The Autobiography of Charles Darwin 1809–1882.* Edited by N. Barlow. New York, 1969.

D'Urville, J. S.-C. D. *Two Voyages to the South Seas.* Edited and translated by H. Rosenman. Melbourne, Australia, 1987.

Jones, A. G. E. *Polar Portraits.*

Plumb, J. H. *The First Four Georges.* Boston, 1956.

Reynolds, W. *Voyage to the Southern Ocean.* Edited by A. H. Cleaver and E. J. Stann. Annapolis, Maryland, 1988.

Ross, J. C. *A Voyage of Discovery.*

Scoresby, W. *An Account Of The Arctic Regions.* London, 1820.

Stamp, T. and C. *William Scoresby, Arctic Scientist.* Whitby, Canada, 1975.

Trevelyan, G. M. *English Social History.* London, 1944.

Weddell, J. *Voyage Towards the South Pole.*

Wilkes, C. *Narrative of the United States Exploring Expedition during the Years 1838, 1839, 1840, 1841, 1842.* Philadelphia, 1845.

Chapter X • Weddell and the Fuegians

Bridges, E. L. *Uttermost Part of the Earth.* New York, 1949.

Cawkell, M. B. R., Maling, D. H., and Cawkell, E. M. *The Falkland Islands.* London, 1960.

Darwin, C. *The Origin of Species.* London, 1859.

———. *The Voyage of The Beagle.* Edited by L. Engel. New York, 1962.

———. *Autobiography.*
Fisher, M. and J. *Shackleton.* London, 1957.
FitzRoy, R. *Narrative of the Surveying Voyages of HMS Adventure and HMS Beagle.* London, 1839.
Mellersh, H. E. L. *FitzRoy of the Beagle.* New York, 1968.
Murphy, R. C. *Logbook for Grace.* New York, 1947.
Shackleton, E. *South.* London, 1920.
Weddell, J. *Voyage Towards the South Pole.*
Worsley, F. A. *Shackleton's Boat Journey.* New York, 1977.

Chapter XI • John Biscoe: The Third Circumnavigation

Biscoe, J. "Recent Discoveries in the Antarctic Ocean from the log-book of the brig Tula." *Geographical Journal.* London, 1833.
Cumpston, J. "The Antarctic Landfalls of John Biscoe 1831." *Geographical Journal.* London, 1963.
Jones, A. G. E. *Polar Portraits.*
Kirwan, L. P. *The White Road.*
Melville, H. *Moby-Dick; or, The Whale.* New York, 1851.
Mill, H. R. *The Siege of the South Pole.*
Murray, G. *The Antarctic Manual.* London, 1901.
Savours, A. "Biscoe's Antarctic Voyage 1830–33." *Geographical Journal.* London, 1982.
———. "John Biscoe, Master Mariner 1794–1843." *Polar Record.* Cambridge, England, 1983.

Chapter XII • Kemp and Balleny: The Last Discovery by Sealers

Balleny, J. "Discoveries of the Antarctic Ocean in February 1839." *Journal of the Royal Geographical Society.* London, 1839.
Bertrand, K. J. *Americans.*
Eden, A. W. *Islands of Despair.* London, 1955.
Jackson, G. *The British Whaling Trade.*
Jones, A. G. E. *Polar Portraits.*
Kerr, I. S. *Campbell Island—A History.* Wellington, New Zealand, 1976.
Kirwan, L. P. *The White Road.*
Mill, H. R. *The Siege of the South Pole.*
Moseley, H. N. *Notes by a Naturalist on HMS Challenger.* London, 1880.
Ross, J. C. *A Voyage of Discovery.*
Spry, W. J. J. *The Cruise of HMS Challenger.* London, 1877.
Stackpole, E. A. *The Sea Hunters.*

GENERAL

Fogg, G. E. *A History of Antarctic Science.* Cambridge, 1992.
Headland, R. K. *Chronological List of Antarctic Expeditions.* Cambridge, England, 1989.
Hydrographic Department. *The Antarctic Pilot.* Taunton, England, 1974.
———. *The Antarctic Pilot.* London, 1948.
———. *The Mariners Handbook.* Taunton, England, 1971.
———. *Ocean Passages for the World.* Taunton, England, 1987.
———. *South America Pilot.* Vol. 2. Taunton, England, 1971.
Jones, A. G. E. *Ships Employed in the South Seas Trade, 1775–1861.* Canberra, Australia, 1986.
Murray, G. *The Antarctic Manual.* Royal Geographical Society. London, 1901.
United States Board on Geographic Names. *Geographic Names of Antarctica.* Gazetteer No. 14. Washington, D.C., 1956.

Index

Italicized page numbers indicate illustrations.

FOR THE BEST IN PAPERBACKS, LOOK FOR THE

In every corner of the world, on every subject under the sun, Penguin represents quality and variety—the very best in publishing today.

For complete information about books available from Penguin—including Puffins, Penguin Classics, and Arkana—and how to order them, write to us at the appropriate address below. Please note that for copyright reasons the selection of books varies from country to country.

In the United Kingdom: Please write to *Dept. JC, Penguin Books Ltd, FREEPOST, West Drayton, Middlesex UB7 0BR.*

If you have any difficulty in obtaining a title, please send your order with the correct money, plus ten percent for postage and packaging, to *P.O. Box No. 11, West Drayton, Middlesex UB7 0BR*

In the United States: Please write to *Consumer Sales, Penguin USA, P.O. Box 999, Dept. 17109, Bergenfield, New Jersey 07621-0120.* VISA and MasterCard holders call 1-800-253-6476 to order all Penguin titles

In Canada: Please write to *Penguin Books Canada Ltd, 10 Alcorn Avenue, Suite 300, Toronto, Ontario M4V 3B2*

In Australia: Please write to *Penguin Books Australia Ltd, P.O. Box 257, Ringwood, Victoria 3134*

In New Zealand: Please write to *Penguin Books (NZ) Ltd, Private Bag 102902, North Shore Mail Centre, Auckland 10*

In India: Please write to *Penguin Books India Pvt Ltd, 706 Eros Apartments, 56 Nehru Place, New Delhi 110 019*

In the Netherlands: Please write to *Penguin Books Netherlands bv, Postbus 3507, NL-1001 AH Amsterdam*

In Germany: Please write to *Penguin Books Deutschland GmbH, Metzlerstrasse 26, 60594 Frankfurt am Main*

In Spain: Please write to *Penguin Books S. A., Bravo Murillo 19, 1° B, 28015 Madrid*

In Italy: Please write to *Penguin Italia s.r.l., Via Felice Casati 20, I-20124 Milano*

In France: Please write to *Penguin France S. A., 17 rue Lejeune, F–31000 Toulouse*

In Japan: Please write to *Penguin Books Japan, Ishikiribashi Building, 2–5–4, Suido, Bunkyo-ku, Tokyo 112*

In Greece: Please write to *Penguin Hellas Ltd, Dimocritou 3, GR–106 71 Athens*

In South Africa: Please write to *Longman Penguin Southern Africa (Pty) Ltd, Private Bag X08, Bertsham 2013*